Service Science: Research and Innovations in the Service Economy

Series Editors
Bill Hefley
Wendy Murphy

More information about this series at http://www.springer.com/series/8080

Service Science: Research and Innovations
in the Service Economy

Jorge Marx Gómez • Manuel Mora
Mahesh S. Raisinghani • Wolfgang Nebel
Rory V. O'Connor

Editors

Engineering and Management of Data Centers

An IT Service Management Approach

Springer

Editors
Jorge Marx Gómez
Department of Computing Sciences
Carl von Ossietzky University Oldenburg
Oldenburg, Germany

Manuel Mora
Department of Information Systems
Autonomous University of Aguascalientes
Aguascalientes, Mexico

Mahesh S. Raisinghani
College of Business
Texas Woman's University Denton
Dallas, Houston
TX, USA

Wolfgang Nebel
Department for Computing Science
Carl von Ossietzky University of Oldenburg
Oldenburg, Germany

Rory V. O'Connor
School of Computing
Dublin City University
Dublin, Ireland

ISSN 1865-4924   ISSN 1865-4932   (electronic)
Service Science: Research and Innovations in the Service Economy
ISBN 978-3-319-87946-8   ISBN 978-3-319-65082-1   (eBook)
DOI 10.1007/978-3-319-65082-1

Printed on acid-free paper

This Springer imprint is published by Springer Nature
The registered company is Springer International Publishing AG
The registered company address is: Gewerbestrasse 11, 6330 Cham, Switzerland

Contents

Contributors

Ammar AlSous Department of Business Information Systems/Very Large Business Applications (VLBA), Carl von Ossietzky University of Oldenburg, Oldenburg, Germany

Atif Amin Dubai Statistics Center, Dubai, United Arab Emirates

Robert Basmadjian Department of Computer Science and Mathematics, University of Passau, Passau, Germany

Sascha Bosse Magdeburg Research and Competence Cluster for Very Large Business Applications, Faculty of Computer Science, Otto-von-Guericke University Magdeburg, Magdeburg, Germany

Cathleen Carey Executive MBA Program, School of Management, Texas Woman's University, Denton, TX, USA

Oswaldo Díaz Group of Systems Engineering, National Institute of Statistics and Geography, Mexico

Kurt J. Engemann Center for Business Continuity and Risk Management, Iona College, New Rochelle, NY, USA

Dora Luz González-Bañales Department of Systems and Computing, Instituto Tecnológico de Durango, Durango, Mexico

Jairo Gutierrez Department of Information Technology and Software Engineering, School of Engineering, Computer and Mathematical Sciences, Auckland University of Technology, Auckland, New Zealand

Johannes Hintsch Magdeburg Research and Competence Cluster for Very Large Business Applications, Faculty of Computer Science, Otto-von-Guericke University Magdeburg, Magdeburg, Germany

Stefan Janacek Smart Resource Integration, OFFIS Institute for Information Technology, Lower Saxony, Germany

Ateeq Khan Magdeburg Research and Competence Cluster for Very Large Business Applications, Faculty of Computer Science, Otto-von-Guericke University Magdeburg, Magdeburg, Germany

William Liu Department of Information Technology and Software Engineering, School of Engineering, Computer and Mathematical Sciences, Auckland University of Technology, Auckland, New Zealand

Teresa Lucio-Nieto Universidad Iberoamericana, ITESM & Universidad Anahuac, Customer Care Associates, Monterrey, Nuevo León, Mexico

Jorge Marx Gómez Department of Computing Sciences, Carl von Ossietzky University Oldenburg, Oldenburg, Germany

Hermann de Meer Department of Computer Science and Mathematics, University of Passau, Passau, Germany

Burkard Meyendriesch IT Services Department, Carl von Ossietzky University Oldenburg, Oldenburg, Germany

Holmes E. Miller Department of Accounting, Business, Economics and Finance, Muhlenberg College, Allentown, PA, USA

Manuel Mora Department of Information Systems, Autonomous University of Aguascalientes, Aguascalientes, Mexico

Mirna Muñoz Mathematic Research Center, Zacatecas, Mexico

Mamta Narang Department of Information Technology and Software Engineering, School of Engineering, Computer and Mathematical Sciences, Auckland University of Technology, Auckland, New Zealand

Wolfgang Nebel Department of Informatics, Carl von Ossietzky University Oldenburg, Lower Saxony, Germany

Florian Niedermeier Department of Computer Science and Mathematics, University of Passau, Passau, Germany

Rory V. O'Connor School of Computing, Dublin City University, Glasnevin, Dublin, Ireland

Ritchie Qi Department of Information Technology and Software Engineering, School of Engineering, Computer and Mathematical Sciences, Auckland University of Technology, Auckland, New Zealand

Mahesh S. Raisinghani College of Business, Texas Woman's University Denton, Dallas, Houston, TX, USA

André Siegling Magdeburg Research and Competence Cluster for Very Large Business Applications, Faculty of Computer Science, Otto-von-Guericke University Magdeburg, Magdeburg, Germany

Klaus Turowski Magdeburg Research and Competence Cluster for Very Large Business Applications, Faculty of Computer Science, Otto-von-Guericke University Magdeburg, Magdeburg, Germany

Klaus Turowski Magdeburg Research and Competence Cluster for Very Large Business Applications, Faculty of Computer Science, Otto-von-Guericke University Magdeburg, Magdeburg, Germany

Raul Valverde Department of Supply Chain and Business Technology Management, Concordia University, Montreal, QC, Mexico

CONAIC, Mexico City, Mexico

Becky White Executive MBA Program, School of Management, Texas Woman's University, Denton, TX, USA

Foundations of Data Center: Key Concepts and Taxonomies

Cathleen Carey, Mahesh S. Raisinghani, and Becky White

Abstract Many corporations use central data centers to avoid building and maintaining a separate data center and are finding and adopting new ways to make the
data centers more energy efficient. This chapter provides a relevant summary of key
concepts for understanding the complexity of data centers and the types and value
of data centers. Its purpose is to provide information and understanding needed to
manage massive data generated every day in the era of internet technology.

1 Introduction

This chapter provides a relevant summary of key concepts for understanding the complexity of data centers. Its purpose is to provide information and understanding needed
to manage massive data generated every day in the era of internet technology. From
huge corporate businesses, share markets to even social media, the amount of data
generated has increased manifold. While internet has been a boon to the world with
the connectivity and the speed it offers, it is only with the help of data centers that
numerous thousands of gigabytes are still generated and stored and still retrieved
quickly from anywhere. Data centers are essential and what's even more necessary is
to have data centers that are environmentally friendly and economic to maintain. With
the growth of business being conducted online, more business systems are classified
as mission-critical. Typically, 58% of the business systems of an organization are classified as mission-critical, and these require additional investments in data center facilities, IT technology, business processes, and IT staff (Cocchiara et al. 2008).

The chapter is organized as follows. The chapter starts with fundamental concepts and then an overview of data centers. Next it describes the evolution of data

C. Carey • B. White
Executive MBA Program, School of Management, Texas Woman's University,
Denton, TX 76204, USA
e-mail: ccarey@twu.edu; bwhite@twu.edu

M.S. Raisinghani (✉)
College of Business, Texas Woman's University Denton, Dallas, Houston, TX, USA
e-mail: mraisinghani@twu.edu

© Springer International Publishing AG 2017   1
J. Marx Gómez et al. (eds.), *Engineering and Management of Data Centers*,
Service Science: Research and Innovations in the Service Economy,
DOI 10.1007/978-3-319-65082-1_1

centers and the various types of data centers. This is followed by the organizational charts for data centers and the taxonomies of services provided and consumed in data centers, and the data center as a service system. Finally the value of data centers is discussed followed by the conclusion section.

2 Fundamental Concepts

Although the Internet keeps the world connected, very few people truly understand how and where the information from this world wide network comes from, or how the personal and professional information is being stored. Data centers are industrialized structures of varied scales in size that are equipped to accommodate the varied needs of servers and their related networking hardware (Pravin 2010). There are many different types of servers such as mail servers, game servers, application servers or data base and web server. Servers are devices or programs that make it possible to share or communicate data over a network via satellite or fiber optic cables that help give servers the capacity to communicate directly with other servers anywhere in the world. Servers host personal or company websites and make the information accessible to visitors all over the world (Pravin 2010). Data centers safeguard this vital equipment that holds all of this information; therefore it plays an integral and necessary part in the functioning of the Internet (McLellan 2013).

Since data centers play such a vital role in the process of getting information all over the globe they have needs in order to function optimally. One such need for data centers is a need for a constant, elaborate power source. The goal of a data center is to be functioning and available around the clock at all times. Another set of needs is related to the physical needs of the environment in which the equipment is stored in. These are needs such as an elaborate climate controlled environment which controls both temperature and humidity. Data centers must also take into account threats of loss from both internal and external factors. This leads to the need for multiple levels of security to protect against catastrophic events. Data centers need knowledgeable personnel to manage this sensitive equipment and a safety guard of backups must be in place at all times to prevent any loss of data or services. Data centers can be housed anywhere in the world and where it can be relied upon around the clock, and the careful management of its needs helps to ensure its quality of service.

3 Overview of Data Centers

According to McLellan (2013), "Data centers range from on premise facilities running traditional enterprise applications to massive outsourced installations offering a variety of cloud services." Data centers came about with the needs of growing internet based businesses as well as the demand for constant communication via email and all types of social media. These growing companies and social media sites needed to be able to provide a constant internet presence to meet the demands of their consumers around the globe. With that came the need to store huge amounts of information for, about and to support their business processes. Data centers provide secure off site locations to hold large quantities of information. The increasing demand for fast internet connectivity, the desire for continuous business operations, and the growing demand for storage space as companies began integrating more automated and/or re-engineered processes in their daily operations; led to building these dedicated facilities to house thousands of servers. All this so that markets that could not otherwise be reached could now be reached at any time, allowing them to expand and grow their business (Carroll 2012). Data centers need to be designed and developed for growth in order to keep up with the demands of advancing technology and the needs of businesses around the world.

4 The Evolution of the Data Center

Business continues to evolve bringing with it the needs for data centers to evolve alongside in order to keep up with the most current needs of the market (Carroll). If we take a look at the evolution of the data center from the mainframe to the current cloud based servers, we will see that the changes in technology have caused big changes in the way we store data. According to McLellan (2013), the twenty-first century data center started in the mainframe housing computer room of the mid-twentieth Century. Both are large facilities, well secured, and built to house complex and expensive IT equipment that requires elaborate power and cooling technology. Today's data centers are designed especially to house this very valuable and massive networking infrastructure, complete with people to maintain the equipment, elaborate backup power sources and very efficient temperature and humidification regulation systems.

The first data center was the ARC net, a loosely configured cluster system that was tied to a local or specific area (Woods 2014). There were 10,000 of these ARC net local area network or LAN installations in commercial use around the world. They remained the main system until the mid to late 80s. During the 1980s, when we saw a rise in the use of the personal computer and Sun Microsystems introduced the network file system protocol, this allowed the operator of a computer to access files over a network (Woods 2014). The early 1990s is when we saw the real change, rooms full of microcomputers acting as servers replaced the old mainframes, then those rooms were labeled as, "Data Centers" (McLellan 2013).

The real birth of the Data Center had begun, the demand and evolution of business needs for fast internet connectivity, and non-stop operation led to the building of dedicated facilities designed strictly for hundreds if not thousands of servers to give its clients the ability for growth required for business. This is when huge data center companies came to be. With the rapid growth of the internet and business during this time, the major advancements in technology started. The building and design of such large data centers brought with it the expense of building, the cost of maintaining, manning and powering such facilities (McLellan 2013).

Mainframe computers were the pioneering technology for data centers. They became the mainstay in commercial areas and were widely accepted as the backbone of data storage and computing. International Business Machines (IBM) is the only company left that makes mainframes; they dominated in that market for years along with a few others. The other significant manufacturers of mainframes were known as BUNCH based on the names of the five mainframe manufacturing companies, i.e., Burroughs, Univac, NCR, Control Data, and Honeywell). These companies were the major vendors for mainframes for many years and were literally the data processing giants for all major U.S. companies.

These mainframe computers were some of the most powerful computers available at the time and offered viable solutions for collecting and processing data. Each generation of mainframes had seen huge progression in speed, capacity, and capabilities solidifying their role in business. Mainframes also had a very high utilization rate, due to the sheer expense of purchasing of mainframes, maintaining, and building data centers to house them. Due to these reasons clients virtually used every bit of computing power they offered at the time, sometimes as high as 90% utilization. One of the biggest benefits of the mainframe was having the ability to run multiple applications on a single machine. The development of workload management by IBM enabled companies to operate more applications and become more efficient and productive. At present, "Data center usage is currently undergoing a transformation due to the increasing use of 'cloud' (i.e. outsourced, external) infrastructure, services and applications (McLellan 2013)." According to surveys conducted in 2012 indicated cloud usage for businesses were already at 38% with an additional 28% having future plans to expand their current use of the cloud. By 2013, Google expanded its global data center network by spending 7.35 billion dollars on one of the largest data center construction efforts in history. Woods continues to add that today's data centers are shifting their model from one infrastructure, hardware and software ownership to a model that is based on virtual space and subscriptions.

5　Types of Data Centers (Tiers I, II, III, IV)

Data systems can be classified into one of a four tier system. Having a tiered system of identification offers a quick and easy way to identify different data system facilities and desired functions for standardized needs such as the TIA-942. According to the Uptime Institute, the four tiers are classified as the following (Beal n.d.):

- Tier 1: composed of a single path for power and cooling distribution, without redundant components, providing 99.671% availability.
- Tier II: composed of a single path for power and cooling distribution, with redundant components, providing 99.741% availability.
- Tier III: composed of multiple active power and cooling distribution paths, but only one path active, has redundant components, and is concurrently maintainable, providing 99.982% availability.
- Tier IV: composed of multiple active power and cooling distribution paths, has redundant components, and is fault tolerant, providing 99.995% availability.

6 Organizational Charts for Data Centers

To ensure proper functionality of a data center, opportunity exists to leverage efficiency with the manpower need for operations. By putting in place an organizational structure that can be outlined by an organizational chart, this can increase efficiency and execution of internal processes. An organizational chart depicts the structure of an organization, including, the various relationships from department to department, person to person, or jobs within the organization used to maintain viability of an organization. It can be thought of as the invisible skeleton of a company. Even though one may not see it on the outside, one knows it's there by the way an organization measures performance outcomes. The evidence of an organization's "skeleton" is seen by the way organization moves. Options vary for defining an organizational structure. Some data center charts can be highly organized at a high-level while some depict organizational design at the frontline. The following two examples illustrate the organizational structures within two different data centers. The first example is a simpler option that contains a data center within the whole of the organization, whereas the second picture is an example of a highly defined structure, wherein the whole of the structure is that of a data center in and of itself (Figs. 1 and 2).

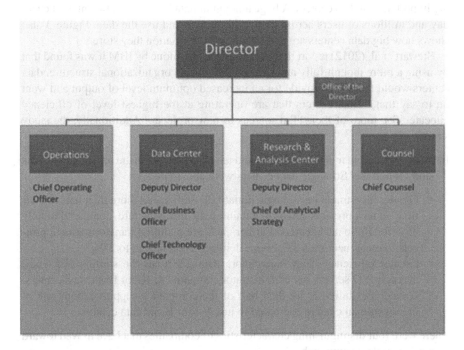

Fig. 1 High-level organizational structure (Source: High-level organizational structure courtesy of www.financialresearch.gov)

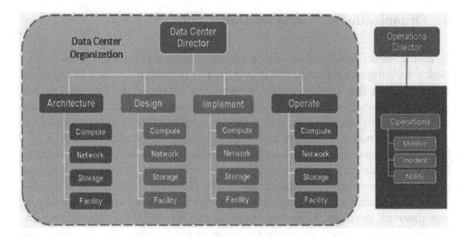

Fig. 2 Cisco IT Data Center Organization: 2008-Today (Source: Front-line organizational structure courtesy of Cisco Systems, Inc)

7   Best Practices for Operational Efficiency

Research is being conducted at present to highlight best practices for the design of organizational charts for data centers. Figure 3 illustrates the growth and the growing importance of data centers. A huge amount of data is placed on the internet every day and millions of users across the world retrieve and use the data. Figure 3 also shows how big data centers are and how much information they store.

Stewart et al. (2012) report that in a study recently done by IBM it was found that by using a more thoughtfully and strategically placed organizational structure, data centers would therefore provide for an increased optimum level of output and went on to say that, "Data centers that are operating at the highest level of efficiency allocate 50% more of their IT resources to new projects." Additionally, the study stated:

Improving data center efficiency can yield tangible benefits to the organization. This study found that Strategic data centers were able to deliver:

- Greater investment on strategic initiatives. Staff spend more than half of their time on new projects versus maintaining the infrastructure, compared to only 35% for Basic data centers. Further, 39% are planning transformational projects to reengineer their IT service delivery as compared to 23%.
- Greater efficiency. They enjoy more than 2.5 times the staffing efficiency, averaging 27 servers per administrator compared to 10 for Basic data centers.
- Greater flexibility. More than half of the companies support a high rate of organizational change compared to just 6% for Basic data centers.

There were four distinguishing characteristics of companies that have moved toward a more strategic approach:

- Optimize the server, storage, network and facilities assets to maximize capacity and availability
- Design for flexibility to support changing business needs
- Use automation tools to improve service levels and availability
- Have a plan that aligns with the business goals and keep it current

In this way, a strategically arranged system of management will yield best outcomes and maximization of positive results.

An alternative perspective to consider the organization of a data center is in terms of the way the storage system itself is set up. Cisco redesigned the system they had in place and had phenomenal results. According to their website, the current structure now consists of:

Cisco has 5 production data centers and 41 engineering data centers worldwide. Two production data centers are located in San Jose, California, and the remaining three are in Research Triangle Park (RTP), North Carolina; Amsterdam, the Netherlands; and Sydney, Australia. The Cisco IT Operations Data Center is the main production data center on the San Jose, California, campus. The IT Operations Data Center supports Cisco's intranet systems; enterprise resource planning (ERP) systems such as financial, data storage, and IP telephony infrastructure; and the many employee-facing applications and databases. It also houses the Operations Command Center (OCC), where business-critical resources within Cisco data centers and across

THE GROWTH OF THE DATA CENTER		
Fueling the Internet	Facebook	500,000,000 active Facebook users on earth ➔ That's 1 in every 13 people on earth
	You Tube	Every second 1,157 people start watching you tube video ➔ That's 100,000,000 videos a day
	Twitter	In Feb. 2011, daily tweets averaged 140 million
Size of Data	509,147 data centers worldwide which is equal to 285,831,541 sq. ft. (that's 5,955 football fields) Every hour enough information is consumed by Internet traffic to fill 7 million DVDs ➔ side-by-side they would scale Mount Everest 95 times	
Failure?	509,147 Data centers worldwide X 2.5 complete outages (average in U.S.) X 134 minutes (average outage duration) = 2,842,737 hours of downtime at an average cost of $300,000 per hour For a total loss of $426 Billion a year	

Fig. 3 The growth and the growing importance of data centers (Source: State of the data- center 2011 [Digital image]. (2011). Retrieved from http://www.emersonnetworkpower.com/en-US/Resources/Market/Data-Center/Library/infographics/Pages/2011DataCenterState.aspx)

Cisco networks worldwide are monitored. Remaining production data centers perform specific functions, as follows:

- The second production data center in San Jose supports the public Website, Cisco. com, and the online applications and tools Cisco provides to customers and partners.
- The production data center in RTP supports application development, testing, and staging environments and serves as a disaster recovery site for the two San Jose data centers.
- In Amsterdam, the Netherlands, the production data center houses systems and databases that support the Europe, Middle East, and Africa (EMEA) region.
- In Sydney, Australia, the production data center houses systems and databases that support the Asia-Pacific region.

The 41 engineering data centers, called server rooms, house servers and databases to support Cisco software and hardware product development. Ranging in size from 20,000+ square feet to server rooms without raised floors with only a few hundred square feet, most of these sites were part of acquisitions by Cisco. Furthermore, Cisco has transitioned over the years to increase staffing and work hours to accommodate an ever-growing need of service to the data centers. According to Cisco's website, "In 2000 there was a staff of 20 handling 400 to 500 incidents per year. Today, the worldwide OCC team consists of 14 members who handle approximately 9000 incidents per year," which they comment has been a great improvement from before.

8   Taxonomies of Services Provided and Consumed in Data Centers

A taxonomy is a classification system, such as the United Nations Standard Products Services Code (UNSPSC), a system specifically for classification of ecommerce goods and services bought and sold. The delineation of classification for "data centers" (UNSPSC 2014) under the UNSPSC lists these identifiers under the "data service" section:

81112000 data service identifiers

[81112001] – Online data processing service
[81112002] – Data processing or preparation services
[81112003] – Data center services
[81112004] – Disaster recovery services
[81112005] – Document scanning service
[81112006] – Data storage service
[81112007] – Content or data standardization services
[81112008] – Cd rom mastering services
[81112009] – Content or data classification services
[81112010] – Data conversion service

Further classifications have been made according to 451 Research, and an organization that focuses on the latest in research and technology for the information sector, they can be divided into segments, such as: premium data centers, regional data centers, local data centers, server rooms, server closets, and hyperscale data centers. Harrington (2014) states that within each segment, the structure can depend on the needs of the area and is not always the same. He explains:

> For example, cloud or outsourcers may consume more premium sites, where enterprises may have a wider mix of server rooms and regional sites. . . The market continues to focus on large facilities, but there are a large number of server closets, rooms and localized datacenters that power millions of enterprises around the world. While these facilities have often been the target of consolidation, they remain a critical part of data center portfolios because branch offices and international sites often require local resources. The different designs and considerable investment in cloud and HPC centers are significant enough to separate.

451 Research defines data center facility types as follows:

- Premium data center – large facility (typically 10,000+ Sq. ft), considered mission-critical and purpose built to provide multiple levels of redundancy for power, cooling and security as part of the design
- Regional data center – Often considered a secondary site (typically 1000–10,000 Sq. ft). A purpose-built facility housing IT systems often used to serve the purpose of supporting regional presence. Differing levels of redundancy fro power, cooling and security.
- Local data center – Often considered a secondary site (typically <1000 Sq. ft) A purpose-built facility housing IT systems often used to provide services for a small number of users. Minimal levels of redundancy for power, cooling and security.
- Server Rooms – Dedicated computer room with some power, cooling and security; typically within an office environment.
- Server Closets – Small room or closet, typically outside of IT control, with little or no security or cooling, within an office environment.
- Hyperscale data center – Large purpose-built facility for serving a limited number of specific applications that require (sometimes massive) distributed IT systems. These facilities often support webscale and HPC applications, and may or may not have multiple levels of redundancy at the facility level.

9 The Data Center as a Service System

Bigelow (n.d.) describes the idea of a data center as a service (DCaaS) system as being a "service [that] is the provision of offsite physical data center facilities and infrastructure to clients. Clients rent or lease access to the provider's data center using the servers, networking, storage and other computing resources owned by the

DCaaS provider." DCaaS provider is typically engaged by a business that can no longer expand its own data center; this may be due to a lack of power or cooling, lack of physical space, lack of capital, lack of experienced IT staff or other factors. By turning to a DCaaS provider, a client essentially outsources some portion (or perhaps all) of its data center to the provider. The client then accesses the provider's computing resources remotely across a wide-area network (WAN).

For example, a business may choose to focus on maintaining a small number of mission-critical applications in-house. Rather than staff up or invest capital in additional computing hardware, the business will rent resources from a DCaaS provider to handle secondary or transient applications.

Some of the biggest concerns with DCaaS providers involve availability and business continuity. For example, provider downtime or WAN disruptions can leave some applications unavailable. Even when availability is clearly defined by a service-level agreement (SLA), the implications of unexpected downtime should be considered carefully. DCaaS providers are also businesses, and they sometimes merge with other businesses, endure staffing issues, and occasionally go out of business, leaving clients with the challenge of recovering or restoring affected applications.

In further research, it is found that data centers as a service describe the services offered in the following list, such as this example from the company, Atos, in Europe:

- Managed Infrastructure – Ensuring all storage and computing resources are fit-for purpose across their lifecycle.
- Server Management Services – Cross platform support (common and legacy operating systems); support of virtual and physical environments on various hardware platforms; fully integrated automated systems management tools.
- Managed Application Storage – Providing customers with a complete enterprise storage service that delivers key business functionality including backup, restore and business continuity.
- Enterprise Management Center Services – Remote centralized monitoring for IT services. Monitoring is provided for hardware and software infrastructure to ensure that any exceptions that arise are identified and handled promptly.

10 Value of Data Centers

The value brought from a data center has greatly increased due to the ability to work more efficiently. Though quite a bit of IT still remains in the traditional network, cloud and virtual data centers are becoming the wave of the future and the wave of the "now." To ensure value-driven results in the future, Hitachi, says, "Data variety and volume have the potential and opportunity to produce great value to businesses. New data value will come from the intersections of rich data varieties. To achieve value, IT must consolidate and pool this data in a form that decision-makers can use for analysis to drive the business forward. Analytics will allow businesses to transform data into information for business innovation, marketing strategies, and other value. "When trying to capture and analyze unstructured information, the criteria are often categorized in to four sections called The Four Vs. The Four Vs are:

1. Volume – Defined as the total number of bytes associated with the data. Unstructured data are estimated to account for 70–85% of the data in existence and the overall volume of data is rising. Benefits of this category include:

   • Turning 12 terabytes of Tweets created each day into improved product sentiment analysis
   • Converting 350 billion annual meter readings to better predict power consumption

2. Velocity – Defined as the pace at which the data is to be consumed. As volumes rise, the value of individual data points tend to more rapidly diminish over time. Sometimes 2 min is too late. For time-sensitive processes such as catching fraud, big data must be used as it streams into your enterprise in order to maximize its value. For example:

   Scrutinize five million trade events created each day to identify potential fraud
   Analyze 500 million daily call detail records in real-time to predict customer churn faster

3. Variety – Defined as the complexity of the data in this class. This complexity eschews traditional means of analysis.

   Big data is any type of data – structured and unstructured data such as text, sensor data, audio, video, click streams, log files and more. New insights are found when analyzing these data types together. With Variety you can:

   • Monitor 100's of live video feeds from surveillance cameras to target points of interest
   • Exploit the 80% data growth in images, video and documents to improve customer satisfaction

4. Variability – Defined as the differing ways in which the data may be interpreted. Differing questions require differing interpretations.

1 in 3 business leaders don't trust the information they use to make decisions. How can you act upon information if you don't trust it? Establishing trust in big data presents a huge challenge as the variety and number of sources grows (Technology Advise 2013)".

Turning the 4 Vs of data growth into business opportunities that drive data value requires a foundation built upon convergence and end-to-end virtualization across server, storage and network resources.

Another important factor is the use of "green" technology to decrease energy consumption and increase energy efficiency. In the data center world, space, energy consumption, security, and hardware are cost barriers to increasing value, with the greatest costs going to servers. The amortized cost of servers comes to $52.5 million dollars per year, with remarkably low utilization of 10% (Greenberg et al. 2009). To increase efficiency, the following steps are necessary:

First, we need to increase internal data center network agility, to fight re-source fragmentation and to get more work out of fewer servers– reducing costs across the board. Second, we need to pursue the design of algorithms and market mechanisms for resource consumption shaping that improve data center efficiency. Finally, geo-diversifying data centers can improve end to end performance and increase reliability in the event of site failures. To reap economic benefits from geo-diversity, we need to design and manage data center and network resources as a joint optimization, and we need new systems to manage the geo-distribution of state (Greenberg et al. 2009).

11   Conclusion

Every industry including healthcare, marketing, retail, and so forth, generates millions of gigabytes of new information in various forms like customer data, revenue, social media, commercial and other videos to name a few. It is important that all the data that is generated worldwide is stored in a place with intense security and should have the ability to retrieve the required data in no time. Data centers have opened doors to numerous opportunities to use technology. However, building data centers with ideal resources is the biggest challenge and different ways to increase the efficiency of data centers have been used and researched upon. Many corporations use central data centers to avoid building and maintaining a separate data center. Thus, data center facilities have been a boon to the technology. Many big corporations are finding and adopting new ways to make the data centers and thus, internet green. Apple has a reputation for energy transparency, commitment to renewable energy, and deployment in IT sector. Apple uses fuel cell installation, its largest privately owned solar farm at its datacenter in North Carolina, geothermal plants for its newest location in Nevada and wind energy in California and Oregon (Cole 2014). This chapter has briefly described the key concepts for understanding the complexity of data centers. And the types and value of data centers.

References

Beal, V.: Data center tiers. Retrieved 15 Apr 2016, from http://www.webopedia.com/TERM/D/data_center_tiers.html (n.d.)
Bigelow, S.: What is data center as a service (DCaaS)? – Definition from WhatIs.com. Retrieved 6 May 2016, from http://searchdatacenter.techtarget.com/definition/data-center-as-a-service-DCaaS (n.d.)
Carroll, A.: The evolution of data centers – Lifeline data centers, July 2. Retrieved 1 May 2016, from http://www.lifelinedatacenters.com/data-center/the-evolution-of-data-centers/ (2012)
Cocchiara, R., Davis, H., Kinnaird, D.: Data center topologies for mission-critical business systems. IBM Syst. J. **47**(4), 695–706 (2008)

Cole, S.: Apple datacenters the most environmentally friendly in tech, says Greenpeace, April 2. Retrieved 25 Sept 2016, from http://appleinsider.com/articles/14/04/02/apple-datacenters-the-most-environmentally-friendly-in-tech-says-greenpeace (2014)

Greenberg, A., Maltz, D. A., Patel, P.: The cost of a cloud: research problems in data center networks. computer communications review, Association for Computing Machinery, Inc. Retrieved 3 May 2016, from https://www.microsoft.com/en-us/research/publication/the-cost-of-a-cloud-research-problems-in-data-center-networks/ (2009)

Harrington, D.: 451 research releases taxonomy for the datacenter market. Retrieved 6 May 06, 2016, from http://www.datacenterconsulting.com/451-research-releases-taxonomy-for-the-datacenter-market-2/ (2014, June 16)

McLellan, C.: The 21st Century Data Center: An overview I ZDNet, April 2. Retrieved 2 Mar 2016, from http://www.zdnet.com/article/the-21st-century-data-center-an-overview (2013)

Pravin.: Data centers concepts, July 5. Retrieved 15 Apr 2016, from http://data-centers.in/data-centers-concepts/#sthash.lyk60xMF.dpuf (2010)

Stewart, D., Buratti, A., Debagnard, P., Bin, X.X., Constant, M.: Data Center Operational Efficiency Best Practices: Enabling Increased new Project Spending by Improving Data Center Efficiency (rep.). IBM Global Technology Services, New York (2012)

Technology Advice: The four vs of big data, May 1, Retrieved 2 Mar 2017 from http://technologyadvice.com/blog/information-technology/the-four-vs-of-big-data/ (2013)

UNSPSC: The United Nations standard products and services code, March 5. Retrieved 1 May 2016, from https://www.unspsc.org/ (2014)

Woods, J.: The evolution of the data center: Timeline from the mainframe to the cloud. Retrieved 26 Mar 2016, from http://siliconangle.com/blog/2014/03/05/the-evolution-of-the-data-center-timeline-from-the-mainframe-to-the-cloud-tc0114/ (2014)

Cathleen Carey is graduate student in the Executive MBA program at Texas Woman's University in USA.

Dr. Mahesh S. Raisinghani, is currently a Professor in the Executive MBA program at the TWU College of Business. Dr. Raisinghani was awarded the 2017 Innovation in Academia award, 2016 Fulbright grant, the 2015 Distinction in Distance Education award, the 2008 Excellence in Research & Scholarship award and the 2007 G. Ann Uhlir Endowed Fellowship in Higher Education Administration. He has edited eight books and he has published over hundred manuscripts in peer reviewed journals, conferences, and book series and has consulted for a variety of public and private organizations on IT management and applications. Dr. Raisinghani serves as the Editor in Chief of the International Journal of Web based Learning and Teaching Technologies; on the board of Global IT Management Association; and as an advisory board member of the World Affairs Council. He is included in the millennium edition of Who's Who in the World, Who's Who among Professionals, Who's Who among America's Teachers and Who's Who in Information Technology.

Becky White is graduate student in the Executive MBA program at Texas Woman's University in USA.

ITSDM: A Methodology for IT Services Design

Manuel Mora, Jorge Marx Gómez, Rory V. O'Connor,
and Burkard Meyendriesch

Abstract The main international Information Technology Service Management
(ITSM) process frameworks such as ITIL V3 and the ISO/IEC 20000-4, includes a
service design process as part of their mandatory set of processes. Nevertheless,
even with such availability of processes, their used nomenclature, their phase-
activity structure, and their granularity level used for their descriptions, are non-
standardized. Consequently ITSM academics are faced with a useful but disparate
and diffused literature, and ITSM professionals lack suitable step-by-step service
design methodologies. In this chapter, we present ITSDM (Information Technology
Service Design Methodology), which is elaborated on best practices suggested in
ISO/IEC 20000-4 and ITIL v3 design processes with the aim to provide a step-by-
step guideline with phases, activities, tasks, roles, controls and input-output artifacts. We illustrate its utilization with a real IT service (Cloud Storage service) that
is ready operational in a German Higher Education Institution. We found that
ITSDM provided qualitative benefits such as: ease of use, usefulness, compatibility
and value. However, given the novelty of this methodology, we encourage for further empirical studies for providing more definitive results.

M. Mora (✉)
Department of Information Systems, Autonomous University of Aguascalientes,
Aguascalientes, Mexico, 20000
e-mail: mmora@securenym.net

J. Marx Gómez
Department of Computing Sciences, Carl von Ossietzky University Oldenburg,
Oldenburg, Germany, 26129
e-mail: jorge.marx.gomez@uni-oldenburg.de

R.V. O'Connor
School of Computing, Dublin City University, Glasnevin, Dublin, Ireland, 9
e-mail: rory.oconnor@dcu.ie

B. Meyendriesch
IT Services Department, Carl von Ossietzky University Oldenburg,
Oldenburg, Germany, 26129
e-mail: burkard.meyendriesch@uni-oldenburg.de

© Springer International Publishing AG 2017   15
J. Marx Gómez et al. (eds.), *Engineering and Management of Data Centers*,
Service Science: Research and Innovations in the Service Economy,
DOI 10.1007/978-3-319-65082-1_2

1 Introduction

IT Service Management (ITSM) refers to a management system of organizational resources and capabilities for providing value to organizational customers through IT services (van Bon et al. 2010). ITSM has become a relevant organizational theme for IT areas in large and mid-sized organizations because it is expected that its utilization, jointly with other IT schemes of processes, deliver a more efficient and effective IT management, and ultimately a better organizational value (Johnson et al. 2007; Gallup et al. 2009). Studies on ITSM impacts (Hochstein et al. 2005; Cater-Steel and Toleman 2006; Potgetier et al. 2005; Cater-Steel et al. 2009) report evidence of positive impacts. Among the main benefits include: a better client/service orientation, a better quality of IT services, a better efficiency of IT processes, and a better visibility on transparency and comparability documentary issues, a more consistent and documented service management process (less negative surprises or omissions), less conflictive SLAs negotiations (smoother), more precise predictions of IT infrastructure warranty issues, and a better management of incidents, changes and testing tasks.

However, to obtain such benefits demand that ITSM practitioners – and their organizations- must firstly to select, learn, and deploy an ITSM process framework such as: ISO/IEC 20000 (ISO 2005, 2010) and ITIL V3 (Cartlidge 2007; van Bon et al. 2010). In this chapter, we are interested in the IT service design process. We consider that for ITSM practitioners and academicians this IT service design implies practically a new problem demanding the adaptation/enhancement of usual software systems development methodologies. The design of an IT service is more complex in general than the design of a software system because an IT service involves several components (hardware, software, DBMS, networks, data, applications, environment, and internal and external teams). Furthermore, few comparative studies on IT service design process have been reported in the literature (Mora et al. 2012, 2014, 2015). Consequently, IT service design processes emerge as a relevant current research problem (Ebert et al. 2007; Weist 2009; Mora et al. 2011, 2012).

In this chapter, we address such a real and academic problematic situation on the lack of a suitable service design methodology, and present ITSDM (Information Technology Service Design Methodology), which is elaborated on best practices suggested in ISO/IEC 20000-4 and ITIL v3 design processes. ITSDM provides a step-by-step guideline with phases, activities, tasks, roles, controls and input-output artifacts. We illustrate its utilization with a real IT service (Cloud Storage service) that is ready operational in a German Higher Education Institution. We found that ITSDM provided qualitative benefits such as: ease of use, usefulness, compatibility and value. ITSDM was designed through a formulative-evaluative conceptual design research method (Glass et al. 2004; Hevner et al. 2004; Mora et al. 2008).

The remainder of this chapter continues as follows: in Sect. 2 we describe the background on core concepts of service and IT service, as well as on the research methodological approach used for designing ITSDM. In Sect. 3, we review the related work on service design process reported in ITIL v3 and ISO/IEC 20000-4:2010.

In Sect. 4 we report the conceptual design and validation of ITSDM. We end this chapter, in Sect. 5 with contributions, limitations and conclusions.

2 Background and Research Approach

The concepts of service and IT service have been defined in different modes by the most recognized ITSM processes frameworks (Mora et al. 2014). In ITIL V3 (OGC 2007), a service is defined, as a means of delivering value to customers by facilitating outcomes customers want to achieve without the ownership of specific costs and risks. An IT service is defined as a service provided to one or more customers by an IT service provider, based on the use of IT and supports the customer's business processes, and is made up from a combination of people, processes and technology and defined in a Service Level Agreement. In ISO/IEC 20000 standard (ISO 2005), the concepts of service and IT service are used implicitly. In ISO 9000:2005 (ISO 2005), a service is an intangible resultant from the interaction of activities between a supplier and a customer.

Design – as a research paradigm- is a prescriptive mode for advancing the performance of systems. In contrast with a knowledge-producing descriptive mode – which pursues to understand their natural behavioral of used systems-, design is a knowledge-using activity pursued for developing useful systems (i.e. IT systems in particular in this studied context) (March and Smith 1995). Design is about *"devising artifacts to attain goals"* (idem, p. 253). Design products are assessed usually using utility or value criteria. Two core activities in design are build and evaluate. *"Building is the process of constructing an artifact for a specific purpose; evaluation is the process of determining how well the artifact performs"* (idem, p. 254). Design –as a substantive- is the generated artifact from design activity. It can be classified either: construct, model, method or implementation.

An IT service must be carefully planned and designed in order to be built as expected. An informal design process cannot establish performance, risk-based, security and cost-effective guarantees to users. Designing IT services helps mainly to avoid costly disruptions in operational settings caused by design flaws, and to produce expected performances. A high quality design implies to achieve it into the design space caused by the application of constrains (usually bounds on available resources) rather attaining the maximum or minimums values without consideration to the attached design constrains.

In ITIL V3 (Rudd and Llyod 2007), service design is the core process of gathering service needs and mapping them to requirements for integrated services, and creating the design specifications for the service assets needed to provide services. In ISO/IEC 20000–4:2010 (ISO 2010), two of the four new processes are linked to service design activities: service requirements where the service needs are established and agreed, and service design where the new or changed service is designed and developed.

Hence, we can refer in general to systems design as a verb and as the intellectual activity to transform a set of system requirements in a set of system specifications which satisfy a set of agreed goals and constrains which will enable the development and building of the designed system. Agreed goals are expected properties for system users (usually related with performance, security, and usability issues), while that agreed constrains are limits (minimums, maximums, or ranges) on characteristics of the design process per se (usually related with the consumption of time-based, financial, organizational, materials, and other related resources used for design, building and operating the expected system). In turn, system design can be defined as the conceptual artifact, which conveys a set of system specifications which enable its further development and building with assumed and extant design resources.

Service design is thus a relevant process for ITSM process frameworks. However, while that the two main international ITSM process frameworks (ITIL V3 and the ISO/IEC 20000-4) include a service design process as part of their mandatory set of processes, their used nomenclature, their phase-activity structure, and their granularity level used for their descriptions, are non-standardized (Mora et al. 2014, 2015). Consequently, ITSM academics are faced with a useful but disparate and disperse literature, and ITSM professionals lack of step-by-step service design methodologies.

ITSDM was designed through a formulative-evaluative conceptual design research method (Glass et al. 2004). March and Smith (1995) indicate that a design research approach can be used to build and evaluate non-trivial, non-naturally created and non-existent artifacts needed for human-being purposes. In design research, a build activity responds to the inquiry: is it feasible to build an artifact X by using a method, materials, and tools Y? and an evaluation activity to the inquiry: does the artifact X fulfill the design range of a set of expected metrics? While March and Smith (1995) does not report guidelines for the build activity, they suggest two critical metrics for the evaluation activity: utility and value, in contrast to truthiness for natural and behavioral sciences. Design research method has been also enhanced by Hevner et al. (2004) guidelines. In Hevner et al.'s framework (2004), seven design research guidelines) and four types of products (design artifacts: constructs, models, methods, or instantiations) are proposed. These recommendations were followed.

A formulative-evaluative conceptual design research method (extended by Mora et al. 2008) was used with five activities as follows: (1) Knowledge Gap Identification, (2) Methodological Knowledge Selection, (3) Conceptual Design, (4) Design Data Collecting, and (5) Analysis and Synthesis. Activities (1) and (2) corresponds to Sect. 3 of this chapter. Activities (3), (4) and (5) are reported in Sect. 4.

3 Theoretical Background on IT Service Design Processes

The design of IT services is based essentially on an IT service architecture design model. This model can be defined as a conceptual representation of a service system, which reports its essential components and interrelationships in an organized and hierarchical mode (Maier et al. 2004; Mora et al. 2014). Modeling IT service architectures can be pursued for several purposes: facilitate human understanding of IT service systems, support IT service systems management, support IT service systems improvement, automate IT service systems guidance and enact automated IT service systems (Curtis et al. 1992; Maier et al. 2004). Given the novelty of IT service systems and the variety of IT service process frameworks, there are also a dispersion of IT service architecture design models. Consequently, IT service academics and practitioners face a fragmented and non-standardized view of what is an IT service architecture design model.

In ITIL v3 (Rudd and Lloyd 2007), the concept of IT service architecture model is reported as a Service Composition Diagram and a Service Relationship-Dependence Model. In Fig. 1 we report an adaptation of both diagrams (Mora et al. 2014).

The core elements derived from both diagrams are the following: (1) business unit, (2) business service, (3) business process, (4) IT service (service utility, service warranty (SLAs)), (5) assets/resources (infrastructure (HW, SW, DBMS, NW), environment, data, applications), and (6) assets/capabilities (IT processes, support teams (OLAs), suppliers (UCs)). The derived interrelationships are the following: R1 a business unit delivers business services; R2 a business service is made up of business processes; R3 business processes (and lately business services) are supported by IT services; R4 an IT service is characterized by service utility and warranty parameters; R5 an IT service is made up of assets/resources and assets/capabilities; R6 assets/resources are infrastructure (HW, SW, DBMS, NW), environment, data, and applications; R7 assets/capabilities are IT processes, support teams and suppliers.

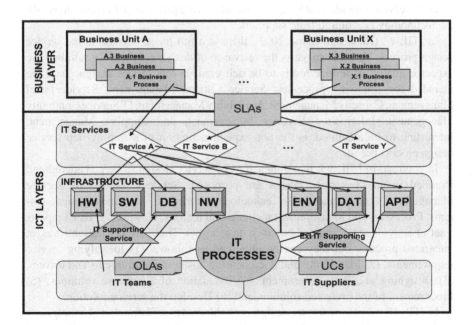

Fig. 1 ITIL v3 service composition model and service relationship-dependence model

Organization X					
	Customer Y - Business Units Layer Business Unit 1, Business Unit 2, Business Unit 3				
	IT Services Layer				
	IT Internal Service Provider Layer				
	Technology / Infrastructure and Service Components				
External IT Service	Servers, mainframes, desktops, storage systems,	Networks, telecommunications, mobile and smart devices	Application s	Managemen t tools and systems	Environmental systems
External Service Provider	IT Service Suppliers Layer				

Fig. 2 ISO/IEC 20000 IT service architecture design model

In ISO/IEC 20000 (ISO 2005, 2010) there is no IT service architecture design model reported explicitly. However, it can be derived one from several insights. Fig. 2 illustrates the derived IT service architecture model. In this model, the core-identified entities are: (1) an organization, (2) a customer, (3) business units, (4) IT services, (5) IT internal or external service provider, (6) technology (hardware, network, applications, systems, and environmental systems), (7) external service provider, and (8) suppliers. The derived interrelationships are the following: R1 an organization has customers; R2 customers have one or several business units; R3 business units use IT services; R4 the IT services are delivered by IT internal or external service providers; R5 the IT internal service provider uses technology; R6 the technology is acquired from suppliers.

In ITIL v3 (Rudd and Llyod 2007), there is a full phase devoted to the service design process. This fact suggests the relevance of design activities for fulfilling the expected quality of service levels to be delivered. In this service design phase are included the following processes: Service Catalog Management, Service Level Management, Capacity Management, Availability Management, IT Service Continuity Management, Information Security Management, and Supplier Management. Interesting to be identified, is the non-explicit definition of a step-by-step service design process per se.

In contrast, in ITIL v3, five dimensions of service design to be considered and included in an IT service design are proposed: Services, Design of Service Management systems and tools, Technology architectures and management systems, Processes, and Measurement methods and metrics. However, ITIL v3 reports a set of activities that grouped pursue a design goal. These are not presented as an integrated process, but they can be identified as follows: (1) Identifying service requirements, (2) Identifying and documenting business requirements and drivers, (3) Designing and Risk Assessment, (4) Evaluation of alternative solutions, (5) Procurement of the preferred solution, and (6) Develop the service solution.

In ITIL v3 the role of service design is established as: '*The design of appropriate and innovative IT services, including their architectures, processes, policies and documentation, to meet current and future agreed business requirements"*. Service design must consider the following elements in ITIL v3: business process to be supported, the service itself, SLAs/SLRs, Infrastructure (all of the IT equipment necessary to deliver the service to the customers and users), Environment (the environment required to secure and operate the infrastructure), Data, Applications, Support Services, Operational Level Agreements (OLAs) and contracts: any underpinning agreements necessary to deliver them, Support Teams, and Suppliers.

The IT service design process in ISO/IEC 20000 appears in the ISO/IEC 20000-4:2010 (ISO 2010). In the three first parts of the ISO/IEC 20000 (ISO 2005) documents, derived from ITIL v2 mainly, does not report on an explicit IT service design phase or process. However, in the new documents, two of the four new processes reported are linked to service design activities. This new category is called Design and Transition of New or Changes Services, and the two linked processes are: Service Requirements, and Service Design.

In Service Requirements, the service requirements are established and agreed. The service may be asked from the Service Catalogue (build for catalogue mode) or as totally new services (build to order mode). Five products are expected of this process: required characteristics and context of service, constraints for a service solution, service requirements, validation of such service requirements, and a set of final agreed and negotiated implemented requirements.

In Service Design, the new or changed service is designed and developed. This process must generate an agreed solution including the service itself and service components. The design must guarantee that the agreed service requirements be satisfied. Four products are expected from this process: a new or changed service design which meets business needs and service requirements, a service specification, a detailed list of infrastructure and service components to support the designed service, and the development of the designed service.

Similarly to ITIL v2, in ISO/IEC 20000 additional processes are partially linked for this service design aim: Service Level Management (SLM), Release Management (RM), and Configuration Management (CM). In SLM the need of defining a service catalogue and service level agreements implies service design activities to be fulfilled. In RM, a final release package must be designed, build and configured. In turn, in CM all technical information of the configuration items (e.g. their components, physical, and logical interrelationships) must be documented.

The Table 1 shows a summary of the core process-activities, roles and related processes of service design in ITIL v3 and ISO/IEC 20000.

In order to assess the extent of support provided by these service design processes in ITIL V3 and ISO/IEC 20000, adapted from Mora et al. (2015), we use a process framework from the systems engineering area: the ISO/IEC 15288 standard (ISO 2007). The ISO/IEC 15288 standard contains four process categories: Enterprise, Project, Technical and Agreement. System engineering is a discipline defined as *"an interdisciplinary approach and means to enable the realization of successful (cost-efficient and trustworthy) systems"* (Sage 2000; INCOSE 2004). For the systems engineering discipline, a system is *"an integrated set of elements that accomplish a defined objective. These elements include products (hardware,*

Table 1 A summary of ITIL v3 and ISO/IEC 20000 service design processes

Service core design process and activities	Service design roles	Service design related activities
ITIL V3: IMPLICIT SERVICE DESIGN (in service design package): A1. Identifying service requirements. A2. Identifying and documenting business requirements and drivers. A3. Designing and risk assessment. A4. Evaluation of alternative solutions. A5. Procurement of the preferred solution. A6. Develop the service solution.	ITIL V3: 1. Service design manager. 2. IT designer/architect. 3. Service design process managers. 4. Customer. 5. User.	ITIL V3: Serv. Catalogue Mgt. Serv. Level Mgt. Capacity Mgt. Availability Mgt. IT Serv. Continuity Mgt. Information security Mgt. Supplier Mgt.
ISO/IEC 20000: Service requirements: A1. Identification of required characteristics and context of service. A2. Identification of constraints for a service solution. A3. Elicitation of service requirements. A4. Validation of service requirements. A5. Agreement of final implementable requirements. Service design: A1. General design of a new or changed service design. A2. Specification of service. A3. Identification of detailed list of infrastructure and service components. A4. Development of the designed service.	ISO/IEC 20000: 1. Service design team. Related roles: 1. Release manager. 2. Service level manager. 3. Configuration manager.	ISO/IEC 20000: Serv. Level Mgt. Release Mgt. Configuration Mgt. Serv. Planning and monitoring

software, firmware), processes, people, information, techniques, facilities, services, and other support elements." (INCOSE 2004). We consider this conceptualization of a system covers adequately the concept of IT service, and thus the ISO/IEC 15288 process standard provides a suitable assessment framework.

The ISO/IEC 15288 standard (ISO 2007) contains four process categories: Enterprise, Project, Technical and Agreement. Each one includes respectively 5, 7, 11 and 2 processes, as illustrated in Fig. 3. In our analysis of the IT service design process for ITILV3 and ISO/IEC 20000 we included only the most related processes with a system design purpose.

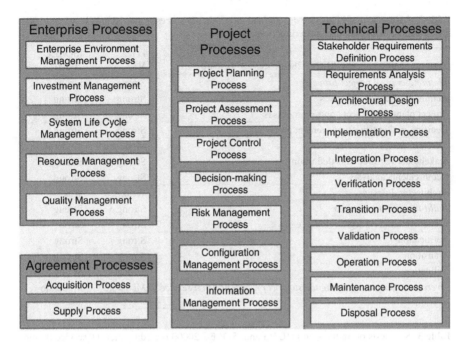

Fig. 3 ISO/IEC 15288 standard from systems engineering

However, given the disparity of views in the two ITSM schemes we consider useful to establish three essential categories of purpose as follows: planning-control, analysis-design, and build-transition. Using this categorization, we were able to select the most related design processes from the four ISO/IEC 15288 process categories to be used as the normative comparative particular model. These selected processes were the following: acquisition and supply processes (from Agreement category); project planning, project control, decision-making, and risk management (from Project category); and stakeholder requirements definition, requirement analysis, architectural design, implementation, integration, verification, transition and validation processes (from Technical category). The Table 2 shows a summary of the service design process evaluation of ITIL v3 and ISO/IEC 20000.

In the Table 3, adapted from Mora et al. (2015) we show a summary of three analyzed issues (foundational concepts of IT services, IT service design architecture layers, and design processes). We found that ITIL v3 has a strong to moderate assessment. In contrast the ISO/IEC 20000 standard was found as moderate to weak, due to the scarce information provided by the consulted documents. As instance, the design process is reported in a text about 450 words.

Hence, we claim that while these two main international ITSM process frameworks include a service design process as part of their mandatory set of processes, their used nomenclature, their phase-activity structure, and their granularity level

Table 2 Assessment of IT service design (and most related) process reported in ITIL v3 and ISO/IEC 20000 from a systems engineering view

Systems engineering ISO/IEC 15288 processes standard	ITIL V3	ISO/IEC 20000
Planning-control project processes	Strong	Strong
Acquisition/supply processes	Strong	Strong
Project planning/project control processes	Strong	Strong
Decision-making/risk management processes	Strong	Strong
Analysis-design processes	Moderate	Moderate
Stakeholder requirements definition	Strong	Strong
Requirements analysis	Strong	Strong
Architectural design	Weak	Weak
Build-transition processes	Strong	Strong
Implementation / integration processes	Strong	Strong
Verification	Strong	Strong
Transition	Strong	Strong
Validation	Strong	Strong
Overall evaluation regarding the support provisioned to it service design purpose	Moderate	Moderate

Table 3 Synthesis of findings on ITIL V3 and ISO/IEC 20000 regarding their IT service design processes

Analyzed issue	ITIL V3	ISO/IEC 20000
Foundational concepts (service, IT service)	Moderate	Moderate
IT service design architecture layers	Strong	Weak
Design processes	Moderate	Moderate
Overall evaluation	Moderate	Weak

used for their descriptions, are non-standardized. Consequently, ITSM academics are faced with a useful but disparate and disperse literature, and ITSM professionals lack of step-by-step service design methodologies.

4 The IT Service Design Methodology: Description and Illustrative Case

4.1 ITSDM Description

ITSDM can be considered an enhancement of the general recommendations reported in ISO/IEC 20000 and as a condensed step-by-step methodology derived from ITIL V3 processes for designing IT services.

The purpose of ITSDM is to provide a systematic and well-defined methodology-based on best practices suggested in ISO/IEC 20000 and ITIL V3 design processes- for designing IT services in medium-sized Datacenters environments.

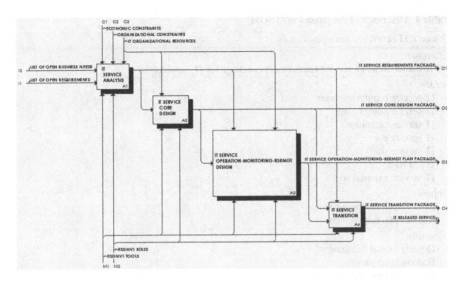

Fig. 4 The IDEF0 Diagram of ITSDM.

ITSDM consists of three phases: (1) IT service requirements analysis, (2) IT service core design, and (3) IT service operation-monitoring-rskmgt planning. The Fig. 4 shows an IDEF0 diagram of the overall process. An IDEF0 diagram (Mayer 1992; Presley and Liles 1995) includes the activities, inputs, outputs, controls and mechanisms (i.e. roles). The IDEF0 diagrams have been widely used for elaborating well-structured process descriptions (Mayer 1992; Presley and Liles 1995) in several domains.

The Fig. 4 shows also a fourth activity named IT Service Transition. This activity is not part of the design process but it is shown for better understandings of the next activities to be performed once complete the design of an IT service.

In the first phase of (1) IT service requirements analysis are conducted three activities: (1.1) Identification of IT service context, (1.2) Elicitation of IT service requirements, and (1.3) Validation-agreement of implementable IT service requirements. In the second phase of (2) IT service core design are conducted two activities: (2.1) Core design of IT service, and (2.2) Specification of IT service components. Finally, in the third phase of (3) IT service operation-monitoring-rskmgt planning are conducted two activities: IT service operation-monitoring-rskmgt planning, and service design overall authorization. These activities are performed by the following roles: IT Service Project Manager, IT Service Design Team, IT Service Customer, IT Service User, IT Service Staff, ITSM Staff and IT Service External Staff. In ITSDM are generated three general artifacts: requirements package, design package, and operation plan package. Each package contains several documents and diagrams. All of them are based on the SysML notation (OMG 2007). SysML has been recommended for designing general systems in the discipline of Systems Engineering.

The Tables 4, 5 and 6 show the general descriptors for the three ITSDM phases. Each descriptor contains the following items: purpose, roles, inputs, controls, activities, outputs and an IDEF0 diagram of activities.

Table 4 Descriptor of the phase I in ITSDM

Phase I: IT service requirements analysis
Purpose:
To elaborate an IT service requirements package for [?] service.
Roles:
IT service project manager
IT service design team
IT service customer
IT service user
IT service staff
ITSM staff
IT service external staff
Inputs:
List of open business needs
List of open requirements
Controls:
Organizational constraints
Economic constraints
IT organizational resources
Activities:
A.11: Identification of IT service context.
A.12: Elicitation of IT service requirements.
A.13: Validation and agreement of implementable IT service requirements.
Outputs: IT service requirements package
IT service system context diagram
IT service use case diagram
IT service requirements diagram
IDEF0 diagram:

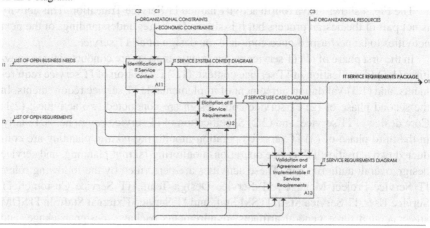

For instance, in the Table 4, the first phase of ITSDM named IT Service Requirements Analysis reports as its essential purpose to elaborate the IT Service Requirements package. This package consists basically of three artifacts: IT Service System Context Diagram, IT Service Use Case Diagram, and IT Service

Table 5 Descriptor of the phase II in ITSDM

Phase II: IT service core design
Purpose: To elaborate an IT service Core design package for [?] service.

Roles:
   IT service project manager
   IT service design team
   IT service customer
   IT service user
   IT service staff
   ITSM staff
   IT service external staff

Inputs: IT service requirements package
Controls: IT organizational resources

Activities:
   A.21: Core design of IT service
   A.22: Specification of IT service components

Outputs: IT service core design package   IT service design block diagram   IT service component specification block diagram
IDEF0 diagram:

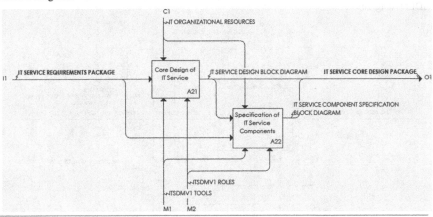

Requirements Diagram. The first two diagrams are widely known and used by software and systems engineers. The third artifact is used in systems engineering and uses a SysML notation (OMG 2007). The first artifact, IT Service System Context Diagram, portrays the essential four design blocks and their key stakeholders from a highest level perspective of the IT service design. These four design blocks are: the IT service block, the served business process block, the IT service system block, and the IT external service system block. These four blocks must be considered in overall in a IT service design. The omission or lack of consideration in some of them can lead a flawed design. For instance, the lack of a care design consideration of the IT external service system block such as ISP (internet service suppliers) or

Table 6 Descriptor of the phase III in ITSDM

Phase III: IT service operation-monitoring-RskMgt design
Purpose: To elaborate an IT service requirements package for [?] service.
Roles: IT service project manager IT service design team IT service customer IT service user IT service staff ITSM staff IT service external staff
Inputs: IT service Core requirements package
Controls: IT organizational resources
Activities: A.31: IT service operation-monitoring-RskMgt planning A.32: IT service design overall authorization
Outputs: IT service operation-monitoring-RskMgt plan packcage IT service operation-monitoring activity diagram IT service design authorization
IDEF0 diagram:

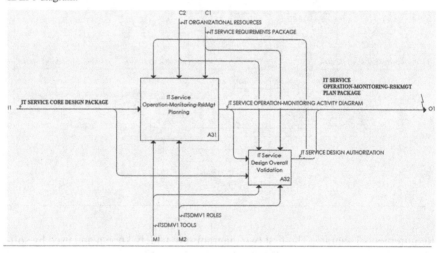

power energy suppliers, or IT suppliers-consulting for some critical IT resources, can lead a failed lately IT service. This Table 4 reports also the participants (in this case the seven ones), the inputs (list of open business needs, and list of open requirements), the outputs (the IT Service Requirements Package), the activities (A.11 Identification of IT Service Context, A.12 Elicitation of IT Service Requirements, and A.13 Validation and Agreement of Implementable IT Service Requirements), and an IDEF0 diagram which shows graphically the interrelationships between activities, inputs, outputs, controls and participants (called mechanisms in IDEF0).

The Tables 5 and 6 reports similar information for the next two phases of IT Service Core Design, and IT Service Operation-Monitoring-RskMgt.

We consider that ITSDM is a step-by-step methodology because it provides well-structured descriptions for each one of the seven activities in ITSDM. The Table 7 for instance shows the step-by-step guide of the first activity A.11 Identification of IT Service Context.

This descriptor contains the following elements: participants, expected duration, inputs, controls, tasks description, outputs and outputs templates. In particular, with the availability of tasks description and output templates, the design of an IT service is guided reducing ambiguity and uncertainty in what steps and what must contain an expected output.

Table 7 Descriptor of the activity A.11 identification of IT service context

Activity A.11 identification of IT service context
Participants:
ITS customer, ITS user, ITS project manager, ITS staff and ITS design team
Expected duration:
Small, simple or well-known IT services: One 1-hr. meeting
Medium-sized, moderate complexity or new IT services: Two or three 1-h meetings
Inputs:
List of open business needs
Controls:
Organizational constraints
Economic constraints
Tasks description:
This is the first formal activity of ITSDM. In this activity, a meeting coordinated by the ITS project manager and with the participation of the ITS customer, ITS user, ITS staff and ITS design team is held.
ITS customer and ITS user are expected to report a set of open business needs. These ones must be specified in a {ITS problem} and a {served business process} descriptions.
Based on such previous descriptions, jointly ITS customer, ITS user, ITS staff and ITS design team must delineate a general and likely {IT service block}.
ITS staff and ITS design team must also to elaborate the general descriptions of the related {ITSM block} and {IT external service block} that will support and deliver the expected {IT service block}.
ITS staff must also complement the descriptions of the stakeholders: ITS customer, ITS user, ITS staff, ITS design team, ITSM staff, IT external services staff}.
Finally, it must be remarked that all descriptions realized in this activity must consider the general organizational and economic constraints reported for both parts (customer/user and technical ones).
Outputs:
IT service system context diagram.

(continued)

Table 7 (continued)

Activity A.11 identification of IT service context

Outputs templates: IT service system context diagram

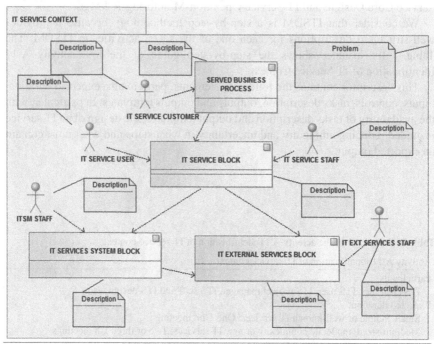

4.2 ITSDM: Illustrative Case

In this section we will report selective evidences on how ITSDM fits a correct IT service design process from a real IT service planned, designed, transitioned and operated currently in the University of Oldenburg. This IT service is named Cloud-Storage: your personal data storage (https://cloudstorage.uni-oldenburg.de/) (Fig. 5).

This IT service is described as follows: *"The data service "cloud storage" allows you to reflect a local directory on your device to the data management system of the university and must be kept in the background sync. The synchronization works not only with one but with any number of devices, so you cannot use the data backup but also to synchronize your data between your devices the service. Additionally, you can put the synchronized folder or parts thereof decidedly individual users for reading or for writing available"* (http://www.uni-oldenburg.de/itdienste/services/datenhaltung/cloudstorage).

In this IT service, we use a reverse engineering to test ITSDM. The IT service Cloud-Storage was already operational at the University of Oldenburg, and we tested the suitability and compatibility of ITSDM on the process followed by IT service design team at University of Oldenburg, which was reported as a mixed of

Fig. 5 Website of the IT service cloud-storage at University of Oldenburg

process based on the best practices of ITIL V3 and ISO/IEC 20000, complemented with the ad-hoc expertise of the IT service team in this university.

However which is relevant for this research is the acceptance of the IT service design team on the lack of step-by-step well-structured guide for this process. Consequently, the IT service design process followed in this case was the particular interpretation of ITIL V3 and ISO/IEC 20000 recommendations and general practices.

By space limitations, we report only some representative evidences on the application (in reverse engineering mode) of the ITSDM process for documenting and validating the design of the IT service Cloud-Storage. The Figs. 6, 7, 8 and 9 show the application of the Phase I of IT Service Analysis, and the artifacts IT Service Systems Context Diagram, IT Service Requirements Diagram, and IT Service Design Block Diagram.

In the Fig. 6 on the application of the Phase I of IT Service Analysis are identified (and documented) the roles (stakeholders), the inputs (list of open business needs, and list of open requirements), and the controls (organizational constraints, economic constraints, and IT organizational resources). In this particular case we can remark that the IT customer was the Vice-President of Administration, and the IT users the groups of research, academic, graduate students, undergraduate students and managerial personnel at the university. Regarding inputs, were identified the next list of open business needs: (1) research groups have national and international collaborations which demand that large quantity of data be shared in an efficient and secure mode, and (2) several groups of stakeholders (academics, graduate students, bachelor students, and management personnel), need data synchronization with their mobile devices. On list of open requirements these were the following ones:

PHASE 1	IT SERVICE ANALYSIS
Purpose	To elaborate an IT Service Requirements Package for: **CLOUD-STORAGE SERVICE**
Roles	• IT Service Project Manager: **General Manager of IT Services** • IT Service Design Team: **Data Center Manager, IT Service Design Engineer** • IT Service Customer: **Vice-president of Administration** • IT Service User: **Research Groups, Academic Groups, Graduate Students, Bachelor Students and Managerial Personnel.** • IT Service Staff: **2 ITS engineers** • ITSM Staff: **2 ITS networking engineers** • IT Service External Staff: **DFN Services Staff**

Inputs	• List of open business needs
	  o **OBN.01 Research groups have national and international collaborations which demand that large quantity of data be shared in an efficient and secure mode.**
	  o **OBN.02 Several groups of stakeholders (Academics, Graduate Students, Bachelor Students, and Management Personnel), need data synchronization with their mobile devices.**
	• List of open requirements
	  o **OR.01 To enable a web-based service of CLOUD STORAGE AND BACKUP which be secure and efficient for all stakeholders (Research groups, Academics, Graduate Students, Bachelor Students, and Managerial Personnel).**
	  o **OR.02 This service must provide the storage service including automatic backup functionality in several SLAs according to type of stakeholder.**

Controls	• Organizational Constraints
	  o **OC.01 The IT service must be released in 6 months and have a useful life over 3 years.**
	• Economic Constraints
	  o **EC.01 To design, activate and release the IT service using affordable enterprise versions of open source available platforms.**
	• IT Organizational Resources
	  o **ITOR.01 IT infrastructure will be limited to the available in the main (at main Campus) and secondary (at Wechloy Campus) data centers.**

Activities	A.11 Identification of IT Service Context. A.12 Elicitation of IT Service Requirements. A.13 Validation and Agreement of Implementable IT Service Requirements.
Outputs	IT SERVICE REQUIREMENTS PACKAGE • IT Service System Context Diagram

Fig. 6 Application of phase I of ITSDM for the IT service cloud-storage at the University of Oldenburg

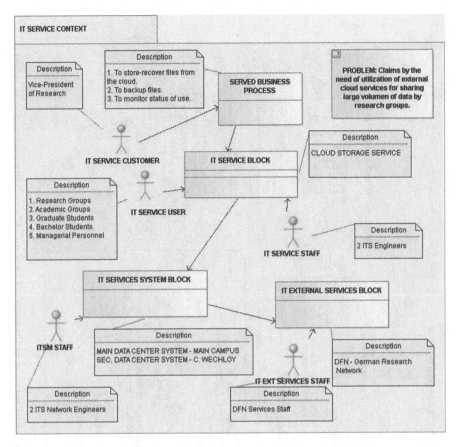

Fig. 7 Application of phase I of ITSDM for the IT service cloud-storage at the University of Oldenburg – IT service system context diagram output

(1) to enable a web-based service of cloud-storage and backup which be secure and efficient for all stakeholders (research groups, academics, graduate students, bachelor students, and managerial personnel), and (2) this service must provide the storage service including automatic backup functionality in several SLAs according to type of stakeholder. This Fig. 6 shows also the main organizational and economic constraints as well as the general IT resources required for the IT service. The organizational constraint was established as: the IT service must be released in 6 months and have a useful life over 3 years. The economic constraint was established as: to design, activate and release the IT service using affordable enterprise versions of open source available platforms. The IT resources constraint was identified as: IT infrastructure will be limited to the available in the main (at main Campus) and secondary (at Wechloy Campus) data centers.

In the Fig. 7 is shown the artifact IT Service Systems Context Diagram. This diagram is useful to highlight the four essential design blocks for an IT service, their

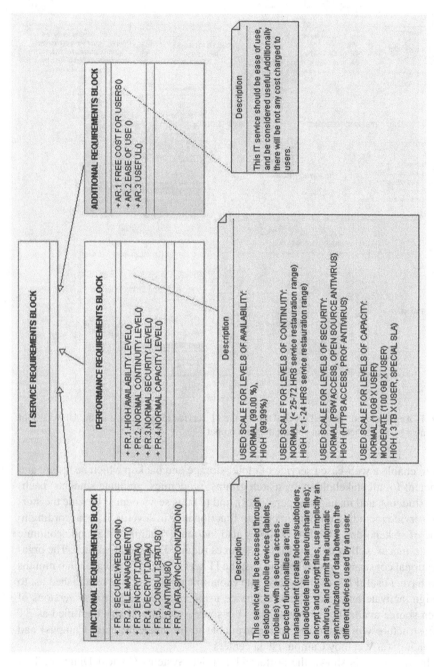

Fig. 8 Application of phase I of ITSDM for the IT service cloud-storage at the University of Oldenburg – IT service requirements diagram output

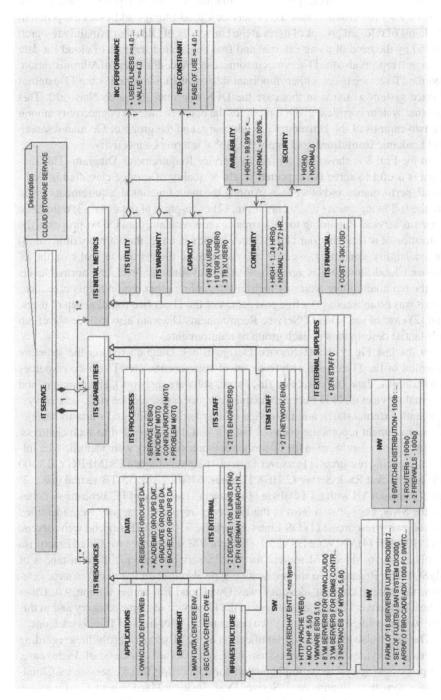

Fig. 9 Application of phase I of ITSDM for the IT service cloud-storage at the University of Oldenburg – IT service design block diagram output

stakeholders and additional relevant information, in a single 1-page document. The Fig. 7 shows for instance, that the IT service Cloud-Storage addresses the problem of claims of relevant groups of users at the University of Oldenburg (mainly research teams) by the need of using external and free but limited services of cloud for data storage. It reports also the IT service customer as the Vice-President of Administration, and the IT service users. Other important design block identified is the IT external service system which is in this case the DFN (German Research Network). This external system is critical given it provides the network internet connectivity among the two campus of the University of Oldenburg, and the group of German research and academic institutions, and lately the global internet connectivity.

In the Fig. 8 is shown the artifact IT Service Requirements Diagram. This diagram is useful to agree the expected levels of quality of service classified in functional, performance and other ones. Among the main functional requirements asked are the following ones: (1) a secure login, (2) encryption of data, and (3) automatic antivirus service. Regarding to performance requirements, the ITSDM proposes the utilization of at least the four ITIL V3 metrics of value (i.e. the warranty dimension) on availability, continuity, security and capacity. In this particular real case the IT service Cloud-Storage was agreed with a high availability level, and normal levels for the remainder three warranty metrics. Regarding other requirements classification it was established: (1) a free cost access of the IT service for all group of users, and (2) ease of use. This IT Service Requirements Diagram also includes brief but substantial descriptions of each group of requirements.

In the last Fig. 9 the IT Service Design Block Diagram reports the structure essential of the IT service with three set of components: (1) IT service resources (applications, data, infrastructure (hardware, software, network), environment, and external services); (2) IT service capabilities (processes, service staff, service system staff, external staff); and IT service initial metrics (utility and warranty ones).

Each element reports the essential but relevant data associated to such elements. For instance for hardware in the IT service resources category were identified the following specific resources: (1) a sever farm of 16 servers Fujitsu PRIMERGY RX300 S8 Dual-Socket Rack-Server (2 HE), 12 cores, 64GB RAM, 15 TB virtual disk; (2) set of Fujitsu SAN with a 1 Petabyte of storage; (3) an array of FC Brocade switches for the SAN. For software also in the IT service resources category were identified the following resources: (1) OS Linux Enterprise 7; (2) HTTP Apache web servers; (3) PHP v.5.5; (4) VMWare ESXI 5.1; (5) eight VM servers for OwnCloud Enterprise Application; (6) three VM servers for DBMS services; and (7) three instances of MySQL 5.6. Regarding to the application type also in the IT service resource category, the unique element identified was OwnCloud Enterprise version 9.0. Other critical element is IT external services in the IT service resource category and in this case were identified two ones: (1) two dedicated X-WiN-links of 1Gbit/s each one.

The Fig. 9 also includes the identification of the IT service capabilities regarding processes, service staff, service system staff, and external services staff. In this case, the processes agreed to be implemented for supporting this IT service of Cloud-Storage were the following ones: Service Desk, Incident Management, Configuration Management, and Problem Management. On the service staff dedicated to this particular service were assigned two IT engineers. It must be remarked that these staff also is responsible of other IT services.

Finally, this Fig. 9 (i.e. the IT Service Design Block Diagram) shows the essential information agreed on IT service metrics: utility and warranty. On utility metrics were established: (1) to increment performance of users measured by perceived value and usefulness from users by using a Likert scale from 1 (very low score) to 5 (very high score); and (2) reduce difficult of utilization of users measured by ease of use with a similar Liker scale from 1 to 5 points. On warranty, several specific metrics were established also for the four dimensions (availability, continuity, security and capacity). An additional category of IT service metrics was added: IT service financial ones. It was established as a total investment for deploying this IT service on at most 30,000 euros.

Hence, this section has presented evidences of the utilization of ITSDM (in reverse engineering mode) for documenting and testing the applicability for designing a real IT service in an organization. In this particular illustrative real case, the IT service considered was a Cloud-Storage service deployed already operational at the University of Oldenburg, Germany. This IT service was planned, designed, built and operated by the IT Service Department of the University of Oldenburg, managed by the fourth co-author of this chapter.

This documentation process was conducted during three interviews by first two co-authors with the IT Service manager, the IT Data Center manager, and one IT principal IT service engineer from the University of Oldenburg, Germany during July 2016, in a research stay from first author. Second and third co-authors reviewed the application of the ITSDM methodology and provide valuable insights for the elaboration of this chapter.

Finally, a quantitative final evaluation was not possible by time restrictions but several positive comments were collected from the IT service team. In overall, they considered the ITSDM methodology as: (1) theoretically well supported from the best ITSM schemes such as ITIL V3 and ISO/IEC 20000; (2) very adequate for the purpose of designing and documenting a new IT service; (3) ease of use; (4) useful; and (5) with interest to be used (with adaptations) in future IT service designs.

5 Conclusions

In this chapter, we have presented a new IT service design methodology named ITSDM. It has emerged from the recommendations from best practices schemes such as ITIL V3 and ISO/IEC 200000. It was motivated for the lack of well-structured step-by-step guides for designing an IT service. ITDSM consists of three phases (IT Service Analysis, IT Service Core Design, and IT Service Operation-Monitoring-RskMgt) and it provides a set of activities, tasks, roles, inputs, controls, and outputs artifacts with specific templates. It considers and it is theoretically compatible with ITIL V3 and ISO/IEC 20000 terminology and conceptual schemes.

ITDSM was tested in a reverse engineering mode for a real IT service implemented in a German university: a Cloud-Storage service. ITSDM was applied for documenting the IT service Cloud-Storage service ((https://cloudstorage.uni-olden-burg.de), through three interviews with IT service department people and research team. We found that ITSDM was capable of including all critical IT service design elements already considered by the IT service department in the German university, and was considered, in overall, as useful and ease of use.

Hence, this chapter provides initial evidence of the usefulness of ITSDM and proposes additional empirical studies for improving it. Given the lack of well-structured and step-by-step IT service design methodologies in the worldwide arena, we consider that ITSDM is a forward step in this direction.

Acknowledgements This research was developed with the financial support of the Autonomous University of Aguascalientes, Mexico (www.uaa.mx) (Project PIINF08-2).

References

Cartlidge, A.: An Introductory Overview of ITIL® V3. Van Haren, Zaltbommel (2007)

Cater-Steel, A., Toleman, M.: Transforming IT service management – the ITIL impact. In: Proceedings of the 17th Australasian Conference on Information Systems, Adelaide, December 6–8, 1–11 (2006)

Cater-Steel, A., Toleman, M., Wui-Gee, T.: itSMF Australia 2009 conference: Summary report of ITSM standards and frameworks survey. In: Proceedings itSMF Australia 2009 Conference, Adelaide, December 6–8, 1–16 (2009)

Curtis, B., Kellner, M., Over, J.: Process modeling. Commun. ACM. **35**(9), 75–90 (1992)

Ebert, N., Uebernickel, F., Hochstein, A., Brenner, W.: A service model for the development of management systems for IT-enabled services. AMCIS Conference, Colorado, August 9–12, 1–8 (2007)

Gallup, S., Dattero, R., Quan, J., Conger, S.: An overview of IT service management. Commun. ACM. **52**(5), 124–127 (2009)

Glass, R., Armes, V., Vessey, I.: An analysis of research in computing disciplines. Commun. ACM. **47**(6), 89–94 (2004)

Hevner, A.R., March, S.T., Park, J., Ram, S.: Design science in information systems research. Manag. Inf. Syst. Q. **28**(1), 75–105 (2004)

Hochstein, A., Tamm, G., Brenner, W.: Service oriented IT management: Benefit, cost and success factors. In: Proceedings of the ECIS 2005, Paper 98, http://aisel.aisnet.org/ecis2005/98 (2005)

INCOSE: Systems Engineering Handbook. INCOSE-TP-2003-016-02. Internet document at www.incose.org (2004)

ISO: ISO/IEC 20000-1 Information Technology – Service Management Part 1 Specification. ISO, Geneva (2005)

ISO: ISO/IEC 15288: Systems Engineering – Systems Life Cycle Processes. ISO/IEC, Geneva (2007)

ISO: ISO/IEC 20000-4 Information Technology – Service Management Part 4 Process Reference Model. ISO, Geneva (2010)

Johnson, M., Hately, A., Miller, B., Orr, R.: Evolving standards for IT service management. IBM Syst. J. **46**(3), 583–597 (2007)

Maier, M., Emery, D., Hilliard, R.: ANSI/IEEE 1471 and systems engineering. Syst. Eng. **7**(3), 257–270 (2004)

March, S., Smith, G.: Design and natural science research on information technology. Decis. Support. Syst. **15**(4), 251–266 (1995)

Mayer, R.J.: IDEF0 Function Modeling – A Reconstruction of the Original Air Force Wright Aeronautical Laboratory Technical Report – AFWAL- TR-81-4023. Knowledge-Based Systems, Inc., College Station (1992)

Mora, M., Gelman, O., Paradice, D., Cervantes, F.: The case for conceptual research in information systems. In: e-Proceedings of the International Conference on Information Resources Management, Niagara Falls, May 18–20, (pp. 1–10) (2008)

Mora, M., O'Connor, R., Raisinghani, M., Macías-Luévano, J.: An IT service engineering and management framework (ITS-EMF). Int. J. Service Sci. Manage. Eng. Technol. 2(2), 1–15 (2011)

Mora, M., Raisinghani, M., Gelman, O.: A comparison of service design processes in relevant international ITSM models and standards. In: Proceedings of the SIGSVC Worksop, Pre-ICIS Conference, Phonix. All Sprouts Content. Paper 516. http://aisel.aisnet.org/sprouts_all/516 (2012)

Mora, M., Raisinghani, M., O'Connor, R., Marx-Gomez, J., Gelman, O.: An extensive review of IT service design in seven international ITSM processes frameworks: Part I. Int. J. Inf. Technol. Syst. Approach. 7(2), 83–107 (2014)

Mora, M., Marx-Gomez, J., O'Connor, R.V., Raisinghani, M., Gelman, O.: An extensive review of IT Service Design in Seven International ITSM processes frameworks: part II. Int. J. Inf. Technol. Syst. Approach. 8(1), 69–90 (2015)

Potgetier, B., Botha, J., Lew, C.: Evidence that use of the ITIL framework is effective. In: Proceedings of the 18th Annual Conference of the National Advisory Committee on Computing Qualifications, Tauranga, NZ, July 10-13, pp. 160–167 (2005)

Presley, A., Liles, D.H.: The use of IDEF0 for the design and specification of methodologies. In: Proceedings of the 4th Industrial Engineering Research Conference, Nashville, TN, May 24-25, 442–448 (1995)

OGC: Glossary of ITIL® V3 terms and acronyms. FGI, Internet Document (2007)

OMG: Systems modeling language specification (SysML), object management group, internet document at: http://www.omg.org/spec/SysML/1.4/PDF/ (2007)

Rudd, C., Lloyd, V.: ITIL Version 3 Service Design. The Stationery Office, London (2007)

Sage, A.: Systems engineering education. IEEE TSMC Part C. 30(2), 164–174 (2000)

van Bon, J., De Jong, A., Kolthof, A., Pieper, M., Tjassing, R., van der Veen, A., Verheijen, T.: Foundations of IT Service Management Based on ITIL® v3, 5th edn. Van Haren, Zaltbommel (2010)

Weist, P.: An AHP-based decision making framework for IT service design. In: *MWAIS 2009 Proceedings*, Paper 11, http://aisel.aisnet.org/mwais2009/11 (2009)

Dr. Manuel Mora is a full-time Professor-Researcher and Coordinator of the CONACYT-PNPC MSc on IT program in the Information Systems Department at the Autonomous University of Aguascalientes (UAA), Mexico. Dr. Mora holds a B.S. in Computer Systems Engineering (1984) and a M.Sc. in Computer Sciences (Artificial Intelligence area, 1989) from Monterrey Tech (ITESM), and an Eng.D. in Engineering (Systems Engineering area, 2003) from the National Autonomous University of Mexico (UNAM). He has published over 90 research papers in international top conferences, research books, and refereed journals listed in JCRs such as IEEE-TSMC, European Journal of Operational Research, Int. Journal of Information Management, Engineering Management, Int. J. of Information Technology and Decision Making, Information Technology for Development, Int. J. in Software Engineering and Knowledge Engineering, and Computer Standards & Interface. Dr. Mora is a senior member of ACM (since 2008), of IEEE SMC Society, of INCOSE, and of the Mexican National Research System at Level I, and serves in the ERB of several international journals indexed by Emergent Source Citation Index focused on decision-making support systems (DMSS) and IT services systems. Dr. Mora has co-edited also four international research books in the topics of DMSS, IT services and Research Methods for prestigious academic publishers like Springer and IGI.

Jorge Marx Gómez is a full-time professor of Business Information Systems at the Carl von Ossietzky University Oldenburg, Germany since 2005. He holds a B. in Computer Engineering and Industrial Engineering at the University of Applied Science of Berlin (Technische Fachhochschule), and a Ph.D. degree in Business Information from Otto-von-Guericke-Universität Magdeburg. In 2004 he received his habilitation for the work Automated Environmental Reporting through Material Flow Networks at the Otto-von-Guericke-Universität Magdeburg. From 2002 till 2003 he was a Visiting Professor for Business Information Systems at the Technical University of Clausthal. Currently, Dr. Marx Gómez is the head of the department Business Informatics (Very Large Business Applications). His personal research interests include Environmental Management Information Systems, Business Intelligence, Material Flow Management Systems, Federated ERP-Systems, Enterprise Systems Engineering, Business Information Systems in Higher Education, Enterprise Tomography, Environmental Data Warehousing, Recycling Program Planning, Disassembly Planning and Control and Life Cycle Assessment. Dr. Marx Gómez is a member of: German Association of Computer Science (Gesellschaft für Informatik e.V., in short GI), OFFIS e.V. (Oldenburg Institute of Informatics), SAP Roundtable for Business Intelligence, German Association of University Professors and Lecturers (Deutscher Hochschulverband, in short DHV), German Forum of Interoperability (in short DFI), German Oracle Users Group e.V. (in short DOAG) and reviewer and expert in DAAD selection committee for Latin-American research proposals.

Prof. Rory V. O'Connor is a Professor of Software Engineering at Dublin City University (Ireland) and a Senior Researcher with Lero, the Irish Software Research Centre. He is Ireland's Head of Delegation to the International Organization for Standardization (ISO) for Software & Systems Engineering (ISO/IEC JCT1/ SC7). He is also editor in chief of the journal *Computer* Standards and Interfaces. His research interests are centered on the processes and standards whereby software intensive systems are designed, implemented and managed. His website address: http://www.roryoconnor.com

Burkard Meyendriesch is the Manager of the IT Service Department at the University of Oldenburg, Germany. He is a senior manager with over 25 years of IT responsibilities in different organizations in Germany.

Using Dashboards to Reach Acceptable Risk in Statistics Data Centers Through Risk Assessment and Impact

Atif Amin and Raul Valverde

Abstract A well designed and integrated database used to present risk management information by using a dashboard interface supported by real time risk management data makes it easy for risk managers to reach a full understanding of the surrounding threats and allows them to find the proper and right controls to mitigate them. The chapter presents a case study for a statistics data center that shows that the calculation of total risk at the organization level is possible by using the proposed risk database that supports decision makers when threats hit the organization. The chapter also shows that presenting the risk level on a dashboard viewer makes risk level clearer for a decision maker in a statistics data center and assists in the creation of a tool to follow-up risk management since the time a threat hits till the time of its mitigation.

1 Introduction

In the modern world the term "Business without a Risk" does not exist (D'Souza and Valverde 2015); with the vast development of technology and science where businesses relies on information technology that depends on internet and unsecure network access, it is almost impossible to achieve total security as there will always be a breaches and vulnerabilities that threaten business and cause damages to

A. Amin
Dubai Statistics Center, Dubai, United Arab Emirates
e-mail: atif_amn@hotmail.com

R. Valverde (✉)
Department of Supply Chain and Business Technology Management,
Concordia University, Montreal, QC, Canada

CONAIC, Mexico City, Mexico
e-mail: raul.valverde@concodia.ca

© Springer International Publishing AG 2017
J. Marx Gómez et al. (eds.), *Engineering and Management of Data Centers*,
Service Science: Research and Innovations in the Service Economy,
DOI 10.1007/978-3-319-65082-1_3

interest. Risk management becomes a necessity to every modern business, organization owners and decision makers implement it wildly to find hidden threats and vulnerabilities in their electronic services and systems and to detect risk before its strike. Monitoring risk level is becoming a trend at every organization in order to protect their assets and interests (Nijburg and Valverde 2011) as early detection of threats would help security staff and risk analysts to build countermeasures and controls that can help to discover vulnerabilities over their systems and business (Wolden et al. 2015). With early detection of risk in organizations, this would give enough time to organizations in order to act and save their interests (Almadhoob and Valverde 2014).

A data center is a facility used to house computer systems and associated components, such as telecommunications and storage systems. Although data centers has been readily adopted and implemented in commercial sectors such as the retail environment, its introduction and implementation for statistics purposes has been growing rapidly particular in the financial market and health care sectors (Khan and Valverde 2014).

The research focuses on conceptual understanding of information technology assets, how assets can be classified and categorized and how to be presented in a risk database for a statistics data center. This research primary focuses on designing and building a successful Information Security Management System (ISMS) module that can help statistics data centers the early detection of business risk. The following steps illustrate the scope of the research work:

1. Categorize assets into tangible assets (hardware, software) and intangible (data, information, Services and company Image)
2. Classify assets (assign access to applications and documents to different levels of management depending on who can access what and when).
3. Group assets in types as (Hardware, Software, Data, Files, Services, Hard Documents… etc)
4. Identify organization's main services and related business processes
5. Build a relationship between assets and business and store information in a relational database.
6. Identify threats, vulnerabilities and possible impacts through risk assessments, history records, and literature.
7. Create an automated Risk Assessment Plan (RAP) that allows the easy retrieval of risk information.
8. A business continuity plan based on assets and risk treatment plan (RAP) and a risk mitigation plan.
9. An ITIL assets management based framework (Assets Managements Database CMDB) for enhancing and maintaining Information security in statistics data centers.

The final result should lead to investigating risk causes using a dashboard viewer that will help IT managers to analyze results and establish proper controls to mitigate risk in statistics data centers.

2   Literature Review

The study focuses on understanding risk components and their related threats over statistics data centers assets; in particular the study is going to explore in more detail the risk's causes and reasons and will attempt to find solutions and controls to protect businesses. The following topics are reviewed:

- Assets
- Threats and Vulnerabilities
- Impact
- Risk management
- Risk Assessment
- Risk Mitigation

2.1   Identifying Risks

Identifying risk can be a very complex and hazard process when it comes to IT industry; one must develop an overall understanding of the business and the surrounding environment where every bit and pieces must count.

Common definitions are shared among related standards and researchers as follows:

- *Risk* is the likelihood of a threat agent taking advantage of vulnerability and the corresponding business impact (Harris 2008).
- *Risk* is the net negative impact of the exercise of vulnerability, considering both the probability and the impact of occurrence (Stoneburner et al. 2002)
- Risk is the combination of the probability of events and its consequences (ISO27001 standard)
- Risks can be defined as the probability of unwanted or unexpected event to occur

IT Systems and Services consist of many related components. In order to understand this relationship we must identify these components and dependent entities. Breaking down the service or system into its components would ease the process of specifying assets hierarchy and levels. Components can be hardware, software, connection while entities can be human, operation and organization image; all can be classified as assets. It is important to classify these assets and group them in categories and grade them. In order to clearly identify Risk levels, we need to assign a value to each asset, one of the key steps to perform a security risk assessment is to determine the value of the assets that require protection (Landoll 2006); this is the first step required by any risk assessment.

The second step is to look for surrounding threats and find their impact values over an asset (Landoll 2006). Impact can be severe causing total damage resulting in business failure or can be acceptable and possible to live with (Stoneburner et al. 2002).

2.2 Identifying Risks

Risk occurs when threats find their way to business infrastructure and environment and when vulnerability is exploited in order to allow threats to penetrate. Understanding threats and their probability of occurrence is important part of risk management. Measuring impact value on assets and finding its volume help to estimate the amount of damage risk can produce.

Another important issue is to have a quick and fast mechanism to act against threats. Building a system that is intelligent enough to predict when the next impact might take place actually would help business owners to develop a disaster recovery action and improve their business continuity plans.

Risk management consists of three major processes (Landoll 2006):

1. *Risk Assessment:* it identifies assets, threats and risk's impacts and recommends measurements through setting controls.
2. *Risk Mitigation:* the processes of accepting, avoiding or transferring risk
3. *Risk evaluation and Assessment:* the process of ongoing risk evaluation

Achieving total security is impossible to reach; this issue has been the debate of many organizations especially those who are involved in military and government activates where security measurements are at the top of their priorities. It is not possible to provide total security against every single risk, but it is possible to provide effective security against most risks (Calder and Watkins 2008).

"No system or environment is 100 percent secure, which means there is always some risk left over to deal with" (Harris 2008). Residual Risk can be defined as "The values of risk remaining after security measures have been applied—namely, the risk that remains after mitigation (countermeasures) has been applied" (Kouns and Minoli 2010).

The Term *Residual Risk* is used as the acceptable level of threat that organization can bear and survives with. It is the acceptable level of threat organization must live with in case of no controls and measures are applied or cannot be applied.

To distinguish Residual Risk from Total Risk, Harris (2008) clarifies it in the next formula.

$$threats \times vulnerability \times asset\ value = total\ risk$$
$$(threats \times vulnerability \times asset\ value) \times controls\ \text{gap} = residual\ risk \qquad (1)$$

Harris (2008) also illustrates Residual Risk as:

$$(threats, vulnerability, \text{and } asset\ value) = total\ risk$$
$$total\ risk - countermeasures = residual\ risk \qquad (2)$$

Accepting part of risk is a process every organization must live with, it is only relevant to how much can be accepted. Sometimes the results of cost benefit analyses indicates that the cost of countermeasures are higher and more expensive than assets that needs to be protected which give the organization no choice but to live and accept this level of risk. Eventually the question that always rises is what degree of residual risk is acceptable to the organization. Organizations must set this level clearly after risk assessment in order to monitor and observe risk level.

2.3 Asset's Attributes for Risk Database

Assets are organization's owned information, or any valuable entities that organization's business depends on. They can also be defined as the property of organization or person. In order to conduct an efficient risk assessment, a classification and categorization of assets are to be conceited and to be well identified. To build a solid design for a risk database many assets dependencies are to be well considered, identified and analyzed. An asset does not refer always to a tangible entity such as hardware or document but it can be none tangible as organization's image, service or a process. It is quite important for the database design to define asset types and subtypes attributes.

Assets types can be as follows:

- Information Assets (electronic files, Data and manuals)
- Paper and hardcopy documents (contracts, Manuals, plans, agreements, correspondences)
- Software assets (applications, systems, codes, Operating Systems)
- Physical assets (Computers, Storages, Network Devices, Cables, RAKS, Power and Cooling Devices)
- People (technical staff, Customers and Clients)

Assets subtype (as proposed in risk database) can be a subcategory of Asset Types, an example of this:

1. Physical asset (Server 004001)
2. Physical asset (Firewall 004005)
3. Information asset (Electronic File 001001)

Assets classification is the act of grouping assets into levels based on their sensitivity and importance to organization. It is useful to categorize or classify assets to organize asset protection requirements, and the vulnerability assessment of assets (Landoll 2006). Some assets might be vital to certain organizations while they are not to others, also classification process can be changed with time, some assets might be top confidential at certain period of time while they can be public at other time. A proposal to win a contract that contains important financial data is very sensitive and classified through bidding while it can be worthless after the bid time is over.

Classification of assets depends on organization methodologies of how its scales and leverage its assets and it can be classified according to different levels. In order to manage and control access to assets, a level of accessibility need to be created where it will govern who assess what. The business owner of an application (and any related data) must define who will have access to that application and, in terms of any data within it, at what level (i.e. read, write, delete, execute) (Calder and Watkins 2008).

Business applications and IT Systems usually consist of many interrelated assets working and communicating together to host business services. Applications like CRM and ERP solutions usually consist of databases, application and web servers and each hosts an operating system, applications and other software communicating though network and filtered by firewalls and network appliances and governed by network core switches via VLANs.

Failure of any asset item might put the service under risk. Some assets can be servers hosting software and data while others are communication channels allowing this data to flow in and out. Eventually each is important to organization. We cannot say one is more important than other, but we definitely realize that losing data storage is more serious than losing communication between two ends, even though both will result in service failure.

To keep assets under observation and monitoring a good management procedure is required. In order to do this the following is to be considered:

- Storage repository to be used as inventory system for these assets. Asset management includes knowing and keeping up-to-date this complete inventory of hardware (systems and networks) and software (Harris 2008).
- To keep good track of assets Configuration Management Database (CMDB) and Assets inventory are to be synchronized in order to keep track of changes and incidents and vulnerabilities (Harris 2008).
- A well defined asset lifecycle and history process starting at requesting and purchasing the asset and ending with assets termination or write-off.

Assets inventory is the source of Risk Management Systems for the determination of assets types, categories, classifications and values that would help to understand their possible threat and eventually propose the proper control. Based on ISO27001 best practices information assets are to be well identified at risk assessment. The asset inventory should identify each asset, including all the software, and describe it or provide such other identification that the asset can be physically identified (wherever possible, it makes sense to reuse whatever fixed asset number has already been allocated) and full details (including maker, model, generic type, serial number, date of acquisition and any other numbers) included in the inventory (Calder and Watkins 2008).

This process can be carried during risk assessment where result can always be compared with organization logistics register. On the other hand many configuration management applications can provide similar information and can be considered as good source of Information Assets inventory.

Incident Management Systems Assets inventory can be a good source to Incident Management System where the last must be updates each time new assets are added, changed or removed.

ITIL CMDB Information Technology Infrastructure Library's Configuration Management Database is also a good example, it is a container and storage for most information assets used in incidents, change and configuration management. A Risk analyst can use assets information in these systems to evaluate risk assessment and load asset data to their processes. Assets historical information must be also stored and obtained in risk management database. Historical data can be very useful in term of understanding asset's nature like age, value, relationship with other assets, and threats history with impacts. This can result in better evaluation and mitigation of risk.

Asset's owners are Individuals (Organization staff) or Entities (department, Section) which approved management responsibility for asset(s) but has no property rights to assets as they are the property of the organization. All information assets should have a nominated owner ('an individual or entity that has approved management responsibility for the assets') and should be accounted for. (Calder and Watkins 2008).

Assets ownership helps in risk assessment process as owners plays the role of custodian where he/she need to be informed before any changes made to asset. Acceptable use are set of rules and controls made to control access to certain asset such as read, edit, print, email, copy, backup, fax, internet usage and using of organization's mobile phones. Acceptable use addresses employee use of the organization's resources for accessing the information, transmitting or receiving electronic mail, general use of software, and system access (Landoll 2006).

2.4 Threats and Vulnerabilities

Threats and vulnerabilities are considered to be the main source of risk, there is no system that is 100% secure. A threat is the potential for a particular threat-source to successfully exercise a particular vulnerability (Stoneburner et al. 2002). The potential for a "threat source" to exploit (intentional) or trigger (accidental) a specific vulnerability (Stoneburner et al. 2002) are:

- Threats usually caused by 'threat source' where the last can be caused by human or nature, it can be deliberate as in hackings, cyber attacks or accidents as human errors, neglecting and lack of training.
- Risk does not occur when a threat source finds no vulnerability,

Threat is the potential to cause damage and harm to organization asset(s), or the reasons behind threats to occur, example of threat source is a human which might cause harm to an asset though computer attacks and unauthorized access.

A threat-source is defined as any circumstance or event with the potential to cause harm to an IT system (Stoneburner et al. 2002). Breaking threats into categories helps to understand them deeper and identify their threat source. The likelihood of threats to occur is considered as important as threat themselves, some threats might impact once a year while others every hour, this parameter (Probability of Occurrence or Likelihood of Occurrence or Likelihood Determination) is to be considered in risk evaluation and assessment.

The terms "Likelihood threat occurrence" or "The probability of threat to occur" are both used to identify the number of times threats might occur. Such information can be gathered from threats surveys, historical system attacks and other source of threats. Based on references (Harris 2008) and (Tan 2002) both qualitative and quantitative risk analysis uses these indicators in risk assessment. Vulnerabilities are weakness in organization security or can be considered as gap that threats can penetrate causing impacts on its assets and business (Stephens and Valverde 2013).

It can "leave a system, or asset, open to attacks by something that is classified as a threat, or allow an attack to have some success or greater impact" (Calder and Watkins 2008).Vulnerabilities can also be defined as situations and gaps that if not controlled or maintained will cause an actual threat. With the fast growing of technology and the demand of new software, threats will always find vulnerable entity or area to practice its impacts and attack. Vulnerability sources could be technical, initiated by human or process. The following could be a good source of vulnerability:

- Previous risk assessment
- Vendor's bugs list and reports
- Previous Incident reports generated by helpdesk system (if exist)
- Quality control testing documents
- Scanning tools and conducting penetration test.

2.5 Impact Analysis

Impact is the volume of damage that result from uncontrolled threat; impact can be estimated and predicted even before it occurs, where it can effect organization's business, operations and even reputation. Measuring impact is a major step in risk assessment, it aims to measure impact volume against asset's confidentiality, integrity and availability (CIA) through identifying impact's magnitude and source and investigating organization's sensitive and critical information, as a result impact analysis should assign a weight to impact where risk values is to be calculated. IT Governance-ISO27001 refers to Impact as "The successful exploitation of vulnerability by a threat will have an impact on the asset's availability, confidentiality or integrity". These impacts should all be identified and, wherever possible, assigned a monetary value based on the cost to the organization of that attribute being compromised" (Calder and Watkins 2008).

Impact can result in damaging and delaying of the following:

- Organization's every day operations.
- Financial loses which results in loss of assets and liabilities.
- Organization's reputation which is considered a major threat.

Impacts that affects assets can vary in magnitude, it is very important to understand and measure the amount of damage a certain impact might cause to systems and services, and how much time and money will be lost and more important is how many times the impact will occur (Likelihood of occurrence/(ARO)). A fast way to explore threats impacts is by identify their critical business processes (related to their core business). Failure of these processes will cause a critical and vital damage to organization.

Table 1 Controls types

Control type	
Detective	Capable to detect threats like IPS, CCTV
Directive	Administrative tasks and policies
Preventive	Prevent threat to occur like IPS, firewall
Corrective	Identify and minimize threat's impacts like applying security policy
Recovery	Controls that associated with disaster recovery and business continuity processes

2.6 Controls

They are set of measurements, activities applied to eliminate, minimize or transfer threats.

"Means of managing risk, including policies, procedures, guidelines, practices, or organizational structures, which can be administrative, technical, management, or legal in nature" (Kouns and Minoli 2010). ISC2 a leaders in information technology describes types of controls as following (Table 1):

Controls also can be implementing sets of operations and procedures to improve security measures or adding new protection asset such as purchasing firewall, antivirus or others.

3 Research Approach

3.1 Risk Management

This research used a case study research method where data was collected from primary and secondary data sources. A case study "involves the investigation of a particular situation, problem, company or group of companies" (Dawson 2009). Secondary data, or supporting data, was collected from related books, journals, online articles, vendors' websites and technology news websites. The case study used for this research is the statistics data center of Dubai.

The design of this study is based on well know risk management methodologies,

1. National Institute of Standards and Technology NIST in their Risk Management Guide for Information Technology System describes a full Risk Management Cycle; NIST Framework is based on three processes and their sub processes or steps:

   - Risk Assessment
   - Risk Mitigation
   - Evaluation and Assessment

2. IT Governance, A manager's Guide to Data Security and ISO 27001/ISO 27002 is based on well defined activates supported by template documents which can

be modified to fit any organization's Information Security Management System ISMS requirements, it is based on the following:

- Gap Analysis
- Identify criticality: the relationships between assets and Objectives
- Identify potential threats and vulnerabilities (likelihood)
- Risk Treatment Plan and the selection of controls and statement of applicability
- Measures of Effectiveness

Based on NIST 800-30 best practices the following figure illustrates risk assessment processes describing inputs and outputs entries (Fig. 1).

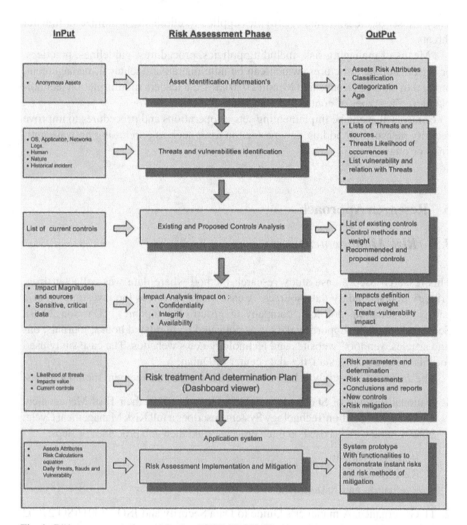

Fig. 1 Risk assessment phases based on NIST SP 800-30

3.2 Information Gathering Methods and Tools

When gathering data, it is quite important to define WHAT is to be collected, and WHO are the involved entities and parties in this process and HOW to collect data.

Before starting the risk assessment, it is important to identify what is to be collected. The following is to be considered:

- Assets data (types, Categories, Classifications, Owners, History data)
- Threats and Vulnerabilities (details description, categories, sources, types, remedy actions, number of occurrences)
- Impacts (details of threats impacts)
- Controls information (description types such as asset, plan, process, prices)

As part of the data collection requirements, it is important to identify the people that can help to speed the process of data gathering as hearing their opinions from different points of views (technical and business) and blend them in one container will help to discover many hidden issues. The process emphasizes on carrying a sequence of interviews with asset's owners, stakeholders, technical teams and risk related organization's members; The interview itself can result in an incredible amount of information if it is conducted properly (Landoll 2006).

The following stakeholders and organization's staff are involved in this process:

- Assets owners
- System and network Administrators
- Database Administrators
- Information Security specialist/Officer
- Business Owners
- Risk Manager/Team (if available)
- Financial Manager
- Top Management

Conducting an interview is considered to be an effective way of data gathering, it allows direct interaction with stakeholders, technical staff and top management, read their impression and understand their concerns not to mention the short time invested in this process. When conducting an interview, it is possible to address any confusion immediately, which minimizes the time lost and the frustration experienced by both sides (Wheeler 2011). Interviews to key personnel help to determine their ability to perform their duties (as stated in policies), their implementation of duties not stated in policies, and observations or concerns they have with current security controls" (Landoll 2006).

Questionnaire is just a passive version of an interview (Wheeler 2011). Questionnaires must be designed in a smart way to cover all to risk assessment process requirements that can be considered as a good input to the risk database for this research. The development of a set of interview questions depends heavily on the security risk assessment method, scope, and budget being applied (Landoll 2006).

All surveys and questionnaires are designed based on Dubai Statistic Center working environment and based on best practices of: Calder and Watkins (2008) and Stoneburner et al. (2002).

Proposed templates, questionnaires and interviews with stakeholders and technical team are to be completed and approved by top management. The following templates are to be used

   (i) Collecting Assets Information using:

      (a) *Assets Classification and Categorization Template.*
      (b) *Assets Information Details from Inventory System.*

  (ii) Collecting threats and vulnerabilities Information using *"General Threats Identification Sheet"*
 (iii) Collecting existing controls using: "Controls" template
 (iv) Collecting Impact Analysis details using:

      (a) *Qualitative Risk Assessment Template*
      (b) *Quantitative risk assessment templates*

3.3 Qualitative Risk Assessment Methodology or Approach

In order to scale assets not based on its marketing value but on its importance to the organization, interviews with business owners were conducted and templates evaluated by related members. The following Table 2 describes how assets are evaluated based on business sensitivity's best practices at Dubai Statistic Center.

Considering the above information and feedback from interviews and questionnaires the following rating is considered (Table 4):

Besides assets' data threats information must be well identified and collected in order to correctly weight their impact values. Threats must be identified, classified by category, and evaluated to calculate their damage potential to the company

Table 2 Assets values based on qualitative approach/Dubai Statistic Center

Assets values	Description
High values assets	Assets involved in core business, stalling or losing them will compromise organization CIA and would result in severe impact and losses such as financial and reputation wise which is unacceptable. An example of this losing organization sensitive information, damaging and ruin its profile
Medium value assets	Any assets that are not part of core business and do not cause a threat to the organization image, impact can be bearable and acceptable Example attendance system, development server and others similar.
Low value asset	Loosing or staling such assets would not compromise organization's CIA and would result in miner disruption Example printer, scanner, telephone device and others similar.

There are other parameters govern assets values which need to be considered also when rating an asset (Table 3).

Table 3 Other parameters effecting assets

Asset parameter	Description
Assets dependency level	Referencing asset's hierarchy and relationship with other assets. Is the asset depending on other assets? (application installed on app server) Does it have children (dependencies)? The more children an asset has, the higher its value as other assets depends on it. (server that hosts different software and data bases should worth more to the organization than a server with a single software that is installed on it)
Assets access level/classifications	What is the classification level for this asset? Is it top classified where losing the asset will damage the organization's reputation or it is public and can be compromised?
Asset age	Represent the number of years that the asset is operating.
Conclusion: in order to assign a value to asset (high, medium, and low) the above parameters are to be considered.	

Table 4 Qualitative asset rating

Asset value	Rate
High	3
Medium	2
Low	1

(Harris 2008). Based on best practices at Dubai Statistic Center threats data can be gathered from the following sources:

- Historical systems attacks
- World wide data
- Surveys and Questionnaires

Threat's historical data can be a good reference to organization's Information Security procedures, it can shows systems and services historical failures and what are the measures taken (if exist) to protect against such threats. This can be treated as the starting point of threats gathering. Threat probability of occurrence can never be 100% accurate after all it is not easy to predict when the next attack will be, however, giving a weight to threat's likelihood of occurrence can lead to better determination of risk value. The likelihood that a potential vulnerability could be exercised by a given threat-source can be described as high, medium, or low (Stoneburner et al. 2002). Based on meetings results with Risk Manager and referencing NIST SP-800-30 (Stoneburner et al. 2002), threats likelihood of occurrence can be measured as following (Table 5):

Identifying the common well known threats is an easy way to start collecting threat information. Table 6 presents common threats data that can exist at most of IT departments.

Table 5 Probability or likelihood of threat to occur

Likelihood of threats occurrence	Description	Weight
Negligible	Unlikely to occur	
Very low	Might occur few times every 5 years	
Low	Like to occur once every year	0.1
Medium	Occurs once every 6 months	0.5
High	Occur multiple times per month	1
Very high	Multiple times every week	
Extreme	More than once every day	

Table 6 General threats list

Threat	Probability of occurrence	Existing control	Applicable assets	Owner
Document theft	Medium	Personal lockers	Bids Technical proposals Technical manuals	System admin Network admin Sales department
Fire	Low	Fire distinguisher	Data Center IT department	Operation section IT department
Power failure	High	UPS Generators	Data Center	Operation section

It would be better to identify major threats over major assets to save time and efforts. Based on asset value to organization and interviews conducted with (Risk Manager, asset's owners), this research measured the impact volume according to its power to stole business or interrupt it. Referencing NIST SP 800-30 (Stoneburner et al. 2002) and based on the Dubai Statistic Center, business sensitivity in the following Table 7 illustrates impact volume measurement.

Based on the previous table, impact values can be presented as following (Table 8):

This approach is based on giving a weight value to each asset, threat's impacts and their likelihood of occurrences as (High, Medium and Low). Risk is calculated in the proposed risk database as follows (Harris 2008):

$$Risk = Asset\ Value \times Impact \times Likelihood\ of\ Threat \qquad (3)$$

3.4 Quantitative Risk Assessment Methodology

In order to gather monetary risk values where assets values are measured in currency, the finance manager and involved team in asset evaluation are to fill a Quantitative Risk assessment questionnaire. Based on interviews with Assets Owners, Financial Manager and Risk Manager, the followings points are to be considered:

Table 7 Impact volume Measurements based on NIST SP 800-30

Impact volume	Description
Insignificant	Almost no impact if threat and vulnerabilities are exploited
Minor	Minor effects on organization's assets and business, recovering is manageable
Significant	Results in some tangible damage, and require some time to recover (example internal service interruption and restored, connection down restored immediately)
Damaging	Noticeable impact that result in large but internal damage, requires time and resources to restore (example internal operation failure)
Critical	The impact could result in high damage of business infrastructure which result total failure to deliver business and require long time and high resources to restore (example production server failure, network down)

Table 8 Impact values

Critical	High	H	3
Damaging	Medium	M	2
Minor	Low	L	1

Financial Cost:

- Market Cost
- Development Cost (in case of Application Software)
- Installation and Configuration Value
- Maintenance and Support Cost
- Replacement Cost
- Operation and running Cost (electricity, License in case of software)
- Depreciation Cost

Non Financial Cost

- Value to organization (like Organization Reputation)
- Asset value to users and customers

Based on previous assets parameters provided, the following formula can be generated and used to set quantitative value to asset.

$$Asset\ Value = Purchasing\ Value - Depreciation\ value + (cost\ of\ time\ to$$
$$recover)\ or\ cost\ to\ replace\ asset\ \text{and put it}\ to\ functioning + loss\ caused\ \text{by} \quad (4)$$
$$service\ stopping + Support\ \text{and}\ Maintenance\ value$$

The *exposure factor (EF)* represents the percentage of loss a realized threat could have on a certain asset (Harris 2008; Kouns and Minoli 2010). Single Loss Expectancy (SLE) is the total amount of revenue that is lost from a single occurrence of the risk (Kouns and Minoli 2010). Annual Rate of Occurrence (ARO) is the normalized rate at which the risk exposure resulting in actual damage occurs during 1 year (Kouns and Minoli 2010).

The *annualized rate of occurrence (ARO)* is the value that represents the estimated frequency of a specific threat taking place within a one-year timeframe (Harris 2008). Qualitative risk is based on assigning monetary value to assets. Based on Harris (2008), Tan (2002) and Wheeler (2011) the quantitative risk formula in the proposed risk database is calculated as below:

$$Single\,Loss\,Expectancy\,(\text{SLE}) = Asset\,Value^{*}Exposure\,Factor\,(\text{EF})$$
$$Annual\,Loss\,Expectancy\,(\text{ALE}) = \text{SLE} \times Annual\,Rate\,of\,Occurrence\,(\text{ARO})$$

(5)

Data for the proposed dashboard viewer can be presented as:

- Charts
- Tables

The proposed study case template to analyze risk data is presented below in Table 9.

4 Case Study and Data Collection

In order to present risk data accurately at any organization, the risk team must have a full picture over organization's main services and its backbone infrastructure where every asset (tangible and none) software and hardware is identified. The above figure demonstrates an IT based service with four VLANs (Virtual Local Area Network) similar to the environment of the Dubai Statistic Center and its components of hardware and software as they are described in details in Fig. 2.

A good understanding of the organization structure leads to a better identification of threats and vulnerabilities areas. The risk team can develop a solid idea on how to plan risk management processes, contacting whom in case of failure, which departments and sections will be out of business in case of threat's impact and what are the losses.

Figure 3 represents part of the Dubai Statistic Center's Departments Organization Chart. Top management approval must be granted before initiating a risk assessment process, the following should be considered:

- All related stakeholders are to be notified.
- All proposed templates, questionnaires and interviews scenarios are to be checked and approved.

Table 9 A proposed study case template to analyze risk data and propose action

Case #	
Name	The case description or the criteria title
Indicators	How this case was explored? What are the risk indicators?
Effective parameters	What are the related parameters? Example asset value, impact value.
Searching criteria	What is the searching criteria, what to look for and where?
Analysis and investigation	This section covers analyzing the case (HOW?) and what indication we need to build our decision on?
Decision and action	Decision and action need to be taken.

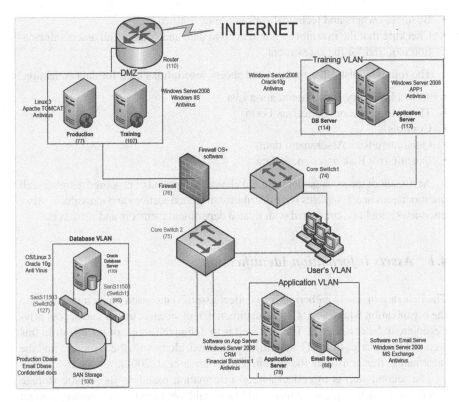

Fig. 2 IT service infrastructures

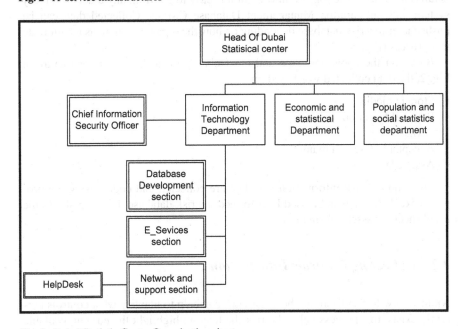

Fig. 3 Dubai Statistic Center Organization chart

- Business owners and technical staff are to be notified.
- Checking that the inventory system is up to date and contains all assets information required for the assessment.

The following lists all templates and sheets descriptions used for data collection.

- Assets Inventory and Classification List
- Threat Information Collection Form
- Controls
- Qualitative Risk Assessment data
- Quantitative Risk assessment data

As a result of top management and stakeholder's approval of proposed templates, all questionnaires and Templates were distributed to related sections and individuals. Also, interviews should be conducted with related department members and managers.

4.1 Assets Information Identification

The first step in assets gathering is to collect assets' data based on its importance to the organization where assets' type, nature, mean of storage, owner and access privileged are to be considered. The first step is to define the scope of the effort. In this step, the boundaries of the IT system are identified, along with the resources and the information that constitute the system (Stoneburner et al. 2002).

The second step is to collect assets' information based on its logistic storage where assets' details are to be recorded like serial No#, brand, maintenance contract details and others. The logistic information is easy to get from any assets inventory system or Configuration Management Database CMDB. Collected data can be pushed later to a risk database depending on how the organization plans to automate this process (Fig. 4).

Based on the above template and the Dubai Statistic Center Infrastructure in Fig. 2, the data collected was based on:

- Storage media
- Physical Location
- Owner
- Acceptable Use and many
- Asset Classification

The required risk information and data are collected and coded using the proposed excel sheets as to be used later to feed the risk database. Figure 5 shows the excel sheet for asset information.

4.2 Collecting Controls Information

An interview to technical and business staff can help to identify what controls currently exists, this process helps the risk the team to highlight the current available countermeasures. Based on best practices and interviews conducted with related

ORGANIZATION (ABC)
ASSET INVENTORY & CLASSIFICATION LIST

					Document No: #	
					Original Issue Date:	
Department: Information Technology					Revision No: 1	
Dept. Incharge Designation:					Revision Date:	

ASSET.No.	INFORMATION ASSET	MEDIUM OF STORAGE	LOCATION	RESPONSIBIT Y	Acceptable Use	Asset Classification
		(Electronic / Hard Copy Documents)	(Computer / Rack / Cabinet etc)	/ OWNER (Designation)		
67	Gateway1		150 (Rack)	System Admin	R-W-X	-3
116	Windows server 2008	E	67	System Admin	R-W-X	-3
115	Trend Micro antivirus	E	116	System Admin	R-W-X	-3
122	Oracle DB Server HW02		150	System Admin	R-W-X	-3
56	RedHat Enterprise Linux	E	122	System Admin	R-W-X	-3
99	Oracle 10g for Windows 2	E	56	DBA	R-W-X	-3
110	Rounter (main)		150 (Rack)	Network Admin	R-W-X	-3

Reviewed by:		Approved by:	
CISO		MD	

Fig. 4 Assets Inventory and Classification List (AICL)

Ast_ID	Ast_Desc 119	Ast_Serial_no	Ast_Model_no	Ast_Brand	Ast_Category	Ast_Service	Ast_Type	Ast_SubType	Ast_Classification	Ast_Access_level	Ast_Qltv_Value	Ast_Age	Ast_Q ntv_Value	Ast_SuppCont_type	Ast_SuppCont_D	Ast_SuppCont_DateF
110	Rounter (main)	xyz	Rt987	15	1	1	1	24	1	-3	3	3	5000	2	2	7/22/2010
	DMZ															
77	Application server_HW01	APP1212X44L	3560	1	1	1	1	1	1	-3	3	3	5600	2	1	1/1/2011
56	RedHat Enterprise Linux Release 3		linux Operating Sys	11	1	1	2	1	1	-3	3	4	2000	2	2	1/22/2010
109	Apachi TOMCAT SW	Tmyvc		11	1	1	2	5	1	-3	3	3		1	1	1/1/2011
3	Trend Micro Antivirus_Linux	Ant L679		2	1	1	2	2	1	-3	3	1	3800	2	2	1/12/2010
107	Training server_HW02	APP1212X44L	3560	1	1	1	1	1	1	-3	3	4	5600	2	1	1/1/2011
37	Win Srv 2008 SW	Tmyvc	Windows Server	4	1	1	2	1	1	-3	3	3	2000	1	3	1/12/2010
108	Win Srv IIS SW	Tmyvc	Windows	4	1	1	2	3	1	-3	3	3		1	3	1/12/2010
105	Trend Micro Antivirus_Windows	Ant W2345		2	1	1	2	2	1	-3	3	1	2000	2	2	1/12/2010
76	ASA 5520	fir1212X47sF	5620	15	1	1	1	20	1	-3	3	4	14000	2	1	1/1/2011
84	OS Firewall	JMX16Z0RK	abc	15	1	1	2	1	1	-3	3	4		2	1	1/1/2011
74	SWITCH -Core01	Sxy12050166	4503	15	1	1	1	5	1	-3	3	4	12000	2	1	1/1/2011
	VLAN Training															
113	Training APP server_HW03	APP1212X44L	3560	1	1	1	1	1	1	-3	3	4	5600	2	1	1/1/2011
114	Win Srv 2008 SW	Tmyvc	Windows Server	4	1	1	2	1	1	-3	3	3	2000	1	3	1/12/2010
106	CRM Software_TSW	App software 1		70	1	1	2	3	1	-3	3	2	25000	2	1	1/1/2011
115	Trend Micro Antivirus_Windows	Ant W2346		2	1	1	2	2	1	-3	3	1	1800	2	2	1/12/2010

Fig. 5 Asset information after coding

members and business owners, the following proposed template in Fig. 6 is used to gather existing controls applied to certain assets

4.3 Collecting Controls Information

Based on the risk formula and previous data collected via assets, threats and controls templates, the following table is produced with risk values against assets before and after the proposed controls (Fig. 7).

	Conrtols Information					
	Control_ID	Asset Id	Control_Desc	Control type	control_est _market Price	
	0		No control on the asset	0		
	1	1	Trend Micro - windows	4		
	4		valid Maintenance Contract	4		
	29		Using Change Management Procedure	4		
	30		Purchase and Install a new san switch	4	15000	
	92		Purchase UPS	1	2000	
	95		Intrusion detections 360	1	35000	
	5		ASA-5520 (Primary) logs	1		
	6		Access Control Policy	2		
	8		Disable ftp port	4		
	9		Disable ssh port	4		
	12		monitor Alert logs	2		
	13		Miror Local Disks	2		
	14		regular System Backup	2		
	15		Hire Qualified DBA	4		
	16		Provide Redundent Server?Cluster	4		
	17		Update Firewall Configuration	4		
	28		Install IPS	4		
	Control_id is a sequeces code					
	Control type : 0 no control 1 Asset 2 Process 3 Plan 4 Action					

Fig. 6 Evaluating control template

											Document No : DSC-02

Date of Issue : 08/10/2010
Revsion No
Date of Revision

Section   : Information technology_
Section Head :

					Asset Info						**Controls Detail**		
seq	asset Id	Asset Description	Date	Asset Value (H,M,L)	Threat_id	Threats description	Impact Value (H,M,L)	status Control	Control_Id	Control Description	Probabil ty of threat	Risk Value	
1	86	SanS11503 (Switch 1)	5/10/2011	3	30	Non redundant SAN Switches	3	0	0		2	9	
2	86	SanS11503 (Switch 1)	5/23/2011	3	30	Non redundant SAN Switches	2	5	30	puchase and install san switch	1	0.6	
3	74	SWITCH -Core01	3/18/2011	2	40	Electrical PS. failure	2	0	0		3	4	
4	74	SWITCH -Core02	3/18/2011	2	40	Electrical PS. failure	2	5	92	Intrusion detections 360	0	0.4	
5	100	IBM SAN Storage	2/17/2009	3	25	Unauthorized access	3	0	0		4	0.9	
6	101	IBM SAN Storage	2/18/2009	3	25	Unauthorized access	3	0	0		6	4.5	
	control Status : 0 current 5: proposed												

Fig. 7 Qualitative risk assessment

4.4 Collecting Quantitative Risk Data

Based on risk formula and previous data collected via assets, values, threats and expected loss factors, a table with risk values in Fig. 8 illustrates the calculation of risk values against asset before and after proposed control.

The template gathers assets information based on asset's financial cost to organization, the calculation formula can be complex and vary from asset to another.

									Document No : DSC-02					
									Date of Issue : 13/10/2010					
									Revsion No :					
Section : Network and support section									Date of Revision :					
Section Head : XXXXX														

		Asset Info								Controls Detail				
seq	sset Id	Asset Description	Asset Value $	Threat_id	Threats description	DATE	Expected lossfactor (EF)	Single Loss Expectancy (SLE)	status	Control	Control_id	Control Description	Annual Rate of Occurrence	Risk Value in $
1	86	SanS11509 (Switch 1)	15000	38	Non redundant SAN Switches	5/10/2011	1	15000	0	0		No control	2	30000
2	86	SanS11509 (Switch 1)	15000	38	Non redundant SAN Switches	5/23/2011	0.5	7500	5	30		Purchase and install a new san switch	1	15000
3	74	SWITCH -Core01	25000	40	Electrical PS. failure	3/18/2011	0.25	6250	0	0		No control	3	18750
4	74	SWITCH -Core02	25000	40	Electrical PS. failure	3/18/2011	0.1	2500	5	92		Purchase UPS	0	7500
5	100	IBM SAN Storage	5000	25	Unauthorized access	2/17/2009	0.1	500	0	0		No control	4	20000
6	101	IBM SAN Storage	5000	25	Unauthorized access	2/18/2009	0.1	500	5	95		Intrusion detections 360	2	1000

Fig. 8 Quantities risk assessment

4.5 Collecting Quantitative Risk Data

Threats data can be collected using surveys and from historical incidents. Software logs if interpreted and reformatted can be another good source of threats, they can show what is the real infrastructure and what are the technical threats surrounding the organization. When it comes to security, these logs can be a good reference for vulnerability and penetration test as well. Other advantage of using system's log is to achieve real time views; risk database can log/accept data from various incident sources. Incident Management Systems and SysLog can be a good example for best practice. The following Figs. 9 and 10 presents electronic threats sources to risk database.

4.6 Design and Build Risk Database

The database design includes entities that define risk processes, attributes which constructs each entity and relationship between entities.

Based on previously provided templates the following entities can be identified:

1. Assets
2. Threats
3. Controls

Going further by breaking down the entities into sub entities based on collected data. The following Table 10 illustrates the major database tables proposed to present risk data. The table also describes the functionality and purposes behind each database table.

This approach is more practical for some organizations while it is not for others but it is still easier and requires less calculation. It is based on surveys and questionnaires provided and it is more achievable when it comes to rate similar hardware that exists in two different businesses (example a Server can be rated as HIGH when it comes to production environment while the same Server can be rated as LOW if it is used for training purposes). Table 11 presents the risk formula calculation in the risk database based on a qualitative approach.

A monetary value presentation of assets, threats and risk, for those who seeks financial numbers can use the Quantitative values which is part of the risk database.

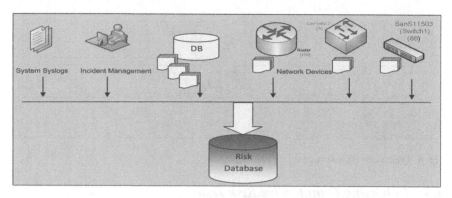

Fig. 9 Sources of threats

Table 12 shows threats and their single Loss Expectancies, Annual Rate of threat's Occurrences and Annual Loss Expectancies.

5 Dashboard and Risk Analysis

A dashboard viewer can provide various risk information that can help the risk team to determine what action needs to be taken. Actions should be based on decisions that's wisely reflects the risk volume and amount of damage that can result.

Three risk scenarios are presented in order to demonstrate the risk dashboard generation for risk management.

5.1 Risk Scenario 1: Threats and Impact Analysis Based on Qualitative Approach

Data at the proposed dashboard viewer can be presented as:

- Charts
- Tables

Table 13 describes the risk scenario 1 that is meant to find high risk based on threat's impact by using a qualitative approach. The risk manager in this case is looking for assets or systems with high impact value and low likelihood of occurrence or high impact value and high likelihood of occurrence.

The results are presented in the dashboard view in Fig. 11.

5.2 Risk Scenario 2: Decisions Based on Historical Risk Data

Risk historical data can be a good source for decision makers and risk analysts for the planning of risk mitigation strategies. The risk database through dashboard views can help to make a better picture of the nature and types of threats for frequent

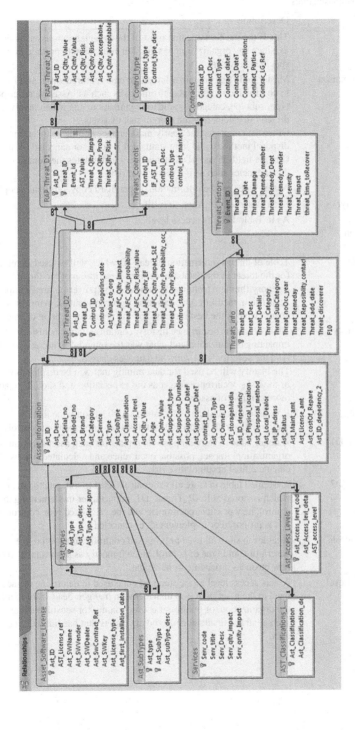

Fig. 10 Database design

Table 10 Database tables

Tables	Description
Services	This is the master table that most of the organizations assets is linked to, since any organization has mission and vision to provide the specified services
Asset _Information	Master table that contain all required data required about all IT assets to control and monitor at real-time risks such as: Asset id, description, type, subtype, category, value to organization, age which involved directly in calculating the current risk to assets. Other data manages the yearly maintenance contracts, location, disposal methods, and item status if it is active or canceled (write-off). One the fields is Ast_ID dependency which relates the item to its dependencies such as if a server is at risk.
Assets_types	Assets types can be information, paper, hard copy, physical, people.
Assets_sub_types	Such as server, software, firewall, ...
Assets_ Classification_ Level	As in Table 1 assets access level
Threats_info	Table of threats information, threat_ID which will be used as reference for the threat in the database, detailed description of the threat, category (human, technical..), subcategory (power failure..), impact scale (high, medium..), access level (top confidential, mangers, section heads) what is the best remedy, and the person or dept. in charge.
Threats_History	Table of threats occurrence history, contains all threats history impacting organization and what was the remedy? Who recovered? And the severity level with the damages caused. The history will be used for data mining that will be displayed if any of the risks occurrences exceeds our expectation and should we add more controls of assets.
RAP_Threat_m	Risk assessment plan master table, which has only the final accumulative risk for all assets items after implementing controls.
RAP_Threat_D1	A detail table to store all possible threats for each asset and values to organization, impact, possible occurrence and calculated risk used to calculate final accumulative risk.
RAP_Threat_D2	A detailed table to store all the controls used to mitigate threats risk's which is stored at RAP_Threat_D1, impact after implementing the control, new possible occurrence and the calculated risk, control status if it is proposed or implemented, or canceled
Threats_Controls	A tables to store all used or proposed controls with a reference, description and type of control, since it mostly as asset item also or a new business procedure or new plan.
Ast_access_Level	Assets access level as the standard code used to determine the access level to the asset item (top management, manger, head section, inside the organization, or public), it is used mainly for sensitive documents such contract, financial data, and any assets that has limited access only.

Table 11 Qualitative risk dependencies and calculation method in the proposed database

Risk dependency	Calculation method
Asset qualitative value AST_QLTV_VALUE	In qualitative approach asset is rated as (HIGH, MEDIUM, LOW) and rated as follows HIGH = 3, MEDIUM = 2, LOW = 1)
Threat impact after controls are applied THREAR_AFC_QLTV_IMPACT	Impact value, can be (HIGH, MEDIUM, LOW) and rated as follows HIGH = 3, MEDIUM = 2, LOW = 1)
Probability of threat to occur or take place it can also be called as the likelihood of threat to occur. THREAT_AFC_QLTV_PROB	The frequency of threat to occur LOW—Occurs once every few years and rated as 0.1 MEDIUM- occurs once every 6 months and rated as 0.5 HIGH- occurs once every month and can be rated as 1
Qualitative risk (calculated value) THREAT_AFC_QLTV_RISK	Risk is calculated in the proposed database using qualitative approach as follows: RISK = ASSET value * impact value * probability of occurrence

attacks and their business impact. Based on the analysis of the dashboard, an analyst can decide if an action needs to be taken towards this risk and to whether add more controls and propose prevention actions or just accept the risk.

Based on the historical table in Risk Database the (qualitative and quantitative view) risk values can shows increases of risk through years as seen in Fig. 12.

Retrieved data filtered by threat number 25 (Unauthorized access), shows that this threat's impact is increasing over the years (2009, 2010, 2011) as indicated in the dashboard view in Fig. 13.

Figure 14 shows a dashboard view that indicates that IBM SAN Storage, MS Exchange Server and Oracle Database server are subject to "Unauthorized Access". This threat is increasing every year.

5.3 Risk Scenario 3: Risk Views at CRM Service Level

The Risk database can provide risk views at the service level (example CRM) where all related assets risk values are added as a sum as shown in Fig. 15 (Table 14).

Based on the previous analysis and investigation to "unauthorized access", a new control is proposed and the next figure illustrates the risk level after the new control is applied (Purchasing IPS) (Fig. 16).

Table 12 Quantitative risk dependencies and calculation method

	Formula
Asset quantitative value (AST_QNTV_VALUE)	There are many ways to measure and calculate asset qualitative value Purchasing value Depreciation value Cost of recovery/replacement time Delay and stepping time cost Ast_Qntv_value = Purchasing value - depreciation value +(cost of time to recover) or cost to replace asset and put it to functioning + loss caused by service stopping + support and maintenance cost
Single loss expectancy (calculated value) Is the quantitative asset value multiplied by exposure factor	Single loss expectancy (SLE) is calculated by multiplying asset quantitative value (calculated in the previous row) by threat exposure factor (EF-the percentage of loss a threat can have over an asset). Example: If asset that worth 20 K is exposed to threat that can damage 30% of the asset such as partial malfunction then single loss expectancy (SLE) = AST_QNTV_VALUE* EF = 20,000 * 0.3 = 6000$
Annual rate of occurrence THREAT_AFC_QNTV_PROB_OCC_ARO	How many time the threat can occur (usually its calculated per year) Value can be between 0 to greater than one
Annual loss expectancy (calculated value)	This value can tell the management how much damage in monetary value can certain threat annually cause to a certain asset, in other word it is the SLE multiplied by ARO = AST_QNTV_VALUE * THREAT_AFC_QNTV_EF * THREAT_AFC_QNTV_PROB_OCC_ARO

The above figure and based on quantitative risk analysis shows drop in risk level to 1000$, 2400$ and 3400$ to IBM SAN Storage, Email Server and Oracle Server respectfully at 2011 and after new control is applied (Fig. 17).

The above figure and based on qualitative risk analysis shows drop in risk level to 0.9, 0.4 and 0.9 to IBM SAN Storage, Email Server and Oracle Server respectfully at 2011 and after new control is applied.

As a result CRM service Level risk is dropped to reach level less than what was in 2009 as shown in Fig. 18.

6   Conclusions

The calculation of total risk at a statistics data center based on qualitative and quantitative analysis is possible using the proposed database that will give decision makers a good insight in order to make better decisions before and when threats hit the

Table 13 Scenario 1

Scenario # 1	
Name	Finding high risk based on threat's impacts/qualitative approach
Indicators	Risk level (high impact and low probability), (high impact and high probability)
Effective parameters	Impact Likelihood of occurrence
Searching criteria	Looking for assets or systems with: High impact value and low likelihood of occurrence High impact value and high likelihood of occurrence
Analysis and investigation	All high impacts values must be taken seriously; IT staff might underestimate risks with low likelihood of occurrence as they might never occur. Example an out of date antivirus on database server, it is a fact that most of database servers are located in a separate VLAN which is isolated from external traffic and the probability of virus attack is very unlikely to occur but that does not mean it is safe to leave the antivirus software out of date. The impact will be very high if the server is attacked.
Decision and action	All high impact values are to be seriously considered even with low probability of occurrence. An immediate action is to be taken for any high impact assets even if the probability of attack was very unlikely to occur.

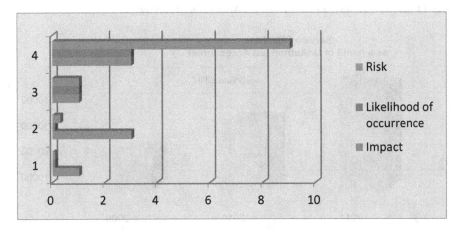

Fig. 11 Dashboard view – high risk based on threat's impacts/qualitative approach

	Ast_ID	Threat_I	Event_year	AST_Value	Threat_Qltv_Impa	Threat_Qltv_Probability_occ	Threat_Qltv_Risk	Threat_Qntv_EF	Threat_(	Threat_Qntv_Probability_occ_ARO	Threat_Qntv_Risk
IBM SAN Storage	100	25	2009	3	3	1	9	0.3	1500	2	3000
IBM SAN Storage	100	25	2010	3	3	1	9	0.3	1500	6	9000
IBM SAN Storage	100	25	2011	3	3	1	9	0.3	1500	9	13500
Email MS Exchange Server_	68	25	2009	2	2	0.5	2	0.1	1200	4	4800
Email MS Exchange Server_	68	25	2010	2	2	0.5	2	0.1	1200	6	7200
Email MS Exchange Server_	68	25	2011	2	2	0.5	2	0.1	1200	9	10800
Oracle DBA-Server-HW02	122	25	2011	3	3	1	9	0.1	1700	9	15300
Oracle DBA-Server-HW03	122	25	2010	3	3	1	9	0.1	1700	6	10200
Oracle DBA-Server-HW04	122	25	2009	3	3	1	9	0.1	1700	4	6800

Fig. 12 Dashboard view—risk values

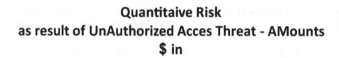

		25	Unauthorized access	
		quantitattive		
		2009	2010	2011
IBM SAN Storage	100	3000	9000	13500
Email MS Exchange Server	68	4800	7200	10800
Oracle DB-Server-HW02	122	6800	10200	15300

Fig. 13 Dashboard view—annual increases of Asset's risk- tabular view

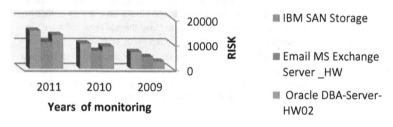

**Quantitaive Risk
as result of UnAuthorized Acces Threat - AMounts
$ in**

Fig. 14 Dashboard view—annual increases of Asset's risk- chart view

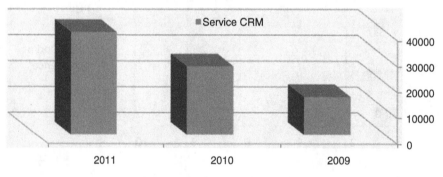

**Service CRM Risk
as a result of UnAuthorised Acces threat**

Fig. 15 Dashboard view—annual unauthorized access risk value –service level –chart view

organization. Predicting threats before they happen by conducting a what if analysis on the infrastructure and calculate the expected risk, take the propriety action as preventing threat from happening or mitigate risk before it happens is possible with a help of a dashboard in a statistics data center. Presenting the risk level on a dashboard viewer makes risk level clearer for a decision maker. The model created with

Table 14 Scenario 3

Case 3	
Area	Risk
Name	Service level risk per threat based on historical data
Indicators	Monitoring risk level
Effective parameters	Threat assets ID and description Events year Asset value (Qltv,Qntv) Impact value (Qltv,Qntv) Risk value (Qltv,Qntv)
Searching criteria	Risk generated by threat number 25 (unauthorized access) since 2009 till 2011
Analysis and investigation	The retrieved data helps risk analysts and security specialists to determine the amount of risk generated by threat 25 since 2009, it indicates as the dashboard shows that the unauthorized access is increases on the related assets (SAN storage, email and database server).
Decision and action	An action need to be taken to protect CRM service Purchasing IPS would be a good solution providing that two out of three assets are rated HIGH (3) which considered important to be protected. Impact value is HIGH (3) for two out of three asset. As a conclusion high level asset with high level impact value is to be considered seriously.

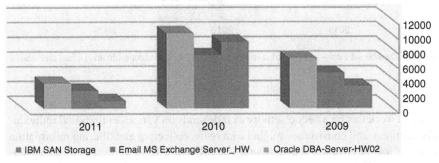

Quantitaive Risk
as result of UnAuthorized Access Threat
after ID 2011

IBM SAN Storage   Email MS Exchange Server_HW   Oracle DBA-Server-HW02

Fig. 16 Dashboard view—Qltv-risk dropped in 2011 to acceptable level-chart and tabular view

the help of managers, head section, risk officers, helpdesk (risk stakeholder) of a statistics data center assisted in the creation of a tool to follow-up risk management since the time it hits till the time of mitigation, and it will give a clear picture for a manager on how subordinates are performing. Historical risk data is considered to be a good and rich source to threats and impacts that surrounds the statistics data center organization. Decisions can be built based on legacy information to provide better protection and controls can minimize manual activities and paper work.

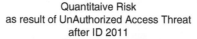

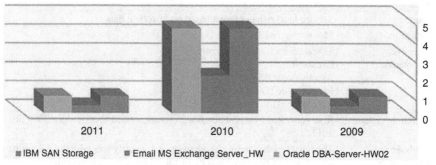

Fig. 17 Dashboard view—Qntv-risk dropped in 2011 to acceptable level-chart and tabular view

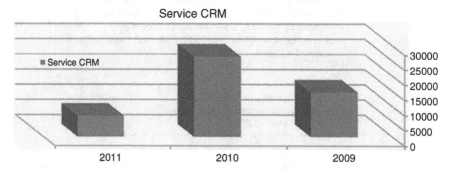

Fig. 18 Dashboard view—service level -risk dropped in 2011 to acceptable level-chart and tabular view

Manual work can be a hectic activity as it depends on various entities and individuals; accuracy and consistency might be an issue, collecting and filtering information requires lots of efforts and man hours. The following Table 15 describes the advantages of a risk database over manual activities:

Finally, a risk database is a good resource for top management to build their conclusions based on collected data and take the proper action against risks at the right time. The senior manager must decide to reduce the risk, accept the risk, or delegate the risk to someone else. A security risk can be reduced by implementing additional security controls or even by improving existing security controls (Landoll 2006).

Table 15 Advantage of risk database

Process	Manual and semi manual work	Proposed design
Assets information gathering/ management	Using surveys, questionnaires and template forms to feed manual and automated processes	Use ITIL CMDB as reference or consider the risk database a good assets repository/inventory which can serve and feed other systems like helpdesk and change and incident systems
Threats dependencies and handling	Generates threat statement based on: Historical data(system attacks) that is collected periodically from different systems and resources Well known attacks by vendors	A full threat's repository for the current existing threats and expected ones based on assets nature vulnerabilities. Automated display (dashboard viewer) for all possible threats, discovery details and existing and proposed controls
Risk mitigation	Qualitative OR quantitative approach. Risk evaluated at asset level only Manual or systematic way of calculation with restriction	Risk evaluation and calculation in both qualitative and quantitative approaches; gives a wide range of evaluation criteria and better understanding of risk A service/system level risk view, with drilling capability to asset level. Automated risk calculation and flexible way to change calculation parameters
Presentation layer	Manuals and hardcopy documents Complicated and very expensive systems	Dashboard viewer that reads directly from the proposed database and required no application.

References

Almadhoob, A., Valverde, R.: Cybercrime prevention in the Kingdom of Bahrain via IT security audit plans. J. Theor. Appl. Inf. Technol. **65**(1), 274–292 (2014)

Calder, A., Watkins, S.: I. T. Governance. A Manager's Guide to Data Security and ISO 27001/ISO 27002. Kogan Page, London (2008)

Dawson, C.W.: Projects in Computing and Information Systems: A Student's Guide. Pearson Education, Harlow (2009)

DeSouza, E., Valverde, R.: An employee-based risk management strategy for reducing security incidents in a Canadian PHIPA regulated environment. In: International Conference on Innovations in Computer Science and Information Technology (ICICSIT -2015), Hyderabad (2015)

Harris, S.: CISSP All-in-One Exam Guide. McGraw-Hill Inc., New York (2008)

Khan, N.A., Valverde, R.: The use of RFID based supply chain systems in data centers for the improvement of the performance of financial institutions. Eng. Manage. Res. **3**(1), 1–24 (2014)

Kouns, J., Minoli, D.: Information technology risk management in entreprise environments. Wiley, Denvers (2010)

Landoll, D.: The Security Risk Assessment Handbook: A Complete Guide for Performing Security Risk Assessments. CRC Press, Boca Raton (2006)

Nijburg, E., Valverde, R.: A business continuity monitoring model for distributed architectures: a case study. Int. J. Appl. Sci. Technol. **1**(2), 5–14 (2011)

Stephens, J., Valverde, R.: Security of e-procurement transactions in supply chain reengineering. Comput. Inf. Sci. **6**(3), 1–20 (2013)

Stoneburner, G., Goguen, A.Y., Feringa, A.: Sp 800-30. risk management guide for information technology systems. National Institute of Standards and Technology, Gaithersburg (2002)

Tan, D.: Quantitative risk analysis step-by-step. SANS Institute, Bethesda (2002)

Wheeler, E.: Security risk management: building an information security risk management program from the ground up. Elsevier, Waltham (2011)

Wolden, M., Valverde, R., Talla, M.: The effectiveness of COBIT 5 information security framework for reducing cyber attacks on supply chain management system. IFAC-PapersOnLine. **48**(3), 1846–1852 (2015)

Atif Amin is an IT manager with the Dubai Statistics Center in Dubai United Arab Emirates. Atif completed a Master of Science in Information Technology at the University of Liverpool in Liverpool England. Atif has international experience in IT from different countries and holds several certifications. Atif's main research interest include business intelligence, data centers and IT management.

Dr. Valverde is a Senior Lecturer in Supply Chain and Business Technology Management at Concordia University and a senior researcher with CONAIC Mexico. He holds a Doctorate in Information Systems from the University of Southern Queensland, Post MBA from McGill University, MSc in Accounting & Financial Management from the University of the West of England, Master of Logistics and Supply Chain Management from Camilos Jose Cela University, MEng in Electrical & Computer Engineering from Concordia University, BS in Electronic Engineering (Intelligent Systems) from ITESM and a BSc in Management Mathematics from Excelsior College of the University of the State of New York. Dr. Valverde's main research interests include IT and Finance in Supply Chain, IT in Finance, Project Cost Management, Risk in IT and Supply Chain and NeuroIS.

Risk and Data Center Planning

Kurt J. Engemann and Holmes E. Miller

Abstract In this chapter, we discuss the issues regarding risk related to data center planning. Organizations are dependent on computing services, which may become unavailable due to the manifestation of threats. These threats include natural disasters, man-made disasters and accidents. Prudent risk management is required to provide for continuation and recovery of operations in the event of a disruption. Risk assessment necessitates an in depth knowledge of the organization and a thorough analysis of the potential events which may have a negative impact on the data center and the associated computing services. Strategy development is discussed as well as preparedness, mitigation, exercises, response and recovery.

1 Introduction

Ongoing trends for ubiquitous computing services have increased the requirement that data centers always be operating. These trends include continued growth in demand for computing power to support desktop and laptop applications, information retrieval, storage, processing demands by customers using mobile devices, and increasing processing demands generated by the "internet of things". These trends have driven the rise of cloud computing and also the demand for instantaneous "always-available" information.

Events such as tornadoes, hurricanes, winter storms, tsunamis, earthquakes, and power outages have underlined our vulnerability to natural disasters. Miller et al. (2006) report that this vulnerability is exacerbated by most organizations' growing reliance on computing and telecommunications technologies, and with trends toward integrating suppliers and business partners into everyday business operations. Engemann et al. (2005) provide a methodology for disaster management in

K.J. Engemann (✉)
Center for Business Continuity and Risk Management, Iona College,
New Rochelle, NY 10801, USA
e-mail: kengemann@iona.edu

H.E. Miller
Department of Accounting, Business, Economics and Finance, Muhlenberg College,
Allentown, PA 18104, USA
e-mail: homiller@muhlenberg.edu

© Springer International Publishing AG 2017   73
J. Marx Gómez et al. (eds.), *Engineering and Management of Data Centers*,
Service Science: Research and Innovations in the Service Economy,
DOI 10.1007/978-3-319-65082-1_4

information technology (IT), exploring the relationship among threats, events, control alternatives and losses. A Disaster Recovery Plan (DRP) is a plan for the IT Department to maintain or restore the systems and communication capabilities of the organization. Disaster recovery planning traditionally was focused on providing resilience to IT, however this led to a process to include all critical areas of an organization. This expanded field of Business Continuity Management (BCM) is a holistic management program that identifies potential events that threaten an organization and provides a framework for building resilience (Engemann and Henderson 2012). BCM describes the processes and procedures an organization must put in place to ensure that mission-critical functions can continue during and after crisis events.

Organizations are dependent on each other and coordinate with partners who are able to provide critical products and services, even when crisis events occur. Stakeholders and regulators seek to gain assurance that proper business continuity plans are in place. Given these requirements, business continuity planning provides a process to enable that the business functions, both in the short term and long term.

Business continuity planning for data centers is critical because organizations today depend on information and depend on data centers that store, retrieve, and process it. Data centers and data center architecture have grown and evolved to meet changing business demands.

A 2015 AFCOM survey of data center professionals identified many trends. Quoting a Gartner Group study, the survey said that, "Global spending on IaaS (Infrastructure as a Service) is expected to reach almost $16.5 billion in 2015, an increase of 32.8 percent from 2014, with a compound annual growth rate (CAGR) from 2014 to 2019 forecast at 29.1 percent, according to Gartner's latest data. It also shows that in 2014, the absolute growth of public cloud IaaS workloads surpassed the growth of on-premises workloads (of any type) for the first time. Gartner's 2015 CIO survey indicates that 83 percent of CIOs consider cloud IaaS as an infrastructure option, and 10 percent are already cloud-first with cloud IaaS as their default infrastructure choice."

The AFCOM study also pointed out that global data center traffic has exploded: "Cisco reports that global data center traffic is firmly in the zettabyte era and will triple from 2013 to reach 8.6 zettabytes annually by 2018. A rapidly growing segment of data center traffic is cloud traffic, which will nearly quadruple over the forecast period and represent more than three-fourths of all data center traffic by 2018."

The survey also showed that redundancy and uptime were key concerns: "Results showed fairly steady trends around redundant power levels spanning today and the next three years. For example, at least 55 percent already have, and will continue to have, N+1 redundancy levels. Similarly, no more than 5 percent of respondents either currently have, or will have, 2(N+1) redundant power systems. For the most part, data center managers are using at least one level of redundancy for "power".

Finally the survey indicated that in the next 36 months, over 80% of the respondents indicated that they would build new data centers (88%), use cloud services (81%), and use collocation/managed services (83%).

A main conclusion from this survey is that data centers need to operate on an ongoing basis and must support growing, ubiquitous demands for information.

These requirements depend on data centers always being available and operating and able to meet capacity demands.

2 Risk Management and Business Continuity Management

Risk management and BCM are closely related and should be regarded in an integrative manner. Risk management is primarily preventative, whereas BCM deals more with consequences. Risk management provides important inputs for BCM and also deals with control for risks, while BCM expands risk management to plan for disasters.

The International Organization for Standardization (ISO) is an independent, non-governmental international organization that brings together experts to share knowledge and develop voluntary, consensus-based, market relevant International Standards that support innovation and provide solutions to global challenges. A standard is a document that provides requirements, specifications, guidelines or characteristics that can be used consistently to ensure that materials, products, processes and services are fit for their purpose. Although application of such standards will vary according to the situation, and therefore need to be customized to fit the organization and environment, such standards provide a good guidelines. ISO provides standards that can be useful in identifying and treating risk related to data centers.

ISO 31000 Risk Management (ISO 2017) provides principles, guidelines, framework and a process for managing risk. It can be used by any organization regardless of its size, activity or sector. Using ISO 31000 can help organizations increase the likelihood of achieving objectives, improve the identification of opportunities and threats, and effectively allocate and use resources for risk treatment. Organizations using it can compare their risk management practices with an internationally recognized benchmark, providing sound principles for effective management and corporate governance.

ISO 22301 Business Continuity (ISO 2017) is a management systems standard for BCM which can be used by organizations of all sizes and types. Organizations can obtain accredited certification against this standard and so demonstrate to legislators, regulators, customers, prospective customers and other interested parties that they are adhering to good practice in BCM. ISO 22301 also enables the business continuity manager to show top management that a recognized standard has been achieved. ISO 22301 may also be used within an organization to measure itself against good practice, and by auditors wishing to report to management. The standard is especially important for multinational firms that need a consistent cross-enterprise approach to BCM. The standard is also easily scalable so it can be adapted to organizations of nearly any size. Its structure and organization also make it a strong audit tool.

Business Continuity Phases are: prevention, mitigation, response, recovery and restoration (Engemann and Henderson 2012). *Prevention* actions may lessen the likelihood of a crisis event. *Mitigation* steps are designed to make the impact of an event less severe. *Response* is the reaction of an organization to an event to address immediate effects. *Recovery* is the stabilization and resumption of critical operations. *Restoration* is the process of returning to normal operations at a permanent location.

BCM is a program consisting of three major stages: development, implementation and maintenance. In this section we disucss the Development phase. Development of a BCM program proceeds from the importance of BCM as perceived by senior management. Senior management assesses organizational objectives and determines the critical products and services necessary to satisfy these objectives. The main components of development include: Business Impact Analysis (BIA), Risk Assessment (RA) and Strategy Development. BIA identifies the importance of the organization's activities by assessing the impact over time of their interruption and establishes continuity and recovery objectives. BIA establishes objectives before, during and after crisis events and examines the infrastructure necessary to conduct operations. RA begins with a systematic process of identifying threats, and determines the risk that each threat poses to the organization. RA then compares risk levels with established risk criteria. RA and BIA are often conducted simultaneously. Strategy Development determines the strategies needed to meet the response, continuity and recovery objectives established during the BIA.

2.1   Business Impact Analysis

BIA focuses on the financial and non-financial effects of an interruption to critical business functions over various durations of time. During BIA, recovery time objectives (RTOs) and recovery point objectives (RPOs) are determined by management. Engemann and Henderson (2012) define the RTO as the prospective point in time when an operation must be resumed before a disruption compromises the ability of the organization to achieve its objectives and the RPO as the retrospective point in time to which information must be restored to ensure objectives can be met.

BIA is a crucial component of an organization's resiliency planning. The resulting report describes the potential risks specific to the organization studied. One of the basic assumptions behind BIA is that every component of the organization is reliant upon the continued functioning of other components, however some are more key than others and require a greater distribution of funds in the event of a disaster.

BIA identifies costs associated with disruptions including: loss of profits, replacement of equipment, incremental salaries, and loss of data. A BIA report quantifies the importance of business components and suggests appropriate fund allocation. The impact of disasters is assessed in terms of life/safety, environmental, asset destruction, loss of current and future business, reputation, and legal compliance. Impact is expressed monetarily for purposes of comparison whenever appropriate. BIA should assess a disaster's impact over time and help to establish recovery strategies, priorities, and requirements for resources and time.

BIA considers the impact on the organization if a business function is unavailable. Although users identify which applications they depend on, they generally are unaware of the other applications and infrastructure those applications rely on. It is important to understand the dependencies on the IT environment: network, servers, storage devices, and applications when determining the significance of applications.

During BIA, previous outages and their impacts are studied, workaround procedures are established, and legal and regulatory constraints are explored. BIA identifies applications supporting critical functions, single points of failure, and costs associated with system failure. The staff and resources necessary for operations to continue, and recovery and restoration time frames are determined.

2.2 Risk Assessment

Risk analysis is the process of identifying events, determining causes, and estimating probabilities and impact (Engemann and Henderson 2012). Risk evaluation is the process of comparing risk levels with established risk criteria. Risk Assessment (RA) is the process of risk analysis and risk evaluation. The purpose of risk assessment is to prioritize planning by assessing the likelihood of events and their potential impact on critical functions. RA is fundamental to identifying vulnerability and is a basis for resource allocation and exposure mitigation.

During the risk assessment phase, the BIA findings may be examined against various hazard scenarios, and potential disruptions may be prioritized based on the hazard's probability and the likelihood of adverse impact to business operations. A BIA may be used to justify investments in prevention and mitigation, as well as disaster recovery strategies.

Risk analysis defines and analyzes the threats to an organization. In IT, a risk analysis report can be used to align technology-related objectives with a company's business objectives. A risk analysis can be quantitative or qualitative. In quantitative risk analysis, an attempt is made to numerically determine the probabilities of crisis events and the impact of the loss if a particular event takes place. Reliability theory and simulation modelling can be applied to result in more robust probability estimates to support the risk analysis phase of the business continuity planning process (Miller and Engemann 2014). Qualitative risk analysis, which is used frequently, does not involve quantitative probabilities or quantitative losses. The qualitative method includes describing the various threats, and determining the general degree of vulnerabilities.

A risk assessment identifies potential hazards and evaluates areas of vulnerability. Threats to a data center include natural disasters, man-made disasters, and accidents. Significant threats which could cause disruptions beyond the RTO require attention are identified during RA. Some threats to consider are listed in Table 1.

Threats can be identified in the general region (e.g. winter storm), in the community (e.g. water outage) and in the building (e.g. HVAC failure). The manifestation of a threat as a crisis may lead to a disruption. In identifying possible

Table 1 Threats

Natural disasters	Man-made disasters	Accidents
Blizzard	Acts of war	Chemical spill
Earthquake	Armed attack	Contamination
Fire	Cyber-attack	Communication outage
Flood	Hacker	HVAC failure
Freeze	Hostage situation	Machine failure
Hurricane	Insurrection	Power outage
Tornado	Kidnapping	Transportation outage
Tsunami	Riot	Water outage
Volcano	Terrorism	
Winter storm	Workplace violence	

disruptions it is helpful to draw upon the information gathered in the BIA. Some outages that should be addressed include:

- Destruction of a building due to a hurricane.
- Damage of a processing area due to a fire.
- Destruction of a building by an earthquake.
- Flooding due to the rupture of a water pipe.
- Inaccessibility to a building due to a fire.
- Evacuation due to a bomb threat.
- Outage of electric power due to a storm.
- Lack of air conditioning due to machine failure.
- No personnel due to a strike.
- Understaffing due to transportation problems.
- Travel restrictions due to a snowstorm.

The electric grid is a vital resource to our way of life. Threats exist that can substantially impact the grid's operation and performance over extended periods of time. The consequences of these events can be extreme and even catastrophic. Organizations can still take action, even though the mitigating effects may be limited (Miller and Engemann 2015). Given the potentially devastating effects of an electromagnetic pulse (EMP), organizations are now looking to EMP ready data center providers to protect their critical data. Underground data centers promote their ability to be EMP resistant, though it is important to note that measures involving securing the entire grid are beyond the scope of any one organization.

Data centers are enticing targets for malevolent hackers attempting to exploit various physical or data security controls. With the tremendous growth of computing devices connected to networks, information systems security is an issue of severe global concern. Developing effective methods for the prevention and detection of network intrusions is essential. Shin (2011) presents a methodology using a game theoretic model, called defensive forecasting, for real-time detection of intrusions. Significant security is aimed at protecting networks from outsiders, but insiders also are a marked threat. An insider threat could be from an employee who takes some action that is detrimental to the organization. Background checks, credit checks, behavior monitoring, and access controls are some means that companies use to manage this threat.

Effective management of shared technology is needed for a cloud data center to securely provide data synchronization service. In cloud data centers, there is a security concern from unauthorized access by malicious attackers. Wi and Kwak (2014) propose a secure data management scheme in cloud data centers by categorization of the data.

Availability, integrity, and confidentiality is a key theme of cyber security. The United States Department of Defense has implemented multiple processes such as an information assurance certification and accreditation process, and has created common criteria and proven baselines to include information assurance controls to protect information system resources (Dawson et al. 2013).

When a business evaluates a cloud service provider, it needs to thoroughly scrutinize the provider's operations and IT environment. In addition, data center and cloud providers need to run risk assessments on any third-party vendors with whom they do business. A provider of cloud software services needs to configure services such that the quality of service is in accordance with the specified requirements, and secondly, the services need to be deployed in the provider's private cloud in a cost and energy-efficient manner (Gullhav and Nygreen 2015). These two sets of decisions need to be taken simultaneously in order to make an optimal decision. Uddin and Rahman (2012) propose a green IT framework for implementing green energy efficient data centers, to save power consumption and reduce the emission of greenhouse gases.

Risk aspects during a data center migration are particularly complex due to a data center's multifaceted system of technology, devices, data, and applications. This is particularly challenging and requires careful planning.

2.3   Strategy Development

Organizations devise strategies to treat risk. Strategies may prevent or reduce the probability of events, or enhance the capability to continue or resume operations following an event. Crisis scenarios are valuable during the analysis process. While developing strategies, focus is placed on what decisions need to be made and on what needs to be accomplished. Organizational activities are divided into business as usual for unaffected areas and recovery activities for affected areas.

The preferred strategies to meet BCM objectives are selected in developing the overall strategy. Recovery strategies need to be evaluated for each critical function, and the selection of a set of strategies depends on costs and benefits. Sometimes, the decision is obvious, as is in cases where the strategies provide protection for a multitude of events and are relatively inexpensive. Sometimes, a strategy may be the only one that could provide for the continuation of a service and the service is so vital that its disruption is unacceptable.

The BCM program should provide contingency plans for all major crisis events. Some strategies cover several crisis events, and cover numerous processing areas. Offsite strategies provide backup for the broadest set of events, while onsite backup could be a cost effective solution for localized events. The evaluation is performed across services when appropriate to determine the usefulness in other operations. Some crisis events may result in consequences which are unacceptable, such as the loss of important customers, fines from regulatory agencies or very high losses. Attaining commitments on contractual agreements is a key part of strategy development.

The advantages and disadvantages of the strategies should be ascertained and the appropriateness of the strategies should be assessed against the BIA. The strategy evaluation criteria include: service level provided, cost, manageability and reliability. Management judgement is used in both assigning ratings and selecting the strategies. Senior management commitment should always be obtained on the recommended strategies.

A detailed cost-benefit analysis may be useful during strategy selection. A strategy usually involves both one-time costs and recurring costs. Quantifying the benefits of a strategy requires studying all the events for which the alternative delivers some security and approximating how it decreases the expected loss of each of these events. The impact of an event depends upon its scope and duration. The net benefit of an alternative is obtained by subtracting the total annual cost of the alternative from its benefit. While a quantitative approach to selecting strategies is valuable there are problems in estimating probabilities and in determining costs and losses. Sensitivity analysis should be used to determine how changes in the estimates of losses, costs, and probabilities would affect the selection of a strategy.

Associated factors such as future business volume, strategic facility relocation and planned growth of processing capacity should be determined. Such factors may have an important impact on the available strategies. For example, if the data center plans to install additional computers, a strategy could be to establish a second data center housing the new computers. This delivers the planned increase in computer capability while also providing a contingency plan for each of the data centers.

A secure data center should be built using the proper construction and in the correct location. Babu and Krishna (2013) apply facility location techniques for evaluating potential locations to determine the optimal facility location of data center facilities. Cloud subscribers would like to verify the location of outsourced data in the cloud data centers to ensure that the availability of data satisfies the service level agreement. Cloud users may not have access to their outsourced data in the event of operational failures in data centers or occurrence of natural disasters and/or power outages. Biswal et al. (2015) propose an enhanced learning classifier geolocation algorithm, which incorporates multiple network measurements to improve the accuracy of geolocating data files in data centers.

Data centers should have redundant utilities such as electricity, water, voice and data. Security should include a buffer zone around the site, crash barriers, and limited entry points. A hardened core with security layers, security devices, surveillance cameras and motion-detector for bomb detection is necessary. Building machinery should be protected, and the building should have secure air handling.

Selecting strategies involves: reviewing business continuity and recovery objectives, identifying potential strategies, assessing strategies against the BIA, consolidating strategies across the organization, determining advantages and disadvantages, conducting cost-benefit analysis and presenting findings for senior management approval. Engemann and Miller (2015) discuss risk and organizational resilience, and provide a paradigm representing the relationship among threats, crises, disruptions and impact. They present a methodology for the selection of risk strategies that incorporates sensitivity analysis of the decision maker's attitude.

A DRP includes planning in the following areas:

- Data Center Controls – to prevent or mitigate the impact of a crisis event.
- Data Center Recovery Plan – to resume data center operations.
- IT Alternate Site – as a backup data center to the primary data center.
- Information Management Plan – for information and critical applications.
- Information Security Plan –to secure data from internal and external threats.

Senior management determines the level of planning and resources that will be devoted to the DRP. This decision is based on the established RTOs, acceptable levels of service degradation and the cost of the planning. Engemann and Miller (2009) provide a computational intelligence methodology, using attitudinal and fuzzy modeling, and illustrate its application as a risk modeling decision technology in the selection of smart technology in critical infrastructure.

Although information systems trends are increasingly focusing on cloud-based applications, with demands for immediate access to much larger amounts of data than in previous years, classical disaster recovery strategies still apply, albeit modified to fit the current environment. Engemann and Henderson (2012) provide an overview of disaster recovery planning strategies. For data centers, alternate sites – either a redundant data center, a hot site, warm site, or a cold site – delineate four basic strategies.

Redundant sites provide instantaneous recovery but are the most expensive. They require duplicate staff, duplicate hardware and also duplicate space. Because of their expense, alternate sites generally make little sense if they are idle unless used in a disaster. A more logical and cost effective strategy is for the alternate site itself to be integrated into an organization's processing stream and for an organization's data centers to be architected such that they provide mutual backup. Ceballos et al. (2012) in a paper focusing on telecommunications technologies, state that, "Many Fortune 500 enterprises and commercial data center service providers require at least two major hubs, which often escalate to more data center pairs spread across the world, and smaller customer sites interconnecting with the larger locations over lower bandwidth links. Due to the fact that the public sector as well as the private sector is highly dependent on data and services provided via such data centers, these facilities form a part of the most critical commercial infrastructure supporting the economy.

A data center facility serving multiple customers can aggregate enough data and applications to represent a significant percentage of business in a city or even a country. Without proper safeguards, a data center failure can put the business infrastructure at risk, and the data center itself may become a target for a terrorist or hacking attack." In their paper they go on to discuss mirrored data centers and the telecommunications challenges facing enabling redundancy. When the mirrored data centers are architected such that a disaster affecting one is unlikely to affect the other, they in essence are both operational for normal processing and also are redundant. A sub strategy organizations follow is also to have the same applications running in multiple data centers, thus ensuring that there are no single point of failures in the organization's overall data center architecture.

Sites can be provided by outside vendors and can also be internally provided. Although vendor provided sites make sense for hot, warm and cold sites, redundant sites often are more cost effective when internally provided, and managed within the organization itself. Internal management ensures hardware and software compatibility and also ensures that architectural changes meet the overall organizational needs. Another option is a mutual aid agreement with another organization (e.g., two different banks). Mutual aid agreements always have been problematic because of hardware incompatibilities, availability issues, capacity issues, and a likelihood the data centers often are geographically close to one another. These problems are magnified today given the likelihood of many real time input and output data feeds for the data centers.

Recovery times for hot, warm and cold sites are not instantaneous and often are significantly longer. For example, Engemann and Henderson (2012) give recovery times of 24–36 h for hot sites (with critical applications perhaps being faster), 24–36 h recovery times for warm sites (with full recovery in 5 or more days), and for cold sites partial recovery in 5+ days and full recovery longer. As a key step in developing a disaster recovery plan is to catalog an organization's applications and each application's criticality, the hot-warm-cold site path would only be feasible for applications without real time processing requirements and/ or characteristics that are deemed non-critical to the organization's overall business objectives.

When hot, warm, or cold sites are used, vendor provided sites are a frequent option. For example, Engemann and Henderson (2012) state that, "A typical hot site vendor will provide space and the supporting infrastructure with appropriate controls and redundancies." The client can specify hardware requirements, which the vendor also will provide. A co-location site is one where the vendor provides facility and infrastructure support but the client provides the hardware. These sites are more of the warm and cold site varieties.

Backup is the activity of copying files or databases so that they will be preserved in case of disaster. Backup is usually a routine part of the operation of businesses.

Cold storage is the retention of inactive data that an organization rarely, if ever, expects to access for years. Remote replication may be either synchronous or asynchronous. Synchronous replication writes data to the primary and secondary sites at the same time. With asynchronous replication, there is a delay before the data gets written to the secondary site. Replication occurs in one of three places: in the storage array, at the host or in the network.

Authentication, the process of determining whether someone or something is, in fact, who or what it is declared to be, is of utmost importance. Authentication is a process in which the credentials provided are compared to those on file in a database of authorized users' information on a local operating system or within an authentication server. If the credentials match, the process is completed and the user is granted authorization for access. Reliable machine authentication is crucial to allow secure communication. In the 'internet of things," almost any conceivable object may be able to exchange data over a network. It is important to realize that each access point is a potential intrusion point. Each networked device needs strong machine authentication and also, despite their normally limited activity, these devices must be configured for limited permissions access as well, to limit what can be done even if they are breached.

3 Discussion

It is very important that a BCM program contain an effective crisis communications plan to address all emergencies. Crisis communications includes disseminating and receiving information within the organization and with outside parties. Internal communications include safety information and emergency instructions for all employees. External communications include information provided to all stakeholders, media, government agencies, suppliers, vendors and other interested parties.

During a crisis event, failed crisis communications can manifest into a problem that can cause a collapse of the entire emergency response. It is essential that crisis communication be delivered promptly and with sufficient detail to initiate the correct response. Acceptable planning, decision-making procedures, and systems must be in place for communications to properly occur over a wide range of situations. Organizations should regularly exercise and update the crisis communication plan, to ensure all participants are able to perform their responsibilities correctly.

Some questions arising in the business continuity planning process are:

- In a hyper-connected economy, how can we prepare for disasters?
- To what extent can disasters be prevented or mitigated?
- How should contingency plans be exercised?
- What response best protects human life and prevents damage to property
- How can organizations recover from disaster and resume operations?

3.1 Preparedness

Preparedness involves putting in place steps called for by the Business Continuity Plan. These include:

- Identifying threats and targeting various scenarios that might manifest themselves. This goes beyond identifying threats such as hurricanes or earthquakes, and highlights the magnitude and duration of various outages and their consequences.
- Identifying critical and non-critical areas and applications. Here, business managers need to be involved and realistic assessments made since any solution has cost/benefit implications.
- Identifying suppliers and customers needed to continue operating and ensuring communications links are operable. Depending on the events, suppliers themselves may be affected. Knowing your partners' business continuity plans is important because their plans may well impact yours. Again, an objective is to avoid any single point of failure and the underlying risk is when those points of failure are hidden.
- Preparing for the possibility that data centers and supplies are inaccessible and addressing this possibility by implementing back-up strategies mentioned above. Hot site and other offsite strategies are particularly vulnerable as in dynamic business and technological environments, what may have been an acceptable solution yesterday may suddenly be obsolete.
- Ensuring that the members of the crisis management team know their roles and understand their responsibility if a disaster occurs. However advanced organizations become, and however dependent on technology they are, when disasters strike people always are important. When roles and murky and responsibilities are ill defined, even the most technologically and architecturally sound plans may be poorly implemented and may result in significant losses.

3.2 Mitigation

When possible mitigation involves preventing hazardous events and when they occur, minimizing the associated losses and damages. Ideally preventing the events is preferred but given their scope, preventing natural disasters is impossible. While preventing events such as hurricanes and earthquakes are impossible, mitigating the impact of those events is possible, given appropriate foresight and planning. Ideally, smart decisions can avoid or minimize losses. Examples are locating data centers away from earthquake fault lines or areas prone to flooding, and choosing architectures that harden facilities such as implementing earthquake-proof buildings.

Mitigation of subsequent events is to be contrasted with mitigation where the event occurs but actions taken and controls implemented mitigate an event's losses. These losses fall in two categories: Losses directly due to the disaster's occurrence and losses incurred after the disaster occurs, such as lost current and future business. Implementing data center strategies, such as those mentioned above, ensure business continuity and address both current and future business losses.

Insuring for catastrophic risk also is an option for transferring risk. Generally, insuring catastrophic risks requires specialized insurance such as earthquake insurance or flood insurance. While insurers offer coverage for uncertain events, adverse selection (e.g., customers able to avoid losses will not purchase insurance and those that do will be the poorest risks) and moral hazard (e.g., insured parties act more recklessly) are to classical problems underlying buying insurance. For natural disasters a third risk is "correlated risk." Hurricanes, floods, and earthquakes may affect many policyholders and in a given area all may simultaneously file claims. This results in insurance companies seeking to leave markets, or pricing products with high premiums. While insurance plays a role – insuring for physical losses and business interruption often makes good sense, yet no organization should rely on insurance to the exclusion of disaster recovery plans. Having well maintained and tested plans often is required to secure insurance in the first place. Moreover, often the biggest risks – such as a business' reputation, customer loyalty, and the public trust – cannot be fully insured.

3.3   Exercises

DRP exercises help ensure that an organization can recover data, restore critical applications and continue operations after a disruption of services. The goal of testing and exercising is to determine how a plan can fail and then take action to solve the problem so that BCM will be successful in an actual event. If an organization doesn't invest in testing and exercising, the plan will likely fail to execute properly when it's actually needed. Data, applications and communications, are typically a focus of all disaster recovery exercises.

Several types of exercises are commonly conducted. A Talk Through Exercise is a presentation and discussion of a particular topic. A Walk Through Exercise is basically a Talk Through exercise but is more physical. These exercises require a minimum financial commitment, a minimum amount of time, and do not interfere with most normal operations. In a Tabletop Exercise, a crisis is described, followed by questions regarding the proper actions that should be taken. Tabletop exercises require a time commitment, a financial commitment, but do not interfere with most normal operations. Drills or Full Scale Exercises require the organization or a segment of the organization to cease normal operations and practice a response to an announced crisis. Some exercises may shut down normal operations for a short period of time. Other Full Scale exercises, such as activating the IT Hot Site, may require teams traveling and restoring operations at a distant location. Disaster recovery exercises should be conducted on a regular basis and should be incorporated into maintenance and staff training.

3.4   Response

Emergency Response includes those immediate actions taken to deal with a disaster or an emergency. The emergency response phase should address the disaster or emergency itself, as well as the problems that are caused by the disaster or emergency. For example, in the case of a flood people must be rescued from flooded buildings. Saving lives and ensuring the safety of all affected personnel is paramount in any emergency response plan. After physical safety has been ensured, emergency response involves ensuring the strategy in the back-up plan is effectively implemented. In the case of a mirrored data center this might be immediate. In the case of a hot site, emergency response steps might be more drawn out and a series of predetermined responses need to be initiated.

Beyond issues of dependency, issues also arise regarding security of information and scalability for recovery in the aftermath of an event. People also are central to the success of any emergency response effort, and must be present in number, skill level, and training. One characteristic of emergency response environments is that invariably people rise to meet the challenges.

Communicating with outside parties also is critical, especially given the interconnectedness of businesses on a local and global scale. To recover from a disaster, all the links in the chain connecting suppliers with customers must be established in the response phase and must function properly.

3.5   Recovery

Resuming normal processing is the objective of the Recovery phase. What is "normal" depends upon the processing objectives as spelled-out in the disaster recovery plan. For example, the overall strategy might call for a select group of critical services to be up and running immediately. Another group might take a week and for significant disasters, another group might take a month or more. In some cases the service might never resume. Regardless of the identity of the applications and the sequencing, the plan will define the recovery process.

Naturally the timing of when operations resume depends upon the underlying event. Each event requires separate actions, and even the same event affects different types of businesses in its own way. Some events, like hurricanes, can be foretold and personnel can be evacuated. Others, like earthquakes, tornadoes, power outages, happen suddenly. Some events place humans at risk and others affect business but not human safety. Regardless of the specific event being planned for, for recovery, some issues discussed above in Sect. 3.4 must be considered: equipment and supplies; people; information and communication; and links with suppliers, customers, and external parties.

People are of particular concern. Even when safely evacuated, issues may surface later on. Individuals rescued and working at a backup facility may still fell the trauma of the event itself; people may be affected experiences of other family members, acquaintances, or coworkers; employees who for the first few days expended "superhuman" effort during the response phase, may suffer burnout during the long term recovery period. The disaster recovery plan must not only include steps for physical recovery, but also for the emotional stability of the workforce.

When a hot or cold site is used, one issue often neglected in the recovery plan is planning to move back to the primary site once processing is restored. For example, a large bank in New York was forced to vacate its processing center due to a fire in a transformer. No physical damage occurred but the building was uninhabitable due to leakage of PCBs. In the middle of the week employees were allowed back in the main complex, but managers realized that they had no plan for moving from the backup site to the primary site! Rather, they waited for a weekend when processing was suspended, and moved their systems and people back.

3.6   Trends and Implications

As discussed in Sect. 1, computing is becoming ubiquitous and data centers now provide information to billions of users via cloud services accessed by cell phones, tablets, and other intelligent devices, in addition to more traditional channels such as laptops and desktops. The implications of this changing landscape are two-fold. First, given the increasing use of Infrastructure as a Service (IaaS) applications, social media, and the growing volume of data stored and the need for immediate data access, the requirements for data centers to be accessible have changed. More data must be available and the data must be available immediately. Moreover, the capability to filter and update information now is more critical than in the past.

Although the methods discussed above are still as relevant as ever, changing customer requirements and resulting risk and impact implications need to be adjusted to fit this faster-paced, data rich, and more data-analytical environment. The key takeaways for managers and practitioners are that the methods discussed above under *Risk Management and Business Continuity Management* must be applied and applied on an ongoing basis. This may involve revisiting plans more frequently, and implementing procedures for ongoing feedback regarding customer needs which inform business impact analysis and risk analysis steps. Also, because of the rapid changes in underlying technologies, strategies must be constantly revisited and if necessary updated, to ensure the plans are congruent with current needs and capabilities.

The second implication concerns the design of the data centers themselves. While this chapter does not address design issues, data center designers need to not only consider issues related to functionality, technology, service and cost, but should augment these by considering implications related to risk management and contingency planning upfront in the process. Given the increasing risks related to hacking and release and possible destruction of sensitive data contained on servers, data center managers in their design and management and risk assessment activities, need to consider these ongoing and increasing risks in the overall design equation, and also in the process of developing and implementing overall data center strategies.

4 Conclusions

Managing risk is no longer an afterthought as business managers now understand that no threat is impossible. Planning and preparation for both the probable and improbable is a necessity. There is a growing body of experience and knowledge drawn from practitioners and academicians making a fundamental contribution to the profession of resiliency. Organizations need to be aware of and manage the risk related to their vital assets, in particular to data centers. It is essential for data centers to increase their efforts to provide security in more comprehensive manner.

References

AFCOM: AFCOM's 2015 state-of-the-data center survey, http://www.afcom.com/news/dcm-digital-issue-afcoms-2015-state-data-center-survey/ (2015). Accessed 22 Feb 2016

Babu, L.D., Krishna, P.V.: Applying operations management models for facility location problem in cloud computing environments. Int. J. Serv. Oper. Manage. 15(1), 1–27 (2013)

Biswal, B., Shetty, S., Rogers, T.: Enhanced learning classifier to locate data in cloud data centers. Int. J. Met. 4(2), 141–158 (2015)

Ceballos, J., DiPasquale, R., Feldman, R.: Business continuity and security in Datacenter interconnection. Bell Labs Technical J. 17(3), 147–156 (2012)

Dawson, M.E., Crespo, M., Brewster, S.: DoD cyber technology policies to secure automated information systems. Int. J. Bus. Continuity Risk Manage. 4(1), 1–22 (2013)

Engemann, K.J., Henderson, D.M.: Business Continuity and Risk Management: Essentials of Organizational Resilience. Rothstein Associates, Brookfield (2012)

Engemann, K.J., Miller, H.E.: Critical infrastructure and smart technology risk modelling using computational intelligence. Int. J. Bus. Continuity Risk Manage. 1(1), 91–111 (2009)

Engemann, K.J., Miller, H.E.: Risk strategy and attitude sensitivity. Cybern. Syst. 46(3), 188–206 (2015)

Engemann, K.J., Miller, H.E., Yager, R.R.: Disaster management of information resources using fuzzy and attitudinal modeling. Int. J. Technol. Policy Manage. 5(4), 388–406 (2005)

Gullhav, A.N., Nygreen, B.: Deployment of replicated multi-tier services in cloud data centers. Int. J. Cloud Comput. 4(2), 130–149 (2015)

ISO: International Organization for Standardization. http://www.iso.org/iso/home/about.htm (2017). Accessed 1 September 2017

Miller, H.E., Engemann, K.J.: Using reliability and simulation models in business continuity planning. Int. J. Bus. Continuity Risk Manage. 5(1), 43–56 (2014)

Miller, H.E., Engemann, K.J.: Threats to the electric grid and the impact on organizational resilience. Int. J. Bus. Continuity Risk Manage. 6(1), 1–16 (2015)

Miller, H.E., Engemann, K.J., Yager, R.R.: Disaster planning and management. Commun. Int. Inf. Manage. Assoc. 6(2), 25–36 (2006)

Shin, H.: Identifying network intrusion with defensive forecasting. Int. J. Bus. Continuity Risk Manage. 2(2), 91–104 (2011)

Uddin, M., Rahman, A.: Validation of green IT framework for implementing energy efficient green data centers: A case study. Int. J. Green Econ. 6(4), 357–374 (2012)

Wi, Y., Kwak, J.: Secure data management scheme in the cloud data center. Int. J. Adv. Media Commun. 5(2/3), 225–232 (2014)

Dr. Kurt J. Engemann is the Director of the Center for Business Continuity and Risk Management and a Professor of Information Systems in the Hagan School of Business at Iona College, USA. He is the Editor-in-Chief of the International Journal of Business Continuity and Risk Management and the International Journal of Technology, Policy and Management. He has consulted professionally in the area of risk modeling for major organizations and has been instrumental in the development of comprehensive business continuity management programs. He has a PhD in Operations Research from New York University and is a Certified Business Continuity Professional.

Dr. Holmes E. Miller is a Professor of Business at Muhlenberg College in Allentown, Pennsylvania and the Chair of the Department of Accounting, Business, Economics and Finance. He teaches courses in operations management, quantitative methods, business and society, and sustainability in business. He received his PhD in Management Science from Northwestern University. Before coming to Muhlenberg, he worked for 15 years in industry for Union Carbide Corporation and Chase Manhattan Bank. He has published extensively in the areas of risk management and decision modeling.

Best Practices in Data Center Management: Case – KIO Networks

Teresa Lucio-Nieto and Dora Luz González-Bañales

Abstract From interviews conducted in KIO Networks (Mexican Data Center) to individuals leading the Human Talent Management and Global Operations Management areas, this chapter presents a set of the best practices at KIO Networks, with a particular emphasis on the value of people and general recommendations on Data Center management. Regarding people, the recruitment, selection and training process is described, as well as the importance of the organization's personnel in developing their competencies that allow them to improve their performance in the mission critical projects they take part in. Regarding processes, KIO considers that having the best human talent is as important as applying the best process certifications. KIO has also found it is important to learn how to recognize, implement and maintain those processes that generate value for the company, its customers, and the organization's human capital.

1 Introduction

In 2009, the Harvard Business Review Latin America magazine published in its July issue (Plant 2009): "Companies that allow a recession to eliminate their own corporate Data Centers might find themselves in an ideal situation to… swiftly reduce their computing capacity, which might provide a significant advantage in volatile times… Data Centers… are not appealing places… they are a jumble of new and obsolete hardware that is often expensive to operate and maintain… Data Center facility costs have been growing at a faster rate than Information Technologies budgets…".

T. Lucio-Nieto (✉)
Universidad Iberoamericana, ITESM & Universidad Anahuac, Customer Care Associates, Degollado Sur 631 Int. 5 Col. María Luisa, Monterrey, Nuevo León, Mexico, 64040
e-mail: tlucio@customercareassoc.com

D.L. González-Bañales (✉)
Department of Systems and Computing, Instituto Tecnológico de Durango, Blvd. Felipe Pescador 1830 Ote., Col. Nueva Vizcaya, Durango, Mexico, 34020
e-mail: doraglez@itdurango.edu.mx

© Springer International Publishing AG 2017
J. Marx Gómez et al. (eds.), *Engineering and Management of Data Centers*,
Service Science: Research and Innovations in the Service Economy,
DOI 10.1007/978-3-319-65082-1_5

In the face of the above outlook, and considering that many companies used to have a Data Center demanding high operation and maintenance costs, in order to reduce such costs, some decided to pass some of their most significant operations onto remote suppliers instead of purchasing costly equipment and applications (Plant 2009). This way, the impact of hiring remote Data Center services meant that, far from disappearing, Data Centers have started to emerge and consolidate to serve nearly all economy sectors: governments, universities, health centers, manufacturing plants, financial services, media and telecommunications and some of them even operate on their own (single-tenant) or through a third-party-controlled service (multi-tenant) in order to obtain necessary connectivity, transaction processing and information management (Alaraifi et al. 2012; Daim et al. 2009).

Based on the above, since the recognition of the ever growing importance of Data Centers for companies from all sectors, research results on Data Centers have been published recently in technical-scientific magazines. It is particularly striking that one of the areas of the most research and, hence, one of the areas for which the most reports have been published is power consumption. A number of studies have shown that Data Centers account for a significant part of the total energy consumption of a modern city (Daim et al. 2009; Fernández-Montes et al. 2015; Nada et al. 2015; Rong et al. 2016; Uddin et al. 2015). Therefore, the environmental impact of Data Centers is one of the most published topics today.

In light of this, it is clear that there is a need to analyze not only the environmental impact of Data Centers, but also other areas such as best practices in the human talent management and process areas from the standpoint of those who hold a central role in Data Centers. This chapter presents a set of best practices regarding Data Center management with the Mexican Data Center KIO Networks as the case of reference.

In this chapter, the KIO Networks background will be described, such as its history, mission, vision, solutions, its "DNA" philosophy, its Data Centers, how they value certifications, the awards they have been granted, its environmental policy and recognition from its clients. A summary of their best management practices is included, with an emphasis on human talent (people) management, presenting their profile, recruitment process, selection, training and coaching and how adequate human talent management has a positive impact on organizational learning. Finally, as a part of the best practices at KIO Data Center Management, a series of recommendations to achieve good performance are presented. The importance of benchmarking, availability and maintenance of technological equipment, operating cost efficiency, as well as the importance of learning how to recognize what processes generate value for the company and its clients are also described.

2   The Importance of Data Centers

Although there is no single definition for a Data Center, we may say in general terms that it consists of facilities for installing computing and data storage equipment, telecommunications equipment, IT systems and related components, such as storage systems and security equipment (Qin et al. 2016). In other words, they are centers where large amounts of data from different organizations are stored to meet their daily transaction processing needs (Rong et al. 2016).

A Data Center includes redundant power sources or security backup systems, redundant data communication connections, environmental control (such as air conditioning and fire extinction) and various security devices (Fernández-Montes et al. 2015). One of their biggest drivers is the growing demand for cloud data processing (*cloud computing*) (Qin et al. 2016), together with breakthroughs in computing, telecommunication and electronic technology (Capozzoli and Primiceri 2015).

To measure the relevance of Data Centers, one must consider the following figures: according to IDC (International Data Corporation), in 2014, the Data Center market was valued at 18 billion US dollars, with 16% growth with regards to 2013 (KIO-Networks 2016).

Data Center importance and growth are undoubtedly related not just to their figures in billions of dollars but also to the constant growth of Data Center Networks (DCN) with hundreds or even thousands of servers with massive storage resources, which are increasingly becoming necessary structures to support cloud computing services and to provide IT environments for Big Data analysis for companies in diverse sectors of various sizes (Ma et al. 2016; Rahman and Esmailpour 2016; Rong et al. 2016; Uddin et al. 2015).

3 KIO Networks Background

This section presents KIO Networks' background, corporate information, mission, vision, solutions, philosophy, representative figures, certifications and recognitions based on interviews and the KIO corporate website (Beguerisse 2016; KIO-Networks 2016; Mejía Resendiz 2016).

3.1 Background

KIO Networks was founded in 2002 with 100% Mexican capital. The company offers an extensive portfolio and infrastructure for a mission critical information technology service. Its offerings adhere to the highest levels of quality and international processes. KIO is the Swahili word for mirror and symbolizes the essential elements of duality and redundancy – core components of mission-critical information technology services.

KIO Networks Group consists of KIO Networks, KIO Business Solutions, MásNegocio, Sm4rt, Dattlas, redIT and Wingu Networks. The group is dedicated to providing highly complex managed hosting services, cloud services, information security, applications on demand, connectivity and Big Data, among other services. It has 32 of the most modern and powerful Data Centers, with one of the highest availability levels of the region. Its facilities are located throughout Mexico, the United States, Central America, the Caribbean, and Europe (KIO-Networks 2016).

3.2 Mission and Vision

KIO Networks' mission centers on being the most trusted partner for its clients on IT systems, providing them with innovative, agile, consistent, customized mission-critical IT services and infrastructure solutions while maintaining operational flexibility.

The company's vision is coupled to its mission; it is oriented towards becoming positioned as the leading expert in the international Information Technologies Market with mission critical IT services and infrastructure solutions in all regions they serve.

3.3 Solutions

KIO Networks provides solutions mostly in Data Center infrastructures, mobile Data Centers, complex managed hosting services, cloud services, corporate and homeland security services, outsourcing applications, fiber optic networks for high capacity data transfer, big data, information security services and business continuity plans (BCP). Its solutions comprise the public and private sectors, as well as enterprise in small and medium businesses. KIO Networks' services are mainly oriented to mission critical solutions.

3.4 KIO Networks DNA

As mentioned, from its foundation in 2002, KIO Networks has cared about providing innovative, agile, consistent, customized mission-critical IT services and infrastructure solutions while maintaining operational flexibility. As a result, the company has become its clients' most dependable partner in IT Systems. KIO Networks has defined this as a part of its DNA (See Fig. 1).

3.5 KIO Networks' Data Centers

KIO Networks built its first Internet Exchange Center (IXP) within one of its Technological Campuses in México City, with an operating investment in the range of 1.5–2 million US dollars.

KIO Network group consists of KIO Networks and its companies: KBS, Sm4rt, Dattlas, redIT and Wingu Networks, which pro-vide a full offering of mission critical information technology ser-vices in six countries: Mexico, Panama, Guatemala, the Dominican Re-public, the United States, and Spain. Sixty-five percent of its clients are in the private sector, and the balance is in the government area.

The Company has 32 Data Centers globally with more than 1500 enterprise clients. KIO services include monitoring, support, continuous security operations for

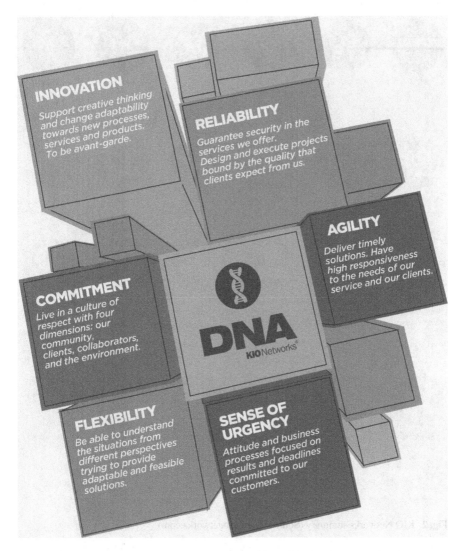

Fig. 1 KIO Networks DNA (Source: KIO Networks (2016))

complex managed hosting, and cloud services. One-half of the company's 32 Data Centers have TIER IV (99.99% Availability) characteristics, and the other half are TIER III (99.98% Availability) (KIO-Networks 2016).

Its Data Centers were designed and developed to meet all of its clients' needs and guaranteeing security by exceeding the seismic regulation requirements for their locations. For instance, being in the TIER III category means maintenance with no break in the server equipment and, for TIER IV, it is assumed that infringement of equipment performance is possible only in the event of an intentional act, fire or the intersection of a series of technical faults (to find out more about this, see (Dumsky and Isaev 2015)). Fig. 2 shows a summary of KIO Networks' Data Centers specifications.

Fig. 2 KIO Networks summary (Source: www.kionetworks.com)

3.6 The Value of Certifications

For KIO Networks, certifications are necessary for the value they add to the organization and, as a consequence, to its clients. The company has found that with a greater the efficiency of certifications, they can offer higher guarantees to their clients about operations and infrastructure security as well as availability and processes.

Thereby, KIO Networks through its 32 centers, has become one of the most robust Data Centers in Mexico, the United States, Latin America and Spain, by guaranteeing a safe and scalable environment. Each one of the company's Data Centers is designed according to international standards and certifications on security, availability, infrastructure and processes, such as the ones below:

- *VMware Certification:* This certification is granted to optimize public cloud solutions for a wide range of applications: seasonal projects, transient workloads, testing/development, and others. These also combine rapid deployment in a public cloud with flexibility to transit between internal and external environments. KIO Networks is the only vCloud Service Provider Partner in Mexico and Central America.
- *Google for Work Partner Premier:* Appointment awarded by Google that allows customers to assess the knowledge and consulting experience of a partner for the implementation of Google products.
- *ICREA:* This certification allows a service provider to guarantee its clients the highest availability in computing room standards with world-class certification (High Security High Availability World Class Quality Assurance Data Center – HSHA-WCQA), a certification issued by ICREA; as well as security in the processes and operation.
- *ISO 20000 IT Service Management System:* This standard, based on ITIL (Information Technology Infrastructure Library), helps consolidate business-aligned IT services delivery, cutting costs and ensuring a continuous improvement framework.
- *ISO 27001 Information Security Management System:* This standard ensures the establishment, implementation, maintenance and continuous improvement of an Information Security Management System (ISMS), with the objective of protecting a company's information and that of its clients.
- *ISO 9001 Quality Management System:* This certification is centered on all quality management elements a company needs in order to have an effective system, thereby allowing it to manage and improve the quality of its products and services. This accreditation means that more than 640,000 companies in the world recognize KIO Networks.
- *ISO 22301 Business Continuity Management System:* This standard provides a framework for managing an organization's business continuity and its recovery from disasters. KIO Networks is the only Mexican company holding this certification.
- *ITIL Operation:* KIO Network's operating framework is based on ITIL. This results in adequate and agile process design, allowing it to cater to the needs and two-way training of its clients while ensuring continuous improvement.
- *PCI Security Standards Council:* This is a certification oriented toward increasing data security in payment accounts by promoting the knowledge of the security standards in the Payment Cards Industry.
- *SAP Certified in Cloud Services:* This is a certification oriented towards making optimum use of Cloud Hosting Services by promoting the integral knowledge of data processing, analysis and hosting.
- *SAP Certified in Hosting Services:* This certification is granted when the technical requirements are met and the requested processes are covered to ensure SP solutions operate properly in a high availability, high security hosting environment. It is worth mentioning that only a small group has this certification in Latin America.

- *SAP Certified in Run SAP Operations:* KIO Networks is the first Mexican Company to be recognized with the Run SAP for Operations certification due to its capacity to produce and manage SAP applications, its highly reliable operation and its warranty of high availability.
- *SSAE16 Completed Type II Audit:* A certification that validates and guarantees the dependability of service level agreements, operations and strict compliance of audit control in providing mission critical technology services.
- *TIER IV:* KIO Networks obtained the certifications for some of its Data Centers from the Uptime Institute, the leading regulating entity for Data Centers worldwide, for its design and construction. This recognition is the only one that has ever been granted in Mexico. TIER IV sites show 99.99% availability, which means that availability is not guaranteed for only 53 min of downtime a year.

In addition to technology and process-related certifications, KIO Networks holds certifications oriented towards an ideal working space and as a socially responsible company and its way of doing business. Some of KIO's most outstanding certifications are:

- *SAP Latin America Excellence Award 2014 for Managed Cloud as a Service*: An award presented by SAP to its best-performing partners in Latin America – those who have made outstanding contributions impacting SAP's overall sales and goal achievement.
- *Intel Cloud Technology*: Intel granted KIO Networks the In-tel.® Cloud Technology certification. This way, KIO Networks became the first company in Spanish-speaking America to be awarded this prize for its large-scale services in mission critical environments for cloud computing.
- *Socially Responsible Company*: As a result of its commitments to the integral development of the country, society, and the environment, KIO Networks was granted recognition as a Socially Responsible Company by the Mexican Center for Philanthropy and Alliance for Social Responsibility in Mexico.
- *Great Place to Work.* KIO Networks was recognized as one of the Best Companies to Work for in Mexico, by the Great Place to Work® Institute, as a recognition for its continuous effort to maintain and promote a friendly work environment and caring for the needs of its collaborators.

3.7   Recognition

In additions to its numerous certifications, KIO Networks has been granted the following recognitions:

- *National Technology Award Premio Nacional de Tecnología)*: An award granted for IT Service Automation and management practices.
- *Datacenter Dynamics Latam Awards*: KIO Networks was recognized in 2 award categories, and was a finalist in 5 out of 7 categories in the 2013 Datacenter

Dynamics Latam Awards 2013 that recognized innovation and leadership in the Data Center industry in Latin America. KIO Networks' SF II technological campus was the winner in the Mega Da-ta Center Innovation category for its topological design, which assures 100% facility availability. Also, KIO Networks' infrastructure team was recognized as the Data Center Team of the Year for high quality and stringency in Data Center design, operation, and management at any stage of installation. These awards position KIO Networks as the industry leader in Latin America for its level of innovation and leadership in this market segment.

- *Gartner Cool Vendor*: Gartner, one of the most important Information Technologies market analysts in the United States, recognized KIO Networks as one of the year's "Cool Vendors" worldwide for its way of doing business in IT services and outsourcing, combining and publishing its offering in an innovative way.

3.8   Environmental Policy: KIO Networks' Green Side

Undoubtedly, one important aspect of a company is its commitment to the environment, and KIO Network is no exception. Since its foundation, the company has been committed to the implementation of actions contributing to a better quality of life based on sustainable development. It is worth mentioning that this is an initiative led by Top Management. When suppliers are selected, they are required to provide documented studies showing that the products they offer meet the current environmental regulations. Additionally, only products that do not have a negative environmental impact are selected.

Regarding personnel, all collaborators – both internal and external – involved in providing IT services must be committed to the control and continuous improvement of operating activities to prevent pollution, reduce negative environmental impacts and contribute to environmental responsibility, with policies and procedures defined and implemented within an Environmental Management System. The company's leading certifications in the environmental area are:

- *ISO 14001 Environmental Management System:* This certification seeks to minimize the impact of company activities on the environment, based on continuous improvement of its operations, optimization of natural resource utilization and strategic planning focused on sustainability.
- *Leadership in Energy and Environmental Design (LEED)*: KIO Networks holds the Leadership in Energy and Environmental Design (LEED) Platinum Level certification, the highest certification granted by the US Green Building Council (USGBC), a non-profit organization dedicated to promoting sustainable buildings.
- *Certified Energy Efficiency in Data Centers Award (CEEDA):* Audited and certified for efficient energy best practices implementation in a Data Center.

3.9   Recognition from KIO Networks Clients

It should be highlighted that, in addition to leading edge technology and the importance and value of certifications, there is an additional element that is just as important for KIO Networks: the value recognized by its clients (Beguerisse 2016). As a company, they do not sell their clients stock in a warehouse, but they seek to meet their client's needs and give integral solutions to their IT needs. Regardless of whether it is the best option from a sales perspective for KIO Networks, the company seeks to provide their clients the best functioning tailor-made solutions.

And so, KIO Networks aims to permanently be a symbol of quality and mission critical practices for its clients. In order to achieve this, the company has experts in all operating areas and makes the necessary investment in high-level training and certification for its personnel, ensuring they are not tied to a brand or solution, in order to provide the necessary flexibility to incorporate as many elements as necessary in order to meet each client's specific needs.

4   Information Collection Method for the KIO Networks Case

Information for this case was collected primarily through interviews and corporate information on the KIO Networks website. Interviews were conducted by Elena Beguerisse, Corporate Director of Human Capital at KIO Networks and by Luis Mejía, Global Operations Director at KIO Networks, responsible for Europe, the United States, Central America and Mexico. Interviews were conducted in person at KIO Networks' (Mexico) facilities.

The recommendations in the Case Study Research Design and Methods book were considered for designing the interview and constructing the sections of this case. The case was divided into the following sections and stages:

- Company background
- Professional interviewee background
- Core reflection area (s)

  - Management
  - Human talent
  - Processes
  - Best Practices

- Questions were designed to collect information on milestones or critical moments in organizational performance and/or stages experienced during solution implementation, the players who had a part in it (people, organizations, clients), and the results achieved. These critical moments in the case were subsequently analyzed considering the following questions:

- What worked out well and why? (successes)
- What could have worked out better and why? (lessons learned)
- What did not work out and why? (failure factors)

- Lessons learned and recommendations: Questions oriented towards lessons and recommendations were asked in a such way as to allow elements to be provided to answer case questions.

5 Best Practices at KIO Data Center Management

KIO Networks' best practices oriented towards properly managing a Data Center are presented in this section. Recommendations on selection, recruitment, and training of human talent, as well as recommendations to achieve the highest performance levels, mostly based on adequate process management prevail.

5.1 People

For KIO Networks' Chief Operating Officer (COO, Mejía Resendiz 2016) the greatest personnel problem in the industry is not that something does not work or that mistakes are made, but not knowing how to make decisions when critical situations arise. Therefore, as stated by the Corporate Director of Human Capital (Beguerisse 2016): "If you want the best, you must have the best talent", this includes decision-making capabilities and that is why this section deals with the importance of people for KIO Networks, by presenting the profile of the person in charge of managing human talent at KIO Networks as well as a description of the recruitment, selection and training process and the way human capital is prepared and motivated to face the significant challenges encountered in the mission critical projects in a Data Center such as KIO Networks.

5.1.1 The Profile of the Human Capital Manager at KIO Networks

To have the best human capital in an organization with the characteristics of KIO Networks, it is necessary to recruit the best talent to achieve the highest performance levels; it also requires adequate leadership and a level of motivation from the Human Capital area leader and, for KIO Networks, from the person leading the Human Management area since 2010 and up to the date this case was documented. The profile is as follows (Beguerisse 2016):

- *Continuous learning,* which must be according to company, client and sector needs, including personalized consultants if required, for gaining a better understanding of the business and providing added value to strategies.

- *Knowing the market's best practices* in order to apply them and adapt them to the needs of KIO Networks and its clients.
- *Experience in various sectors:* financial, educational, retail, health and automotive sectors among others, as well as local and federal government
- *Experience in mission critical and strategic projects*
- *Capability to project long-term actions,* not just for here and now, but also the ones that will be required 5 years into the future and, additionally keep preparing the company's human capital and the necessary resources to always remain at the leading edge of technology and human talent.
- *Constant attention to attract the best human talent,* considering the mission critical essence of KIO Networks, it is necessary to have the best human talent, those who are able to handle not just the technology being used by the company, but also the leading edge practices in the market overall.
- *Conducting benchmark activities on a permanent basis,* and attending congresses, both domestic and international, in order to identify the best practices and then implement them within the organization, taking into account the company and client needs so as to be able to project the necessary resources.
- *Being a manager with the ability to find and manage the necessary resources* to carry out corporate strategy.
- *Having skills and power to participate in the corporate strategic vision.*

5.1.2   The Recruitment and Selection Process at KIO Networks

As previously mentioned, KIO Networks permanently seeks to have the best human talent. The recruitment process is one of the pillars to achieve this. The elements that KIO Networks considers essential in its personnel recruitment and selection process are presented below. It is a meticulous process that is focused on the requirements of the company and its clients because, for KIO Networks, human talent is an important part of its "DNA". Some of the considerations regarding the profile of the human capital to be recruited and selected are as follows (Beguerisse 2016):

- Having the necessary technical competencies for subsequent development in the company.
- Having the following five drivers: (1) fast learner (self-driven); (2) self-taught; (3) teamwork capacity; (4) sense of "dissatisfaction" and hunger for learning; (5) being a person who fully enjoys his/her work (because KIO Networks is a company where there are no working hours but deliverables).
- Willingness to work under pressure. It is sought that, rather than being related to economic need, this point has to do with being willing to do one's best.
- Being a self-directed person, with decision-making capabilities. This is an important point in the selection process and one where KIO Networks is more punctilious, as once the ideal candidate has been selected, projections are made regarding candidate suitability for the next higher position, rather than for the position the candidate is applying for, because he/she may be promoted in the short term.

The human talent recruitment and selection process is summarized below (Beguerisse 2016):

- *Recruitment begins with an online interview.* KIO Networks has a tool where people interested in a job receive an email with directions on how to access a prerecorded interview. Candidates then record themselves and return the result of the interview. Interviews are the first screen to schedule appointments for candidates.
- *Personal interview.* In a more personal interview, candidates are questioned to verify if they have the required technical knowledge, the five divers and to make sure that they fit into the company's DNA. Questions like the ones below are asked in the interview:

  - "Describe a situation in your former jobs where you have laughed a lot about something that happened to you". If the candidate cannot tell about a time when he laughed at himself/herself, he/she is not the kind of person KIO Networks is looking for.
  - "Describe your career plan, not within the company but your personal plan". The intent is to know the career and institutional plan, because in order to be selected, although KIO Networks will not be responsible for career and individual plans, it will provide the resources to carry them out.
  - "Tell me what your career plan is, where do you envision yourself in the technology area, how would you go about it to get there, what would you need?" From these questions and based on his/her capacity to create that mental map, the person can be considered as a candidate.
  - "If you have to develop your technical competencies, what resources would you use? Where would you go?" If he/she is a technology person, they should at least know where they can get knowledge.
  - Taking into account that it is sought that the candidate is a *"team player"*, questions are asked regarding the person's leadership to work in a team, what a team means to them, what would be a team's objective. If the person is a *"team player"*, he/she must be able to identify the differences between individualism and teamwork.

Based on the interview process, once the personnel has been selected, work will be done on them through a training process and internal marketing. The latter is considered as important as external marketing because KIO Networks believes that personnel act as "ambassadors" outside the company, and so they are expected to be proud of the place where they work. Evidence of this is KIO Network's *"Great Place to Work"* certification, in addition to being recognized as a socially responsible company. Both certifications are considered the most significant ones in the human capital area.

5.1.3 Training and Coaching Process

After completing the selection and recruitment process, training and coaching actions are conducted. It is stressed that at KIO Networks, when the need for training arises, they seek to have the best, delivered by the best people, and, when required, tailor-made training and coaching sessions are conducted.

With regards to training actions, four of them stand out: the first one is that each person is responsible for increasing their knowledge; the second is a Performance Bonus that is measured based on the person's knowledge, what the person has learned and who the person has taught. The third action is oriented towards ensuring no one in KIO Network's personnel fails to receive training at least once a year, rather than measuring training in terms of man-hours Here, it is stressed that, at KIO Networks, training expenses are not limited, as providing such training is relevant to what KIO Networks and its clients need, based on the projects to be executed. Finally, the fourth action is that persons who will be taking care of a project have the duty of studying the client's business, what they do and their line of business. So purely technical training does not suffice, they must also get trained in knowing the business of the client they will be serving in order to provide added value solutions.

In addition to the above, it is important to emphasize that KIO Networks also provides coaching support for its personnel in various areas and for various purposes. One of its methodologies is the *Nine Box Grid* which, although not exclusive to KIO Networks (it was developed by McKinsey and improved by General Electric), it means for instance, that if someone in the company is under development training (growth employee), they may move onto the next level (see Fig. 3).

On the other hand, training on how to coach collaborators is also provided. For this purpose, courses such as *"trainer of trainers"* are delivered, so that project leaders can train their collaborators because they must know not just how to conduct the technical side but also a human capital area called *"happiness"*. When required, an external consultant and/or coach paid by KIO Networks is brought in and assigned a space in the company so that personnel can consult him or her when needed.

Additionally, there are more specialized coaching programs for managers. This type of program consists of two phases. The first one is when a new director is hired and he/she is assigned a coach for *on boarding* for the purpose of supporting the new director in becoming adapted to KIO Networks ecosystem. The second phase is assisted coach-

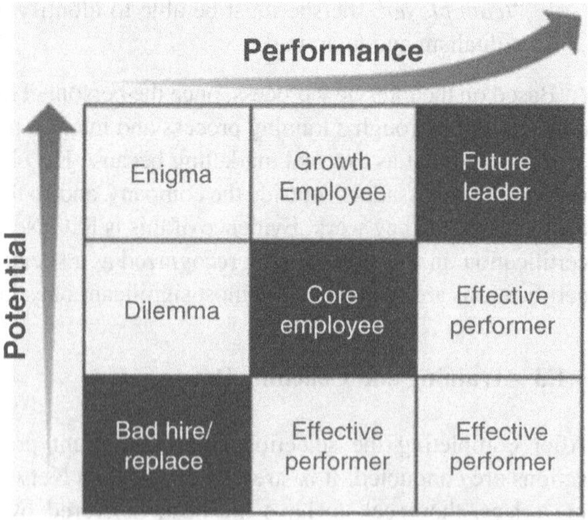

Fig. 3 Nine Box Grid (Source: http://intelligentexecutive.com/)

ing, and is intended to "debug" a particular topic that the director would like to discuss with a coach on issues such as knowing how to delegate, being more empathic and how to get the best out of collaborators; everything is organized around their agenda.

5.1.4 What KIO Networks Knows Is Best to Do with Its Human Talent

There is no doubt that great achievements and high customer satisfaction indexes in a company are elements that show what a company does best, and to KIO Networks, the basis for this is its human talent, which is chiefly characterized by the following elements:

- *Development of human talent.* Everyone working at KIO Networks values the formation they are provided with. This is how in-house intellectual and corporate capital is built, giving the company added value in the market.
- *Talent retention.* KIO Networks has learned that personnel retention is not always achieved through higher wages, but through complements such as work spaces that are pleasant and fun, getting people to feel proud of working for the company and through personalized training plans. In other words, by being a place where one can grow and apply one's knowledge, a place for making decisions and assuming responsibility for them and, most importantly, that collaborators are aware that they are a key element that adds value to the company.
- *Flexible work environment.* Considering that, at KIO Networks, the work is done based on objectives, Flex Office & Home Office work environments are ideal as they make it possible to have no arrival or leaving times.
- *Anytime, anywhere any device.* High-level connectivity allows collaborators to work within their facilities anywhere, anytime and from any device.

5.1.5 KIO Networks' Personnel-Related Organizational Lessons Learned

Every person and every generation going through an organization leaves behind lessons in human capital areas. Below are some of KIO Networks' lessons learned in the last 10 years, in its human capital selection, recruitment and development processes:

- *A new generation of collaborators known as the "Millennials" is recognized.* Recognizing and valuing millennials as a part of their company's personnel has resulted in low personnel turnover rates at KIO Networks, and in persons who work there wishing to stay. The company seeks to have a work environment adapted to them. For instance, 90% of KIO Networks Millennials personnel like things to be agile, "On & Off" stuff, innovation, they dispose of things really quickly: they just get used to something and, all of a sudden, they want something different. Also, they seek to promote values within the company with an approach adapted to this generation.

- *They have learned to get the best out of people,* always aiming for a win-win scheme, and making personnel feel comfortable at their work environment and fostering a passion for their job.
- They have seen that *learning is never enough* and one must always remain at the leading edge.
- *Benchmarking* must not be against one's own company, but also against the market, one must know what the best ones are doing.
- *The "soft" side of technical persons must be developed* so they can become leaders. Considering that KIO Networks is growing so fast, they have realized that leaders for the future must be developed, not just on their technical side also on their "soft" side of managerial and leadership skills.
- *A company must not neglect being a seed bed.* This is why KIO Networks takes care to always keep its personnel in training for their next upper level. Being a seed bed implies seeking for the highest-grade students in universities and the best talent in order to start developing and turning them into future leaders through agile approaches allowing them to initiate their leadership careers in technological areas as soon as possible.

5.1.6 What has Not Worked Out for Developing Human Talent

KIO Networks acknowledges that not all of its practices intended to develop human resources have been successful. Although they consider that a large percentage of its personnel are "Millennials" who seek for agile learning, they have found that some online courses have not worked out, maybe because is not the best vehicle for their development, and so, at times they have had to switch over to in-person training formats after the self-taught methods.

Regarding communication systems, attempts have been made to work with some online formative tools, but they have not worked too well because these tools happen to be unattractive and something more sophisticated and agile is required. It was observed that sometimes, if they provide too formal communication, trainees just wouldn't focus their attention on this, even when monitoring what they look and what was catching their attention in course material. Therefore, an agile internal training scheme had to be generated where they could learn how the company is doing, what it is doing and what is going to be done.

5.2   The Keys Factors for Good Performance

Considering that Data Centers are critical elements for organizations using their services nowadays (Dumsky and Isaev 2015; Fernández-Montes et al. 2015), a Data Center must, in addition to having high quality and technological performance, manage its services and processes adequately. Therefore, below are KIO Networks recommendations and best practices intended to guarantee the best performance in its processes for mission critical projects, which are the ones a Data Center usually deals with (Mejía Resendiz 2016).

5.2.1 Benchmarking

Some of KIO Networks' considerations to achieve adequate Data Center performance include the recognition of benchmarking against industry standards as a best practice.

An example of this is the number of servers per FTE (Full time Equivalent). According to figures provided by Gartner, about 70 servers can be managed per FTE; at KIO Networks one person may be in charge of as many as 100 servers, a workload that may vary as a function of server-related aspects such as whether they are virtual or physical, fault level and the types of transactions or operations to be conducted because, for instance, it a server for the banking or finance sector can be different from one for the government sector.

And so, based on the above, KIO Networks has realized that the fact that a person has competencies to handle technologies in the government area does not necessarily mean that this person has competences for a different sector and that this could even result in waste and inadequate use of knowledge, resources and time.

5.2.2 Availability and Maintenance of Technological Equipment

There are two other aspects to be considered as a best practice, in addition to adequately assigning human talent: availability and adequate maintenance of technological equipment. If these aspects are not taken care of and monitored in a timely manner, the results may impact not just a company's operation level, but also its costs such as those related to maintenance. It is important to have information that identifies the time a technology is becoming obsolete and/or when it is showing high fault indexes that, in time, will lead to non-viable, costly operation.

5.2.3 Increasing Operating Cost Efficiency

Another best practice proposal by KIO Networks in order to increase operating cost efficiency is the one presented in Fig. 4, where the proposal is to solve a larger number of incidents at the base of the pyramid, so that strategic problems and projects are solved at the top of the pyramid by specialists with 6 or 7 years of experience. In some cases, there are operations that run on an inverted pyramid, whereby basic incidents are solved at the top by specialists, increasing the costs of Human Resources.

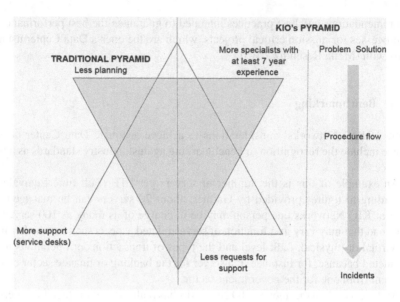

Fig. 4 KIO Networks' Pyramid to increase operating cost efficiency (Source: Mejía Reséndiz (2016))

5.2.4 Considerations for Good Human Talent Performance

One best practice for a Data Center is undoubtedly its human talent. KIO Networks' recommendations to achieve adequate personnel performance in the IT service management area are summarized below (Mejía Resendiz 2016):

- *IT service manager with prior experience in Data Centers.* Prior experience in Data Center management allows applying previously acquired knowledge by adapting and scaling it.
- *Personnel capacity to cope with high responsibility levels.* Operations at a Data Center with high performance KPIs (*Key Performance Indicators*) calls for high levels of responsibility and an ability to make decisions.
- *Quest for high levels of personal commitment.* A work environment centered on order and discipline must be created; it motivates personnel to do their best in the face of the high performance levels a Data Center such as KIO Networks calls for. All this is intended to keep the organization from being stressed.
- *Continuous growth within the organization.* Economic incentives through wage rises are not the most important factor for KIO Networks personnel, because they value their growth within the organization more, and one of the most valued incentives is the personal and professional growth each employee sets for himself/herself as a goal.
- *High level project-customized training.* One of the aspects KIO Networks cares for is that every project is carried out by the personnel that most closely meet the required profile, every person involved in a project decides what training they require in order to generate maximum value in terms of a person's work and, therefore, in terms of results.

- *Decision-making capability.* Having a high performance human team that is able to work under critical levels and high availability calls for high levels of decision-making capability when critical situations are faced and, at the same time, requires a mix of processes that they are trained in, in addition to a culture promoting decision-making, continuous process improvement and certifications.
- *Fast thinking.* What makes work special every day in KIO Networks are the challenges that collaborators face daily, which keep their mind open to fast changes, inviting them to increase their knowledge and improve their skills as well. This allows consistently and almost immediately developing innovative and creative solutions that solve complex requirements of demanding customers, increasingly specialized solutions that require more speed and correlation technology.
- *Closeness among all organizational levels.* Closeness and interaction among the various organizational levels is a fundamental element to promote communication and effective achievement of results.

5.2.5 Considerations for Good Process Performance

KIO Networks has come to know through experience what processes generate value. They have even learned that when a process is not clear or when it does not exist, it must be created, but paying attention is important so processes are just filed away and never used. With regards to creating new processes, one of the ways to support project creation is through an induction course that is mandatory for all personnel. For instance, ITIL (Information Technology Infrastructure Library) is the framework for implemented processes; training is online and mandatory. Subsequently in-person certification is carried out. Internal ITIL instructors are available as a supportive resource (Beguerisse 2016).

On the other hand, when selecting and creating processes, one must learn not to lose sight of the level of scalability and flexibility the company has and, most importantly, one must be alert to the technical personnel for they are rather prone to solve things immediately and on their own – especially newly hired personnel, who, due to a lack of knowledge for the short time they have been in the company, may fail to realize that it may adversely affect other areas. That is why KIO Networks has deemed it fit to have highly strict training so that people working for the firm have the capacity to know what they can and what they cannot modify, and are aware of the scope and impact their decisions may have at the various levels of escalation. Also, through its various levels of certification, they should only work on modules or processes that make sense in their daily activities and projects (Beguerisse 2016).

In addition to the above, according to KIO Networks, there are four other elements that contribute to good process performance (Mejía Resendiz 2016). The *first one is a constant quest for continuous improvement of the processes oriented towards customer care,* for the purpose of making customer care easier and faster so that customers feel they are being taken care of without so much bureaucracy.

The *second element is process follow-up.* It is not enough to implement them, it is also important to follow up on them, in addition to monitoring those processes to uncover any weaknesses, otherwise there might be an adverse impact on the success level of other processes and operations (Mejía Resendiz 2016). Because KIO

Networks considers that processes that are not useful or do not add value, hinder and become obstacles (*"stoppers"*) for decision making, they recommend that one must be able to identify processes that do not contribute to and adversely affect a business critical mission (Beguerisse 2016).

Going back to the topic of the above paragraph, the *third element has to do with continuous process improvement*, which is a mandatory element considering the demand for high level decision making when critical situations are faced. This calls for a culture promoting continuous process improvement and their associated certifications.

Finally, *good processes performance is also related to the availability and resiliency of technological equipment*. In simple terms, this means the capacity of a solution to go on working within acceptable parameters when facing various types of problems (Mejía Resendiz 2016).

5.2.6 Value-Generating Process Frameworks

One of the process frameworks that have been implemented and are considered to generate value for the organization is ITIL, for which incident management, problem management, change management and configuration management are being used to sell their clients solutions with high availability technology and ticket closing within the established response and restoration levels when any incident occurs.

Finally, just as there are process frameworks that generate value for an organization, as far as KIO Networks is concerned, there are certifications that are not necessarily critical for KIO processes, such as ISO 9000, because it is not considered in the best practice category but rather as a supportive element for process documentation. Regarding ISO 20000, rather than turning it into a certification, it represents a supportive element to follow up on a process operation.

6 Summary of Implications for Research and Practice

In this section, based on the KIO Networks case, we describe the main implications for research and practice of Data Center managers in two main areas: Information Technology Service Management (ITSM) and Human Resource Management.

Considering an adequate Data Center performance, the key lessons learned for research and practice are: permanent benchmarking against industry standards. KIO Networks has realized the fact that just because a person has competencies to handle technologies in the government area does not mean he/she has competencies for different sectors and that impacts an inadequate use of knowledge, resources and time. Availability and adequate maintenance of technological equipment is mandatory; and strategic problems and projects must be supported and solved by specialists with experience.

Regarding the proper personnel performance in the IT service management area, the recommendations are: the IT service manager must have prior job experience in

Data Centers; every project is carried out by the personnel that most closely meet the required profile; every person involved in a project decides what training they require in order to generate maximum value, especially when critical situations are faced; a high training level allows to the organization to have the capacity to know what they can and cannot do. Implementing processes is not enough, it is also relevant to monitor them to identify processes that do not contribute to or even adversely affect a business's critical mission; there is a strong culture promoting continuous process improvement and their associated certifications.

For Data Center Human Resource Managers, KIO lessons shows that having high technical knowledge is not enough, and some of the main key factors for a better personnel performance are: they need to know how to make decisions when critical situations arise; requires adequate leadership and a level of motivation from the Human Capital area leader; fast learning; self-taught; teamwork capacity; sense of "dissatisfaction"; hunger for learning; fully enjoy his/her work; constant training and coaching; and a flexible work environment.

Considering all the above, each of these key factors could be researched to find which of them is the most influential in a higher level performance of processes and human capital of a Data Center.

7 Conclusions

Data Center Networks (DCN) have become gradually strategic technological partners for their clients because these centers provide them with services ranging from data storage to *cloud computing* and Big Data analysis environments.

Although having the best technological infrastructure underlies the trust level and strategic partnership existing between a Data Center and its clients, that is not all there is to it; the organizational and management aspects of a Data Center, such as the following ones, are just as important: its business model, its way of managing its technological and human resources, its level of social responsibility, its commitment to protect the environment, its capacity to manage mission critical projects, and always being at the leading edge of technology.

Considering the above, in the conclusions of this case, the most outstanding best practices for Data Center management and good performance are, on one hand, having a work environment that promotes, among the individuals comprising a company's human capital, capabilities to take care of mission critical services and projects, decision making and innovation. A key element is having the best human talent and a continuous training and certification process in accordance to the needs and challenges contingent to the nature of the projects of a Data Center such as KIO Networks and, on the other hand, although a Data Center calls for adequate technical, technological and even environmental management, the management of its information technology services and the utilization of adequate process frameworks for this kind of center is just as important. Care must be exercised to select and implement those that actually generate value for the organization and its clients.

Hence, we consider that this paper contributes information for those who are closely involved in the technological side of a Data Center, mainly for those who are on the managerial side. This case provides a view on how this kind of organization managed its human resources and strategic processes, considering these kinds of companies are highly involved in managing mission critical projects. The case also provides a view of the information technology management frameworks (ITSM) that best fits a Data Center.

Finally, existing and emerging Data Centers will face new challenges, and innovative value added solutions that best fits their clients needs, for example (Schmidt 2016):

- Now the focus has shifted to analyzing and processing data for on-demand access. The rise of mobility and wearable technology creates requirements for latency that has previously never been seen.
- The large wave of growth will be in point of presence (PoP) Data Centers, supporting content delivery networks for service providers as well as promoting network virtualization and software defined networks. A combination of growth within PoP and co-location will increase the need for interconnecting or peering between service providers.
- The world has shifted towards an app-driven world where users look at the data hundreds of times a day in shorter durations. Users are starting to feel that data should be predictive and instantly serve up information from the cloud.
- Data Centers cannot be inefficient; they need to know exactly where everything is, how it is being used and powered. Any form of inefficiency in the Data Center can be costly so Data Center infrastructure management (DCIM) will be paramount in helping keep these Data Centers running without problems.
- The streaming, uninterruptable, low latency services of music, video, and information are spurring the growth of hyperscale (ability of an architecture to scale appropriately as increased demand is added to the system).
- Users want streaming information without delay.
- Data exists in multiple places to provide static information without latency.

Considering all the above, more published research is needed so that Data Centers can share their best practices and lessons learned, not only in the technological side but also in their process and human resource management. In that sense, in this chapter, KIO Networks shared three important issues: Data Centers require highly talented human resources with the ability to make decisions on mission-critical projects; higher performance technology is needed; and managerial leadership is essential.

References

Alaraifi, A., Molla, A., Deng, H.: An exploration of data center information systems. J. Syst. Inf. Technol. **14**(4), 353–370 (2012)
Beguerisse, E.: Interview: Elena Beguerisse, Corporate Human Resources Director, KIO Networks (2016)

Capozzoli, A., Primiceri, G.: Cooling systems in data centers: state of art and emerging technologies. Energy Procedia. **83**, 484–493 (2015)

Daim, T., et al.: Data center metrics: An energy efficiency model for information technology managers. Manage. Environ. Qual. Int J. **20**, 712–731 (2009)

Dumsky, D.V., Isaev, E.A.: Data centers for physical research. Phys. Procedia. **71**, 298–302 (2015)

Fernández-Montes, A., et al.: Energy wasting at internet data centers due to fear. Pattern Recogn. Lett. **67**, 59–65 (2015)

KIO-Networks: KIO networks web page. *Web Page*. Available at: https://kionetworks.com/almacenamiento-privado-de-datos-crece-75-kio/#.VyLAb_l97IU (2016). Accessed 1 May 2016

Ma, L., et al.: Probabilistic region failure-aware data center network and content placement. Comput. Netw. **103**, 56–66 (2016)

Mejía Resendiz, L.: Interview: Luis Mejía Resendiz, Chief Operating Officer, KIO Networks (2016)

Nada, S.A., Elfeky, K.E., Attia, A.M.A.: Experimental investigations of air conditioning solutions in high power density data centers using a scaled physical model. Int. J. Refrig. **63**, 87–99 (2015)

Plant, R.: ¿El centro de datos en proceso de desaparición? *Harvard Business Review América Latina*, (July) (2009)

Qin, Y., et al.: Analysis for TCP in data center networks: Outcast and incast. J. Netw. Comput. Appl. **68**, 140–150 (2016)

Rahman, M.N., Esmailpour, A.: A hybrid data center architecture for big data. Big Data Res. **3**, 29–40 (2016)

Rong, H., et al.: Optimizing energy consumption for data centers. Renew. Sust. Energ. Rev. **58**, 674–691 (2016)

Schmidt, J.: Key trends for data centers. *Data Center Dynamics*. Available at: http://www.datacenterdynamics.com/core-edge/key-trends-for-data-centers/95679.article (2016)

Uddin, M., et al.: Evaluating power efficient algorithms for efficiency and carbon emissions in cloud data centers: A review. Renew. Sust. Energ. Rev. **51**, 1553–1563 (2015)

Teresa Lucio-Nieto is CEO at Customer Care Associates. She is experienced in design and implementation of strategies for IT Service Management, IT Governance, Process Reengineering, Customer Quality and Service in the areas of Information Technology, Quality and Manufacture, Distribution and Customer Care Centers for various organizations such as Coca-Cola, Instituto Federal Electoral (IFE), Petroleos Mexicanos (Pemex), and others. She has been a professor in the graduate programs at Tecnologico de Monterrey and Universidad Anahuac (Mexico). She holds a Bachelor's Degree in Computer Systems from Tecnologico de Monterrey (Mexico), and Master's Degrees in Computer Sciences and System Management from Tecnologico de Monterrey (Mexico), and a PhD from Carlos III University in Madrid, Spain. She is certified in ITIL Expert Project Management (Carnegie Mellon University); Benchmarking (Purdue University); an Internal Auditor ISO 9000; Certified Auditor and Consultant in the ISO/IED 20000 standard.

Dora Luz Gonzalez-Bañales is full-time professor and researcher in the Department of Systems and Computing at the Instituto Tecnologico de Durango, México. Dr. Gonzalez-Bañales holds a Master's Degree in Information Technology Management from Monterrey Tech (ITESM, Campus Monterrey, México) and a PhD in Integration of Information Technologies in Organizations from the Polytechnic University of Valencia, Spain (2007). Her research interests include: User eXperience, usability, human-computer interaction, design thinking, educational technology, project management, B-learning, flipped learning, incorporation and use of information technologies in organizations.

QoS in NaaS (Network-as-a-Service) Using Software Defined Networking

Ammar AlSous and Jorge Marx Gómez

Abstract Network-as-a-Service (NaaS) is one of new and promising cloud service models, through which the network infrastructure is offered to cloud customers as a service. Quality of Service (QoS) criteria play a significant role in the Service Level Agreement (SLA) for pricing and evaluation. This chapter describes NaaS service model and focuses on QoS criteria and issues in NaaS as well as for networking in general. A description about Software Defined Networking (SDN) has been presented, this promising network paradigm, which is considered one of programmable network designs, that depends on decoupling the control and data planes in order to achieve easier manageable networks. Finally, a deep research about applying a QoS policy in cloud and normal networks using SDN has been conducted, that shows the main categories for achieving the required QoS level. Their advantages and disadvantages have been mentioned, which in turn helps in choosing the best model according to multiple factors: the current network hardware, the traffic data type, the budget, etc.

1 Introduction

Cloud computing is considered one of the most important research areas nowadays, through adopting the resource sharing concept it saves many costs for users. The resources utilization rate is optimized (Rittinghouse and Ransome 2016) and the required service level is delivered to the end user without any hardware or maintenance responsibilities from his side. In the last decade, using cloud services became more common for companies and individual users as well, where these services are able to serve different levels and needs. Network-as-a-Service (NaaS) is one of the

A. AlSous, MSc (✉)
Department of Business Information Systems/Very Large Business Applications (VLBA),
Carl von Ossietzky University of Oldenburg, Oldenburg 26129, Germany
e-mail: ammar.alsous@uni-oldenburg.de

J. Marx Gómez
Department of Computing Sciences, Carl von Ossietzky University of Oldenburg,
Oldenburg 26129, Germany
e-mail: jorge.marx.gomez@uni-oldenburg.de

© Springer International Publishing AG 2017   115
J. Marx Gómez et al. (eds.), *Engineering and Management of Data Centers*,
Service Science: Research and Innovations in the Service Economy,
DOI 10.1007/978-3-319-65082-1_6

new offered cloud service models, in which the cloud provider's network is also offered as a service, with a related Service Level Agreement (SLA) that specifies the service details and limitations according to the payment.

Software Defined Networking (SDN) is a network promising paradigm, that depends on decoupling data and control planes. The control plane consists of a controller (or multiple controllers), which has a global view about the whole network, and is responsible of sending commands to network devices in order to apply the required protocols or policies. The data plane (which is called "the forwarding plane" as well) consists of simple network devices which can receive controller's commands, and interpret them as rules in their rule tables (Neto 2011). As a result, the controller is the network's master that controls everything, and the network devices become simple forwarding devices responsible of following the rules without applying network protocols locally as in the traditional networks. That gives the applications more ability and flexibility to participate in deciding the network behavior according to their requirements, without many complications as before, where network configurations should be applied in each network device individually.

One of the most important parts in a NaaS's SLA is the Quality of Service (QoS) level, which is considered from of the main factors that affect services pricing. Recently, many researches have been conducted in order to use SDN features to apply and guarantee QoS requirements in NaaS services.

This chapter analyzes the previous points and presents a deep research about the academic works in these fields. It is organized mainly as the following: Sect. 2 summarizes the cloud services and focuses on NaaS and their features. Section 3 speaks about QoS criteria in networks in general and the special requirements for NaaS. Section 4 identifies SDN principles and structure. Finally, Sect. 5 conducts a deep research about using Software Defined Networking to apply the required QoS in a network, and the main categories for current researches and their limitations.

2 Theoretical Background on Cloud Computing Services

The cloud computing concept has come from the idea of using the internet to access the offered services by service providers, in order to utilize the resources according to customers' demands and to price services accordingly. This environment consists of a pool of shared resources, and by offering these services, the cloud provider could achieve a very high optimization level of resource utilization. Moreover, it helps in reducing management efforts, because separated data centers require separated human resources for each site, and that can be reduced in a central could data center. The cloud services could be at different levels, i.e. computing, storage, software, etc. (Neto 2011).

There are three major service models for cloud services:

- *Infrastructure as a Service (IaaS):* The offered services in this model include computers (or mostly virtual machines), that are used by the user remotely regardless any details related to a real physical infrastructure, security, backup etc. At the service provider level, there is a Hypervisor (or pool of hypervisors) that is responsible of managing the infrastructure and offering the required machines to the users, with the ability to scale the offered services according to users' requirements and their current usage level. Then the users can install an operating system and needed applications as well (Neto 2011; Buyya et al. 2010). Amazon Web Services (Cloud 2011) is an example for could providers that can offer this service model.

- *Platform as a Service (PaaS):* This model suits developers who seek for an environment to develop their own software solutions without taking into consideration an infrastructure's complexity and cost. The offered services by vendors include a computer platform with an installed operating system and some extra tools that are necessary for software solutions development. The PaaS user can configure the software-developing environment without worrying about servers, networks, operating systems and storage management operations (Neto 2011; Buyya et al. 2010). Google AppEngine ('App Engine – Platform as a Service|Google Cloud Platform' n.d.) is PaaS cloud service provider, in which developers can build web and mobile applications.

- *Software as a Service (SaaS):* In this service model the cloud provider offers an infrastructure with a platform and the desired application software. It is more efficient, cheaper and simpler for users to use the offered software without any responsibilities regarding its installation, license, management, maintenance and support. Those software applications can support multitenancy, which means that multiple users can use the same application separately (Neto 2011; Buyya et al. 2010). Salesforce ('Salesforce.com: The Customre Success Platform To Grow Your Business.' n.d.) is an example for SaaS service providers, it offers CRM, where the user can subscribe and use the software without responsibilities of maintenance or license.

Network-as-a-Service (NaaS) could sometimes be separated from the main three service models and considered a standalone service. It is one of new offered services by cloud vendors that considers the network transport connectivity as a service, and offers it to customers (on-demand network connectivity) with the ability to achieve a higher optimization level of resource allocation (Costa et al. 2012). Those resources include computing and network resources. There is a strong relation between the NaaS and the IaaS concepts. However, the NaaS can make it much easier and more efficient for end users not to deal directly with the infrastructure. In this service model, the tenants can access the network devices (switches and routers) through the service, also they can apply customized network traffic decisions regarding forwarding, blocking and any other type of supported network decisions. As a result, the cloud network infrastructure will be provisioned as cloud services, and will be utilized more efficiently according to tenants' requirements, where the current network status plays a primary role in that (Ayadi et al. 2013).

Distributed applications' components can use this type of service model to achieve a better performance (e.g. VPN, VLAN, etc.). There are many advantages of using NaaS model: the customer is charged according to pay-as-you-use model, which is more efficient without management responsibilities for the customer. Moreover, the cloud provider can maximize the utilization of computing and network resources by using some optimization techniques, which affects the services' prices. Furthermore, service providers can take care of multiple issues at the same time because they own the infrastructure (high computing, routing, security, etc.) (Costa et al. 2012; Ayadi et al. 2013).

Virtual Private Network "VPN" is considered one of NaaS services that can be offered by a cloud provider with many advantages over normal VPN services. The public or shared network can be used as a private network with capabilities of QoS guarantee and on demand bandwidth reservation. Aryaka is one of NaaS providers ('Network as-a-Service|At a Glance|Aryaka' n.d.), with offering IPsec VPN it provides a private connection to Microsoft Azure ('Microsoft Azure: Cloud Computing Platform & Services' n.d.) and Amazon Web Services (AWS) ('Amazon Web Services (AWS) – Cloud Computing Services' n.d.), that includes many other features like: QoS level, TCP optimization, real time network visibility and smart link (link aggregation and load balancing).

2.1 NaaS Functionality

NaaS functionality can be determined by: network visibility, custom forwarding and in-network processing (Costa et al. 2012):

- *Network visibility:* In the internet and any other open environments, the applications use the Black-Box model regarding the network design for communicating. While the White-Box model is used in Data Centers (DCs), where the provider knows the logical and physical topologies, and he can optimize the utilization of his infrastructure. Because of the high oversubscription level in Data Centers (Benson et al. 2010), the mapping between logical and physical topologies has an important effect on the performance.
- *Custom forwarding:* The applications can manage forwarding rules in the switches, and choose the suitable routing algorithm to be applied. As a result, the network traffic paths in the DC are optimized according to applications' requirements and the current network state.
- *In-network processing:* The cloud applications performance can be improved by using packets aggregation, which can be applied between network stages in order to reduce the overall traffic processing in a cloud network. This feature depends on the used applications, e.g. distributed computing platforms (Dean and Ghemawat 2008), real time streaming systems and search engines (Borthakur et al. 2011).

In order to use the NaaS model efficiently in current DCs, there are some require-ments should be fulfilled (Costa et al. 2012): it is better not to force the provider (sometimes it is inapplicable) to change the old expensive network infrastructure, which is typically not programmable, in order to adopt the NaaS model. Moreover, the NaaS should offer high level model for software developers, without showing the complexity at the packet processing level, and without exposing the internal design of the DC's internal network. Furthermore, the ability of network resource isolation is an important point, which should be applied between the simultaneously running applications. This isolation should be better than the previous routing soft-ware solutions (Lu et al. 2011; Rizzo et al. 2012).

There are multiple researches have been done in order to suggest network virtual architectures that can be used in the NaaS model (Bari et al. 2013a). One of these researches is CloudNaaS (Benson et al. 2011), which offers a cloud networking system that can be used by developers and can grant them wider access to network functions, i.e. network isolation, service differentiation (QoS) and other functions.

3   Network Quality of Service (QoS)

The service level agreement (SLA) between customers and providers determines the guaranteed service level that is offered by the provider, according to the cus-tomer's payment and other factors. For NaaS and any other network service models, there are some general criteria for pricing and service evaluation processes. In other words, network QoS means the managed unfairness in the provider's network according to delay sensitivity, packet loss tolerance and any other criteria (Szigeti et al. 2013, p. 5). In general, internet routers and network switches use the 'best effort' model for QoS, which means that each network flow can obtain a variable bandwidth, round trip time (RTT) and other QoS standards, depending on the cur-rent network state and without any guarantees from the provider (Peuhkuri 1999). Because there are different priorities for different network services and each service has its own QoS requirements (bandwidth, delay, etc.), the network traffic should be separated and prioritized according to network provider's priorities, where the low-est prioritized traffic is categorized as a 'best effort'. Combining guaranteed and best-effort traffics together is very hard to be achieved (Goossens et al. 2002).

There are several points should be taken into consideration in order to evaluate the QoS in a network, and they can be summarized as the following (Peuhkuri 1999; Sambanis 2001):

- *Network bandwidth (Data rate):* The rate of carrying the traffic by the network. The available bandwidth might not be enough to serve every service, and some services like video streaming need a minimum amount of available bandwidth in order to work properly. For other services like downloading a file, the limitation in the available bandwidth will affect the download speed. And here is the role of the network provider to prioritize the flows according to the current customers, their flows types and the current network status. Usually it is measured in bits per second.

- *Latency:* The needed time for one packet to reach its destination. The packets can be handled differently by network devices according to the used protocol, the application, the user, etc. That is because of multiple reasons, e.g. the assigned routing path for a specific packet could not be the shortest one, in order to avoid a congestion or a long waiting time in some network devices. The latency is measured by milliseconds.
- *Jitter:* The variation in the packets' delay between the same source and destination, where the packets can take different routes and wait in different queues. As a result, the destination receives out-of-order packets and it needs some strategies to deal with that (Frnda et al. 2013). Some services can deal with the jitter by using a buffer at the receiver side to gather and reorder the packets, however, some services like voice and video streaming, need a constant bit rate, where gathering the packets in a buffer then reordering them affects the quality of these services directly and degrades them. The jitter is measured in milliseconds and happens mainly in packet switching networks.
- *Packet loss ratio:* The ratio of network packets that are discarded by network devices or lost because of any other reasons. Some services can tolerate a specific level of packet loss, like voice and video streaming services, where other services like file transfer is very sensitive for any packet loss. The packet loss is measured by the lost percentage of the total sent packets.

3.1   QoS in Cloud Network Services (NaaS)

The QoS requirements for Network-as-a-Service could be summarized in QoS awareness and Guarantees of application flows (Ayadi et al. 2013). The real network usage by NaaS applications could be changed over time, and as a result, the network might be overprovisioned and the QoS level will be degraded. For that, the QoS contract is important and should be defined in the conceptual phase, in order to manage the offered services and guarantee the QoS level for network services according to the network's state (self-manage and self-control). Moreover, the cloud services can be offered in a heterogeneous environment that has different applications with different network requirements. Some applications need high throughput and no packet loss (e.g. data transfer applications), and others need low latency and can tolerate a certain level of packet loss (e.g. real time voice/video streaming). That is why, an effective mechanism to differentiate the services is needed, in order to optimize the network utilization and taking into account services' requirements.

4 What Is Software Defined Networking (SDN)?

The idea of programmable networking has come from the need to more flexible and easier manageable networks, Software Defined Networking (SDN) paradigm is one of the promising approaches in the computer networking field, which gives the network administrator the ability to program the network. SDN depends on the concept of decoupling the data plane (forwarding hardware devices) and the control plane (network management and network decisions). The network, as a result, can be managed in simpler way with a higher ability for innovation and evolution by developers (Nunes et al. 2014).

4.1 SDN Principles

The SDN principles can be summarized as the following (Open Networking Foundation (ONF) 2013):

- *Separation (Decoupling) the control plane and the data plane:* Removing the control part from network devices (data plane) and put it in a separated level (control plane). There is a control plane interface (CPI) between the controller and each network element in the data plane, in which the control plane can authorize the network element (NE) to do some tasks under its supervision.
- *Central control and management:* The central controller has a better and wider image about the network, and that leads to enhance management decisions. Scalability can be improved by centralizing the controller, where there is more global and less detailed view of the network hardware.
- *Giving applications the ability to control network resources:* The controller can give the applications a certain level of access to the network hardware, which makes the development process more flexible to access and configure the data plane, in order to ease the network resource optimization process.

In order to apply SDN in a network: the control plane should be added as a separated layer, and the network devices should be able to support the used protocol by the controller, in order to interpret the sent commands by the controller.

4.2 SDN Architecture

The main components that form the SDN architecture (Fig. 1) as they have been introduced in (Nunes et al. 2014; Open Networking Foundation (ONF) 2013) are:

- *Application Plane:* Includes SDN applications that can deal directly with the network through the SDN controller. They can send their requests and get the required view of the current network.

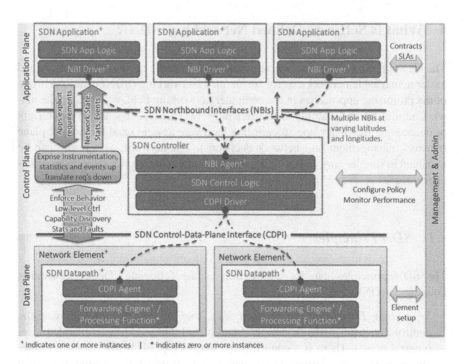

Fig. 1 SDN architecture (Open Networking Foundation (ONF) 2013)

- *Control Plane:* The control plane is logically centralized, and includes one or more controllers. The SDN controller works between SDN applications and network elements. It can interpret applications' demands to the data plane as orders, and it can transfer the relevant data from the data plane to the applications e.g. statistics.
- *Data Plane:* The data plane consists of SDN-enabled network elements. These devices include switches, routers and any physical network equipment. They can be called "forward devices", while mostly they are represented as basic forwarding network devices. The data plane might be called in some cases "forward plane".
- *SDN Control to Data-Plane Interface (CDPI):* CDPI is an interface between the control plane and the data plane. It can transfer programmed instructions to network hardware elements, and it supports path advertisements, statistics and notifications for events.
- *SDN Northbound Interfaces (NBI):* NBI is an interface between applications (Application Plane) and the control plane. It transfers applications' requirements to the controller, and the network's state and views to applications.
- *Interface Drivers & Agents:* The driver represents the hardware infrastructure side and the agent represents the application side of this pair, which is implemented for each interface.
- *Management & Admin:* This plane is responsible of higher tasks, which are beyond SDN scope (application, control and data planes).

4.3   OpenFlow

OpenFlow (McKeown et al. 2008) is the most common communication protocol for SDN, it defines rules and standards between the control and data planes. OpenFlow transfers controller's instructions to network devices regardless devices' vendors, which makes it more easy and efficient to control network elements from one centralized place. Controller commands could be interpreted into rules and actions in network devices' flow tables, that is based on a global view of the network and applications' requirements. The flow table exists in each network element and contains rules that should be checked for passing packets before taking the forward decision. When there is no match with any rule, these packets are forwarded to the controller for checking, then the controller can decide to modify the existing rules or add new rules to the flow table in one or more network devices in order to handle this packet or flow in the next time.

5   QoS and Software Defined Networking

This chapter includes a research about the main techniques that used to apply QoS criteria in networks, before and after the SDN. It focuses mainly on SDN approaches which still under development. After mentioning the main SDN approaches, a summary about the main researches has been conducted, which could be applied in normal or cloud networks, with their advantages and disadvantages.

5.1   QoS Before Software Defined Networking

Before using SDN, there were two main QoS approaches, that can be used to differentiate flows' classes in a network: IntServ and DiffServ.

Integrated services (IntServ) (Braden et al. 1994) IntServ approach depends on per flow resource reservation technique, through which each network device (switch or router) has to reserve the required resources for each network flow, in order to provide guaranteed QoS for applications or users. It uses Resource reservation protocol (RSVP) (Zhang et al. 1997) in order to reserve resources in network elements. There are two main problems in this technique concerning scalability and high computational resources. It's hard to be applied in the internet, because it needs that each router on the path supports IntServ and reserves the required resources. Because that routers should reserve resources for each flow, that requires many computational resources in order to handle all network flows and reserve resources in large-scale networks. For these issues, IntServ can be applied in small-scale networks. One solution for the scalability problem, is to use aggregation of RSVP (Baker et al. 2001), which means that flows could be aggregated and transmitted as groups of flows according to QoS requirements. IntServ is considered a fine-grained QoS approach, where each application has its own reserved resources.

Differentiated services (DiffServ) (Blake et al. 1998) DiffServ approach is used to aggregate and classify network flows in order to provide QoS for them. For that, it uses the differentiated services code point (DSCP) in the IP header, which is 6-bits and can be used to differentiate 64 classes. For each packet, the forward decision is taken in network elements according to its class, that makes it simpler and more scalable to classify the network traffic, and it's possible to apply DiffServ in large-scale networks because of the limited number of classes. DiffServ is static, there is a fixed and limited number of classes, without the ability to tune it (and network paths for each class) dynamically or increase it beyond the limit, and that is considered as a disadvantage when there is a need of classes flexibility or high number of classes (Serban et al. 2002). Moreover, there is a lack in the ability to assign QoS per flow, it can just deal with classes. DiffServ cannot guarantee end-to-end QoS when there are multiple domains on the path. In (Zhang et al. 1999), the authors have introduced the Bandwidth Broker as a solution for end-to-end QoS using DiffServ, through a cooperation between network domains, in order to achieve a suitable policy for each one that satisfied the required QoS. DiffServ is coarse-grained QoS approach because of the aggregation.

The traffic engineering concept is missed in DiffServ and IntServ, where the shortest path is determined by routing algorithms. Multiprotocol Label Switching (MPLS) has solved this problem partially. However, it uses inflexible underlying protocols, and as a result, it is hard to configure and manage the MPLS network (Tomovic et al. 2014). For all of that, these QoS techniques are not deployed widely (Egilmez et al. 2013), and there is a need for more flexible QoS and traffic engineering techniques.

5.2   QoS Improvements Using Software Defined Networking

The next generation of QoS methods can be applied using Software Defined Networking. Because of its concept of separating the control and data planes, there is no need to apply low level configurations in network elements by the network administrator. Using the SDN concept for QoS makes it more flexible to manage the required QoS policy, without facing the previous restrictions in the traditional methods (IntServ, DiffServ, etc.). There is no limit for classes' number (e.g. max 64 classes in DiffServ) and QoS rules can be applied per flow. Everything is controlled and managed by the controller, and is sent to forwarding devices as rules (Mirchev 2015).

Based on this concept, the QoS policy can be applied either per customer flows (flows related to specific tenant or customer), or per application flows. There are four main categories for QoS frameworks using SDN (Mirchev 2015): Resource Reservation, Per-flow Routing, Queue Management and Policy Enforcement.

5.2.1   Resource Reservation

The most common approaches to provide QoS using SDN is by using resource reservation technique. In order to apply resource reservation, there are two main modules: The packet classifier module, which checks packets and assigns appropriate priorities according to a predefined classification policy by the controller; and the rate shaper module, which is responsible of sending resource reservation rules to network elements in order to serve network packets according to their priorities (after classification).

Network devices (like switches) should support OpenFlow protocol to be part of SDN-based QoS system. The latest versions of OpenFlow protocol (1.3 and 1.4) provide simple QoS mechanisms that can be applied to flow packets directly, like controlling a flow rate (Sharma et al. 2014).

FlowQoS (Seddiki et al. 2014) is one of QoS frameworks that depends on the Resource-Reservation concept. It has been designed for home and small networks with low computation resources. It consists of Flow-classifier and Rate-controller in order to perform per-flow and application-based QoS. The user can prioritize applications, and the controller is responsible of installing the required rules in forwarding devices. The Flow-classifier has a table with some keys in order to identify the packets (source IP, destination IP, protocol, source port, destination port). It has two modules for classification: the first module is for web traffic, and the second is for other flows. The Rate-controller installs rules in the data plane based on a previous classification. According to these rules, the network element chooses the forwarding path, the queue and the appropriate rate for this application flow.

In (Sharma et al. 2014), the authors have proposed a new and complete QoS framework based on (Braun et al. 2008). It supports SDN and is considered one of Resource-Reservation frameworks for large scale networks. The bandwidth is managed on-path and off-line. On-path means the resource management across multiple Autonomous Systems (ASs). And off-line means the resource management is applied in off-line software (not connected to forwarding network elements). There are three queues: The highest priority queue is for control traffic, then the second priority queue is for high priority traffic, and the third queue is for best-effort traffic. It can differentiate high and best-effort traffics by using the Type Of Service (TOS) field. The standard routing protocols (BGP, OSPF) can be applied by the controller in forwarding routers.

5.2.2   Per-flow Routing

Per-flow Routing is the second category of QoS solutions using SDN. The solutions in this category of QoS frameworks don't use resource reservation in each network element, rather they place the high priority traffic on a QoS guaranteed path. So, the general concept is about checking the available paths, and try to divide the network traffic into these paths according to flows' priorities (not according to paths' availability). In (Egilmez et al. 2012), the authors used this method to prioritize multimedia traffic over normal traffic in order to fulfill the required QoS. In resource reservation methods, the best-effort traffic is given the lowest priority with a possibility for high latency and packet loss. Per-flow Routing methods have an advantage in this aspect by reducing latency and packet loss possibilities for non-QoS flows. These methods are not complex as the standard QoS methods, and that is considered another advantage (Egilmez et al. 2012). On the other hand, it is hard to apply these methods when there are many priority levels. Moreover, these frameworks require continuous links monitoring in the network in order to obtain an accurate network state, which is necessary to choose the appropriate routes (guaranteed QoS). That generates a scalability challenge, because gathering and processing the data needs significant computational resources in large networks, i.e. controller overhead. For all of that, Per-flow Routing Frameworks are suitable when the QoS should be guaranteed for a specific application traffic in small-scale networks (e.g. voice or video streaming).

5.2.3 Queue Management and Packet Scheduling

The third category of QoS solutions using SDN depends on Queue Management and Packet Scheduling concepts. OpenFlow does not support queue creating (Sharma et al. 2014), it supports only First-In-First-Out (FIFO) queuing (Ishimori et al. 2013). FIFO queuing is not suitable for prioritizing network flows, where each packet should wait the previous arrived packets to be served. In QoS enabled networks, network flows should be processed according to their priorities, not to their arrival time. OpenFlow 1.3 supports some QoS mechanisms (e.g. rate limiting), but that is not enough with FIFO queuing to support QoS. Some proposed frameworks tried to use the programming ability in SDN networks in order to create new queuing system that supports QoS. In (Ishimori et al. 2013), a packet scheduling framework has been proposed with new queuing mechanism. It contains multiple packet schedulers with three QoS features: (1) HTP packet scheduler for splitting the real bandwidth virtually into different FIFO queues (different priorities). (2) Stochastic Fairness Queueing (SFQ) for fair queuing by assigning network flows to different hash buckets according to their priorities. (3) Random Early Detection (RED) for congestion avoidance, where it performs smart tail drop in FIFO queues, which helps in controlling the dropping strategy by considering the flows' priorities and queues.

This framework depends mainly on Linux features to provide these services to network flows in switches, and that can be considered as a disadvantage, because not all switches can run a Linux distribution.

As mentioned before, the current version of OpenFlow does not support creating priority queues. In (Palma et al. 2014) and by using OVSDB protocol, an extension to an OperFlow controller (Floodlight) has been proposed, in order to create multiple queues to serve multiple QoS classes.

5.2.4 Policy Enforcement

The last category of QoS solutions using SDN depends on Policy Enforcement. The main idea in this category is about modifying the QoS policy dynamically, and without applying one static policy as in the previous methods. The network state might change, and application requirements might change as well. It proposes a mechanism to change the SLA (QoS policy) using Northbound API, and assigning the new policy to the data plane using the Southbound API. The authors in (Bari et al. 2013b) have proposed PolicyCop, a QoS framework that adds a management plane over the control plane. It can apply the QoS policy per flow, and it supports dynamic flow aggregation. In addition, PolicyCop offers through its management plan the ability of adding new traffic classes dynamically at the runtime. Where traditional QoS techniques do not allow a dynamic change of predefined priority classes. The traditional methods require high computational resources when there is a need for multiple protocols as well, in order to offer the QoS services. PolicyCop can reduce this overhead by offering multiple services in one programming step. Moreover, it is easy to be deployed, it just requires the data plane switches to support the same version of OpenFlow. The proposed management plane consists of Policy Validator and Policy Enforcer (Bari et al. 2013b). The *Policy Validator* is responsible of a continuous network monitoring to detect any policy violations. After determining the monitoring interval and its metrics for each network segment that should be monitored, the data will be collected and processed by the Traffic Monitor module. Then, the Policy Checker module compares the collected data with the QoS policy and detects if there are any policy violations. From a predefined list, the Event Handler module determines the event for any detected violation, and send it either to the network manager to be handled manually, or to the Policy Enforcer (exactly to Policy Adaptation module) for automatic handling. The *Policy Enforcer* depends on Policy Validator's detections, and according to the violation type and the current network state (topology, resource utilization), the Policy Adaptation module in Policy Enforcer specifies the suitable action and forwards it to the Resource Provisioning module. The Resource Provisioning module applies changes to the network by modifying (increase or decrease) the allocated resources, in order to remove the violation and satisfy the QoS policy again.

For example, when the 'packet loss' QoS parameter is violated, the Policy Adaptation module decides either to reconfigure the queue (maybe the queue is dropping packets), or to choose other route (lower packet loss rate). When the 'Throughput' parameter is violated, the Policy Adaptation decides to make changes to rate limiters. (Bari et al. 2013b).

The PolicyCop depends on different dynamic techniques in order to achieve the required QoS for each flow, with the ability to apply changes dynamically and according to the current network state. This type of processing generates overhead and that in turn produces scalability problems in large-scale networks (Mirchev 2015).

5.3   QoS Approaches Using SDN in Normal Networks

After defining the main categories for applying QoS in SDN networks, this sub-chapter summarizes some applied solutions. There are many approaches that use the advantages of the SDN in order to apply QoS requirements in normal networks (without SDN).

The authors in (Wallner and Cannistra 2013) have proposed a QoS approach that can be applied in the Floodlight SDN controller as a new module. The main objective is to apply traditional QoS techniques in SDN-based networks, i.e. Differentiated Services Code Point (DiffServ DSCP) (Babiarz et al. 2006) and common queueing methods. It uses the DSCP value in the packet's header to specify the "class of service" for this flow in this network segment. This new module can be added to the original Floodlight architecture ('Architecture – Floodlight Controller – Project Floodlight' n.d.), and is responsible of applying the QoS policy by determining flows' classes (based on the DSCP and a predefined classes list) and applying the suitable queuing technique in data plane switches (see Fig. 2). This module also can check and verify policies duplicates at the data plane level, and it can detect topology changes that may violate QoS parameters. The module adds different queues to data plane elements in order to support different QoS levels (multiple queues with different rate limits), an incoming packet is forwarded to one of these queues after a Flow-base classification and according to its class of service.

An SDN controller framework has been proposed in (Tomovic et al. 2014). It gives the highest priority to multimedia traffic, with the purpose of optimizing the

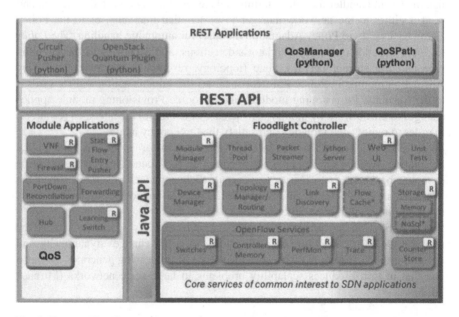

Fig. 2 The new Floodlight architecture with QoS module (Wallner and Cannistra 2013)

Fig. 3 SDN with QoS support (Tomovic et al. 2014)

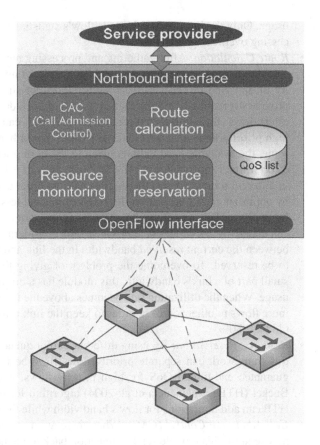

network performance for best-effort traffic. Previous researches focused on dynamic rerouting for video traffic in SDN networks (Egilmez et al. 2013) without giving significant attention to best-effort traffic. SDN, by supporting per-flow traffic control, makes it easier and more flexible to differentiate network flows, which helps in overcoming the complexity and dynamism limitations of traditional QoS methods, through which changes to QoS parameters need separated configurations in network elements. This research proposes a framework design for SDN controller with automatic and fine grained QoS control and with a guarantee for high priority classes (see Fig. 3). It uses a new technique (not the traditional shortest path algorithms) in order to improve the network performance for best-effort traffic. OpenFlow is the used protocol in communications between the data and control planes. This research supports the QoS only for two classes: priority flows (with specific bandwidth requirements) and best-effort.

The new architecture has the following modules in the controller:

- *Resource Monitoring:* This module gathers the required information about the current network state, and some traffic statistics. Per-flow and per-interface data are processed in order to get accurate details about network flows and links usage. Only the ingress switch sends flow's statistics in order to reduce the processing overhead in the controller.

- *Route Calculation:* After gathering and processing network state data, the route calculation module uses this data and applies a routing algorithm (with the ability of applying more than one routing algorithm simultaneously) in order to provide the required QoS for each class, which includes priority flows and best-effort flows. Based on the current network state, it calculates the best route for high priority flows (shortest path with the required bandwidth). In the shortest route, the available bandwidth is given to the high priority traffic and the best-effort traffic is given a lower priority. That's why, it is better to spread the traffic in different routes (not just the shortest path) in order to get a better performance by optimizing links utilization (less congestion and less delay). That is achieved by applying Dijkstra algorithm on a weighted graph. The links' weights are calculated by an equation, that takes into consideration the maximum value between the current reserved bandwidth in the link and the supposed bandwidth to be reserved. To overcome the problem of giving the best-effort traffic very small part of a link's bandwidth, this module has a utilization threshold for links usage. When the utilization rate becomes above the threshold, it redirects one or more flows to other routes in order to keep the link utilization under the threshold (e.g. 80%).
- *Resource Reservation:* By using different output queues in data plane switches, this framework can separate priority flows from best-effort flows. In order to guarantee end-to-end QoS for high priority flows, it uses Hierarchical Token Bucket (HTB) (Valenzuela et al. 2004) algorithm for queue scheduling, where HTB can add limitations for flow's bandwidth while the queues are being served.
- *Call Admission Control (CAC):* When there are no enough resources to serve a new request, this module sends a rejection back to the user.

For testing, the authors used an SDN testbed, that consists of POX controller ('About POX' n.d.) for the control plane and Open vSwitch ('Open vSwitch' n.d.) for data plane switches.

In (Akella and Xiong 2014), an approach for QoS in SDN networks has been proposed. This research focuses on multimedia applications (VoIP and video streaming), and ensures end-to-end QoS by proposing a new approach. The traditional routing solutions are divided into two categories: static and dynamic routing (Marzo et al. 2003). In static routing, the algorithms compute route paths previously and regardless the parameters that can be changed with the passage of time (current state of the links and network elements). The dynamic routing takes these parameters into consideration and calculates route paths according to them. The proposed approach considers end-to-end delay and dynamic changes in the network state in order to achieve end-to-end QoS at the service level.

This approach focuses on supporting QoS for multiple cloud services by using a new metric for paths evaluation. The suggested metric takes three parameters into consideration: Bandwidth, Round Trip Time (RTT) and path length (hops number). For each service and by using a specific equation, it gives each parameter an appropriate weight in order to evaluate possible paths for this service and choose the most suitable one. The data plane consists of Open vSwitch devices ('Open vSwitch' n.d.) which supports OpenFlow. Open vSwitch supports two queuing techniques: Hierarchical Token Based (HTB) (Devera n.d.) and Hierarchical Fair Sequence Curve (HFSC) (Rechert et al. 2005). The HTB allows the network controller to specify min and max values for each queue (bandwidth limits), and assign the rest bandwidth to queues according to their priorities. The HFSC is similar, however, there is no priority bandwidth allocation and it deals with delays. The proposed approach, and by using the Open vSwitch, supports QoS for different services to the same user. That's why it uses application, protocol and port as input parameters for queueing system. The network traffic is separated into QoS and best-effort. The QoS traffic can be at one of three levels according the its priority. This procedure is applied in each hop according to the status of the connected links to this network element.

This approach monitors the network performance continuously and in case of any QoS violations (Bandwidth, RTT or path length), it can dynamically search and choose other path that satisfies all QoS parameters for this flow. For Bandwidth violations, it compares the current value to the minimum bandwidth for this service, and it assigns the excess bandwidth to the current flows according to their priorities.

5.4   QoS Approaches Using SDN in Cloud Environment

Finally, and after summarizing how to apply QoS criteria using SDN and QoS approaches that use SDN in normal networks, this section focuses on other researches, which aimed to achieve QoS requirements in a cloud environment using SDN.

The author in (Duan 2014) has proposed an approach to deal with end-to-end QoS provisioning using Service Oriented Architecture (SOA), which in turn leads to NaaS service model. As mentioned before, the NaaS paradigm offers the network as services to users and that helps in achieving end-to-end QoS. In SOA architecture, functions can be defined as separated and independent services. Each service has its own state and is accessible by standard interfaces and messaging protocols. That is very useful in heterogeneous systems where services can be invoked regardless compatibility checks, which keeps both sides independent and each one has its own requirements. NaaS model includes different networking services at different levels, that some of them could be gathered and form one service. According to the SDN nature, it is very useful to use the NaaS model to improve the SDN performance and to make it more efficient and more flexible. Network elements in the data plane could exist in different autonomous systems, and this SDN network has the ability to use different controllers in its domains, where each controller communicates with an upper SDN level that is a service orchestration module, which abstracts network functions as services in this domain regardless the controller. In this way, the network service orchestration module takes applications' requirements from the application layer, and communicates with heterogeneous controllers using abstracted NaaS services in order to ensure end-to-end QoS through these domains, that is achieved by sending resource reservation requests. Because that this module has a global network view, it can process the data more accurately in order to achieve optimal QoS solutions.

The NaaS network services in this approach have two functions: connectivity and capacity. The connectivity is used to check if there is a connection between two network elements in the network. The capacity is to know the connection's capacity between two network devices. It uses Latency-rate Servers model (Stiliadis and Varma 1998) in order to calculate and guarantee rate and latency. Other main functionality for network orchestration module is bandwidth reservation, which should be according to the applications' requirements and the current state of the network.

By using the advantages of SDN and NaaS, this approach is very helpful in large scale networks, like the internet, where there are multiple heterogeneous domains and it is not easy to communicate with all of them in order to organize resource reservation requests among them for end-to-end QoS. The SDN centralizes the management of each domain, and the NaaS provides a network service abstraction between network domains (even when there are different SDN controllers).

Currently, many service providers use Multiprotocol Label Switching (MPLS) (Rosen et al. 2000) for tunneling and traffic engineering purposes. It uses labels instead of network addresses in order to give the network administrator more capabilities in controlling flows' paths in the network. The authors in (Manthena et al. 2015) have proposed a combination between MPLS networks and SDN in order to offer NaaS services. The main idea is about applying SDN concept in edge network devices and keeping the core MPLS network as it was (to be applicable in the current wide spread MPLS based networks). The normal Label Edge Routers (LERs) have been replaced by OpenFlow-enabled network devices. The core network contains Label Switching Routers (LSRs) connect to each other in mesh model (not dynamic) by Label-switched Paths (LSPs). In this way, an edge OpenFlow network device performs the complex labeling tasks, and the core network acts as before. The edge routers are sFlow (Phaal et al. 2001) devices, which are common and wide spread OpenFlow devices. The core network is managed using Simple Network Management Protocol (SNMP) (Harrington et al. 2002) as a normal MPLS network, that can be managed using SNMP. The edge routers are part of an SDN network, which needs a control plane for these network devices (data plane). The control plane includes an SDN controller, that has the ability to provide edge routers with the needed rules, and to handle the network traffic per flow dynamically. The control plane contains sFlow analyzer, in order to monitor and analyze network flows. In addition, it contains a network configuration system that is responsible of resources configuration. In order to deal with this SDN network as a NaaS, the control plane should be accessible through abstracted APIs. For the core network, it's easier to do it with SNMP functions through APIs of core's analyzer.

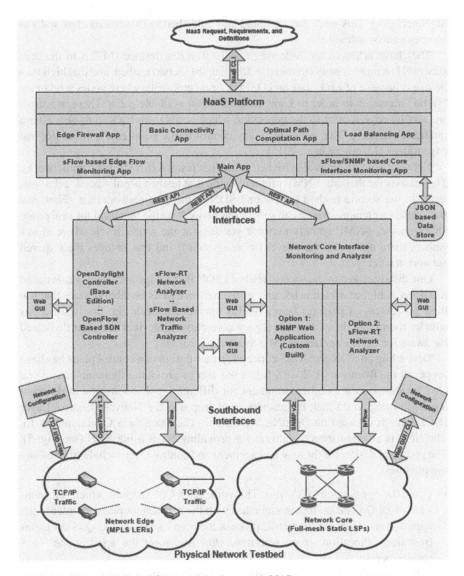

Fig. 4 The design of Proof of Concept (Manthena et al. 2015)

The authors used the Proof of Concept (PoC) in order to test the proposed architecture (see Fig. 4). Tests were conducted in two physical testbeds: The first testbed is equivalent to the proposed architecture (SDN for managing edge devices and normal MPLS in the core network). The second testbed adopted SDN architecture for all network devices in the network (edge and core network elements). In both testbeds, OpenDaylight controller (The Linux Foundation n.d.) is used as SDN controller, and sFlow-RT (InMon Corp n.d.) is used as a network analyzer (just for

SDN network). This work can be found and published in (Manthena et al. n.d.) as an open source software.

They have achieved the following results: The first testbed (MPLS in the core network) has more control overhead traffic than the second testbed, and that high traffic rate is because of Link-state and OSPF routing protocols, where nodes send many "Hello" messages in order to know neighbors and available paths. These messages are sent by edge routers to the controller, which sends them back to routers after a multicast checking. That generates many control traffic between the controller and edge routers (Manthena et al. 2015).

Network core traffic is also higher in the first testbed (SNMP for core network). The reasons for that are: SNMP protocol in the first testbed is pull-based technique, while in the second testbed (sFlow and SDN in the core network) the sFlow is a push-based technique, which can reduce the network traffic that used for analyzing. Other reason, SNMP gathers network statistics at the router level, where sFlow gathers them at the interface level (more specific), and that reduces the required network traffic.

One disadvantage in the second testbed (SDN in the edge and core) is that round trip delay is higher, which is because of the network SDN-enabled devices that use their processors to perform heavy MPLS operations, while the first testbed has smaller round trip delay, because legacy core network devices use their dedicated hardware for MPLS operations (Manthena et al. 2015).

Depending on SDN and NaaS concepts, a new design of a control plane has been proposed in (Bueno et al. 2013). It has the aim of providing dynamic end-to-end QoS guarantee in a cloud environment for different applications and at different levels. In order to do that, the authors have proposed the Network Control Layer (NCL) which is based on OpenNaaS platform (The OpenNaaS Community n.d.). The NCL is an open source platform for providing NaaS using SDN (see Fig. 5). The proposed design for the new management and control layer includes the following modules:

- *QoS SDN Application (SDNapp):* This is the main QoS module, which is responsible of all QoS tasks. It communicates with the application plane in order to get applications' QoS requirements, process them and generate the QoS decisions (resources allocation, route selection, etc.) that meet the applications' QoS requirements.
- *SDN Controller:* The SDN controller is the main component of the control plan. It is responsible of communicating with data plane devices and sending them required forwarding rules and resource allocation decisions using OpenFlow protocol.
- *SDN Monitor:* This module collects data about the current network state, analyzes them and send them as statistics to the SDNapp module. That is an important feedback in order to take suitable QoS decisions according to the current network state.

OpenNaaS platform gives capabilities for utilizing network devices through web services. By using SDN with OpenNaaS, the management layer can apply QoS

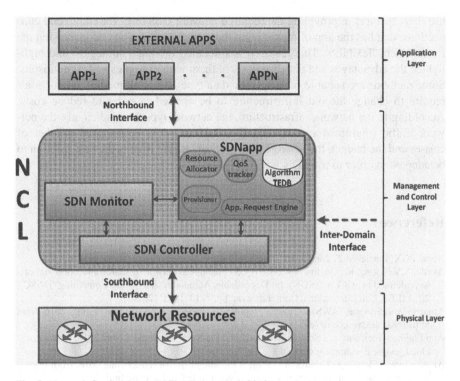

Fig. 5 Network Control Layer (NCL) (Bueno et al. 2013)

requirements in easier and more flexible way, and it can react to changes in network state more efficiently.

6   Conclusion

In this chapter, a research about the cloud services and especially the Network-as-a-Service (NaaS) model has been conducted. It started by explaining the main three cloud service models: (IaaS, PaaS and SaaS), which followed by a brief description of the NaaS and its functionality. Then the Quality of Service (QoS) concept has been defined especially for network services, the main criteria for these services and the special requirements for cloud network services. Software Defined Networking (SDN) principles and its architecture have been presented, this promising program-mable network paradigm, that depends on decoupling the control and data planes in order to give the network management process more flexibility and capabilities. Finally, a deep research about applying QoS using SDN has been conducted, that includes a study concerning using SDN specially in cloud service providers' net-works for QoS purposes. There are many techniques have been applied in order to use SDN features in providing the required network QoS level for end to end connections, that has the aim of maximizing the network utilization and increasing the management flexibility. This research has detailed the main strategies, and highlighted the advantages and disadvantages of them with examples and comparisons. Some methods are suitable for a specific data type (e.g. multimedia), others don't require to change the old infrastructure to be applied in order to reduce costs. According to the network infrastructure, the network type (normal/cloud), the network traffic (multimedia streaming, file sharing, etc.), the required number of classes and the budget, the network manager can decide what is the best solution to be adopted in order to use SDN with QoS support.

References

About POX: Retrieved 27 June 2016, from http://www.noxrepo.org/pox/about-pox/ (n.d.)
Akella, A.V., Xiong, K.: Quality of service (QoS)-guaranteed network resource allocation via software defined networking (SDN). In: Dependable, Autonomic and Secure Computing (DASC), 2014 IEEE 12th International Conference on, pp. 7–13. IEEE (2014)
Amazon Web Services (AWS) – Cloud Computing Services: Retrieved 11 November 2016, from https://aws.amazon.com/ (n.d.)
App Engine – Platform as a Service|Google Cloud Platform: Retrieved 8 May 2016, from https://cloud.google.com/appengine/ (n.d.)
Architecture – Floodlight Controller – Project Floodlight: Retrieved 23 June 2016, from https://floodlight.atlassian.net/wiki/display/floodlightcontroller/Architecture (n.d.)
Ayadi, I., Simoni, N., Diaz, G.: NaaS: QoS-aware cloud networking services. In: Network Computing and Applications (NCA), 2013 12th IEEE International Symposium on, pp. 97–100. IEEE (2013)
Babiarz, J., Chan, K., Baker, F.: Configuration guidelines for DiffServ service classes (2006)
Baker, F., Iturralde, C., Le Faucheur, F., Davie, B.: Aggregation of RSVP for IPv4 and IPv6 Reservations.. Retrieved from https://tools.ietf.org/html/rfc3175 (2001)
Bari, M.F., Boutaba, R., Esteves, R., Granville, L.Z., Podlesny, M., Rabbani, M.G., Zhang, Q., Zhani, M.F.: Data center network virtualization: a survey. IEEE Commun. Surv. Tutorials. 15(2), 909–928 (2013a)
Bari, M.F., Chowdhury, S.R., Ahmed, R., Boutaba, R.:PolicyCop: an autonomic QoS policy enforcement framework for software defined networks. In: Future Networks and Services (SDN4FNS), 2013 IEEE SDN for, pp. 1–7, Trento: ICT Labs. IEEE (2013b)
Benson, T., Akella, A., Maltz, D.A.: Network traffic characteristics of data centers in the wild. In: Proceedings of the 10th ACM SIGCOMM conference on Internet measurement, pp. 267–280. ACM (2010)
Benson, T., Akella, A., Shaikh, A., Sahu, S.: CloudNaaS: a cloud networking platform for enterprise applications. In: Proceedings of the 2nd ACM Symposium on Cloud Computing, p. 8. ACM (2011)
Blake, S., Black, D., Carlson, M., Davies, E., Wang, Z., Weiss, W.: An architecture for differentiated services (1998)
Borthakur, D., Gray, J., Sarma, J. S., Muthukkaruppan, K., Spiegelberg, N., Kuang, H., Ranganathan, K., Molkov, D., Menon, A., Rash, S., Schmidt, R: Apache Hadoop goes realtime at Facebook. In: Proceedings of the 2011 ACM SIGMOD International Conference on Management of data, pp. 1071–1080. ACM (2011)
Braden, R., Clark, D., Shenker, S.: Integrated services in the internet architecture: an overview (1994)

Braun, T., Diaz, M., Gabeiras, J.E., Staub, T.: End-to-End Quality of Service over Heterogeneous Networks. Springer Science & Business Media, New York (2008)

Bueno, I., Aznar, J.I., Escalona, E., Ferrer, J., García-Espín, J.A.: An opennaas based sdn framework for dynamic qos control. In: Future Networks and Services (SDN4FNS), 2013 IEEE SDN for, pp. 1–7, Trento: ICT Labs. IEEE (2013)

Buyya, R., Broberg, J., Goscinski, A.M.: Cloud Computing: Principles and Paradigms, vol. 87. Wiley, Hoboken (2010)

Cloud, A.E.C.: Amazon web services. Retrieved November, 9, 2011 (2011)

Costa, P., Migliavacca, M., Pietzuch, P., Wolf, A.L. NaaS: network-as-a-service in the cloud. In: Presented as part of the 2nd USENIX Workshop on Hot Topics in Management of Internet, Cloud, and Enterprise Networks and Services (2012)

Dean, J., Ghemawat, S.: MapReduce: simplified data processing on large clusters. Commun. ACM. **51**(1), 107–113 (2008)

Devera, M.: HTB Linux queuing discipline manual-user guide, May 2002. Retrieved from http://luxik.cdi.cz/~devik/qos/htb/manual/userg.htm (n.d.)

Duan, Q.: Network-as-a-service in software-defined networks for end-to-end QoS provisioning. In: 2014 23rd Wireless and Optical Communication Conference (WOCC), pp. 1–5. IEEE (2014)

Egilmez, H.E., Civanlar, S., Tekalp, A.M.: An optimization framework for QoS-enabled adaptive video streaming over OpenFlow networks. IEEE Trans. Multimedia. **15**(3), 710–715 (2013)

Egilmez, H.E., Dane, S.T., Bagci, K.T., Tekalp, A.M.: OpenQoS: an OpenFlow controller design for multimedia delivery with end-to-end Quality of Service over Software-Defined Networks. In: Signal & Information Processing Association Annual Summit and Conference (APSIPA ASC), 2012 Asia-Pacific, pp. 1–8. IEEE (2012)

Frnda, J., Voznak, M., Rozhon, J., Mehic, M.: Prediction model of QoS for triple play services. In: Telecommunications Forum (TELFOR), 2013 21st, pp. 733–736, Belgrade: SAVA Center. IEEE (2013)

Goossens, K., Wielage, P., Peeters, A., Van Meerbergen, J. Networks on silicon: combining best-effort and guaranteed services. In date, p. 423. IEEE (2002)

Harrington, D., Wijnen, B., Presuhn, R. An architecture for describing simple network management protocol (SNMP) management frameworks (2002)

InMon Corp: InMon: sFlow-RT. Retrieved 30 June 2016, from http://www.inmon.com/products/sFlow-RT.php (n.d.)

Ishimori, A., Farias, F., Cerqueira, E., Abelém, A.: Control of multiple packet schedulers for improving QoS on OpenFlow/SDN networking. In: 2013 Second European Workshop on Software Defined Networks, pp. 81–86. IEEE (2013)

Lu, G., Guo, C., Li, Y., Zhou, Z., Yuan, T., Wu, H., Xiong, Y., Gao, R., Zhang, Y.: ServerSwitch: a programmable and high performance platform for data center networks. In: 8th USENIX Symposium on Networked Systems Design and Implementation (NSDI), vol. 11, pp. 2–2, Boston (2011)

Manthena, M.P.V., van Adrichem, N. L., van den Broek, C., Kuipers, F.: An SDN-based architecture for network-as-a-service. In: Network Softwarization (NetSoft), 2015 1st IEEE Conference on, pp. 1–5. IEEE (2015)

Manthena, M.P.V., van Adrichem, N. L., van den Broek, C., Kuipers, F. GitHub – TUDelftNAS/SDN-NaaSPlatform. Retrieved 30 June 2016, from https://github.com/TUDelftNAS/SDN-NaaSPlatform (n.d.)

Marzo, J.L., Calle, E., Scoglio, C., Anjah, T.: QoS online routing and MPLS multilevel protection: a survey. IEEE Commun. Mag. **41**(10), 126–132 (2003)

McKeown, N., Anderson, T., Balakrishnan, H., Parulkar, G., Peterson, L., Rexford, J., et al.: OpenFlow: enabling innovation in campus networks. ACM SIGCOMM Comput. Commun. Rev. **38**(2), 69–74 (2008)

Microsoft Azure: Cloud Computing Platform & Services: Retrieved 11 November 2016, from https://azure.microsoft.com/en-us/ (n.d.)

Mirchev, A.: Survey of concepts for QoS improvements via SDN. In: Future Internet (FI) and Innovative Internet Technologies and Mobile Communications (IITM), vol. 33, (2015)

Neto, P.: Demystifying cloud computing. In: Proceeding of Doctoral Symposium on Informatics Engineering (2011)

Network as-a-Service|At a Glance|Aryaka: Retrieved 11 November 2016, from http://info.aryaka.com/rs/477-WNL-836/images/network-as-a-service-at-a-glance.pdf (n.d.)

Nunes, B.A., Mendonca, M., Nguyen, X.-N., Obraczka, K., Turletti, T.: A survey of software-defined networking: past, present, and future of programmable networks. IEEE Commun. Surv. Tutorials. 16(3), 1617–1634 (2014)

Open Networking Foundation (ONF): SDN Architecture Overview. Retrieved from https://www.opennetworking.org/images/stories/downloads/sdn-resources/technical-reports/SDN-architecture-overview-1.0.pdf (2013)

Open vSwitch: Retrieved 24 June 2016, from http://openvswitch.org/ (n.d.)

Palma, D., Goncalves, J., Sousa, B., Cordeiro, L., Simoes, P., Sharma, S., Staessens, D.: The QueuePusher: enabling queue management in OpenFlow. In: 2014 Third European Workshop on Software Defined Networks, pp. 125–126. IEEE (2014)

Peuhkuri, M.: Ip Quality of Service. Helsinki University of Technology, Laboratory of Telecommunications Technology, Espoo, 2–0 (1999)

Phaal, P., Panchen, S., McKee, N. InMon corporation's sFlow: a method for monitoring traffic in switched and routed networks (2001)

Rechert, K., McHardy, P., Brown, M.A.: HFSC scheduling with Linux. Linux Magazin, 28–37 (2005)

Rittinghouse, J.W., Ransome, J.F.: Cloud Computing: Implementation, Management, and Security. CRC Press, Florida (2016)

Rizzo, L., Carbone, M., Catalli, G.: Transparent acceleration of software packet forwarding using netmap. In: INFOCOM, 2012 Proceedings IEEE, pp. 2471–2479. IEEE (2012)

Rosen, E., Viswanathan, A., Callon, R.: Multiprotocol label switching architecture (2000)

Salesforce.com: The Customre Success Platform To Grow Your Business: Retrieved 8 May 2016, from https://www.salesforce.com (n.d.)

Sambanis, K.: Quality of service for IP-Based Networks. DTIC Document (2001)

Seddiki, M.S., Shahbaz, M., Donovan, S., Grover, S., Park, M., Feamster, N., Song, Y.-Q.: FlowQoS: QoS for the rest of us. In: Proceedings of the third workshop on Hot topics in software defined networking, pp. 207–208. ACM (2014)

Serban, R., Barakat, C., Dabbous, W.: Dynamic resource allocation in core routers of a Diffserv network. In: Annual Asian Computing Science Conference, pp. 153–167. Springer (2002)

Sharma, S., Staessens, D., Colle, D., Palma, D., Goncalves, J., Figueiredo, R., Morris, D., Pickavet, M., Demeester, P.: Implementing quality of service for the software defined networking enabled future internet. In: Software Defined Networks (EWSDN), 2014 Third European Workshop on, pp. 49–54. IEEE (2014)

Stiliadis, D., Varma, A.: Latency-rate servers: a general model for analysis of traffic scheduling algorithms. IEEE/ACM Trans. Networking (ToN). 6(5), 611–624 (1998)

Szigeti, T., Hattingh, C., Barton, R., Briley Jr., K.: End-to-End QoS Network Design: Quality of Service for Rich-Media & Cloud Networks. Cisco Press, Indiana (2013)

The Linux Foundation: OpenDaylight 'HYDROGEN' Base Edition. Retrieved 30 June 2016, from https://wiki.opendaylight.org/view/Release/Hydrogen/Base/User_Guide (n.d.)

The OpenNaaS Community: OpenNaaS. Retrieved 1 July 2016, from http://www.opennaas.org/ (n.d.)

Tomovic, S., Prasad, N., Radusinovic, I.: SDN control framework for QoS provisioning. In: Telecommunications Forum Telfor (TELFOR), 2014 22nd, pp. 111–114, Belgrade: SAVA Center. IEEE (2014)

Valenzuela, J.L., Monleon, A., San Esteban, I., Portoles, M., Sallent, O.: A hierarchical token bucket algorithm to enhance QoS in IEEE 802.11: proposal, implementation and evaluation. In: Vehicular technology conference, vol. 4, pp. 2659–2662 (2004)

Wallner, R., Cannistra, R.: An SDN approach: quality of service using big switch's floodlight open-source controller. In: Proceedings of the Asia-Pacific Advanced Network, vol. 35, pp. 14–19 (2013)

Zhang, L., Berson, S., Herzog, S., Jamin, S.: Resource ReSerVation protocol (RSVP)–version 1 functional specification. Resource. Retrieved from http://tools.ietf.org/html/rfc2205.html (1997)

Zhang, L., Nichols, K., Jacobson, V.: A two-bit differentiated services architecture for the internet. Retrieved from https://tools.ietf.org/html/rfc2638 (1999)

Ammar AlSous studied Informatics Engineering at Damascus University, and he has obtained the BSc degree in 2007. In 2013 he has received his Master degree in Informatics Engineering (computer networks and systems) at Damascus University. Since 2015 he is a Ph.D scholarship holder at the department of Business Information Systems/Very Large Business Applications (VLBA) at the Carl von Ossietzky University Oldenburg, Germany. His research interests include Cloud Networking, Software Defined Networking, Quality of Service, Computer Systems and Security.

Jorge Marx Gómez studied Computer Engineering and Industrial Engineering at the University of Applied Science of Berlin (Technische Fachhochschule). He was a lecturer and researcher at the Otto-von-Guericke-Universität Magdeburg where he also obtained a PhD degree in Business Information Systems with the work Computer-based Approaches to Forecast Returns of Scrapped Products to Recycling. In 2004 he received his habilitation for the work Automated Environmental Reporting through Material Flow Networks at the Otto-von-Guericke-Universität Magdeburg. From 2002 till 2003 he was a Visiting Professor for Business Information Systems at the Technical University of Clausthal. In 2005 he became a Full Professor of Business Information Systems at the Carl von Ossietzky University Oldenburg. He is the head of the department Business Informatics (Very Large Business Applications). His personal research interests include Environmental Management Information Systems, Business Intelligence and Big Data, Material Flow Management Systems, Federated ERP-Systems, Enterprise Systems Engineering, Business Information Systems in Higher Education, Enterprise Tomography, Environmental Data Warehousing, Recycling Program Planning, Disassembly Planning and Control and Life Cycle Assessment.

Optimization of Data Center Fault Tolerance Design

Sascha Bosse and Klaus Turowski

Abstract Balancing costs and quality of offered IT service is a challenging task for data center providers. In the case of availability, fault tolerance can be applied by introducing redundancy mechanisms into the service design. Redundancy allocation problems can be defined as combinatorial optimization problems to identify cost-effective redundancy configurations in which availability objectives are met. However, these approaches should be flexible to trade-off effort and benefit in a specific scenario. Therefore, a redundancy allocation problem is proposed in this chapter that is capable of modeling the specific characteristics of the IT system to be analyzed. In order to identify suitable design configurations, a generic Petri net simulation model is combined with a genetic algorithm. By defining the solution algorithm adaptively to the complexity of the considered problem definition, users are able to reduce modeling as well as computational effort. The suitability of the approach is demonstrated in the use-case of an international application service provider.

1 Introduction

In recent years, the concept of IT services increasingly replaces the concept of IT products (Krcmar 2015). In this context, the importance and workload of data centers is growing since computations are no longer performed at the client site. In order to describe the relation between service providers and consumers, service level agreements (SLA) are formulated (Lewis 1999). Besides a functional description of the obtained service, these agreements also include guarantees for non-functional properties such as availability, performance, and IT security. Meeting these guarantees is crucial to a service provider as violations can lead to penalty

S. Bosse (✉) • K. Turowski
Magdeburg Research and Competence Cluster for Very Large Business Applications,
Faculty of Computer Science, Otto-von-Guericke University Magdeburg,
Universitaetsplatz 2, 39106 Magdeburg, Germany
e-mail: sascha.bosse@ovgu.de; klaus.turowski@ovgu.de

© Springer International Publishing AG 2017
J. Marx Gómez et al. (eds.), *Engineering and Management of Data Centers*,
Service Science: Research and Innovations in the Service Economy,
DOI 10.1007/978-3-319-65082-1_7

costs and loss of reputation decreasing long-term competitiveness (Callou et al. 2012; Emeakaroha et al. 2012).

One of the most important quality metrics is the availability of an IT service defined as the probability that a service is capable to respond correctly to a customer request (Franke et al. 2014). As a concept of fault-tolerance, redundancy mechanisms can be introduced to increase availability (Shooman 2002). For that purpose, functionally equivalent components are introduced to cover the failure of primary components. This approach, however, can lead to high costs. Therefore, the costs of redundancy mechanisms have to be balanced with the gains in availability.

In traditional system reliability engineering, redundancy allocation problems can be defined for that task in which the optimal combination of redundancy mechanisms is sought. In order to map the specifics of IT systems, these definitions have been continuously extended. However, evaluation methods and solution algorithms are problem-dependent so that the transferability of these approaches is limited. In this chapter, a flexible redundancy allocation problem is defined that is solved using a combination of Petri net simulation models and meta-heuristics. Using this approach, data center managers are able to model their IT systems on the required detail level without the need to adapt solution algorithms. Thus, effort and benefit of the optimization approach can be better balanced.

2   Related Work

In this section, the related work of this chapter is discussed by introducing the availability management process, availability modeling techniques as well as definitions and solution algorithms for the redundancy allocation problem.

2.1   Availability Management and Modeling

The availability management is an important process of the design stage in IT service management (ITSM) and is included in ITSM frameworks such as the IT Infrastructure Library (Hunnebeck 2011). Its objective is to ensure that an IT service meets its availability objectives cost-effectively. In order to increase the availability of a system, four principle approaches can be distinguished: fault forecasting, fault removal, fault prevention, and fault tolerance (Laprie 1995).

Fault forecasting means that a running system is carefully monitored to estimate future faults so that counter-measures can be applied. Fault removal approaches aim at minimizing the time to recover after a fault occurred. Thus, these two approaches can be applied in the operational phase of an IT service (reactive approaches). On the other hand, fault prevention and fault tolerance techniques can be introduced into the design phase (proactive approaches). However, the effectiveness of fault prevention, as an approach aiming at minimizing the fault probability, is limited since faults can never be excluded (Lee and Anderson 1990). As fault tolerance is defined as an approach ensuring availability even in the presence of faults, this is an effective approach for designing high-availability systems. Normally fault-tolerance is achieved by introducing redundancy mechanisms in which spare components are installed to cover the fault of a primary component (Shooman 2002).

Since important decisions are made in the service design stage that are costly to be corrected afterwards (Terlit and Krcmar 2011), availability modeling techniques should be applied in order to estimate the future service availability (Hunnebeck 2011). For this purpose, measurement- or model-based approaches can be distinguished.

In measurement-based or black-box approaches, no knowledge about the inner structure and behavior of a system is required. Data mining and machine learning techniques are applied to model the relation between input (design parameters) and output values (availability, costs), e.g., in Hoffmann et al. (2004), Silic et al. (2014). Although these approaches are very effective, training examples have to be provided that require running instances of comparable systems which may not be available (Immonen and Niemelä 2008).

In this case, additional information about the system internals has to be utilized which leads to model-based or white-box approaches. Depending on the underlying model, these can be further classified into combinatorial, state-space-based, and hierarchical approaches (Trivedi et al. 2008). In combinatorial models, all components can be characterized by an availability value. On the basis of probability theory assuming independent component faults, system availability can be computed fast and easily. An example are reliability block diagrams which model a series-parallel system (Anon 1981). Redundant components of the same function form subsystems (parallel system) all of which are all crucial for system availability (series system). System availability is defined as the probability that at least one component is available in each subsystem.

However, the assumption of independent faults limits the accuracy of these approaches, especially for software systems (Callou et al. 2012; Trivedi et al. 2008) which may lead to wrong decisions (Littlewood 2006). Examples of dependent fault behavior are common-cause failures (Shooman 2002), systematic bugs (Chi and Kuo 1990), or imperfect coverage (Milanovic and Milic 2011). Furthermore, a major part of IT system failures is induced by operator errors (Oppenheimer et al. 2003) which cannot be mapped in combinatorial approaches.

In order to encompass such aspects, a state-space-based approach can be applied in which all possible states of a system and the corresponding transition rates are modeled (Callou et al. 2012). In this context, Markov approaches, such as continuous-time Markov chains (CTMC), are often used. However, the problem of state-space explosion affects these types of models even for medium-sized problems serverly, leading to difficulties in constructing, storing, and evaluating these models (Sachdeva et al. 2008). Alternatively, the state-space of a system can be modeled implicitly, e.g., using Petri nets. If such models are evaluated by the means of a Monte Carlo simulation instead of using an analytical evaluation, the problem of state-space explosion can be effectively contained (Zille et al. 2010). For that purpose, the (random) behavior of the model is analyzed in a number of replications to gain statistically significant results. Since these replications are independent, massive parallelization can be applied to reduce the time effort (Sachdeva et al. 2008). Another advantage of simulation in comparison to analytical evaluation is the ability to perform dynamic analyses which means that not only mean values but also variances can be computed (Jewell 2008). Especially in the management of service levels, statements about variance are important (Franke 2012).

Besides pure state-space-based modeling approaches, low-level state-space and high-level combinatorial models can be combined in order to reduce model complexity while not affecting accuracy which is defined as a hierarchical approach (Trivedi et al. 2008).

2.2 The Redundancy Allocation Problem

While redundancy has been identified as an effective approach for increasing availability of a system, it is also a costly one since the utilization of redundant components is usually very low. Therefore, the introduction of redundancy for a component should be justified by the increase in availability. Besides the question of which components should be covered by redundancy, other aspects have to be considered, too.

On the one hand, redundancy can be homogeneous or heterogeneous. In the former case, all redundant components are equal to the primary component in each characteristic, while characteristics are different in the latter case (except functional ones). Although heterogeneous redundancy is often associated with higher costs, the probability of common-cause failures may be reduced.

On the other hand, active and passive redundancy can be distinguished. Components in active redundancy are fully operational and can replace a defect component immediately. If the state of a redundant component is not fully operational and its time to activation is greater than zero, the component is said to be in passive or standby redundancy. Depending on the time to activation, cold-, warm-, and hot-standby can be differentiated (Ardakan and Hamadani 2014; Chambari et al. 2012). Usually, failure rate and operational costs of components can be reduced with increasing time to activation (Orgerie et al. 2014; Shooman 2002).

In order to identify suitable redundancy designs of all these possible combinations, a redundancy allocation problem (RAP) can be defined and solved.

2.2.1 Definitions

In 1962, Kettelle was one of the first researches to define an RAP (Kettelle 1962) in which dynamic programming has been utilized to minimize system cost subject to an availability constraint. Alternatively, RAP can be used to maximize system availability subject to a cost constraint or for multi-objective optimization of costs and availability. Often, other linear constraints are introduced mapping, e.g., volume or weight limitations.

Even a simple RAP is an NP-hard optimization problem as Chern could prove for the following definition (Chern 1992):

(i) A system contains n serially connected subsystems that are required for the system to be working.
(ii) In a subsystem, a number of components can be operated in active redundancy (series-parallel system).
(iii) A component can either be working or failed (binary state), component faults are independent and identically distributed within a subsystem (homogeneous redundancy).
(iv) The number of components in each subsystem has to be chosen so that availability of the system has to be maximized subject to linear constraints.

In subsequent years, RAP definitions have been continuously extended to increase applicability, especially for IT systems. Examples for these extensions include

- Heterogeneous redundancy, e.g., in Chen and You (2005), Coit and Konak (2006), Coit and Smith (1996), Liang and Smith (2004), Lins and Droguett (2009), Onishi et al. (2007), Sooktip et al. (2012),
- Passive redundancy, e.g., in Ardakan and Hamadani (2014), Chambari et al. (2012), Sadjadi and Soltani (2015), Taguchi and Yokota (1999),
- Multi-state components, e.g., in Abdelkader et al. (2013), Ouzineb et al. (2008), Ramirez-Marquez and Coit (2004), Tian et al. (2009),
- Complex system designs, e.g., in Chen (2006), Ravi et al. (1997), Sahoo et al. (2010), Ziaee (2013),
- Inter-component dependencies (Bosse et al. 2016; Chi and Kuo 1990; Lins and Droguett 2009), and
- Parameter uncertainty.

In order to introduce uncertainty, stochastic, fuzzy, interval, and stochastic-fuzzy variables can be utilized (Soltani 2014). While stochastic variables model uncertainty as a result of randomness, e.g., in Painton and Campbell (1995), fuzzy variables model it as a result of vagueness, e.g., in Garg and Sharma (2013), Jiansheng et al. (2014), Wang and Watada (2009). Interval variables are simpler to handle since only interval boundaries have to be considered, e.g., in Taguchi and Yokota (1999). However, if uncertainty is a result of randomness and vagueness, fuzzy-stochastic approaches should be applied (Wang and Watada 2009). This can be done by defining random fuzzy variables (Zhao and Liu 2004) or fuzzy random variables (Kwakernaak 1978).

2.2.2 Solution Algorithms

In order to identify suitable design configurations on the basis of an RAP definition, mathematical programming, heuristics, and meta-heuristics can be applied (Soltani 2014). Mathematical programming includes linear, dynamic, and non-linear programming techniques which can be applied for exact or approximate solution of an

RAP, e.g., in Cao et al. (2013), Caserta and Voß (2015), Kettelle (1962), Onishi et al. (2007). However, these approaches often restrict the search space massively due to problem complexity (Coit and Smith 1996). The need for more flexible and efficient solution methods led to the application of (meta-)heuristics (Kulturel-Konak et al. 2003).

Heuristics are algorithms that are constructed for a specific problem class, so their transferability to other problem classes is normally limited (Soltani 2014). On the contrary, meta-heuristics are general solution algorithms that can be applied to arbitrary optimization problems by defining problem-dependent operations, e.g., for a neighborhood search. Although meta-heuristics usually require more parameter settings, they produce better results in general (Coit and Konak 2006). Examples for meta-heuristics that have been adapted to solve RAP are genetic algorithms, tabu search, simulated annealing, particle swarm optimization as well as ant and bee colony optimization (Soltani 2014).

Some of the problem-dependent operations to be instantiated in order to apply a meta-heuristic are common for several meta-heuristics. This includes a fitness function to determine the suitability of a solution candidate as well as operations for local neighborhood search, random global search, and recombination of solutions.

Since meta-heuristics aim to maximize the fitness of solutions, in the context of RAP, availability or negative costs may be used as fitness values. However, in order to result in feasible solutions, a generation-dependent penalty function should be defined to decrease the fitness of infeasible solutions without discarding these totally in the search process (Coit and Smith 1996). In case of a multi-objective RAP, a solution's fitness may be computed by integrating all objectives into one value. This requires a weighing of the objectives which may be difficult to define and will lead to problems if the trade-off function is concave (Fonseca and Fleming 1995). In this case, Pareto-based approaches can be applied in which a fitness tuple is assigned to each solution according to the number of objectives. In order to decide if a solution is better than another, the concept of Pareto dominance is utilized: a solution x with fitness $(f_1(x), \ldots, f_m(x))$ dominates another solution y with fitness $(f_1(y), \ldots, f_m(y))$ if and only if there is a k for which $f_k(x) > f_k(y)$ with $\forall i \neq k : f_i(x) \geq f_i(y)$ holds (expressed by $x \succ y$).

The operations for constructing, altering, and recombining solutions are normally defined on the basis of a binary or integer encoding of fixed length. As an example, in Coit and Smith (1996) a maximum number of components per subsystem c is defined so that the encoding has the length $n \cdot c$ representing all possible component slots in each subsystem. The values of each slot indicate which component is used in a slot or if a slot is unused. Alternatively, the encoding length may be determined by the number of different component types that are available in a subsystem (Lins and Droguett 2009). In this case, the integer values represent how many components of this type are used. A third example encoding is derived from (Ardakan and Hamadani 2014) in which the encoding has the length n representing the subsystems. Values of the encoding, however, are vectors of different lengths including the components of a subsystem. Although operations can only be defined on the level of subsystems in this encoding, additional information, e.g., about redundancy types, can be integrated easily.

On the basis of a suitable encoding, solutions can be generated by choosing random components for each subsystem. Recombination of solutions is performed by applying uniform crossover, i.e. the random exchange of encoding values (Coit and Smith 1996). The neighborhood of a solution is usually defined as all solutions that can be reached by changing a single value of the encoding.

These operations are normally applied on a set of solution candidates concurrently and in several iterations. The fitness values are used to guide the search process to promising regions of the search space. Eventually, a meta-heuristic results in a single solution candidate for a single-objective problem or in a set of mutually non-dominated solutions in case of Pareto optimization. In order to ensure that the result considers the global optima that have been found, so-called elitism mechanics can be implemented.

3 A Flexible Redundancy Allocation Problem for Data Center Design

While numerous extensions have been developed for the RAP in order to increase its applicability to IT systems, also the complexity of the problems has grown. Possible users, such as data center designers, may have problems balancing effort and utility of the different RAP definitions and solution approaches. In the following section, first the different characteristics of RAP definitions are discussed before a flexible problem definition and solution algorithms are presented.

3.1 Requirements Analysis

The requirements for a flexible RAP for data center design can be classified into aspects addressing the description of possible design alternatives, the estimation of IT service availability and costs as well as identifying a (sub)optimal design from the possible alternatives.

3.1.1 Description of Possible Design Alternatives

In order to define a search space for design alternatives, the decision variables of a data center design have to be determined. Normally, an RAP is applied to a series-parallel system, although some works have dealt with hierarchical or complex system designs in specific scenarios. To provide the maximum flexibility for the system specification, a generic complex system should be defined to compute system availability from subsystem availabilities. This generic complex system can be described by a directed graph in which a dedicated starting and end node are connected by different series of subsystems as depicted exemplary in Fig. 1.

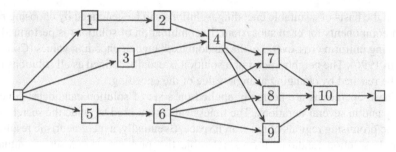

Fig. 1 Subsystem graph of the complex system analyzed in Sahoo et al. (2010)

Based on such a graph, all possible paths from the starting to the end node can be determined. The system is considered as available if all subsystems on at least one path are available.

While the system of subsystems is considered as constant, the subsystem configurations are different for each solution candidate. The possible configurations can be defined by providing components and redundancy mechanisms that can be selected for each subsystem. In addition to that, number and type of operators can be defined as decision variables since IT systems often require manual interaction and operator errors are one of the major causes of unavailability (Oppenheimer et al. 2003).

On that basis, the combination of components and redundancy mechanisms for the subsystems as well as number and type of operators characterize a solution candidate and the set of all possible combinations forms the search space.

3.1.2 Estimation of IT Service Availability

The availability of an IT service depends on the availability of its subsystems which again depends on its components' characteristics. Thus, the state-space of a single component has to be modeled which can also include more than two states in order to map performance degradation of components (Abdelkader et al. 2013). Additionally, there may be several possible transitions between two states in order to model different fault types such as transient, intermittent, and permanent failures (Bondavalli et al. 2000). The transition times should be distributed according to arbitrary random variables as especially recovery times are not exponentially distributed (Chellappan and Vijayalakshmi 2009). Furthermore, transition times may be uncertain, e.g., due to optimistic manufacturer information (Pinheiro et al. 2007).

In a subsystem, components with different state distributions can be operated in parallel. The state distributions differ between different component types but are also depending on the selected redundancy type. In addition to that, inter-component dependencies may be defined in which the state change of a component can lead to state changes of another component to model, e.g., common-cause failures or systematic bugs. Operator interaction can also influence the state distribution of a component if it is required for certain transitions. Thus, limited operator capacities or operator errors should be included in the problem definition.

3.1.3 Estimation of IT Service Costs

In a data center, capital and operational expenses can be distinguished (Barroso et al. 2013). Capital expenses are costs that can be depreciated over a timeframe, e.g. for the acquisition of IT components. Other capital expenses, e.g., for the construction of a data center site, are normally fixed and subsequent limitations can be formulated within the constraints of the optimization problem.

The variable operational expenses for different redundancy configurations are mainly composed of running costs for components, costs for personnel such as operators, and recovery costs for failed components. The running costs for components and especially the energy costs should be dependent on the state distribution of the component (Fan et al. 2007).

3.1.4 Design Optimization

While the former requirements address the search space and the objective functions, it has to be defined which solutions from the search space are sought. For an RAP, three different optimization objectives can be identified:

- Maximize availability subject to a cost constraint.
- Minimize costs subject to an availability constraint.
- Multi-objective optimization of availability and costs.

Besides the mentioned constraints whose values are non-linearly dependent on the decision variables, linear constraints can be introduced, e.g., to map volume or weight constraints.

3.2 Problem Definition

The IT service to be optimized is comprised of n subsystems. An adjacency matrix $M \in \{0, 1\}^{(n+2) \times (n+2)}$ describes the subsystem graph (cf. Fig. 1). Additionally, the IT service is characterized by a load function $l : \mathbb{R}_+ \to \mathbb{R}_+$.

For each subsystem i, a number m_i of components can be defined. A component has s possible states and a function $tp : \{1, \ldots, s\} \to \mathbb{R}_+$ describes the component's throughput in each state. A similar function op describes the running costs of the component depending on its current state for a timestep Δt. Furthermore, the acquisition costs ac and the component's weight for additional constraints $\vec{w}$ characterize a component.

In order to describe the availability characteristics of a component, sets of redundancy mechanisms R and state transitions T can be defined. A redundancy mechanism is described by a standard state $s_0 \leq s$, a throughput threshold tp_{min}, a random variable TTA, a Boolean value ω, an integer value ρ, and an error probability p_{err}. If a subsystem has a current throughput above the defined threshold, the component will be operated in its standard state. Otherwise the component will be set to the state of highest throughput after a time distributed according to TTA. If operator interaction is necessary for the failover (indicated by ω), an operator will be assigned with priority ρ. The error probability is the likelihood that a task has to be repeated after the time to activation has passed.

A state transition changes the component's state from s_{start} and s_{end} in a time distributed according to a random variable TT. Parameters ω, ρ, and p_{err} describe possibly required operator interactions. For a transition, costs rec arise to map recovery costs. In addition to that, dependencies can be associated with a transition. A dependency is characterized by a set of components whose states may be changed after a time distributed according to a random variable TTD with probability p. This is described by a function d mapping possible state changes.

For the IT service, operators can be employed for recovery and failover tasks. Different operator types can be defined that differ in their wage for a timestep Δt and a factor e describing how error probability for tasks is scaled. In order to map uncertainty in the model, each random variable can be characterized by two random distributions which only differ in a single parameter value. In relationship to the concept of random fuzzy variable (Zhao and Liu 2004) these two distributions describe a random interval variable which is easier to handle.

The problem definition is graphically illustrated as a UML class diagram in Fig. 2. In this graphic, mandatory as well as optional classes and attributes are distinguished. In order to support a data center designer in trading-off effort and utility for the design optimization, several standard definitions for attributes are defined so that problem complexity is flexible. For instance, if no adjacency matrix is given, a series-parallel system is assumed. Load and timestep are set to 1, a redundancy mechanism activates a component if throughput reaches zero, and no operator interaction is assumed for a task. A standard component has a binary state-space between throughputs 0 and 1 as well as no operational costs.

3.3   Availability and Cost Prediction

The mandatory and optional information to define an RAP for data center design form up the search space of possible design solutions. In order to predict the availability and costs of the different designs, a model-based approach is utilized. Using a hierarchical simulation approach, the flexibility of the problem definition can also be incorporated into the model construction and evaluation process. As model type, generalist stochastic Petri nets (GSPN) have been chosen, cf. e.g., Ciardo et al. (1989).

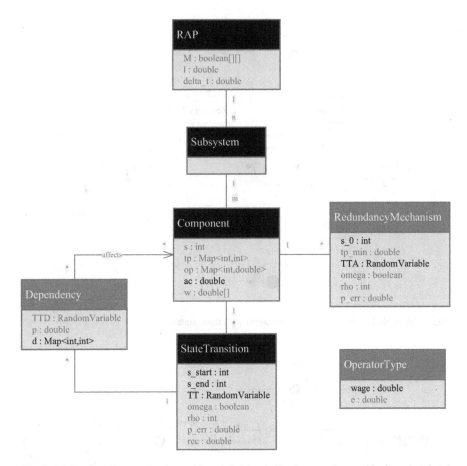

Fig. 2 UML class diagram for the problem definition indicating mandatory (*black*) and optional (*gray*) classes and attributes

A solution candidate is characterized by a selection of components and redundancy mechanisms for the different subsystems. In order to map the state space of a component, s places are generated for each of the possible states. Between these states, transitions are placed according to the defined state transitions. If operator interaction is required for a transition, an operator place is constructed before and after the corresponding transition. An example of a component model (in active redundancy) is illustrated in Fig. 3.

If a component is operated in passive redundancy within a solution candidate, an additional standby place indicates that the component is not failed and disables recovery. In Fig. 4, an example GSPN of a component in standby redundancy is depicted.

In order to map different types of operators, colored tokens can be used. All operator tokens are initially allocated to a place called operator pool. From the pool, immediate transitions are connected to the operator places associated with recovery

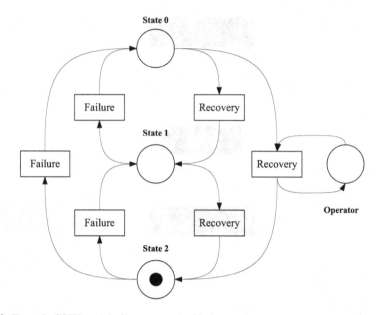

Fig. 3 Example GSPN model of a component with three states

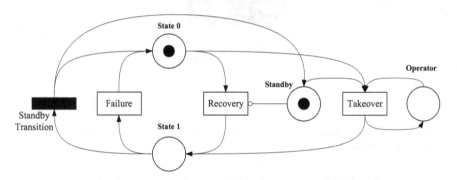

Fig. 4 Example GSPN of a standby-redundant component

or failover activities. These immediate transitions are only activated in case that operator interaction is required for a certain task. After an activity has been completed, there is a probability according to p_{err} that the task has to be repeated, i.e., no state transition occurs. After an activity has been completed and the state change has been performed, another immediate transition returns the operator token to the pool. An example of this behavior is modeled in Fig. 5.

Dependencies between components are modeled using dependency places from which two immediate transitions are connected. One of them has no succeeding elements and fires with probability $1 - p_{err}$. Otherwise the other transition fires and an immediate transition changes states of affected components according to the function d of the dependency. In Fig. 6, an example GSPN of a dependency is

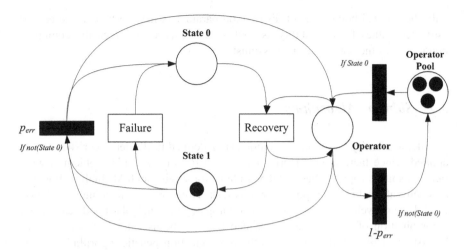

Fig. 5 Example GSPN of operator interaction

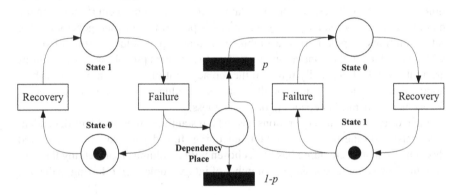

Fig. 6 Example GSPN of an inter-component dependency

given in which the failure of one component may cause the failure of another (common-cause failure).

On the basis of the constructed GSPN models, values for availability and costs can be estimated. In case of availability, the current system throughput is related to its load. When a state change happens, the new point availability is computed and interval availability is updated. Acquisition and personnel costs can be computed independently of the simulation. For recovery costs, a global variable is used that is updated by impulse rewards of firing state transitions. The operational costs are updated by rate rewards depending on a component's state.

If the problem definition contains at least one random interval variable, two GSPN have to be created for both an optimistic and a pessimistic model. For that purpose, a random interval variable has to be associated with a comparator indicating whether a lower value for the parameter interval is optimistic or not. Using this approach, only the interval boundaries of distribution parameters have to be considered and estimated values for availability as well as for costs are between the computed boundaries of the optimistic and pessimistic model.

3.4 Solution Algorithms

In order to identify (sub)optimal solutions to a defined RAP, meta-heuristics can be applied. Since there is no superior meta-heuristic for a specific problem, a wide range of solution approaches could be suitable for solving an RAP. In the following, a genetic algorithm is proposed for this task. However, an encoding of solution candidates as well as operations for random generation, neighborhood search, and recombination of solutions are presented that can be used to apply other meta-heuristics easily. In Algorithm 7.1, the plus selection genetic algorithm (GA) is presented.

First, a number μ of solutions is generated randomly (initialization). These solutions are evaluated in terms of their suitability to solve the problem (fitness). In the main loop, a number $maxGen$ of generations is performed. In each generation, the set of solutions (population) is recombined to create λ new solutions (the offspring) which are added to the population. According to a defined probability p_{mut}, solutions are mutated which normally refers to the replacement of a solution by a neighborhood solution. After the fitness of all solutions is evaluated, μ solutions are selected for the next generation depending on their fitness.

Each of the mentioned operations has to be instantiated with problem-dependent mechanisms on the basis of a suitable encoding. In order to provide the required flexibility, a matrix encoding has been chosen with n columns representing the subsystems. Each column consists of a number of integer tuples (i,j) referring to the fact

Algorithm 7.1 Plus selection genetic algorithm

Input: $maxGen$, μ, λ ($\lambda > \mu$)		
Output: pop		
1:	$gen = 0$	
2:	$pop = \text{INIT}(\mu)$	
3:	$\text{EVALUATE}(pop)$	
4:	**for** $1 <= gen <= maxgen$ **do**	
5:		$pop = pop \cup \text{RECOMBINE}(pop, \lambda)$
6:		$pop = \text{MUTATE}(pop)$
7:		$\text{EVALUATE}(pop)$
8:		$pop = \text{SELECT}(pop, \mu)$
9:		$gen = gen + 1$
10:	**end for**	
11:	**return** pop	

that the ith component is selected in the jth redundancy mode for the subsystem. Thus, an example encoding for a solution candidate may look as follows:

$$\begin{pmatrix} (1,1) & (3,1) & (1,1) \\ (1,2) & & (2,1) \\ & & (2,2) \end{pmatrix}$$

The fitness of a solution is determined by the estimated values for availability, costs, and the values for the linear constraints. While it is desired to gain feasible solutions as a result, considering infeasible solutions can improve the quality of the solution algorithm (Coit and Smith 1996). This can be done by defining a penalty function depending on the degree of constraint violation. For the negative cost fitness with an availability constraint, the fitness function would look as follows, cf. Kulturel-Konak et al. (2006):

$$f(x) = -C(x) - \left(C_{feas} - C_{all}\right)\left(\frac{\max\left(0, A_0 - A(x)\right)}{NFT_A}\right)^2$$

The so-called near feasibility threshold NFT controls which degrees of violations are tolerable. To scale the penalty for the objective value, the difference between the best feasible (C_{feas}) and the best objective value (C_{all}) is used.

Similar to this function, other objective values and constraints can be addressed. Thus, a solution's fitness can be defined as

- Negative costs minus penalty for cost minimization,
- Availability minus penalty for availability maximization, or
- A tuple of costs and availability minus penalty for multi-objective optimization.

In order to initialize a random solution, a parameter *subSize* is required which characterizes the mean of an exponential distribution. For each subsystem, a random value for the number of components is computed and random components and redundancy mechanisms are selected until this number is reached. According to this procedure, the parameter *opNum* describes the mean number of operators for random solutions.

The neighborhood of a solution is defined as all solutions that can be generated by applying a single operation to the original solution. Valid operations are the addition, removal, and exchange of a component-redundancy tuple. A random neighborhood solution (e.g., for the mutation operator) is generated by applying a random operation to a solution.

Solutions are recombined using a uniform crossover. Hence, subsystem vectors from the matrix encodings are exchanged randomly to form two new solutions.

The applied selection algorithm depends on the chosen objectives: if the RAP is defined as single-objective, tournament selection will be applied. For that purpose, μ tournaments are performed in which t randomly chosen solutions are compared regarding their fitness. The kth fittest solution is selected for the next generation with a probability $p_t(1 - p_t)^{k-1}$. In the end, the fittest solution in the population is returned as the optimization result.

In the case of multi-objective optimization, a solution is characterized by two fitness values for availability and costs. A Pareto approach is used to perform the multi-objective optimization. For that purpose, the Fast Non-Dominated Sorting Genetic Algorithm (NSGA-II) selection approach can be applied (cf. Deb et al. 2000).

4 Use-Case Example

In order to demonstrate the suitability and flexibility of the proposed approach, an RAP is defined for the multi-objective optimization of an IT service hosted by an international application service provider (ASP). Using this service, nearly 500 customers can access SAP ERP systems for educational and research purposes. For the optimization, the approach has been implemented as a prototype in the java-based simulation framework AnyLogic 6.8.1.

The IT service is modeled as a series-parallel system of 11 subsystems covering infrastructure, supporting systems, and applications. In Table 1, more information is presented regarding the subsystems as well as the available components and redundancy mechanisms.

In order to define the characteristics of components and redundancy mechanisms, information of the ASP has been utilized. Additionally, statistical data from the Los Alamos National Lab covering failure data of a computing cluster from 1995 to 2011 as well as data from literature, e.g., Milanovic and Milic (2011), Schroeder et al. (2011), have been used to define state transitions. For the operational costs, two benchmarks have been analyzed: the SPECpower and the HP Power Advisor.

Table 1 Subsystems, components, and redundancy mechanisms for the use-case scenario

Subsystem	Components	Redundancy mechanisms besides "active"
ERP system	SAP ERP 6.0	Hot standby
ERP host	HP ProLiant BL620c	Warm standby
DB system	IBM DB2	Hot standby
DB host	HP ProLiant BL460c	Warm standby
Proxy server	SAP router	Warm standby
Storage system	HP StorageWorks EVA 6400	Warm standby
Load balancer	SAP adaptive computing controller	Hot standby
Storage mgmt.	HP storage essentials	Hot standby
WAN access	ISP connection	
LAN	Network equipment	
Power supply	Power connection & UPS	Warm standby (only UPS)

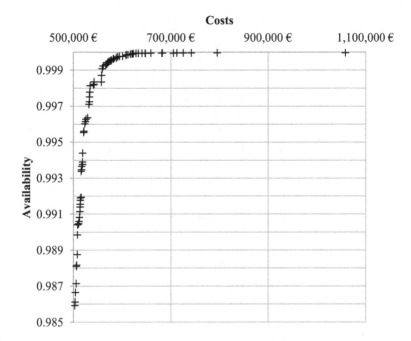

Fig. 7 Pareto front of the use-case results

Regarding the optional RAP attributes, multi-state components, passive redundancy, operator interaction, and dependencies have been modeled. For instance, a failure dependency has been defined between the database and the ERP systems while the latter can also be affected by a common-cause failure. On the other hand, all random variables are defined as certain distributions and a series-parallel system is assumed in which all subsystems have to be available. Furthermore, no additional constraints are introduced so that the multi-objective optimization is unconstrained.

The GA has been performed in ten iterations with $maxGen = 100$, $\mu = 30$, $\lambda = 60$, $p_{mut} = 0.3$, $subSize = 1$, $opNum = 1$, and the simulation has been performed for 8760 h in 100 replications. The ten resulting Pareto sets are aggregated into a single one including all non-dominated solutions which is displayed in Fig. 7. Three exemplary solutions of this set are presented in Table 2.

In this table, a cell $n + m$ refers to the fact that n components are operated in active redundancy and m components in passive redundancy. The first line represents the naïve solution of only one active component in each subsystem and is, thus, the lower bound for availability and costs. In the second line, the cheapest solution achieving 99.9% availability is displayed. The third line describes a high-cost, high-availability solution in which many components and two operators are used. On the basis of this information, a decision-maker can identify the optimal trade-off between availability and costs for a specific use-case.

Table 2 Three exemplary non-dominated solutions

Operator	ERP	ERP host	DB	DB host	Proxy	Storage	Load balancer	Storage mgmt.	WAN	LAN	Power	Availability	Costs
1	1	1	1	1	1	1	1	1	1	1	1	0.98592	503,039
1	1 + 1	1 + 1	2	1 + 1	1	1 + 1	1 + 1	1 + 1	1	2	1	0.99908	559,238
2	7 + 1	2 + 1	2 + 4	2 + 3	2 + 1	2 + 1	2 + 3	2 + 2	1	3	2 + 1	0.99996	1,058,974

5   Conclusion

Data center providers have to ensure that service level agreements of offered IT services are met at low cost. In case of IT service availability, introducing redundancy mechanisms is an effective approach to increase quality. However, a high number of possible redundancy design alternatives and dependencies exacerbate the identification of a suitable trade-off between costs and availability. In this chapter, the redundancy allocation problem (RAP) has been described as a combinatorial optimization problem addressing this task.

Nonetheless, the availability of data center IT services may be dependent on a variety of aspects such as performance degradation, operator interaction, or inter-component dependencies. In order to allow a data center designer to introduce the relevant aspects of a specific scenario as well as to minimize modeling effort, a flexible RAP definition and solution algorithms have been proposed. This approach can be utilized to optimize availability or costs of an IT service hosted by a data center as it has been demonstrated in the use-case of an application service provider.

In future work, different application scenarios should be optimized in varying level of details in order to analyze the effects of definition complexity on the results. Furthermore, on the basis of the proposed solution encoding and operations, other meta-heuristics can be defined to analyze which approaches are most suitable for solving RAP.

References

Abdelkader, R., et al.: Search Algorithms for Engineering Optimization, pp. 241–258. InTech, Rijeka, Croatia (2013)

Anon: Military Standard: Reliability Modeling and Prediction (MIL-STD-756B), U.S. Department of Defense, Washington D.C., USA (1981)

Ardakan, M.A., Hamadani, A.Z.: Reliability–redundancy allocation problem with cold-standby redundancy strategy. Simul. Model. Pract. Theory. **42**, 107–118 (2014)

Barroso, L.A., Clidaras, J., Hölzle, U.: In: Hill, M.D. (ed.) The Datacenter as a Computer, 2nd edn. Morgan & Claypool Publishers, San Rafael (2013)

Bondavalli, A., et al.: Threshold-based mechanisms to discriminate transient from intermittent faults. IEEE Trans. Comput. **49**(3), 230–245 (2000)

Bosse, S., Splieth, M., Turowski, K.: Multi-objective optimization of IT service availability and costs. Reliab. Eng. Syst. Saf. **147**, 142–155 (2016)

Callou, G., et al.: A petri net-based approach to the quantification of data center dependability. In: Pawlewski, P. (ed.) Petri Nets - Manufacturing and Computer Science, pp. 313–336. InTech, Rijeka (2012)

Cao, D., Murat, A., Chinnam, R.B.: Efficient exact optimization of multi-objective redundancy allocation problems in series-parallel systems. Reliab. Eng. Syst. Saf. **111**, 154–163 (2013)

Caserta, M., Voß, S.: An exact algorithm for the reliability redundancy allocation problem. Eur. J. Oper. Res. **244**, 110–116 (2015)

Chambari, A., et al.: A bi-objective model to optimize reliability and cost of system with a choice of redundancy strategies. Comput. Ind. Eng. **63**, 109–119 (2012)

Chellappan, C., Vijayalakshmi, G.: Dependability modeling and analysis of hybrid redundancy systems. Int. J. Qual. Reliab. Manag. **26**, 76–96 (2009)

Chen, T.-C.: IAs based approach for reliability redundancy allocation problems. Appl. Math. Comput. **182**, 1556–1567 (2006)

Chen, T.-C., You, P.-S.: Immune algorithms-based approach for redundant reliability problems with multiple component choices. Comput. Ind. **56**, 195–205 (2005)

Chern, M.-S.: On the computational complexity of reliability redundancy allocation in a series system. Oper. Res. Lett. **11**, 309–315 (1992)

Chi, D.-H., Kuo, W.: Optimal design for software reliability and development cost. IEEE J. Sel. Areas Commun. **8**(2), 276–282 (1990)

Ciardo, G., Muppala, J.K., Trivedi, K.S.: SPNP: stochastic petri net package. In: Proceedings of the 3rd International Workshop PNPM, pp. 142–151. IEEE Computer Society (1989)

Coit, D.W., Konak, A.: Multiple weighted objectives heuristic for the redundancy allocation problem. IEEE Trans. Reliab. **55**, 551–558 (2006)

Coit, D.W., Smith, A.E.: Reliability optimization of series-parallel systems using a genetic algorithm. IEEE Trans. Reliab. **45**, 254–266 (1996)

Deb, K. et al.: A fast elitist non-dominated sorting genetic algorithm for multi-objective optimization: NSGA-II. In: Proceedings of the 6th International Conference on Parallel Problem Solving from Nature. Lecture Notes in Computer Science. Springer, Berlin/Heidelberg (2000)

Emeakaroha, V.C., et al.: Towards autonomic detection of SLA violations in cloud infrastructures. Futur. Gener. Comput. Syst. **28**(7), 1017–1029 (2012)

Fan, X., Weber, W.-D., Barroso, L.A.: Power provisioning for a warehouse-sized computer. In: Proceedings of the 34th International Symposium on Computer Architecture. San Diego, CA, USA, pp. 13–23 (2007)

Fonseca, C.M., Fleming, P.J.: An overview of evolutionary algorithms in multiobjective optimization. Evol. Comput. **3**(1), 1–16 (1995)

Franke, U.: Optimal IT service availability: shorter outages, or fewer? IEEE Trans. Netw. Serv. Manag. **9**, 22–33 (2012)

Franke, U., Johnson, P., König, J.: An architecture framework for enterprise IT service availability analysis. Softw. Syst. Model. **13**, 1417–1445 (2014)

Garg, H., Sharma, S.P.: Multi-objective reliability-redundancy allocation problem using particle swarm optimization. Comput. Ind. Eng. **64**, 247–255 (2013)

Hoffmann, G.A., Salfner, F., Malek, M.: Advanced Failure Prediction in Complex Software Systems. Informatik-Bericht 172 der Humboldt-Universität zu Berlin (2004)

Hunnebeck, L.: ITIL Service Design 2011 Edition. The Stationery Office, Norwich (2011)

Immonen, A., Niemelä, E.: Survey of reliability and availability prediction methods from the viewpoint of software architecture. Softw. Syst. Model. **7**, 49–65 (2008)

Jewell, D.: Performance modeling and engineering. In: Liu, Z., Xia, C.H. (eds.) pp. 29–55. Springer, Boston (2008)

Jiansheng, G., et al.: Uncertain multiobjective redundancy allocation problem of repairable systems based on artificial bee colony algorithm. Chin. J. Aeronaut. **27**(6), 1477–1487 (2014)

Kettelle, J.D.J.: Least-cost allocations of reliability investment. Oper. Res. **10**(2), 249–265 (1962)

Krcmar, H.: Informationsmanagement, 6th edn. Springer, Berlin (2015)

Kulturel-Konak, S., Smith, A.E., Coit, D.W.: Efficiently solving the redundancy allocation problem using tabu search. IIE Trans. **35**, 515–526 (2003)

Kulturel-Konak, S., Smith, A.E., Normal, B.A.: Multi-objective tabu search using a multinomial probability mass function. Eur. J. Oper. Res. **169**, 918–931 (2006)

Kwakernaak, H.: Fuzzy random variables-I. Definitions and theorems. Inf. Sci. **15**(1), 1–29 (1978)

Laprie, J.-C.: Dependable computing: concepts, limits, challenges. In: 25th IEEE International Symposium on Fault-Tolerant Computing. Pasadena, CA, USA, pp. 42–54 (1995)

Lee, P.A., Anderson, T.: Fault Tolerance: Principles and Practice, 2nd edn. Springer-Verlag, Wien (1990)

Lewis, L.: Service level management definition, architecture and research challenges. In: IEEE Global Telecommunications Conference, pp. 1974–1978 (1999)

Liang, Y.-C., Smith, A.E.: An ant colony optimization algorithm for the redundancy allocation problem (RAP). IEEE Trans. Reliab. **53**, 417–423 (2004)

Lins, I.D., Droguett, E.L.: Multiobjective optimization of availability and cost in repairable systems design via genetic algorithms and discrete event simulation. Pesqui. Oper. **29**, 43–66 (2009)

Littlewood, B.: Comments on "Reliability and performance analysis for fault-tolerant programs consisting of versions with different characteristics" by Gregory Levitin. Reliab. Eng. Syst. Saf. **91**, 119–120 (2006)

Milanovic, N., Milic, B.: Automatic generation of service availability models. IEEE Trans. Serv. Comput. **4**(1), 56–69 (2011)

Onishi, J., et al.: Solving the redundancy allocation problem with a mix of components using the improved surrogate constraint method. IEEE Trans. Reliab. **56**(1), 94–101 (2007)

Oppenheimer, D., Ganapathi, A., Patterson, D.A.: Why do internet services fail, and what can be done about it? In: 4th Usenix Symposium on Internet Technologies and Systems (USITS) (2003)

Orgerie, A.-C., De Assuncao, M.D., Lefevre, L.: A survey on techniques for improving the energy efficiency of large scale distributed systems. ACM Comput. Surv. **46**(4), 1–35 (2014)

Ouzineb, M., Nourelfath, M., Gendreau, M.: Tabu search for the redundancy allocation problem of homogenous series–parallel multi-state systems. Reliab. Eng. Syst. Saf. **93**, 1257–1272 (2008)

Painton, L., Campbell, J.: Genetic algorithms in optimization of system reliability. IEEE Trans. Reliab. **44**, 172–178 (1995)

Pinheiro, E., Weber, W.-D., Barroso, L.A.: Failure trends in a large disk drive population. In: Proceedings of the 5th USENIX Conference on File and Storage Technologies (FAST) (2007)

Ramirez-Marquez, J.E., Coit, D.W.: A heuristic for solving the redundancy allocation problem for multi-state series-parallel systems. Reliab. Eng. Syst. Saf. **83**, 341–349 (2004)

Ravi, V., Murty, B.S.N., Reddy, P.J.: Nonequilibrium simulated annealing-algorithm applied to reliability optimization of complex system. IEEE Trans. Reliab. **46**, 233–239 (1997)

Sachdeva, A., Kumar, D., Kumar, P.: Reliability analysis of pulping system using Petri nets. Int. J. Qual. Reliab. Manag. **25**, 860–877 (2008)

Sadjadi, S.J., Soltani, R.: Minimum–maximum regret redundancy allocation with the choice of redundancy strategy and multiple choice of component type under uncertainty. Comput. Ind. Eng. **79**, 204–213 (2015)

Sahoo, L., Bhunia, A.K., Roy, D.: A genetic algorithm based reliability redundancy optimization for interval valued reliabilities of components. J. Appl. Quant. Methods. **5**, 270–287 (2010)

Schroeder, B., Pinheiro, E., Weber, W.-D.: DRAM errors in the wild: a large-scale field study. Commun. ACM. **54**, 100–107 (2011)

Shooman, M.L.: Reliability of Computer Systems and Networks – Fault Tolerance, Analysis, and Design. Wiley, New York (2002)

Silic, M., et al.: Scalable and accurate prediction of availability of atomic web services. IEEE Trans. Serv. Comput. **7**(2), 252–264 (2014)

Soltani, R.: Reliability optimization of binary state non-repairable systems: a state of the art survey. Int. J. Ind. Eng. Comput. **5**, 339–364 (2014)

Sooktip, T., et al.: Multi-objective optimization for k-out-of-n redundancy allocation problem. In: International Conference on Quality, Reliability, Risk, Maintenance, and Safety Engineering (ICQR2MSE), pp. 1050–1054. IEEE, Chengdu (2012)

Taguchi, T., Yokota, T.: Optimal design problem of system reliability with interval coefficient using improved genetic algorithms. Comput. Ind. Eng. **37**, 145–149 (1999)

Terlit, D., Krcmar, H.: Generic performance prediction for ERP and SOA applications. In: Proceedings of the 18th European Conference on Information Systems (ECIS) (2011)

Tian, Z., Levitin, G., Zuo, M.J.: A joint reliability–redundancy optimization approach for multi-state series–parallel systems. Reliab. Eng. Syst. Saf. **94**, 1568–1576 (2009)

Trivedi, K. et al.: Achieving and assuring high availability. In: Nanya, T., et al. (eds.) 5th International Service Availability Symposium (ISAS). Lecture Notes in Computer Science, pp. 20–25. Springer Verlag, Tokyo/Berlin/Heidelberg (2008)

Wang, S., Watada, J.: Modelling redundancy allocation for a fuzzy random parallel-series system. J. Comput. Appl. Math. **232**, 539–557 (2009)

Zhao, R., Liu, B.: Redundancy optimization problems with uncertainty of combining randomness and fuzziness. Eur. J. Oper. Res. **157**, 716–735 (2004)

Ziaee, M.: Optimal redundancy allocation in hierarchical series–parallel systems using mixed integer programming. Appl. Math. **4**, 79–83 (2013)

Zille, V., et al.: Simulation of maintained multicomponent systems for dependability assessment. In: Faulin, P., et al. (eds.) Simulation Methods for Reliability and Availability of Complex Systems, pp. 253–272. Springer, Berlin/Heidelberg (2010)

Sascha Bosse (born 1986) achieved his Master's degree with distinction at the Faculty of Computer Science of the Otto von Guericke University Magdeburg in 2011. Since 2012, he has been working as a researcher at the Magdeburg Research and Competence Cluster (MRCC) and received his doctorate (Dr.-Ing.) in 2016. After his doctor studies, Sascha Bosse now coordinates the research activities at the MRCC. He is author of more than 20 international scientific publications in the field of IT systems engineering, published, for instance, in the Reliability Engineering and System Safety Journal or the European Conference on Information Systems (ECIS).

Klaus Turowski (born 1966) studied Business and Engineering in Karlsruhe, achieved his doctorate at the University of Münster and habilitated in Business Informatics at the Otto von Guericke University Magdeburg. In the year 2000, he held the Chair of Business Informatics at the University of the Federal Armed Forces München and, from 2001, he headed the Chair of Business Informatics and Systems Engineering at the University of Augsburg. Since 2011, he has been heading the Magdeburg Research and Competence Cluster which encompasses the world's largest SAP University Competence Center (SAP UCC Magdeburg).

Energetic Data Center Design Considering Energy Efficiency Improvements During Operation

Stefan Janacek and Wolfgang Nebel

Abstract Designing a modern data center is not only an engineer's challenge, but also always a try to predict the future. A data center must provide resources to operate the current state of applications, but it must also provide additional potential for upcoming tasks and requirements. Applications, their demands and the technology of servers change rapidly. However, data center infrastructure, which is costly to acquire, has a much slower cycle of renewal. Hence, these devices, mainly power supply and cooling, must be able to fulfil future requirements. But overestimating demands and provisioning these devices by unrealistic loads may lead to serious energy wasting. During the last years several power saving techniques have evolved that allow data centers to save energy and costs during operation. However, these techniques may be significantly enhanced by considering them during the data center design process and also when hardware device updates are planned. To combine the power saving techniques with an intelligent design method, the following questions need to be answered first: Which energetic interdependencies exist in the data center in terms of electrical and thermal energy? How can these be controlled, regulated and systematically exploited to save energy and still preserve future potential? Therefore, this chapter will provide some basic information about data center energy flow and interdependencies. Based on this, an improved data center design method is presented that does not deviate too much from existing approaches, but enables significant power savings by following only a few new design choices. It is analyzed in what data center usage concepts the proposed energetic improvements may be used and how they can be exploited during operation. A special focus is placed on

S. Janacek (✉)
Smart Resource Integration, OFFIS Institute for Information Technology,
Escherweg 2, 26121 Oldenburg, Lower Saxony, Germany
e-mail: janacek@offis.de

W. Nebel
Department of Informatics, Carl von Ossietzky University Oldenburg,
Ammerländer Heerstr. 114-118, 26129 Oldenburg, Lower Saxony, Germany
e-mail: wolfgang.nebel@uol.de

© Springer International Publishing AG 2017
J. Marx Gómez et al. (eds.), *Engineering and Management of Data Centers*,
Service Science: Research and Innovations in the Service Economy,
DOI 10.1007/978-3-319-65082-1_8

the combination of server consolidation strategies with improvements of the cooling infrastructure. But these can only be fully exploited if the described design methods and improvements are implemented.

1 Motivation

In the modern world, data centers play a significant role in our lives. We use Internet services and mobile applications that base their success on the availability of huge computing resources, located in a data center at some place in the world. The data center market keeps growing; new data centers are built and the existing ones are constantly renewed, enlarged or modernized. The servers, which are the main resource a data center offers, are also subject of new trends, developments and entirely new concepts. In the last years, the computing power of a single server increased while the power demand remained almost constant for a single processor. However, new technologies that allow for a very compact design of servers, now consisting of multiple processors with a dozen of cores, lead to a constant increase of the power density in a server and thus in the racks inside a data center.

These trends are also reflected in the design process and operation of data centers and the concerns operators have about these. Figure 1 shows the results of a survey from Emerson Network Power amongst data center operators (Emerson Network Power 2012). 48.2% of the interviewed raise serious concerns about energy efficiency, 34.8% about the heat density of the racks and the appropriate cooling and 27.4% about the power density, the ability to supply all servers in the data center with the needed power. Considering this yearly repeated survey, it is for the first time

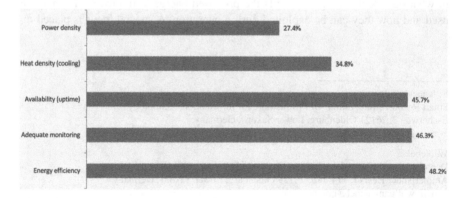

Fig. 1 Main concerns of data center operators, data from (Emerson Network Power 2012)

that the operators considered energy efficiency as the number one concern. Rising energy prices and significantly increased power demand of data centers are the main reasons why energy efficiency has become such an important topic. Besides the aspects of energy efficiency, power distribution and density, there are numerous other topics that need to be considered in the process of the data center design. However, this text focuses on the energetic aspects and combines them with runtime optimization strategies. When designing a data center today, there are numerous technologies available that improve the efficiency of data center infrastructure devices, like cooling or power supply. This chapter describes some of the common cooling solutions applied today, the benefits and the limitations they imply. Uninterruptible power supply (UPS) devices are also a device class that holds potential for efficiency improvements, but the cooling devices are still the major power consumers besides the servers. However, designing a data center with all kinds of efficiency improvements in mind but operating it as conservatively as always might only form an interim solution, at best. Efficient hardware devices and an operation that allows for a consideration of the dynamic behavior of data centers will not only save energy, but also helps improving the thermal stability of the data center operation. During the last years, several concepts for power saving in data centers have emerged, most of them applying some kind of server consolidation. This concept involves adjusting the number of running servers to the current needs. In this chapter, data center design is combined with the strategy to apply server consolidation during operation. The chapter gives hints about design decisions that must be reviewed if consolidation is used and explains some possible consequences and possibilities to further improve the efficiency of the data center. A special focus is put on the optimization by combining traditional server consolidation with an intelligent server and application placement inside the server rooms and across the server rooms in the data center. Also, the importance of choosing power proportional devices that adapt their efficiency and power consumption to the current needs is explained. Data center design methods and processes are changing fast and new technologies, especially regarding data center cooling, emerge constantly. Many of these new technologies claim to provide significant energy savings, but are still under development or research topics without practical experiences. It is not in the scope of this text to describe these technologies. Instead, the chapter focuses on currently applied and matured concepts that offer the most promising results regarding stability and energy efficiency.

The chapter is structured as follows: In Sect. 2, some data center basics are explained and also some detailed data center energy facts are presented. Section 3 explains a common way of state of the art data center design and focuses on cooling technologies and concepts and their influence on the energy efficiency. Section 4 presents data center power saving concepts that are applied during operation and combines these concepts with the data center design and the choice of placing servers inside the server rooms in the data center. Finally, Sect. 5 gives a conclusion.

2 Basics

Data centers include different device categories that all need a certain amount of power. Mainly these are the servers, cooling or air conditioning, emergency power supplies and UPS. Additionally, there are storage devices, network devices such as switches and routers, power distribution units (PDU) and other infrastructural devices, i.e. lighting, alarm or monitoring systems. Figure 2 shows a power consumption breakdown of these devices. In efficient data centers, most of the power should be consumed by servers whereas the air conditioning should consume less power; nevertheless, this is one of the main areas besides the servers that needs a significant amount of energy.

The air conditioning includes all devices used to create cool air, distribute it and extract the hot air from the server rooms. A common misconception is that only the servers generate waste heat and need to be chilled. It is true that the servers are the major heat producers, but each other device that consumes electric energy dispenses warm air, heating up the surrounding air and thus the entire room. If the electric components cannot be provided with enough cold air, serious hardware damage may result. Besides the servers, the UPS devices generate a significant amount of heat that needs to be transported out of the data center. Basically, according to the physical law of conservation of energy, the energy going into a system is equal to the energy coming out of the system. For a data center this means the energy in the form of power consumed must leave the data center, normally in the form of heat transported by hot air or water. This is one of the major facts one needs to keep in mind when designing a data center. Even if smaller devices like network switches consume less power than the servers, they still need to be accounted for when

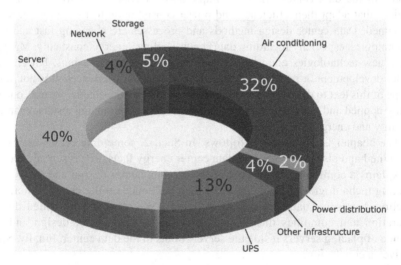

Fig. 2 Power breakdown of typical data centers by device categories, data taken from (Hintemann 2010)

dimensioning the data center's power distribution and heat extraction. A very common metric to assess the efficiency of a data center and its cooling is the Power Usage Effectiveness (PUE) (Avelar et al. 2012). It relates the total data center power to the power consumed by IT equipment. However, the metric fails if modern efficiency optimizations are applied (Schlitt et al. 2015). Another important aspect is the approached usage concept of the data center, since this may have significant influence on design choices and runtime parameters.

2.1 Data Center Usage Concepts – of Contracts and Payment Models

When designing and planning a data center, it is always crucial to be clear about the desired usage concepts. In general, one can differentiate between four types (Pulvermueller 2008):

- Own operation: The data center operator is also the owner of the building and all servers. He also controls and operates the applications running on the servers in the data center. The operator has all options to design the data center, chose power supply and cooling devices and the capacities and types of the servers. He can define service level agreements (SLA) and alter them as he needs to. He is also able to apply power saving technologies while operating the data center.
- Hosting: The data center operator offers complete applications or virtual machines to his customers (this also includes cloud applications). Contracts include the availability and maximum downtimes of the systems as well as support. The operator can directly chose, influence and maintain the hardware in the data center. He determines the type and capacity of the servers and is able to apply power saving technologies.
- Co-location operation: The data center operator only provides the data center building and all required infrastructure for the operation of the servers. The servers themselves are chosen and placed by the customers. The operator is forced by contracts to keep all data center parameters stable, like power supply and room temperatures. He is not able to influence the operation of the servers.
- High Performance Computing (HPC): The servers in the data center are mainly used to solve scientific simulations, medical calculations or other highly numerical operations. Often, special servers are used, which are adjusted to the use cases. In most cases, power saving is not an option for these data centers.

Depending on the chosen concept, designing the data center will differ significantly. Data centers designed for own operation or for hosting purposes can be fully customized to the operators own needs. Choosing and positioning the servers as well as planning the energetic dimensions of the server rooms and all supplying devices can be made with the desired server capacities in mind. However, co-location operation involves planning only with the infrastructure. The operator does not even know what kind of servers will be placed in the racks. Also, power saving strategies cannot be applied by the operator, since he has no influence on the servers and their working state. This is similar when designing a HPC data center. Here, the focus is on the availability of computing resources for complex calculations; it is rather uncommon that HPC data centers have idle servers that might be turned off for energy saving reasons.

2.2   *Impact of Virtualization*

Although data centers are mainly defined by hardware and infrastructure devices, some software trends have still had a major influence on the data center operation. One of them is the virtualization technology. This allows the separation of physical servers and virtual machines that run the applications provided to the users or customers. One physical server can execute several different virtual machines at the same time, since these share the physical machine's resources. Virtualization was originally introduced to improve the maintainability and flexibility of the servers. With virtualization, operators can migrate virtual machines to different servers without stopping the running services. Old or faulty servers can be relieved in this way and then get substituted by new ones. However, virtualization has much more potential than originally thought. Live migrations allow the transfer of virtual machines between servers with practically no service downtime (in millisecond range) and within small time ranges of a few seconds. A recent trend has emerged that applies this concept to move as many virtual machines as possible to a single server and switch off currently not needed, "empty" servers. This is commonly known as server consolidation and allows significant energy savings. The data center's operator must still guarantee to a certain extent that the execution of its services will proceed without problems. The operator therefore signs contracts with his customers that define terms as quality of service and availability. These so called Service Level Agreements (SLA) thus form the legal base of the cooperation between data center operators and customers. In the context of energetic optimizations in the data center, the quality of service defined in the SLA is of special importance and needs to be fulfilled. Variations in application load profiles may lead to resource shortness on a physical machine when there are too many demanding applications. In this case, an early switch-on of additional servers is needed to migrate some virtual machines to them, just enough to allow the accurate operation of all applications and to comply with the SLA terms. This concept is known as dynamic load management and is currently the subject of heavy research and development, with some solutions already on the market. Virtualization has thus a significant impact on the design and operation of today's data centers. The impact of the already existing fluctuations in application loads are fortified by the concentrated and consolidated operation states. Supporting devices like UPS and air conditioning need to adapt to rapidly changing power demands of a changing set of servers.

3 State of the Art Data Center Planning

The design of a data center depends on many aspects, some technical and energetic, and some mostly regarding the infrastructure and security of the building. In general, when looking at popular design guidelines (Bell 2005; CISCO 2014), at least the following categories have to be considered:

- Location and building site, physical safety of the property and possible impact of natural influences
- Building architecture and material selection
- Power distribution and dimensions
- Network layout, topology and scalability
- Cooling technologies and dimensions
- Fire detection and suppression systems

However, it is not in the scope of this chapter to cover all these aspects. Instead, it focuses on the power and cooling subsystems. Before the dimensioning and technology of the power and cooling subsystems are chosen, the desired data center tier level or category has to be defined. These definitions describe the level of redundancy necessary, possible failure durations and other security and stability related aspects. They can be summarized in four data center categories:

- Category A: Small data center or server room, almost no redundancy and no emergency power, cooling is simple and non-redundant, maximum duration of outage: 12 h
- Category B: Small data center with redundant power supply and emergency power supply for 24 h, redundant cooling, maximum duration of outage: 1 h
- Category C: Data center with full redundancy on all levels and device categories, emergency power supply for 72 h, maximum duration of outage: 10 min
- Category D: Large data center with full redundancy plus additional emergency systems for all devices (power supply, cooling), emergency power supply for at least 72 h, maximum duration of outage: less than 1 min

While the duration of emergency power supply has almost no influence on the design decisions of the data center's server rooms, the level of redundancy has. Also, the power density in the racks often defines the design process: all power distribution units and power supplies as well as uninterruptible power supplies are chosen to be able to supply the servers, including redundancy.

3.1 Data Center Power Design: The Architecture of (Uninterruptible) Power Supply

The availability of the data center is a serious concern and one of the main worries the operators have. Several redundant systems for supplying the servers are used to guarantee an almost uninterrupted availability. The power supply system is often

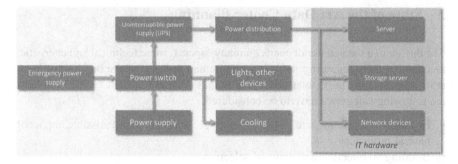

Fig. 3 Typical data center power path

heavily redundant. To circumvent total power blackouts, on-site emergency power generators are used for a mid-term power supply. These are normally Diesel-fueled generators, which are located near the data center's main facility.

For easier understanding, a power path of a typical data center is shown in Fig. 3. Inside the data center, UPS systems are used to secure the power supply of the most important IT devices, which are the servers, storage and network devices. Modern UPS systems are able to power these devices in case of power shortages for a few minutes. For this, they can fall back on a grid of battery packs. Similar to Diesel generators, they need regular testing and maintaining. However, merely supplying power is not the only task for UPS systems in data centers.

3.1.1 Uninterruptible Power Supply

From an energetic point of view, the UPS devices do not only provide the power supply, but they also apply some kind of power preparation. Depending on the UPS's topology, the device can correct voltage and frequency fluctuations, protecting the supplied servers from power surges or similar incidents. This functionality is mostly the reason for their own power demand and the power loss that UPS devices might bring. The efficiency of an UPS device is thus describing the relation of the supplying power load and the UPS device's own demand. Normally, the higher the load, the better the efficiency. Table 1 shows some of the most commonly applied UPS topologies and there possibilities. In modern data centers, especially in bigger ones, double conversion or delta conversion UPS systems are mostly used, since only these provide all the functions these data centers need. Only very small data centers tend to the off-line or in-line variants (Ton and Fortenburry 2005; Govindan et al. 2010; Govindan et al. 2012). The efficiency of the UPS devices depends on the power needs of the supplied devices, mostly the servers. When planning a data center, the dimensioning of the UPS must be in accordance to the estimated power demand of the servers and all other devices behind the UPS. However, even if these power dimensions are considered, the chances that the UPS devices

Table 1 UPS topologies, their functionality and advantages, data from (Ton and Fortenburry 2005)

Topology	Function	Efficiency	Corrections
Off-line/standby	Simple switch between the battery and grid	–	None
In-line/line-active	Converter and battery parallel to power grid, allowing voltage corrections	Load dependent	Power fluctuations
Double conversion	Double power conversion: AC to DC and back, resulting in smoothed power; full electrical isolation of supplied devices possible	Load dependent	Frequency and power fluctuations
Delta conversion (APC 2004)	Patented system, "delta converter" regulates secondary voltage and main transformer, results in direct regulation of voltage and frequency	Load dependent	Frequency and power fluctuations

will operate in a high and efficient load state are low. Several studies have shown that UPS devices in data centers are running with low load. For example, 80% of the investigated UPS devices had a utilization of less than 50%, the mean utilization was at 37.8% (Ton and Fortenburry 2005). These low utilizations lead to inefficient operations. However, it is hard to avoid them, mainly because of these reasons:

- Redundancy: Redundancy of the UPS devices prevents a high utilization of each single device. Since multiple devices share the load, but still must be able to handle the load alone in case of an emergency, the devices will never reach a high utilization.
- Centralized design: Many (bigger) data centers have a centralized UPS room with all the devices needed to supply the entire data center or at least a part of it. These centralized devices are often dimensioned according to the maximum power demand that all connected server rooms may need. However, due to fluctuating server utilizations, this maximum is seldom reached. This leads to another reduction of the UPS utilization.
- Dimensioning of the UPS devices: Dimensioning the UPS devices is often done taking into account the maximum plate power all the connected servers and devices have. This power is, however, almost never reached.
- Take into account for future demands: When planning the data center, the UPS devices should be dimensioned considering possible future demands.

All these points are hard to circumvent and thus will lead to a low utilization of UPS devices. To prevent decreasing the energy efficiency of the data center, modern modular UPS devices should be used that have improved efficiencies when operating in rather low utilization states compared to traditional (older) UPS devices. Some also offer the ability for extensions when power demand grows. However, keep in mind that UPS optimizations during runtime are hardly possible. Once a

UPS system is chosen, it will operate within its possibilities. Dynamic energy optimizations during runtime should focus on the servers and the cooling instead.

3.2   Data Center Cooling

As already stated in the motivation of this text, the cooling of data centers has become one of the main concerns of data center operators, partly because of the increasing heat load and heat density (BITKOM 2010; Patel et al. 2003) and because of its general high power consumption. Looking at the heat load per area, it is observable that the number increased from 1 kW/m^2 in the year 2000 to about 6 kW/m^2 in the year 2014 (prognosed) (Schwalfenberg and Schmidt 2008). Data center and server room cooling need to remove this heat from the servers and all the devices inside the data center. For this task, the cooling devices need a significant amount of energy, but they also need clever design choices to prevent thermal failures and problems. This chapter bases on one of the currently most used cooling chains in data centers and takes a special look at the server room air conditioning. Before handling these topics, free cooling is explained shortly that allows for a significant power usage reduction by using outside cold air for data center cooling.

3.2.1   Free Cooling

If the data center is placed at a location where the outside air temperature during the year is often below a certain threshold, free cooling can be used to provide the cooling and air conditioning of the data center. The concrete temperature threshold depends on many parameters, like the desired server room temperatures, the total cooling capacity needed and the type of the cooling devices. In general, two main concepts can be followed (BITKOM 2010), which must be chosen at the design stage and significantly influence the further design process:

- Direct usage of outside air: The outside air is directly used as cold air in the server rooms and for the servers (Zhou et al. 2012). This possibility can be used, if the outside air temperature is below the needed air temperature in the server room. In case of an outside air temperature that is too low, additional heating up of this air might be necessary. However, this concept has some problems. The air going into the server rooms and directly into the servers must be filtered, since dust particles and other dirt is not allowed to enter the data center's rooms (BITKOM 2010). It is also important to keep the humidity of the air constant within specified limits. Solving these problems is expensive and also needs additional maintaining. Hence, the majority of the data centers does not use direct outside air for cooling purposes. However, since this approach claims to offer significant energy savings, it is subject of current research (Zhou et al. 2012; Xu et al. 2015).

- Usage of cold outside air to provide chilled water: This common concept keeps the climate in the server rooms, as it uses the existing air in the rooms and cools it down with chilled water. Heat exchangers in the server rooms cool down the room's air using the chilled water. This water is chilled using cooling towers and the low temperatures of the outside air (Pelley et al. 2009).

Using cold outside air to provide chilled water is the common and suggested method, especially for huge data centers (BITKOM 2010). Possible energy savings depend on the capacity of the cooling tower, the outside air temperatures of the location during the year and the desired cold air temperatures in the server rooms (BITKOM 2010; Pelley et al. 2009). However, there are suggestions and models provided by the green grid (Harvey et al. 2012) and ASHRAE (ASHRAE 2011), which calculate possible temperature thresholds for free cooling. According to them, even an outside temperature of 35 ° C still offers possibilities of free cooling. This is, however, only possible if the highest server room temperatures suggested by ASHRAE are used. The rest of this work assumes that free cooling is used with outside air to provide chilled water. When the outside air temperatures are too high, chillers provide the chilled water. In any case, the entire cooling chain in the data center must be designed to be able to provide enough cooling capacity for the data center and its devices inside. The details of this cooling chain, dimensioning the devices and the influences on the energy efficiency are described in the next sections.

3.2.2 Cooling Chain in the Data Center

Small data centers or single server rooms often apply room-based air conditioning with computer room air conditioning (CRAC) units. However, data centers with multiple server rooms should establish a cooling chain with computer room air handlers (CRAH) in the server rooms and a centralized chiller compartment. This will lead to a higher efficiency and also allows for the possibility of free cooling. Figure 4 shows a simplified view of such a cooling chain. A chiller or a free cooling device takes care of the cold water provisioning. Pumps dispatch this cold water to the CRAH units in the server rooms. These units use a heat exchanger to cool down air

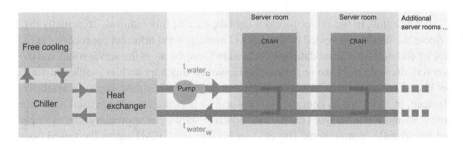

Fig. 4 Common cooling concept in data centers using a cool chain with free cooling, chiller and CRAH units in the server rooms

using the cold water supplied from the chiller. Using ventilators, the air is then distributed in the server room and to the servers in the racks. Warm exhaust air from the servers is drawn back to the CRAH units and cooled down. During this process, the cold water's temperature rises, since the heat energy is transferred from the warm air to the water. This returned warm water must then be chilled by the chiller or free cooling respectively. The amount of cooling capacity available in the cooling chain is directly depending on the temperature of the cold water t_{waterc} and the flow rate. However, due to limitations in the CRAH units and in the entire chain, the flow rate is normally kept constant. Additionally, the chiller's energy demand depends directly on the desired temperature t_{waterc}. This demand can be estimated with the coefficient of performance (COP) (Moore et al. 2005). Increasing this temperature leads to significant energy savings.

Especially since the chillers consume a major part of the energy needed in the cooling chain, a concentration on the cold water temperature should be made during the design process as well as during operation. However, the temperature t_{waterc} is the same for all CRAH units in all server rooms, since they share the same cooling chain. When planning the data center, this fact should be kept in mind, since a distribution of the heat load over the server rooms may allow for a higher cold water temperature. Such an optimization can be made during the planning phase, when the locations for the servers are defined, but also during the operation when application load is distributed in the data center. This optimization will be explained later in this chapter.

3.2.3 Air Conditioning

Server room air conditioning is responsible for removing the heat produced by all electrical devices in the server rooms. These are mainly the servers, but also devices like network switches or power distribution units. According to the physical law of conservation of energy, this text assumes that all energy that enters a server room in form of the electrical power P_{el} will be converted to the heat Q_{therm} and must be removed from the server room:

$$Q_{therm} = P_{el}.$$

CRAH units in the server rooms must take care of this removal. To actually distribute the cold air provided by the CRAH units, several different approaches exist. Older and non-optimized data centers used to blow the air in the server room and the servers drew them in using their fans. However, this approach is inefficient since cold and warm air mix, lowering the entire amount of cooling capacity available. Instead, in today's data centers cold or warm aisle containments are used to isolate the cold and warm air from each other. Figure 5 shows this approach at the example of a cold aisle containment. The cold air leaving the CRAH enters the raised floor and leaves it to the cold aisle containment. The servers draw the air in and use it to cool down their electrical components.

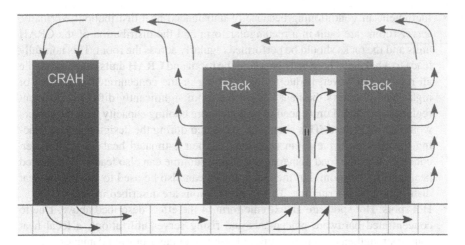

Fig. 5 Concept of cold-aisle containment

This process heats up the air, which then leaves at the back of the servers and the racks into the open room. The CRAH takes in this warm air and cools it down again. This concept significantly enhances the cooling efficiency (Patel et al. 2001; Patel et al. 2002). Often, several CRAH units exist in one server room. Depending on the level of redundancy desired, it may be possible that a single CRAH unit must be able to supply enough cold air for the entire room. During the design phase of the data center, the amount of cooling in each server room must be predicted by defining the maximum power density of all racks, since it defines the number and dimension of the CRAH units and of the rest of the cooling chain. When designing the data center, it is also helpful to define the environmental parameters the server work with. This is especially true for the temperatures of the warm and cold air the servers can handle. The US organization ASHRAE published guidelines for these temperatures that should be used to achieve a high cooling efficiency. The temperature of the air entering the server should be between 18 °C and 27 °C, allowed are 15 °C and 32 °C (ASHRAE 2011). In general, the temperatures should stay in these ranges, but should be kept as high as possible. In later sections in this chapter, it is shown that significant energy savings can be achieved, if the temperature is increased.

3.2.4 Thermal Emergencies and Cooling Failures

Although the cooling technologies have evolved during the last years, there are still some thermal problems occurring, often because of non-optimal hardware placements or missing thermal management. The most common thermal failures or emergencies are these:

- Inefficient air conditioning because of unbalanced heat distribution: Normally, server rooms are built in a rectangular form and the distribution of the CRAH units and the racks should be performed regularly across the room. This normally leads to a balanced heat distribution in the room and CRAH units can thus handle all regions. However, if due to load shifting or the concentrated placement of high density servers the heat load in the room significantly differs in different regions, the CRAH units need to provide more cooling capacity than the servers would actually need. This should be prevented during the design phase by placing the servers in the room according to their estimated heat load. However, consolidation and load management during runtime can also lead to unbalanced heat load in the room, but the technologies can also be used to correct the heat distribution during runtime. These optimizations are described in Sect. 4.
- Hot spots: Hot spots are an extreme form of the effect described above. Due to concentrated hardware placements and rising server utilizations, a local heat source strengthens and may result in hardware outages or even damages.
- Air recirculation: The aisle containment in the server rooms should isolate the warm and cold air. However, if there are holes in the containment or empty places in the racks are not closed, both air sides can mix and thus reduce the cooling efficiency (Capozzoli et al. 2015; Qouneh et al. 2011). This effect should be avoided in any case. However, sealing the containment should be done when building the data center, since the effect of recirculating may be hard to correct. However, there are several research approaches that try to at least avoid recirculation during runtime by a special placement of the servers and the workloads (Pakbaznia and Pedram 2009; Tang et al. 2006).

Preventing air recirculation is one of the major faults when building aisle containments and should be targeted during the design and building phase. During operation, empty locations in racks should be closed using panels. Optimizing the heat distribution in the data center and especially in the server rooms is a complex topic and is even more complex if runtime optimizations of the data center are applied. The placement of the servers and the load distribution in the data center are keys to a stable and efficient cooling. The following section describes the major impacts, influences and measures that should be performed to improve data center air conditioning.

4 Combining Data Center Design and Dynamic Optimization Techniques

This section describes the consequences that arise when data center design is confronted with runtime optimization technologies that lead to a high dynamic of the data center's power consumption. Therefore, server consolidation and thermal influences are first briefly explained. Then, the combination of these optimizations with further improvements that reflect data center design decisions of the infrastructure are described.

4.1   Data Center Power Saving with Dynamic Server Consolidation

The rising energy demand of data centers and the increase in heat density lead to further research of energy saving technologies. In combination with the success of virtualization technologies, the development of server consolidation and dynamic load management emerged. Server consolidation technologies try to concentrate the applications, which are executed in virtual machines, on as few servers as possible. Servers that do not operate any virtual machines can be switched off or can be put into sleep modes. Due to the dynamic utilization of applications and thus of virtual machines, the number of active servers in the data center can significantly differ. In times of high load, it might be possible that all servers are switched on and utilized, while in times of low load only a small fraction of the servers might be switched on. Dynamic load management algorithms observe the application's utilizations in the data center and constantly re-plan the allocation of virtual machines to physical servers. Using this approach, current research showed that the power consumption of the servers might decrease by up to 50% (Hoyer et al. 2011). This also leads to lower utilizations of the UPS and cooling devices. If a data center is designed today, these energy saving technologies and the resulting energetic dynamic must be taken into account while dimensioning and choosing the devices in the data center. A challenge is not only the resulting fluctuation of the power consumption, but also its rapid change. Modern dynamic load management algorithms may lead to several different operating states on one day with significantly different power consumptions (Hoyer et al. 2011; Janacek and Nebel 2015). While traditional server consolidation tries to minimize the number of active servers, some research has also focused the thermal aspects of server consolidation and the resulting heat distribution. The results of these researches are clear: Cooling efficiency and thermal stability increase significantly if a well-balanced heat distribution is achieved in the server rooms (Moore et al. 2005; Sharma et al. 2005; Tang et al. 2008). The cited research has simulated different thermal situations in a server room using computational fluid dynamics simulations (CFD). The results are reason enough to take a closer look at the placement of servers and application load in the data center, during the design phase as well as during operation.

4.2   Placing Servers in IT Rooms: An Energetic View

Dynamic load management that takes these thermal results into account will thus consider the individual amount of each server's exhaust heat that will occur under a specific utilization. An example is shown in Fig. 6. In situation a) (top), the distribution of the virtual machines on the servers lead to several heat concentrations, possibly leading to hot spots. In situation b) (bottom), the virtual machines are almost equally allocated to the server in the room, which results in a balanced amount of exhaust heat in each rack.

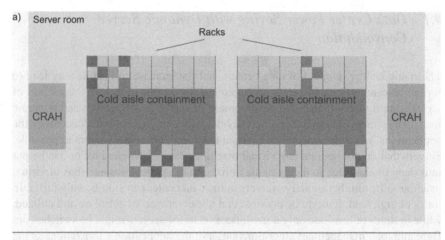

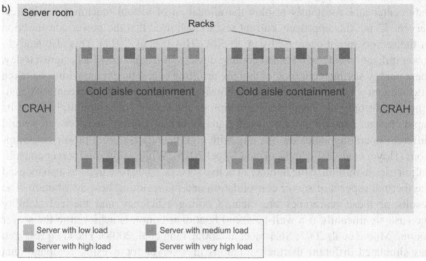

Fig. 6 Two different heat distribution situations in the same server room: Situation (**a**) (*top*) has concentrated server loads, which may lead to thermal emergencies. Situation (**b**) (*bottom*) has a well-balanced distribution of the servers and the load according to the amount of exhaust heat

However, in a data center there normally exist several different servers with different capacities and individual energy efficiencies. Dynamic load management will always try to prioritize the most energy efficient servers with the biggest resource capacity. These servers can operate a greater amount of virtual machines and often lead to the deactivation of multiple smaller servers. If these efficient servers are, however, all located at a single spot or in a single region in a server room, thermal considerations prevent the usage of all of these efficient servers. Instead, other servers have to be switched on to circumvent thermal incidents. It is thus crucial during the design and building phase of the data center to place the servers in the server rooms and racks according to their efficiency and amount of exhaust heat. Clearly, servers with high energy density should be placed between servers with lower density (Bell 2005). If this hint is considered when placing the servers in the data center, air conditioning will start with a higher efficiency and this will even increase if dynamic load management is applied. The following section proposes an energetic optimization of the data center's cooling chain, but this can only be applied, if the thermal situation in the server rooms is optimized as shown in the Fig. 6. An unoptimized distribution leads to an increased cooling capacity necessary, which prevents the further optimizations.

4.3 Matching IT Room Power and Cooling Capacity

Keeping in mind the power consumption breakdown from Fig. 2 it is obvious that a major part of the power consumption belongs to the air conditioning. Here, the chillers consume most of the energy. As stated in Sect. 3.2.2, the chiller's power consumption directly depends on the desired temperature of the chilled water and the total amount of heat to remove. Increasing this temperature allows for significant energy savings, but the temperature must be low enough to be able to provide enough cooling capacity to all the server rooms. At this point - again - the distribution of the exhaust heat in the data center is the key element to optimize the cooling and thus decrease its energy demand. An example for the needed optimization is shown in Fig. 7. The first situation (a)) again shows the unoptimized state, where the heat distribution across the server rooms is unbalanced and leads to a very high amount of exhaust heat in server room 1 while other rooms are almost idle. The result is a chilled water temperature that needs to be able to provide enough cooling capacity for server room 1, but the rest of the server rooms need far less capacity. However, if the heat distribution can be balanced across the rooms (situation b)), the maximum amount of heat that has to be removed in a single server room decreases and the cooling capacity for all server rooms approaches the actual need, thus reducing "wasted" cooling capacity. The regulation of the cooling capacity is performed here by increasing the cold water temperature. In general, the chilled water temperature t_{waterc} depends on the maximum of the amount of exhaust heat of all connected rooms:

$$t_{waterc} = f\left(\max\left(Q_{r1}, Q_{r2}, \ldots, Q_{rn}\right)\right).$$

In this formula, the function f is a fictional model function for the corresponding cooling chain that needs to be characterized for each cooling chain individually. The optimization process shown in Fig. 7 b) leads to a decrease of the maximum. This allows the increase of t_{waterc}. However, there are even further improvements possible. If all server rooms are individually controllable, in times of low application demand,

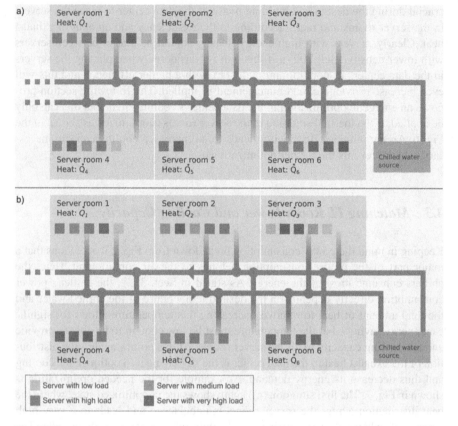

Fig. 7 The unoptimized situation (**a**) (*top*) leads to a significantly greater amount of necessary cooling capacity in server room 1, while the other server rooms will waste this capacity. Situation (**b**) (*bottom*) has a well- balanced heat distribution, which leads to less required cooling capacity, resulting in direct energy savings

entire server rooms can be put to sleep by migrating all the virtual machines to the servers in a subset of the data center's server rooms. During the design phase, the steps to support this optimization are:

- Placement of servers across server rooms: Servers with high power density should be available in all server rooms; they should not be concentrated in a single server room.
- Flexibility of supporting devices: Supporting hardware devices, especially the UPS, should be able to endure the deactivation of all devices in a single server room. Again, these devices should be as modular and flexible as possible. Such devices are commonly referred to as power proportional devices that can adapt their power consumption to the current needs.

Dynamic load management that optimizes the operation of the data center must be able to consider the location of the servers and estimate the resulting power consumption and amount of exhaust heat for each server room. Then, the algorithm can calculate a maximum temperature t_{waterc} for the cold water that guarantees the provisioning of enough cooling capacity for all server rooms, but also allows for energy savings of the chillers.

4.4 Energy Saving Potential

This section briefly shows the saving potential that the described optimizations may lead to. The results were achieved by analyzing an existing data center with 12 server rooms, cold aisle containment in the rooms and the cooling chain described in this chapter. On the basis of this data center, a simulation was created that included all IT and network devices and the cooling chain. The real data center showed a mean utilization of fewer than 30%. The first optimization step was to apply the dynamic load and power management from (Hoyer et al. 2011). This leads to a significant reduction of the power demand. In the original operation, each server room had a designed power capacity of up to 130 kW, the cold water temperature required to provide the necessary cooling capacity was set to approximately 6 °C.

However, when looking at the actual measured power consumption in the server rooms, this maximum was never reached; it did not even get close to the value. The mean power consumption per server room was at approximately 50 kW. By simulating the running services and the hardware, a consolidation algorithm was developed that was able to guarantee enough cooling capacity even when load peaks occur with a cold water temperature of 14 °C. Considering the maximum possible power consumption per server room as shown in Fig. 8, each server room could have a real power consumption of up to approximately 80 kW.

Figure 9 shows the chiller's power consumption depending on the necessary cold water temperature. According to the simulation results, this improvement reduced the mean power demand of the chillers from more than 700 kW to 310 kW, which is a decrease of 56%. Depending on the application load profiles and cooling devices, the yearly cooling costs can be decreased by the same percentage. This significant power consumption reduction was possible, because the original data center had an entirely unoptimized operation. However, looking at Figs. 8 and 9 shows that even slightly increasing the cold water temperature leads to enormous power savings.

5 Conclusions

This chapter explained some of the challenges that arise when designing the energetic aspects of a data center. The text concentrated on the server and air conditioning devices and showed ways to increase the energy efficiency of these devices and thus of the entire data center. Especially the distribution and location of servers in the data center have significant influence on the general energy efficiency but this

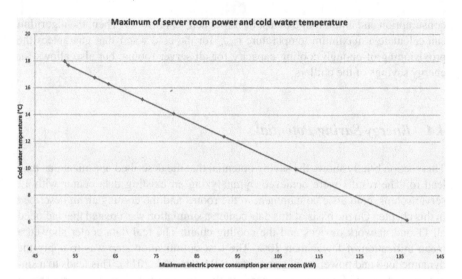

Fig. 8 Maximum electric power consumption possible for each server room depending on the cold water temperature

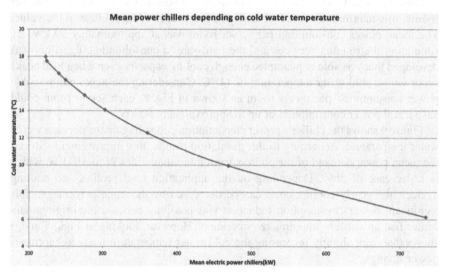

Fig. 9 Mean power consumption of the chillers depending on the necessary cold water temperature

influence increases when dynamic load management is applied. To keep the operation of the data center stable in terms of thermal incidents, this placement has to be well thought. In short, these measures should be taken into account:

- Balanced server distribution in the server room: In each server room, the servers should be placed according to their power demand and the amount of exhaust heat. Servers with high power density should be placed next to low density servers. The distribution should be equally across the server room and there should be no regions with an excessive amount of exhaust heat.
- Distribute servers across the server rooms: All the server rooms in the data center should have a similar power demand and thus a similar amount of exhaust heat. Even if in the planning stage this calculation is considered, during operation the actual demand often differs and fluctuates. Hence, the application's load profiles should be taken into account as soon as possible to provide a well-balanced power distribution across all server rooms.
- Use virtualization and apply dynamic load management: Since many of the servers typically only show a low utilization during operation, significant power savings can be achieved if virtual machines can be migrated to as few servers as possible and the rest of the servers are switched off.
- Dynamic load management must take into account the infrastructure: Significant energy savings at the cooling devices can only be achieved if the power demands in the server rooms remain balanced.

If these approaches are realized, the data center can save a significant amount of energy and still guarantee the thermal stability during operation. Also bear in mind that common efficiency metrics like the power usage effectiveness (PUE) often fail to achieve realistic results if these optimization measures are realized (Schlitt et al. 2015). New and load dependent metrics should instead be used to assess the data center's efficiency gain (Schlitt and Nebel 2012).

References

APC: Understanding Delta Conversion Online "The Difference". APC Application Note 39 (2004)

ASHRAE: 2011 thermal guidelines for data processing environments expanded data center classes and usage guidance. Whitepaper prepared by ASHRAE Technical Committee (TC) 9.9, Mission Critical Facilities, Technology Spaces, and Electronic Equipment (2011)

Avelar, V., Azevedo, D., French, A.: PUE: a comprehensive examination of the metric. The Green Grid whitepaper (2012)

Bell, M.: Use Best Practices to Design Data Center Facilities. Gartner Research, ID Number: G00127434 (2005)

BITKOM: Energieeffizienz im Rechenzentrum – Ein Leitfaden zur Planung, zur Modernisierung und zum Betrieb von Rechenzentren, Band 2. Schriftenreihe Umwelt und Energie (2010)

Capozzoli, A., Chinnici, M., Perino, M., Serale, G: Review on performance metrics for energy efficiency in data center: the role of thermal management. Energy efficient data centers. In: Third International Workshop, E2DC 2014, Cambridge, UK, June 10, 2014, Revised Selected Papers, 2015

CISCO: Data Center Technology Design Guide. CISCO August 2014 Series, CVD Navigator (2014)

Emerson Network Power: Data center users' group special report - energy efficiency and capacity concerns increase. Emerson Network Power Whitepaper, Data Center Users' Group, Fall 2012 Survey Results (2012)

Govindan, S., Wang, D., Chen, L., Sivasubramaniam, A., Urgaonkar, B: Modeling and analysis of availability of datacenter power infrastructure. Technical Report CSE-10-006, The Pennsylvania State University, Philadelphia, PA, USA (2010)

Govindan, S., Wang, D., Sivasubramaniam, A., Urgaonkar, B.: Leveraging Stored Energy for Handling Power Emergencies in Aggressively Provisioned Datacenters. SIGARCH Comput. Archit. News. **40**(1), 75–86 (2012)

Harvey, T., Patterson, M., Bean, J.: Updated air-side free cooling maps: the impact of ashrae 2011 allowable ranges. The Green Grid (2012)

Hintemann, R.: Die Trends in Rechenzentren bis 2015. Ergebnisse einer neuen Studie im Auftrag des Umweltbundesamtes (2010)

Hoyer, M., Schroeder, K., Schlitt, D., Nebel, W.: Proactive dynamic resource management in virtualized data centers. In: Proceedings of the 2nd International Conference on Energy-Efficient Computing and Networking (2011)

Janacek, S., Nebel, W: Expansion of data center's energetic degrees of freedom to employ green energy sources. In: Selected and Extended Contributions from the 28th International Conference on Informatics for Environmental Protection, Springer, Heidelberg, Germany (2015)

Moore, J., Chase, J., Ranganathan, P., Sharma, R.: Making scheduling "cool": temperature-aware workload placement in data centers. In: Proceedings of the Annual Conference on USENIX Annual Technical Conference, ATEC '05 (2005)

Pakbaznia, E., Pedram, M.: Minimizing data center cooling and server power costs. In: Proceedings of the 14th ACM/IEEE international symposium on Low power electronics and design (2009)

Patel, C.D., Bash, C.E., Belady, C., Stahl, L., Sullivan, D: Computational fluid dynamics modeling of high compute density data centers to assure system inlet air specifications. In: Proceedings of IPACK'01, The Pacific Rim/ASME International Electronic Packaging Technical Conference and Exhibition (2001)

Patel, C.D., Sharma, R., Bash, C.E., Beitelmal, A: Thermal considerations in cooling large scale high compute density data centers. In: The Eighth Intersociety Conference on Thermal and Thermomechanical Phenomena in Electronic Systems, 2002. ITHERM 2002 (2002)

Patel, C.D., Bash, C.E., Sharma, R., Beitelmal, M., Friedrich, R.: Smart cooling of data centers. Adv. Electron. Packag. **2**, 129–137 (2003)

Pelley, S., Meisner, D., Wenisch, T.F., Vangilder, .W.: Understanding and Abstracting Total Data Center Power. In: Proc. of the 2009 Workshop on Energy Efficient Design (WEED) (2009)

Pulvermueller, P.: Bestandsaufnahme effiziente Rechenzentren in Deutschland. eco Verband der deutschen Internetwirtschaft e.V. (2008)

Qouneh, A., Li, C., Li, T.: A quantitative analysis of cooling power in container-based data centers. In: 2011 IEEE International Symposium on Workload Characterization (IISWC) (2011)

Schlitt, D., Nebel, W.: Load dependent data center energy efficiency metric based on component models. In: 2012 International Conference on Energy Aware Computing, pp. 1–6 (2012)

Schlitt, D., Schomaker, G., Nebel, W.: Gain more from PUE: assessing data center infrastructure power adaptability. Energy efficient data centers, Lecture Notes in Computer Science, vol. 8945, pp. 152–166. (2015)

Schwalfenberg, V., Schmidt, M.: Infrastruktur im energieeffizienten Rechenzentrum. RITTAL White Paper, V10 (2008)

Sharma, R.K., Bash, C.E., Patel, C.D., Friedrich, R.J., Chase, J.S.: Balance of power: dynamic thermal management for Internet data centers. Internet Comput. IEEE. **9**(1), 42–49 (2005)

Tang, Q., Mukherjee, T., Gupta, S.K.S., Cayton, P.: Sensor-based fast thermal evaluation model for energy efficient high-performance datacenters. In: Proceedings - 4th International Conference on Intelligent Sensing and Information Processing (2006)

Tang, Q., Gupta, S.K.S., Varsamopoulos, G.: Energy-Efficient Thermal-Aware Task Scheduling for Homogeneous High-Performance Computing Data Centers: A Cyber-Physical Approach. IEEE Trans. Parallel Distrib. Syst. **19**(11), 1458–1472 (2008)

Ton, M., Fortenburry, B.: High Performance Buildings: Data Centers Uninterruptible Power Supplies (UPS). LBNL (2005)

Xu, H., Feng, C., Li, B.: Temperature Aware Workload Management in Geo-Distributed Data Centers. IEEE Trans. Parallel Distrib. Syst. **26**(6), 1743–1753 (2015)

Zhou, R., Wang, Z., McReynolds, A., Bash, C.E., Christian, T.W., Shih, R.: Optimization and control of cooling microgrids for data centers. In: 2012 13th IEEE Intersociety Conference on Thermal and Thermomechanical Phenomena in Electronic Systems (ITherm), pp. 383–343 (2012)

Stefan Janacek is a full-time researcher at the OFFIS Institute for Information Technology in Oldenburg, German. He studied computer science at the Carl von Ossietzky University of Oldenburg until 2008. His research focus is on data center energy efficiency and optimization technologies as well as modelling and simulating cyber-physical systems. He has published several research papers, articles and book chapters in international top conferences, research books, and journals.

Wolfgang Nebel holds a chair on "Embedded HW/SW Systems" as a full professor at Carl von Ossietzky University Oldenburg. He is chairman of OFFIS – Institute for Information Technology, a 250 employee think tank in Oldenburg. Further Nebel is member of the Board of edacentrum e.V., Hanover, chairman of EDAA – European Design Automation Association, Vice President of Deutsche Industrieforschungsgemeinschaft Konrad Zuse e.V., member of acatech – National Academy of Science and Engineering, member of ACM, fellow of DATE, member of GI, and fellow of the IEEE.

Nebel's research interest is on design methodologies for robust and energy efficient cyber physical systems. He holds four patents and is author of more than 200 publications.

Demand-Side Flexibility and Supply-Side Management: The Use Case of Data Centers and Energy Utilities

Robert Basmadjian, Florian Niedermeier, and Hermann de Meer

Abstract Lately power grids have been subject to one of their major evolutions since their design and conception. The traditional structure of electricity being generated by a small number of huge and centralized power plants is being defied by the increasing penetration of renewable energy sources. The major drawback of such sources is their intermittent behavior rendering power generation planning even more cumbersome. This problem can be alleviated through the implementation of intelligent energy management systems (EMS) whose main objective is to exploit demand-side flexibilities for the purpose of better supply-side management and planning. Data centers, on one hand due to their significant power (in the order of up to 200 MW) as well as energy demand, and on the other hand thanks to their highly automated ICT infrastructure providing flexibilities without human interventions, have been shown to be excellent candidates for participation to such EMS. To this end, in this chapter we study such energy management systems by considering the use case of data centers both from local as well as coordinated management perspectives. For each considered perspective we describe thoroughly the concept as well as give its corresponding architectural building blocks. Furthermore, we specify the mechanisms and strategies that can be used for the case of data centers in exploiting demand-side flexibilities.

1 Motivation

The electricity grid has become a critical infrastructure which modern society cannot do without. Traditionally, the responsibility to maintain the equilibrium of power generation and demand lay solely at generation side. As generally demand was perceived as *non-controllable*, electricity generation had to be continuously

R. Basmadjian (✉) • F. Niedermeier • H. de Meer
Department of Computer Science and Mathematics, University of Passau,
Innstrasse 43, 94032 Passau, Germany
e-mail: robert.basmadjian@uni-passau.de; florian.niedermeier@uni-passau.de;
hermann.demeer@uni-passau.de

© Springer International Publishing AG 2017 187
J. Marx Gómez et al. (eds.), *Engineering and Management of Data Centers*,
Service Science: Research and Innovations in the Service Economy,
DOI 10.1007/978-3-319-65082-1_9

adapted through orchestration of different types of power plants. Those power plants were grouped into three major classes: base-, medium- and peak-load. Base-load power plants are used to cover the baseline power demand in the grid. Power generation using base power plants, like nuclear and large coal power plants, is cheap, however their power output adaptability is low and therefore these power plants are not fit to cope with sudden changes in power demand. Medium- and peak-load power plants are much more flexible regarding their power output adaptation, however fuel costs are higher and they are often not environmental friendly in terms of CO_2 emissions. Typical medium and peak power plants are gas or fossil-based diesel generators.

The limitations of a power grid in its traditional form are recently becoming increasingly apparent in the light of new requirements arising from, e.g., power feed from high amounts of renewable energy sources such as photovoltaic, windmills, etc. The volatile nature of these energy sources requires fundamental changes to the electricity infrastructure to ensure future stability of the power grid. Some of the most important changes include a finer monitoring granularity in the grid and increased automation of grid management using information and telecommunication technology (ICT). These requirements lead to the provision of the so-called "Smart Grid" which interconnects ICT with power grid technology to improve its efficiency and reliability.

The emergence of Smart Grids however raises two intrinsic characteristics of this latter. On the one hand, the intermittent behavior of renewable energy sources leads to less certainty and controllability of the power generation from supply-side. This compels the need to accurately *forecast generation* as well as requires *flexibilities* on demand-side. On the other hand, the power generation management at supply-side as well as the exploitation of flexibilities provided by demand-side necessitate regular exchange of information in both directions. As mentioned earlier, ICT plays a prominent role in enabling such an intelligent Energy Management System (EMS) for Smart Grids. To this end, Demand Response (D/R) mechanisms have been proposed lately with the objective of exploiting demand-side flexibilities managed by energy utilities in order to partially substitute power generation controllability lost on supply-side due to an increased use of renewable generation. More precisely, D/R (Anon 2010) deals with the interaction between supply- and demand-side for the purpose of the latter to change its power usage pattern as well as magnitude. Furthermore, D/R describes different schemes in incentivizing the demand-side to participate in such an energy management program. In general, three different kinds of incentives for D/R exist: (1) economic/market driven, (2) environment driven, and (3) efficiency driven.

Among several stakeholders in the energy market, Distribution System Operators (DSO)[1] have the most beneficiary interest to set up D/R mechanisms in order to control to a certain extend the energy load of their customers. This is due to the fact that DSO's main objective is to ensure that the power grid is operated in the most

---

[1] http://userwikis.fu-berlin.de/display/energywiki/distribution+system+operator

stable manner. To guarantee power grid's stability, DSO is faced with making investments on upgrading the infrastructure, which are costly and a very complex incremental process. Furthermore, generally DSOs have internal power generation sources such as renewables and fossil-based generators. Due to lack of sufficiency, they also have contract with bigger energy suppliers (e.g. EDF, e-on, etc.) to feed power to their grid. Such contracts are signed on a yearly-basis and enforce the DSO to pay extremely high penalties every time the bound agreed upon in the contract is exceeded (even for 1 s). As a matter of fact, this leads to another reason for DSOs to adopt D/R mechanism.

Data centers are emerging as focal points for Green IT, due to their current position as consumers of about 1.5% of the world's energy consumption. Because of the recent trend of outsourcing IT services to the cloud or traditional computing data centers, their total carbon footprint is estimated to increase from 14% in 2002 to 18% in 2020 (Anon 2009), thus being the only ICT sector whose relative magnitude is growing (Schomaker et al. 2015). Given the importance of the topic, several initiatives were taken in order to study the potential of data centers in reducing their power demand. It has been shown that data centers are excellent candidates to participate in D/R mechanisms due to several reasons (Ghatikar et al. 2010; Basmadjian et al. 2012a):

1. Their significant power demand which ranges from 200 kW (medium-sized) to more than 2500 kW (large-sized) (Hintemann et al. 2010), reaching to orders of MWs such as Google Data Hotel.
2. The availability of highly automated frameworks able to manage the IT infrastructure without any human intervention.
3. The presence of quickly reacting (in the order of seconds) strategies providing flexibilities such as uninterruptible power supply (UPS), cooling down/heating up by altering temperature set points, migrating or shifting workload, etc.
4. The capability of data centers to store energy in case of excess of power from renewables.

In general, there exist three different types of data centers, each having its own intrinsic characteristics as we demonstrate next: *high performance computing* (HPC), *traditional computing* (TC) and *cloud computing* (CC). In HPC-type data centers, workloads are executed on dedicated physical machines, which require high computation time and powerful physical resources. Consequently, no virtual machines (VM) and hence virtualization techniques are considered in such type of data centers. In CC-type data centers, physical resources are subject to virtualization so that they can be shared among different customers. Numerous "as a Service" models have been proposed such as Infrastructure as a Service (IaaS), Platform as a Service (PaaS), Software as a Service (SaaS), etc. Hence, workloads are presented by VMs which can share the same physical machine during their execution. Between high performance and cloud computing, TC-based data centers provide a computational environment by mixing the two world together where it can execute certain workloads on virtualized resources and others on physical ones. It is worth mentioning that each of the above mentioned three data centers has its own specific service level agreements (SLAs). As we point out in Sect. 3, the more stringent the SLA is, the less data center provides flexibilities and hence possibilities to participate in D/R mechanisms.

In this chapter, we illustrate different ways of data centers participating in D/R both from local and coordinated management perspectives. The remainder of this chapter continues as follows: We describe the different considered concepts for the energy management system in Sect. 2. The concrete processes as well as strategies exploiting the flexibilities provided by data centers are presented in Sect. 3. The architectural building blocks for the implementation of the different energy management systems are given in Sect. 4. We conclude this chapter by mentioning certain prospects and challenges in Sect. 5.

2 Perspective Description and Concepts

On the top level, we differentiate data center power and energy management regarding the scope of interaction with other parties in the system. In the following, several concepts will be covered, starting from a local approach with an increasing level of interaction.

2.1 Local Energy Management

Data center (DC) energy management in an entirely local setting is limited to adaptation within its local scope. Therefore, cooperation with outside entities or orchestration by such entities is not possible. However, local optimization still is highly attractive to DC managers as it may reduce TCO through energy saving. Local energy management may be performed in different ways: static and dynamic. Static (or long term) energy management is concerned with improving the overall data center energy-efficiency. This could be, e.g., investments in highly energy-efficient hardware, which may be beneficial to overall power demand while achieving the same performance as standard hardware. Static energy management requires careful capacity planning, anticipating growth and peak load, while at the same time avoiding over provisioning ("right-sizing"). In contrast, dynamic energy management is concerned with improving energy-efficiency at runtime by adaptively optimizing operating parameters. Limitations on energy conservation mainly consist of technical limitations of DC equipment and data center SLAs. The former consist mainly of restrictions regarding operating conditions, e.g. temperature, which limits energy savings possible by reducing cooling. SLAs require DCs to guarantee a certain service quality for the services offered. This requires a tight monitoring of service performance and hardware utilization in order not to violate SLA limits while distributing services on available substrate hardware in an optimal way.

2.2 Coordinated Energy Management

In contrast to local energy management, coordinated approaches aim to provide data center power demand flexibility to achieve a higher level goal. To this end, information exchange with an entity governing the grid is required. This may be a Distribution System Operator (DSO) in charge of medium and low voltage grid stability and power quality or, in a future smart grid scenario, some other more general energy management authority (EMA). In contrast to consumers, this entity has access to current and forecasted information regarding generation and demand in the power grid. By sharing certain pieces of this information, an EMA may guide the power demand of consumers inside its power grid. Two different possibilities of this guidance are discussed in the following.

2.2.1 Cooperation Through On-demand D/R

A possible approach towards coordinated power demand adaptation is on-demand D/R. In this setting, an EMA may request its consumers to increase/decrease their power demand at some point in the future for a certain duration. Several different concrete implementations exist, e.g. price-based, incentive−/event-based and demand reduction bids (Siano 2014). This way, electrical load can be reshaped during certain time intervals to, e.g., avoid peaks in power demand. Outside the D/R time periods, participating consumers are not bound by any restrictions except those in their standard contracts, which allows for local energy management mechanisms to be applied. In on-demand D/R, adaptations usually occur rather rarely (e.g., a few times per month). Therefore, power adaptation techniques which exhibit long recovery times are still applicable, however the enactment needs to be reliable. From the perspective of an energy utility sending D/R requests, challenges mainly arise in communicating D/R events and in accounting. The latter is not trivial as special measurement and verification (M&V) techniques need to be used to proof that an actual adaptation of power demand is performed (Goldberg and Agnew 2013).

2.2.2 Cooperation Through Continuous D/R

Another approach based on a tighter coupling of EMA and DC is continuous D/R. In this setting, the desired power demand of a consumer is communicated continuously by an EMA. This "power plan" needs to consider one major additional aspect compared to on-demand D/R: consumers need to be able to continue their business operations without major interruption while implementing a power plan. This is a significant challenge, as several power planner properties have to be avoided: First, strong deviations from the consumers' baseline power demand profile may be hard to implement as flexibility in power demand is limited. Second, high frequency changes in a power plan may be hard to implement as accessing flexibilities may require ramp times. Finally, low lead time changes to a power plan have to be avoided as rescheduling of flexibilities on short notice may be impossible or costly (Niedermeier et al. 2016).

3 Mechanisms and Strategies for Flexibility

Any demand-side entity, participating in power adaptation collaboration with the supply-side, needs to clearly identify the potential flexibilities that it provides to the latter. For this purpose, it is crucial to precisely describe the kind of operations and processes that a specific demand-side entity daily operates on. In the context of data centers as demand-side entity, we next illustrate the operational considerations for participating in D/R mechanisms. Furthermore, for each identified process, we specify its technological enabler, technical requirements, impact as well as the needed reaction time.

3.1 Workload

In a data center, we can identify two major types of workload: *elastic inelastic*. Unlike inelastic loads, elastic ones do not have very stringent constraints in terms of their time of execution, interruptibility, as well as response time. Example of typical inelastic workloads are the ones executed in HPC data centers. In this case, the workload is submitted in the form of jobs where start and end times as well as required resources are well defined. Hence, the SLAs of a typical inelastic workload do not provide any room of flexibility without breaching the agreement. Elastic workloads have much more relaxed constraints in terms of SLA. For instance, the SLA related to back-up services specifies the frequency (e.g. daily) of the back-up operation and leaves the exact time (e.g. at night) of this operation undetermined. These relaxed constraints pave the way for data centers to provide a certain level of flexibility. To this regard, there are four techniques to deal with elastic workloads for the purpose of providing flexibilities: consolidation, shifting, migration and frequency scaling.

3.1.1 Consolidation

Consolidation is a technique building on a virtualization-enabled data center infrastructure. By packing several different workloads (encapsulated in virtual machines) of the data center on a subset of its IT equipment, the number of switched-on physical IT resources may be reduced. This is desirable, as the power demand exhibited by typical IT equipment is highly non-linear with regard to its utilization (an idle server may consume up to 50% of its maximum power demand (Basmadjian et al.

2012b)). While drastically decreasing the overall power demand of operated IT equipment, this technique may also degrade performance of running services especially in dense consolidation scenarios. Regarding the reaction time for consolidation, this mainly depends on the data centers' configuration and workload size. It is assumed to be in the order of minutes (e.g. 1–3 min). Typical virtualization technologies implemented in data centers are KVM, XEN, and VMware hypervisors.

3.1.2 Shifting

As mentioned in Sect. 3.1, the SLA of certain elastic workloads may focus on functional aspects without putting hard constraints on execution time. For instance, as long as the SLA guarantees 99.99% availability (security), it may not be concerned with the exact time of the backup (or anti-virus check) operation being carried out (e.g. at noon or night). Under such circumstances, it is possible to shift the workload temporally. By shifting we mean rescheduling the IT workload to a time outside of the D/R event window. As a consequence, this technique decreases IT workload for a certain period of time. Subsequently, it may enable consolidation of workload to a lower number of servers, which in turn saves additional power as more servers may be shut down. The most appealing characteristic of such a technique is that its reaction time is instantaneous.

3.1.3 Migration

This term (Fischer et al. 2011) refers to the technique of geographically shifting IT workload from one data center to another not currently being in a D/R period. The major requirement for this technique to work is the technical compatibility of source and destination data centers, meaning both are capable of executing the migrated workload. Furthermore, both data centers should be equipped with virtualization technology. As a consequence, this technique mitigates the burden from one geographical utility and puts it on the hosting data center's one. Also, it has an impact on service downtime. Concerning the reaction time, this largely depends on several factors such as the size of the workload, the bandwidth of the network as well as the mode of migration (e.g. cold, warm, live (Clark et al. 2005)). For instance, in live migration we can have in optimal cases a downtime of only in the order of seconds.

3.1.4 Frequency Scaling

Consists of clocking down the frequency and voltage of the processor during low to medium workload utilization periods. For this technique to work, the underlying IT equipment need to be capable of Dynamic Voltage and Frequency Scaling (DVFS) technology (Basmadjian et al. 2016). Note that current major processor vendors such as Intel and AMD provide their own implementation of DVFS. This technique has the same impact as the one for consolidation by reducing the power demand as well as the performance of the running services. However, unlike consolidation, the reaction time for this technique is instantaneous.

3.1.5 Summary

There exist in practice four flexibility providing techniques related to IT workload: consolidation, shifting, migration and frequency scaling. The amount of flexibility that each one provides is highly dependent on the service level agreement of the corresponding workload. Such techniques are viable with elastic workloads whose SLA provides some sort of flexibilities. Next, we describe two techniques, namely HVAC and UPS that provide flexibilities without having any impact on the SLA of data center services.

3.2 HVAC

Power provisioned to IT systems is dissipated as heat. In densely equipped environments like data centers, this heat must be removed in order to keep IT equipment within acceptable temperature ranges. Overheating of IT equipment may result in decreased performance (thermal throttling), loss of availability (emergency shutdown) or even hardware damage. Traditionally, there exist two methods for cooling (Evans 2004): Computer Room Air Conditioners (CRAC) and Computer Room Air Handlers (CRAH). Those traditional methods have been enhanced with free cooling mode which is capable of exploiting the outside air. In addition, liquid-based cooling technology is frequently combined with air-based systems in order to take advantage of the excellent specific heat capacity of liquid coolant (e.g. water) compared to air. Those techniques are known as hybrid cooling. Numerous optimization approaches have been proposed in the literature which exploit the energy-efficient usage of the cooling systems (Pore et al. 2015; Patterson and Fenwick 2008; Li et al. 2014). This is due to the fact that energy demand for the purpose of cooling may amount up to 40% of the overall energy demand of a data center (Meijer n.d.). Consequently, the main objective behind this technique is to alter the temperature set points of the IT infrastructure. However, in order for this technique to be usable, a data center needs to be provided with different cooling technologies (e.g. air- and liquid-based, free cooling). Furthermore, the different temperature set points must be inside an acceptable temperature range (between 18 °C and 30 °C in compliance with the standards suggested by American Society for Heating and Air-Conditioning Engineers (ASHRAE) for IT equipment (Kuusisto 2011)). As a direct impact, by exploiting the temperature set points, it is possible to reduce significantly the energy demand of the data center. It is worth pointing out that this technique can also be used for energy storage purposes. For instance, in times of renewables' power surplus, it is possible to decrease the temperature set points to create a thermal buffer, which can later be used to reduce cooling during future D/R periods. Reaction time of this technique depends on data center size and cooling system details. Typically, it can take up to 5 min to cool down or heat up a given data center.

3.3 Uninterrupted Power Supply

Traditionally, UPS systems are used in data centers as a backup power supplier in case of blackouts or disconnection of a data center from the power grid. For this reason, most data centers are equipped with such systems able to provide power to the whole data center for a short period of time until either the local diesel generator is powered on or other external sources of power are made available. Despite its normal operation purpose, a UPS may be used in order to supply a data center for a short period of time with power during D/R periods. Furthermore, it can be used as an energy storage during power surplus situations by charging its battery. For this technique to be applicable in practice, it is necessary that the UPS system to be controllable from automation framework of data center. Such frameworks send control signal to the UPS in order to put this latter in the most suitable mode of operation during D/R period. As a consequence, this technique contributes in reducing the power demand and in certain cases to go off grid for a short period of time. Concerning the reaction time, it is instantaneous however depending on the actual status of the battery.

In summary, the flexibility techniques provided by HVAC and UPS for D/R purposes inside a data center can be employed independent of the service level agreements of its running services. Furthermore, those techniques can be used as energy storage facilities during power surplus situation from renewables. Also, both techniques are in practice very well integrated within the automation framework of data centers. Hence, these can be controlled without any human intervention.

3.4 Green Agreements

3.4.1 Green SLA

Besides the above mentioned mechanisms and strategies, which provide data centers with flexibilities that can be used for the purpose of D/R, the customers of those data centers play an even more essential role. This is reflected by them being flexible and accepting the alteration of the agreed quality of their running services. More precisely, service level agreements (SLA) traditionally specify the amount of commitment that data centers guarantee to their customers in terms of performance, availability, etc. of their services. To this end, Green SLAs were proposed that have shown their high potential in Green IT (Klingert et al. 2012). The main concept of

Green SLA is the fact that customers may not require all the guaranteed commitments of their rigid SLA and agree to its degradation during D/R periods. Hence, an example of a Green SLA can be high performance during weekdays between 9 AM and 9 PM and medium performance for other times of the day as well as during weekends. To realize this concept in practice, it requires data centers to incentivize their flexible customers. To this end, reward and penalty schemes have been proposed that grant monetary rewards to customers based on their provided and implemented flexibilities and penalties in case any of the agreed terms of Green SLA is breached.

3.4.2 Green SDA

The major inconvenience of conventional energy tariffs, between an energy utility and its customers, is their lack of flexibility. In other words, the customers of an energy utility sign a contract specifying a fixed basic fee, a power charge varying with the highest power required in the billing period and an electricity price for each consumed kWh, on a yearly basis regardless of the power grid's operational state. Such an inflexibility at contract level diminishes the possibilities of provisioning demand-side flexibilities. Hence, Green Supply Demand Agreement (Green SDA) has been proposed in (Basmadjian et al. 2013b) as an agreement that replaces the legacy energy tariffs as well as contracts, and determines the conditions under which the supply-side entity may request power adaptation actions from its customers. Among others, its contractual terms contain the amount of maximum and minimum power the demand-side (e.g. data centers) can adapt for a specific duration of time. Also, it specifies the number of consecutive requests that the supply-side is allowed to send to the demand-side as well as the number of times this latter can reject a request from the former. Note that all the agreed terms are on a monthly basis. The concept is generic and can be applied to any industry. For the use case of data centers, it accounts for specific mechanisms (e.g. workload, HVAC, UPS) which are highly flexible and reactive. The origin of the Green SDA concept lies in technical contracts that specify guaranteed quality of a service like response times or reliability. As for the case of Green SLA, here too reward and penalty schemes are well defined, rewarding the flexibility providing demand-side entities and penalizing those that breach the contractual terms specified in Green SDA.

3.4.3 Summary

On one hand, Green SLA is an agreement between the data center and its customers helping the former to take decisions regarding the energy demand that may affect the quality of the provided services. On the other hand, Green SDA is an agreement between the energy utility and its customers (e.g. data centers) specifying the bounds of their power adaptation collaboration. It is worth pointing out that both Green SDA and Green SLA complement one another and primordial for any D/R mechanism to be set in place.

4 EMS Architecture

In order to take the most energy-efficient decisions, the ecosystem consisting of both demand- and supply-side entities needs to be supported by an intelligent Energy Management System (EMS). Such a system can be realized through the software implementation of the considered requirements of the ecosystem. In this section, we demonstrate the architectural building blocks of an EMS for the case of data centers. We first start by describing the relevant components of an EMS for local energy management and then illustrate the ones for coordinated management both for on-demand and continuous cases.

4.1 Local Energy Management

Figure 1 illustrates the architectural overview of an energy management system specialized in locally optimizing (e.g. reducing) the energy demand of a given data center (Basmadjian et al. 2010). As it can be seen, the "Orchestrator" plays the prominent role of a middleware capable of enacting the decisions taken by the "Optimizer" into the ICT resources through the "Automation Tools" of each data center. It is worthwhile to note that the "Orchestrator" needs to be agnostic to the

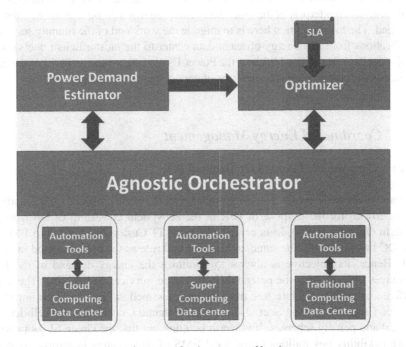

Fig. 1 Architectural overview of a system for the purpose of local energy management

automation framework of the data centers so that the same optimization concepts and methodologies can be adopted to different data center type, being it cloud, super or traditional computing. This can be realized by the development of customizable connectors containing the specifics of each data center's automation framework as well as the internal data structure of the "Orchestrator".

The major optimization problem to which the "Optimizer" finds solutions is formulated in the following manner: "Given a set of ICT resources each having its own energy-efficient characteristics, as well as given a set of services/applications running on those resources where each such service/application has its own QoS requirements specified by SLAs, what is the minimum number of ICT resources needed for those services to run such that no SLA is breached?" From this formal description, the "Optimizer's" main objectives are to (1) pack as much as possible services/applications on most energy-efficient and minimal number of ICT resources without violating any SLA, (2) turn off unutilized or idle resources to save energy demand. In pursuing those objectives, the "Optimizer" needs to consult regularly "Power Demand Estimator", whose main goal is to predict the power consumption of the ICT resources. Hence, such a predictor has to have an in-depth overview of the resources found inside a data center. To this end, schemas based on standard ontologies were proposed in (Basmadjian et al. 2011) (Janacek and Nebel 2016) that describe the infrastructural details of a data center in terms of servers and their compartments such as racks, enclosures, etc., as well as networking and storage equipment.

In case federation of different data centers for the purpose of energy demand optimization is taken into account, the "Orchestrator" of each data center needs to cooperate with its counterpart of the other data centers so that a *global optimized* solution is found. The main intuition here is to migrate the workload of the running services/applications from less energy-efficient data center to the most efficient one(s). The major decisive factor, in addition to the Power Usage Effectiveness (PUE) of the data center, is the cost of migration in terms of energy and downtime periods.

4.2 Coordinated Energy Management

4.2.1 Cooperation Through On-demand D/R

Figure 2 gives an overview of an energy management system proposed in (Basmadjian et al. 2013a) for the purpose of D/R in the ecosystem consisting of Distribution System Operator (DSO), Data centers (DC) and IT Customers (ITC). The EMS in the DC has essentially the same architecture and role as the one presented in Sect. 4.1. Hence, its objective is always to minimize the energy demand of the ICT resources by exploiting the potentials in hardware, services and cooling. The main differentiator of this architecture from the one presented in Sect. 4.1 is the introduction of Green SLAs (see Sect. 3.4.1 for more details), coupled with well-defined reward and penalty schemes. It is worth pointing out that the Green SLAs provide more flexibility possibilities to the local EMS of data centers in terms of further

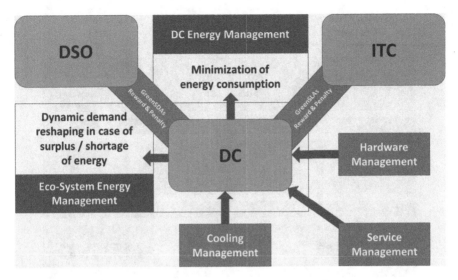

Fig. 2 Architectural overview of a system for the purpose of coordinated energy management through on-demand D/R

optimizing (e.g. minimizing) the energy demand. On the other side of the spectrum, lies the power adaptation collaboration between the DSO and DC through the implementation of Green SDAs, coupled with reward and penalty schemes. To this end, two essential aspects of the EMS for the eco-system DSO – DC need to be considered: bidirectional communication and DC scheduling policies. The former is necessary to exchange information between the DSO and DC before or during D/R periods. In this context, OpenADR (Piette et al. 2009) was proposed which specifies communications' data model with the purpose of realizing automated demand response. Note that OpenADR is an open (freely available) specification allowing everyone to implement D/R mechanisms. Its current version is 2.0 and has been used by different stakeholders in energy market. DC scheduling policies define the ordering in which a DSO selects a set of DCs during D/R periods. This selection process is based on the Green SDA implementation of each DC. Among different policies proposed in (Basmadjian et al. 2014), the "fair" approach ensures that the burden of power adaptation collaboration is shared evenly among the different participating DCs.

4.2.2 Orchestration Through Continuous D/R

Continuous D/R, in contrast to its on-demand counterpart, requires a tighter coupling between energy authority and data center. The main differentiator of this approach from that of Sect. 4.2.1 is the fact that data center's power demand is not only adapted during certain time frames (e.g. D/R periods), but rather in a continuous manner. This, first and foremost, requires a power plan, meaning a continuous plan on *when* to consume *which* amount of power. Deriving such a plan is a non-trivial task: on the

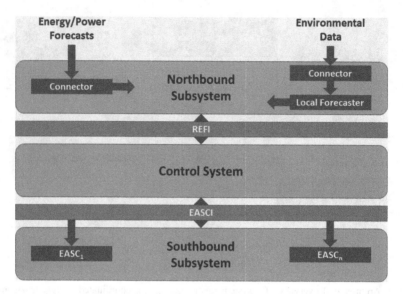

Fig. 3 Architectural overview of a system for the purpose of coordinated energy management through continuous D/R

one hand, a responsible energy management authority needs to fulfill its target overall power demand by superimposing power plans of participating data centers. At the same time, all power plans must be implementable by the respective data centers, meaning their service quality needs to be sustainable while following their power plans. Figure 3 gives an example of a possible architecture for continuous D/R, developed in the course of (Klingert et al. 2015). The depicted system consists of three major components, cyclically executed in the following order: "Northbound Subsystem", "Control System" and "Southbound Subsystem". The former is responsible for deriving power plans based on monitoring data of power generation and goals defined by an EMA. These power plans are handed to the "Control System", which finds a suitable adaptation of available flexibilities to follow a given power plan. The adaptations are then executed by the "Energy Adaptive Software Controllers" (EASCs) or power adaptive infrastructure components.

5   Prospects and Challenges

Generally speaking, reducing energy consumption and increasing performance of the running services are two conflicting objectives of any optimization problem. In order to cope with SLAs of the running services, most of the time ICT resources in a given data center are over provisioned. This paves the way of energy optimization by either (1) minimizing the number of resources and thus finding the optimal mapping of resources to the services without violating SLAs or (2) introducing flexibilities at the customer side and hence the implementation of Green SLAs. In either case, the most relevant metric used to qualify the efficiency of a given data center is its Power Usage Effectiveness or PUE (Belady et al. 2008). In short, this metric indicates the ratio of total energy spent in data center to the energy usage of its IT resources and has an optimal value of 1 (i.e. nearly all of the energy is used for computing) (Pedram 2012). For instance, a PUE of 2 indicates that for every watt of IT power, an additional watt is consumed to cool and distribute power to the IT equipment.

In practice, there have been several initiatives to reduce the energy demand of data centers. These can be classified into two groups: Proof-of-Concept and industrial implementation. The former deals with projects funded by institutions such as European Commission's initiatives of FP 7 framework programs, Lawrence Berkeley National Laboratory, to name it few. The latter deals with initiatives implemented by well-known commercial IT companies such as Google, Facebook, etc. Lessons learnt from those is the fact that both methodologies have shown the potential reduction of energy demand in data centers and hence the improvement of the respective PUE. For instance, Google has improved the efficiency of its data centers by reducing the PUE from 1.25 in 2008 to 1.11 in 2016. It is worth pointing out that the amount of reduction in energy demand is highly related to the type of considered data centers where HPC-based ones can have reductions between 4% and 10%, whereas CC- and TC-based data centers can sometimes achieve reductions of about 45%.

As a matter of fact, energy efficiency in data centers is not a *myth* but rather a *must*. Similar to car manufacturer emission groups (e.g. EURO 4, 5 and 6), we believe that in the near future regulations will classify data centers to efficiency groups and respective additional taxes will be leveraged.

In the last decade, it has been crucial to maintain the stability of the power grid especially after the advent of the intermittent renewables. This burden needs to be shared among different stakeholders of the energy market from Transmission System Operators (TSO), Distribution System Operators (DSO), retailers to the end consumers. Each stakeholder has in its turn a certain role to play. From DSO's perspective, based on some regulations we believe that guaranteeing the quality of the power grid will become the ultimate obligation in the near future. The main indicator of the power grid's quality is the discrepancy or fluctuation of the frequency and voltage with respect to the nominal ones. Technically speaking, this fluctuation is due to the fact that power demand does not match to the generation. Demand Response has shown its significant potential in mitigating such a problem. Among several initiatives, Open ADR Alliance formed by industrial stakeholders has its main objective to foster the development, adoption, and compliance of the Open Automated Demand Response (OpenADR) standards through collaboration, education, training, testing and certification. To the best of our knowledge, apart from Proof-of-Concept projects, there has been no efforts of integrating data centers in power adaptation collaboration with energy suppliers to perform D/R mechanisms. The main reason for this is due to the stringent business commitments that commercial data centers such as Google, Facebook, Amazon, etc. have with their customers. We believe that this can be significantly improved by incentivizing all the parties of eco-system through monetary benefits and rewards through the well implementation of Green SDA and Green SLA concepts. Furthermore, we strongly argue that *energy storage* will play in the near future an imminent role in enabling D/R despite energy price fluctuations. This can be in practice realized through the implementation of battery storage systems. However, the major inconveniences that such systems are suffering from are (1) high battery costs and prices and (2) short lifetime of the battery with respect to return on investment (ROI). Thus, data centers with their capability of storing energy through UPS and HVAC mechanisms are an excellent alternative to battery storage systems until those latter become both technologically and economically feasible.

Total cost of ownership (TCO) in a DC consists of capital (Capex) and operational (Opex) expenses. The former refers to investments (e.g. construction costs of DC, purchase of IT equipment, etc.) made that will be later subject to depreciation. The latter denotes to the recurring monthly expenses (e.g. electricity costs, repairs and maintenance, salaries, etc.) of running the DC services. It was shown in (Barroso et al. 2013) that the dollars per watt cost of server hardware is trending down, whereas electricity and construction costs are increasing. Hence, over long term, the authors believe that the DC facility costs which are proportional to power consumption will become the prominent fraction of total costs. Current best practices in data centers aim to reduce operational costs while guaranteeing high system availability. To create an ecosystem beneficial to all stakeholders, flexibilities offered by data centers have to be adequately rewarded by DSOs. This is, at least in some European countries, not directly possible due to a forced separation between grid operation and energy reseller. Therefore, offering flexibility is only feasible as an ancillary service.

The ecosystem may also be expanded to include data center customers. While it is already common that costumers pay according to guaranteed uptimes/performance of services in data centers, offering specific green SLA agreements at a lower rate is currently not common practice. Including end users in the system may further increase overall DC flexibility, which enables higher profits for DCs offering these flexibilities. By passing on these profits to costumers in form of lower prices, DCs participating in D/R programs may create an environment which is beneficial to all stakeholders.

All measures of energy saving/flexibility of course are subject to certain limitations. First and foremost, DC operators have to ensure service availability/performability, i.e., services have to be able to respond to requests and fulfill them in a specific strictly defined time limit. To this end, services need to be provisioned with a set of computing resources, usually proportional to their respective current workload. To provide the required resources, a lower threshold of operating servers, network and storage devices and support infrastructure needs to be operational, which in turn leads to a lower bound on potential energy savings.

From a data center IT manager perspective, the will to participate in a D/R program may be supported by choices made in IT acquisition and operation. By deciding to use equipment that operates close to energy proportionality (as proposed in (Hölzle and Barroso 2007)), maximum flexibility in power demand is increased. Also, idle servers, which may be required to act as hot standby, require less power and generate less heat. On software side, virtualization should be applied wherever possible to gain additional flexibilities, e.g., move services between hardware, consolidation of services, etc.

References

Anon: Smart 2020: Enabling the Low Carbon Economy in the Information Age. The Climate Group, London (2009)

Anon: Assessment of Demand Response and Advanced Metering. Federal Energy Regulatory, Washington, D.C. (2010)

Barroso, L.A., Clidaras, J., Hölzle, U.: The Datacenter as a Computer: An Introduction to the Design of Warehouse-Scale Machines, 2nd edn. Morgan & Claypool, San Rafael (2013)

Basmadjian, R., et al.: Fit4Green – Energy Aware ICT Optimization Policies. COST Action IC0804 (2010)

Basmadjian, R., et al.: A Methodology to Predict the Power Consumption of Servers in Data Centres. ACM, New York (2011)

Basmadjian, R., De Meer, H., Lent, R., Giuliani, G.: Cloud Computing and Its Interest in Saving Energy: the Use Case of a Private Cloud. J. Cloud Comput. Adv. 1(5), 1–25 (2012a)

Basmadjian, R., Niedermeier, F., De Meer, H.: Modelling and Analysing the Power Consumption of Idle Servers. IFIP (2012b)

Basmadjian, R., et al.: A Generic Architecture for Demand Response: The ALL4Green Approach. IEEE, New York (2013a)

Basmadjian, R., et al.: Green SDAs Leveraging Energy Adaption Collaboration Between Energy Provider and Data Centres. IFIP (2013b)

Basmadjian, R., Mueller, L., De Meer, H.: Data Centres' Power Profile Selecting Policies for Demand Response: Insights of Green Supply Demand Agreement. Ad Hoc Netw Spec Issue Energy Aware Data Centers Archit. Infrastruct. Commun. 25, 581–594 (2014)

Basmadjian, R., Niedermeier, F., De Meer, H.: Modelling Performance and Power Consumption of Utilisation-based DVFS Using M/M/1 Queues. ACM, New York (2016)

Belady, C., Amd, A.R., Dell, J.P., Spraycool, T.C.: Green Grid Data Center Power Efficiency Metrics: PUE and DCIE, the green grid. (2008)

Clark, C., et al.: Live Migration of Virtual Machines. (2005)

Evans, T.: The Different Types of Air Conditioning Equipment for IT Environments. APC (2004)

Fischer, A., Fessi, A., Carle, G., De Meer, H.: Wide-Area Virtual Machine Migration as Resilience Mechanism. IEEE (2011)

Ghatikar, G., et al.: Demand Response and Open Automated Demand Response Opportunities for Data Centers. Lawrence Berkeley National Laboratory, Berkeley (2010)

Goldberg, M.L., Agnew, K.: Measurement and Verification for Demand Response. US Department of Energy, Washington DC (2013)

Hintemann, R., Fichter, K., Stobbe, L.: Materialbestand der Rechenzentren in Deutschland. Umwelt Bundesamt (2010)

Hölzle, U., Barroso, L.A.: The Case for Energy-Proportional Computing. Computer. 40(12), 33–37 (2007)

Janacek, S. & Nebel, W., 2016. Expansion of data centers' energetic degrees of freedom to employ green energy sources. In: Advances and New Trends in Environmental and Energy Informatics. s.l.Cham :Springer, 21–38

Klingert, S., et al.: Sustainable Energy Management in Data Centers Through Collaboration. Springer, Berlin/New York (2012)

Klingert, S., et al.: Renewable Energy-Aware Data Centre Operations for Smart Cities – The DC4Cities Approach. IEEE (2015)

Kuusisto, O.: Thermal Guidelines for Data Processing Environments – Expanded Datacenter Classes and usage Guidance. ASHRAE (2011)

Li, L., Zheng, W., Wang, X. Wan, X.: Coordinating Liquid and Free Air Cooling with Workload Allocation for Data Center Power Minimization. (2014)

Meijer, G.: Cooling energy-hungry data centers. Science. **328**(5976), 318–319 (n.d.)

Niedermeier, F., Kazhamiaka, F., De Meer, H.: Energy Supply Aware Power Planning for Flexible Loads. ACM, Waterloo (2016)

Patterson, M.K., Fenwick, D.: The State of Data Center Cooling: A Review of Current Air and Liquid Cooling Solutions. Intel Corporation (2008)

Pedram, M.: Energy-efficient datacenters. IEEE Trans. Comput. Aided Des. Integr. Circuits Syst. **31**(10), 1465–1484 (2012)

Piette, M.A., et al.: Open Automated Demand Response Communications Specification (Version 1.0). (2009)

Pore, M., Abbas, Z., Gupta, S.K.S., Varsamopoulos, G.: Techniques to achieve energy proportionality in data centers: a survey. In: Handbook on Data Centers, pp. 109–162. Springer, New York (2015)

Schomaker, G., Janacek, S., Schlitt, D.: The energy demand of data centers. In: ICT Innovations for Sustainability, pp. 113–124. Springer, Cham (2015)

Siano, P.: Demand response and smart grids—a survey. Renew. Sust. Energy Rev. **30**, 461–478 (2014)

Robert Basmadjian holds a Ph.D. from University of Toulouse on data replication. After completing his doctorate, in 2009 he joined University of Passau and since then he has been as a postdoctoral fellow, where his main research interests are large-scale energy management systems (Smart Grid), and performance modelling of computing systems (queuing theory). He has more than 25 scientific publications in the respective fields. He was a scientific and technical contributor to EU FP7 FIT4Green and ALL4Green projects related to Demand Response in data centers. Moreover, he was an active member of WG 2 and 3 of COST ACTION 804, EURONF and EINS.

Florian Niedermeier achieved his Diploma degree in computer science at the University of Passau in Germany in 2009. Since then, he is research and teaching assistant as well as PhD student at the chair of computer networks and communications, led by Prof. Hermann de Meer. He is interested in research on energy systems, virtualization and smart grids. He was involved in several national and international projects concerning energy efficiency and demand side management, recently EU FP7 projects "All4Green" and "DC4Cities".

Hermann de Meer received his PhD degree in Computer Science from University of Erlangen-Nuremberg. He held postdoctoral research positions at Hamburg University, UT at Austin, Duke University and Columbia University. After his Readership at University College London (UCL) he was appointed Professor at University of Passau in 2003. His area of research comprises Computer Networking and Energy Systems. Special focus has been on Network Virtualization, IT-Security of the Smart Grid, Demand Side Management, E-Mobility, Industry Automation, Resilience and Risk Management of Distributed Systems.

DevOps: Foundations and Its Utilization in Data Center

Mirna Muñoz and Oswaldo Díaz

Abstract Nowdays the importance of the term DevOps (Developer Operations) has been increasing around the world, and Mexico is not the exception. This chapter describes the DevOps approach established in a Data Center of Mexico of a large Mexican governmental organization. The DevOps approach proposed aims to produce a seamless bridge and path between the software development teams and the release and deployment teams at Data Centers for developing and releasing software products. The approach was developed taking into account the process, the people and the technology. Therefore, the foundations, phases, activities, roles and artifacts are described. Besides, the chapter also reports benefits and challenges found in two illustrative real cases implemented in a large Mexican governmental organization data centers. Finally, the main recommendations and cautions in the implementation of a DevOps approach are reported.

1 Introduction

Nowadays, enterprise applications are so diverse and composed of multiple technologies, databases, end-user devices, and so on that integration targeting product delivery, continuous testing, quality testing, feature development, and releases are performed by large organizations in order to improve reliability and security and provide faster development and deployment cycles. In this context, the term DevOps arises as a solution.

The term DevOps is a mix of two words, developers and Operations that arises from the need of building software systems with a reduction on the time for market delivery. According to Lwakatare, et al. in (Lwakatare et al. 2015) DevOps has been

M. Muñoz
Mathematic Research Center, Av. Universidad no 222, 98068 Zacatecas, Mexico
e-mail: mirna.munoz@cimat.mx

O. Díaz (✉)
Group of Systems Engineering, National Institute of Statistics and Geography,
2301 Aguascalientes, Mexico
e-mail: oswaldo.diaz@inegi.org.mx

© Springer International Publishing AG 2017   205
J. Marx Gómez et al. (eds.), *Engineering and Management of Data Centers*,
Service Science: Research and Innovations in the Service Economy,
DOI 10.1007/978-3-319-65082-1_10

identified as key aspect toward a continuous deployment paradigm. Besides, Manish in (Virmani 2015) mention that DevOps arises as a solution to the problem of optimize the delivery lifecycle, so that, all the pieces of the delivery lifecycle can work as a well-oiled machine.

DevOps (Development Operations) is a process for software development whose emphasis is on collaboration, communication, automation and integration being a way of how the cooperation between the IT professional and the software developers can be reinforced. In this process, there is interdependency between the members of the software development team. Due to this, the development team finds possible to develop and deliver software rapidly and to improve the performance of various operations through the software development cycle.

DevOps is based on the lean and agile principle, which encourages the collaboration of business owners and the development, operations, and quality assurance departments to deliver software in a continuous way, so that, it enables the business to get a quickly advantage of the market opportunities and to reduce the time needed to include customer's feedback.

Based on the above mentioned, this chapter aims to provide a DevOps approach developed in a large Mexican governmental organization, where, DevOps allowed establishing integration between the processes and procedures based on information technologies in accordance with a specific vision and strategy of tolerance for change in continuous improvement.

The rest of the chapter is structured as follows: after introduction, Sect. 2 gives a brief introduction to the DevOps history; Sect. 3 presents the proposed DevOps approach; Sect. 4 provides a set of examples of how the approach has been implemented in the organization; Sect. 5 reports a set of the main recommendations and cautions in the implementation of a DevOps approach, and finally, Sect. 6 present the conclusions.

2 Data Centers

A Data Center is a facility within an organization that centralizes the organizational operations and the IT equipment in which the information is stored, managed and deployed (Robertazzi 2012). Data Centers host the most critical systems of an organization, so that they are of vital importance for the day-to-day operation continuity (Robertazzi 2012). Therefore, reliability and security have a high priority in data centers (Kant and Mohapatra 2004).

Although data center designs are unique, they can be classified according to their domain of application in two types: internet-oriented and enterprise or internal (Callou et al. 2014). On the one hand, the internet-oriented data centers support few applications typically browser-based and they often have many unknown users. On the other hand, the enterprise data centers support more applications that go from standards to customized applications, and, they have few well-known users.

Data Centers' requirements and architectures may differ significantly, e.g. a cloud service provider data center satisfies requirements of facilities, infrastructure and security significantly different from a private data center. However, independently of its classification, an effective operation in a data center is achieved through a balanced investment in the facilities and the allocated equipment. The elements that regulate data center services are:

- *Physical architecture:* it refers to the usable location and/or space that is available to the IT team. The access to the information makes data centers some of the most energy-consuming facilities in the world. Then, special emphasis is made on the design to optimize the space and the environmental control to keep the equipment within the temperature and humidity range specified by the manufacturer. Additionally, an environmental control (air conditioners, ventilation – heating) must be implemented for the servers.
- *Support Infrastructure:* it refers to the equipment that contributes to safely maintaining the highest possible level of availability. The Uptime Institute defines four levels of data centers regarding the availability ranging from 99.671% to 99.995%. Therefore, uninterruptible power supplies such as redundant battery bank must be implemented.
- *Computer equipment:* it refers to the real equipment for performing IT operation and organization's data storage, including the servers and hardware storage, as well as a variety of information security items (e.g. biometrics and video recording systems).
- *Operating staff:* it refers to the staff that share, monitor and maintain IT and equipment infrastructure available all day according to specific and strategic schedules depending on the business process.

Figure 1 presents an IT data center infrastructure.

It is important to mention that data centers have evolved significantly in recent years, adopting technologies such as virtualization to optimize the resources utilization and to increase the IT flexibility (Callou et al. 2014).

As IT organizations' needs continue to evolve toward on-demand services, progress in data centers are being made toward cloud-based services and infrastructure (Fylaktopoulos et al. 2016).

In this context, attention has also been focused on initiatives to reduce the great amount of energy consumption in data centers by incorporating more efficient technologies and practices in the management of data centers in order to minimize the environmental impact (Cook et al. 2012). Data centers built in accordance with these standards are refered as "Green Data Centers" (De Meer et al. 2012).

3 DevOps Approach

3.1 Introduction

In 1961, NASA enlisted Margaret Hamilton to lead the development of critical software. To provide a solution to write the critical software, she instituted a set of requirement gathering that included (Debugging all individual component, testing individual components prior to assembly, and integration testing).

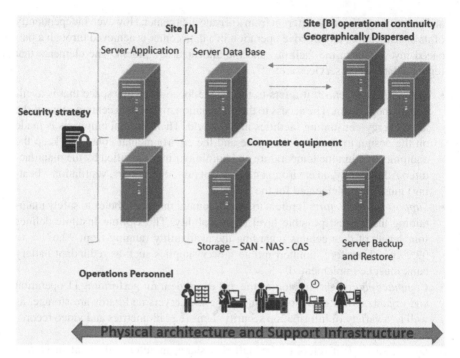

Fig. 1 Example of IT data center infrastructure

In 1968, at the NATO Software Engineering Conference, the key problems with software engineering were identified including (defining and measuring success, building complex systems requiring large investment and unknown feasibility, producing systems on schedule and to specification, economic pressures on manufacturers to build specific products).

The DevOps approach arose from the need of the IT department to give an agile response regarding the implementation and operation of software engineering and hardware projects, so that, it allowed the IT department the adoption of a culture in which the life cycle is accelerated, a set of best practices, focused on reducing risks in critical projects, are integrated in a framework and, the productivity is increased.

The DevOps was implemented with the goal of providing a communication-collaboration strategy that enabled the institution to establish a feedback based on best practices of project management and risks management processes regarding the processes and procedures automation, taking into account people and technologies, so that it was possible the establishment of quantitative and qualitative service levels, fault-tolerance agreements, continuous improvement, as well as the project management life cycle that allows adopting software engineering practices in an efficient way.

3.2 DevOps Approach

The DevOps approach proposed in this chapter was developed taking into account three key elements: the process, the people and the technology. To achieve the goal for establishing the strategy the best practices provided by the framework workflow secure development lifecycles and Risk management proposed in (Curphey and Groves 2015) was taken as the strategy base, so that, the developed strategy involves:

- *People:* the definition of a set of roles and responsibilities.
- *Process:* the definition of a set of activities, deliverables and control methods.
- *Knowledge:* the adaptation of knowledge contained on standards and guidelines, compliance and transfer methods according to the organization's business process.
- *Tools and Components:* the definition of development support, assessment tools and management tools.

As Fig. 2 shows, it consists of three phases: development, quality assurance and technology operations. Next, the three phases are briefly described.

3.3 Development (Software Engineering)

In a DevOps context, the development cycle involves the use of software engineering practices that give a solution to the problem slow releases (Lwakatare et al. 2015; Virmani 2015; Bass et al. 2015; Forsgren and Humble 2016). Then, the use of agile methods is strongly linked with the use of a DevOps strategy.

The company used to use waterfall methodology that develops software with an emphasis on a sequential progression from one stage of the methodology to the next and that each phase of the methodology should be completely finished before starting the next. Besides, this methodology promotes the idea that is better to fix bugs at the earlier stages in which they are discovered.

The original stages performed in the company to develop software were: requirements specification, design, implementation, integration, testing, installation, and maintenance, in which the progress of the project was visualized as flowing from one stage to the next.

To achieve a development that reduces the time of release, our strategy changes from a waterfall methodology to an agile methodology. The selected methodology was scrum.

Scrum is an agile methodology that emphasizes in collaboration, functioning software, team self-management, and the flexibility to adapt to emerging changes (Gloger 2014). In a DevOps context from the software-development viewpoint, scrum focuses on sprint cycles that allow frequent hassle-free deployments (IBM Software 2014).

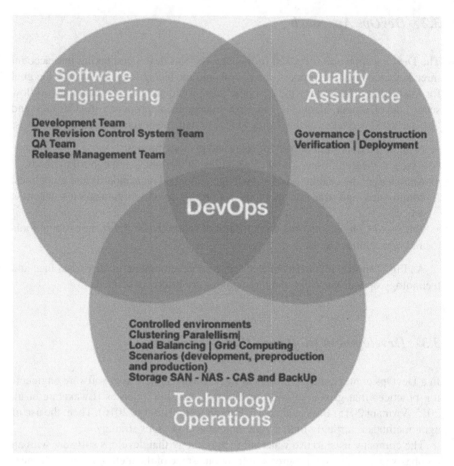

Fig. 2 Phases of the DevOps strategy

3.3.1 Scrum Interaction Workflow Framework

The scrum workflow defined for the organization contains six phases: requirement gathering and feedback, design, development, testing, deployment and retrospective. As Fig. 3 shows all phases are performed in an interactive way. Besides, Table 1 briefly describes each phase.

It is important to mention that the use of scrum allows starting a change propagating it through the continuous delivery pipeline toward test systems and beyond when it is deemed ready enough to start that journey (IBM Software 2014).

Moreover, the use of the scrum methodology reinforces the team's work because teams should have a meeting every day in the morning to select the set of activities to be performed from a dashboard in which all the project activities are included by sprint cycles. Besides, during this daily meeting all restrictions or contingencies that arise through the progress of the project should be analyzed and resolved.

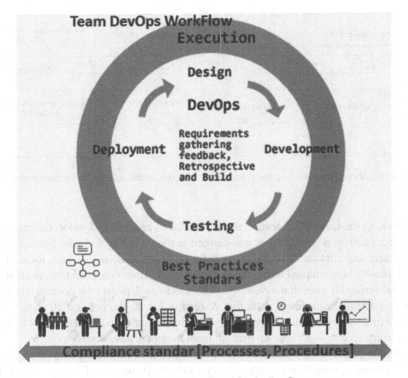

Fig. 3 Scrum interaction workflow framework tailored for the DevOps strategy

Table 1 Scrum interaction workflow framework definition

Phase	Description
Design	In this phase the team defines compliance rules and a schedule with commitment dates according to the requirements of the process to be automated to publish them in an IT controlled environment.
Development	In this phase the team develops the automated process based on software engineering practices and taking into account the hardware that is defined as part of the "Design", so that a significant advance named as "Beta" is delivered to interact with the testing process.
Testing	In this phase the team makes a strategic plan and specific tests based on the project requirements and taking into account the "Beta" version and the feedback of all detected eventualities
Deployment	In this phase the team publishes and controls the version of the project named as "Release" in a controlled IT environment.
Retrospective	In this phase the team makes an assessment of the risk analysis based on eventualities detected in the testing phase and takes the decisions to mitigate or to face the risks.
Requirements gathering and feedback	In this phase the team performs an interactive face to face meeting to determine the project performance, of both progress and delay, in order to speed-up the processes and procedures so that the delivery schedule can be met.

Development (1)				Testing (2)				Deployment (3)				(4) Requirements gathering & Feedback			
To do	In Process	To validate	Done	To do	In Process	To validate	Done	To do	In Process	To validate	Done	To do	In Process	To validate	Done
Involved Role (5)				Involved Role (6)				Involved Role (7)				Strategies and Current Issues (8)			

Fig. 4 Dashboard for analyzing and reporting the progress of the agile project management

To help the team to achieve it, the dashboard to analyze and report the progress of the agile project management was defined as shown in Fig. 4. As the figure shows, the dashboard contains 10 columns as follows: From column 1 to 4 are focused on each phase of the adapted scrum development cycle; from column 5 to 8 are focused on registering all roles that have responsibilities in each phase; the column 9 is used for registering requirement gathering & feedback and; the column 10 is used for registering strategies and current issues. It is important to mention that this form is performed as a digital sheet, so that, all team members have access to it.

Besides, a set of best practices were established to reinforce the adoption and use of our scrum interaction workflow framework. Next, the set of best practices are described:

- *The project progress and agreements under workflow are analyzed in the daily morning meeting to size new requirements or eventualities:* in today's workplaces, with increasing demands for both improving the product performance and reducing the costs, individuals face a great amount of competing demands. Therefore, they should be able to focus their time and attention on what their goals are. Besides, the conflicts that will arise from these demands will need to be resolved somehow. Then, these practices helps to reinforce negotiation styles such as competing, collaborating, compromising, avoiding and accommodating helping the team members to build a better relationship.
- *Avoiding unnecessary competition:* competition occurs naturally where people are coexisting or sharing the same space. It's not necessarily a negative thing, but the lack of shareable goals means that it does not lead them toward accomplishing the same goals. If people on a team are focused on competing without any kind of collaboration, the results of the team performance will be less optimal with increased time to market, decreased innovation, and decreased morale.
- *Look for avoidance dynamics:* avoidance dynamics can be observed in multiple ways such as high tension between individuals; lack of depth in communication and issues resolution; a deficient or a lack of set goals; unfulfilled commitments; and missed deadlines. A monitoring to identify avoidance dynamics should be defined to implement corrective actions.

Tool	Use rules for Communication channels				
	URGENCY	AUDIENCE REACH	INVESTMENT	CONTEXT REQUIRED	ORGANIZATION
email	Low	High	Medium	High	Medium
Impromptu in-person (or video)	High	Low	Medium	Low	Low
Chat	Medium	Medium	Low	High	Low
Meeting	Very Low	High	High	Low	High
Twitter	Low	Medium	Low	High	Low
Github pull request	Low	Medium	Medium	Medium	Medium
Post-it notes	Very Low	Medium	Low	High	Low
pagerDuty pages	High	High	High	Medium	Low
Nagios Alters	Medium	High	High	Medium	Low
Books or Blog post	Very Low	Low	Medium	Medium	High
Pictures, graphs and gifts	Low	Low	Low	High	Low

Fig. 5 Rules used to select communication channels and tools (Davis and Daniels 2015)

- *Reinforce the individual's compromise:* it involves individuals of the team helping one another by each giving up something of value to get something of value. It is important that each team member understand that when only one side is giving something up, this is not a true compromise.
- *Reinforce the individual's collaboration:* it involves individuals of the team working to achieve shared goals including the knowledge sharing and learning as well as building consensus among the individuals involved.
- *Reinforce communication:* it involves the provision of adequate communication channels because without effective communication channels, neither the shared goals, nor strategies taken to improve the team, nor the contingency plans can be successful. The use of the communication channels and tools are addressed by the rules defined in (Davis and Daniels 2015) and are shown in Fig. 5.

3.3.2 Roles

To be able to perform in a correct way our DevOps strategy, it was necessary to define a set of strategic roles. Table 2 shows a summary of the roles defined. Besides, next to the table, each role is briefly defined. As Table 2 shows, four areas defined the strategy roles so that all the phases of our framework are covered. The areas are development team, monitoring and control system team, quality and assurance team, and release management team in which a total of 11 roles were defined.

Development Team Strategic Roles The team of this area is focused on developing software within production environments. In the ideal context, this team should have production-like environments available to work with in both locally on their workstations or laptops. Depending on the type of software that is being developed, this might actually be possible, but it's more common to simulate, or mock the parts

Table 2 Strategic roles

Development team	The revision and control system team	QA team	Release management team
Architect UML strategies by source code. [objects, class and apps] Architect database information [relational and no-relational]	Continuous integration Source management Artifact repository control version by process and calendar strategy	Staging environments Integration testing [performance and scalability] Management repository information issues and solutions	Operation team SysAdmin [system operation + storage + network] DBA's [database administration] Webmaster deployment environments production

of the production environments that are hard to replicate, for example, the development of systems such as external payment systems or phone hardware.

Working with DevOps and depending on if you emphasize on simulate or mock the parts of the production environments, it is better to have a prepackaged developer environment and work with it. This is a best practice since otherwise developers might spend a lot of time in creating their development environments.

For this team, two roles were defined:

- *Architect UML role:* it is responsible for implementing a strategy to automate processes based on diagramming the processes according to the business goals and the software engineering requirements in order to transform them in objects, class and apps.
- *Architect Database Information role:* it is responsible for sizing the project requirement based on data modeling best practices and taking into account relational and non-relational strategies.

The Revision Control System Team Strategic Roles The team of this area is often the heart of the development environment. They are in charge of storing the code that forms the organization's software products. Besides, they store the configurations that form the infrastructure. And, working on hardware development, this team might also store the designs of the revision control system being a vital part of the organization's infrastructure.

Working with DevOps and taking into account that there is a surprisingly little variation in the choice of product, it is common that organizations use Github or are switching to it, especially those using proprietary systems reaching end-of-life. For this team, three roles were defined:

- *Continuous Integration role:* it is responsible for integrating and performing ongoing reviews to avoid delays in the tasks assigned to the team.
- *Source Management role:* it is responsible for implementing a strategy based on the record of logbooks to control the versions issued by the working group.
- *Artifact Repository Control Version by process and calendar strategy role:* it is responsible for implementing a software version control based on delivery dates and relevant changes taking into account the project management life cycle.

QA – Team Strategic Roles The team of this area installs the artifacts into the test environments. After the build server has stored them in the binary repository. It is important to highlight that the test environments should normally be as production-like as feasible.

When working with DevOps, it is desirable to install and configure test environments with the same methods as production servers were installed. For this team, three roles were defined:

- *Staging Environments role:* it is responsible for installing new releases on the staging servers, checking that everything works, and then, swapping out the old production servers and replace them with the staging servers, which will then become the new production servers. The activities performed by this team are sometimes called the blue-green deployment strategy.
- *Integration Testing role:* it is responsible for implementing a strategic plan based on testing best practice indicators for decision-oriented performance and scalability of the IT infrastructure decisions.
- *Management Repository Information Issues and Solutions role:* it is responsible for implementing a strategy to generate a knowledge database regarding the eventualities - issues that have arisen in the operation flow of the project processes based on software engineering, in order to learn from mistakes.

Release Management Team Strategic Roles The team of this area controls the IT infrastructure scenarios (pre and production) where the projects are hosted based software engineering. For this team, four roles were defined:

- *Operation Team role:* it is responsible for maintaining the operation of the project in the established scenarios, based on business processes service levels agreements.
- *SysAdmin role:* it is responsible for maintaining the operation of the IT infrastructure based on network connectivity, telecommunications, storage and other necessary items for integrating the information based on the software engineering implemented components.
- *DBA's role:* it is responsible for managing the managers (DataBase Administration – software) where organizational information is housed. Also, it is responsible for implementing cleaning mechanism and data extraction (ETL's) for data integrity.
- *Webmaster role:* it is responsible for publishing projects environments (pre and production) based on software engineering of the IT infrastructure implemented in the organization.

Finally, Fig. 6 shows the integration of the roles and Scrum interaction workflow framework for our DevOps strategy. As figure shows, the development team strategic roles are involved in the requirement phase; the revision control system team strategic roles are involved in the development and build phases; the QA team strategic roles are involved in the testing phase and, finally, the release management team strategic roles are involved in the deployment and execution phases.

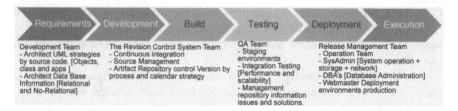

Fig. 6 DevOps lifecycle processes [Notation: Porter's Value Chain] (Bass et al. 2015)

3.4 Quality Assurance (QA)

In a DevOps context, the quality and assurance involves getting the ability to measure the development process by incorporating a set of metrics that allows seeking insights regarding the quality of the software processes and usefulness of software functionality but using real time performance and data of software functionality in the production environment so that, this area helps to increase the efficiency in the product development (Lwakatare et al. 2015).

To achieve it, there were established a set of processes were defined. It is important to highlight that the implemented strategy also includes a process that contains a set of best practices for security information. Therefore, our QA covers both the quality assurance and security.

The set of processes established as a part of our DevOps strategy are: governance, constructions, verification and deployment. Moreover, the processes definition was based on the methodology OWASP's Software Assurance Maturity Model (Owasp SAMM)[1] (Curphey and Groves 2015). Next, each process is briefly defined.

3.4.1 Governance

The governance process is focused on the activities related to how the organization manages overall software development activities. More specifically, this process includes the management of issues that can arise among cross-cut groups involved in development as well as business processes that are established at the organization level.

The governance process allows our DevOps strategy having quantitative and qualitative indicators based on the compliance policies and controls, so that, control dashboards for decision-making are generated.

---

[1] It is a methodology that enables organizations to steadily improve their software security posture over the time. As a result organizations of all sizes and across every industry rely on web, mobile and cloud applications as a source of strategic differentiation and competitive advantage.

The process has three main activities:

- *Implemented strategy and metrics:* it involves the overall strategic management of the software assurance program as well as the instrumentation of processes and activities to collect metrics about an organization's security position.
- *Implemented Policy & Compliance:* it involves setting up a security and compliance control; as well as, an audit framework throughout the organization to achieve an increasing assurance in software under operation and construction.
- *Implemented Education & Guidance:* it involves increasing the security knowledge of the software development personnel through training and guidance on security topics relevant according to individual job functions.

3.4.2 Construction

The construction process is focused on activities related to how the organization defines goals and creates software within development projects. In general, this process includes the product management, requirements gathering, high-level architecture specifications, detailed design, and implementation.

The construction process allows our DevOps strategy setting the security levels taking into account internal and external policies based on the organizational standards, as well as, the technological trends in hardware and software in which the organization has maturity, so that that, the adoption of them does not imply a delay in performing the organization's projects.

This process has three main activities:

- *Threat Assessment:* it involves an accurate identification and characterization of potential attacks upon an organization's software in order to achieve a better understanding of the risks and therefore, facilitate the establishment of risk management.
- Security Requirements: it involves promoting the inclusion of security-related requirements during the software development process in order to specify the correct software functionality since the beginning of its development.
- *Secure Architecture:* it involves reinforcing the design process with activities that promote secure-by-default designs and the control of them over the technologies and frameworks in which the software is built.

3.4.3 Verification

The verification process is focused on the activities related to how an organization checks and tests the artifacts produced throughout software development. This process typically includes quality assurance activities such as testing, but it can also include other activities related to review and assessment.

The verification process allows our DevOps strategy to establish a test plan in conjunction with the team leader and to take into account project aspects regarding the best practices of code engine and the performance profile focused on the compliance of base lines established by the organization (example: Model–View–Controller (MVC[2])).

This process has three main activities:

- *Design Review:* it involves the inspection of the artifacts created from the design process to ensure the provision of adequate security mechanisms and their adherence according to the organization's security expectations.
- *Code Review:* involves assessment of an organization's source code to aid vulnerability discovery and related mitigation activities as well as to establish a baseline for secure coding expectations.
- *Security Testing:* it involves testing the organization's software in its runtime environment in order to discover both the software vulnerabilities and a minimum standard that should be established for the software releases.

3.4.4 Deployment

The deployment process involves the activities related to how an organization manages the software releases. This process involves shipping the products to end users, deploying products to internal or external hosts, as well as the normal operations of software in the runtime environment.

The deployment process allows our DevOps strategy to establish fault tolerant environments for the publication of projects, managing vulnerabilities and exceptions based on computer security metrics, performing hardening[3] level layers for the components involved in the project, and having a monitoring of processes, resources, and the staff involved in the organization.

This process has three main activities:

- *Vulnerability Management:* it involves establishing consistent processes for managing internal and external vulnerability reports to limit exposure and gathering data to improve the security assurance program.
- *Environment Hardening:* it involves implementing controls for the operating environment that surrounds the organization's software to strengthen the security posture of applications that have been deployed.
- *Operational Enablement:* it involves identifying and capturing security-relevant information needed by an operator to properly configure, deploy, and run the organization's software.

---

[2] It is a software design pattern for implementing user interfaces on computers. It divides a software application into three interconnected parts, so that it is possible to separate internal representations of information from the way that information is presented to or accepted by the user.

[3] In computing, hardening is usually the process of securing a system by reducing its vulnerability, which is larger when a system performs more functions. A single-function system is more secure than a multipurpose one. Reducing available ways of attack typically includes changing default passwords, the removal of unnecessary software, unnecessary usernames or logins, and the disabling or removal of unnecessary services.

3.5 Infrastructure Technology

In a DevOps environment it should be taken care of the infrastructure based on the visualize processing, information storage, and the specific and strategic information transfer requirements with the goal of spreading the products or services generated in a safely and timely way. To achieve it, that, the next consideration should be taken into account:

3.5.1 Controlled Environments

Controlled environments should be established for the development, preproduction and production sceneries that aim to separate the applications and the databases in order to reduce the risk. Next, a list of them is included:

- The servers' services can be physical or virtual, depending on the needs and economic budget.
- The storage should be divided using access policies and taking into account technologies such as Storage Area Network (SAN), Network Attached Storage (NAS) or Content Attached Storage (CAS).
- A strategy for load balancing should be established when the project has concurrent users.
- Policies for backup and restore contingency plans should be established.
- Strategies for risk reduction based on the organization needs should be established.
- Security mechanisms should be taken into account for the infrastructure defined by the organization such as: High availability grid computing and/or a cluster; Active Directory; System Operation; Sensors; RFID; Virtual Machine; Web Server; App Server; Database Server; Security Devices and Network Geographic.

3.5.2 DevOps and ITIL

ITIL is an acronym of Information Technology Infrastructure Library. It is a set of practices for IT Service Management (ITSM) that focuses on aligning IT services with the business needs. Its current version contains a series of five core volumes, each volume covers a different ITSM lifecycle stage (ITIL/OGC 2010).

ITIL describes processes, procedures, tasks, and checklists that are not defined by a specific organization, but that can be applied by an organization for establishing integration with the organization's strategy, delivering value, and maintaining a minimum level of competency (ITIL/OGC 2010).

ITIL allows the organization to establish a baseline for planning, implementing, and measuring. Moreover, it is used to demonstrate services levels compliance and to measure their improvement (ITIL/OGC 2010).

In our DevOps strategy ITIL v3 enables the operation of IT infrastructure, so that, IT infrastructure is referenced using qualitative and quantitative indicators to generate information for decision-making based on best practices. Therefore, the next qualitative and quantitative indicators for managing IT infrastructure were described:

- *Incident Management:* it allows restoring and/or resolving as quickly and efficiently as possible any incident that causes an interruption in service.
- *Problem Management:* it covers both the reactive and the proactive problems. For reactive problems, it allows analyzing the incidents to discover their cause and to propose solutions. For proactive problems, it allows monitoring the quality of the IT infrastructure and analyzing its configuration in order to prevent incidents even before they occur.
- *Change Management:* it allows solving known errors, developing new services and improving existing services.
- *Release Management:* it allows implementing and controlling quality of all software and hardware installed in the production environment.
- *Assets Management:* it allows maintaining assets inventories for decision-making based on the acquisition processes, the life cycle of projects and the technology trends.
- *Service Level Management:* it allows maintaining the quality of IT services, aligning the technology with business processes at a reasonable cost for the organization.

4 Examples of DevOps Approach Implementation

4.1 Mood of the Tweeters from the Twitter Social Network in Mexico

- *Overview:* as part of the activities performed by the National Institute of Statistics and Geography (INEGI, by its spanish acronym) (National Institute of Statistic and Geography 2014a) it was necessary to identify indicators in practical applications of Data Science aimed to solve Big Data problems for decision-making based on quantitative and qualitative behavior using tools based on software engineering.
- *Business need:* in order to manage all elements involved in the work teams such as people, processes and technology, it was necessary to implement a collaborative way of work among various government institutions to feedback the data for processing.
- *Solution:* implementing a DevOps strategy enabled INEGI to generate a collaborative environment based on software engineering standards; best practices and the information technology and infrastructure, that is implemented in fault tolerant controlled environments and in environments of risk management. Figure 7 shows the DevOps solution.

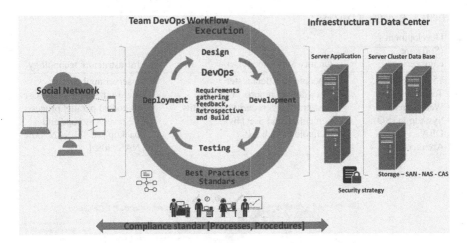

Fig. 7 DevOps processes (drill down in expertise)

- *Benefits:* the benefits of implementing the DevOps solution are shown in Table 3.
- As the table shows, the DevOps solution enabled the organization to manage the workflow in two Data Centers (one in tier 3 and other in tier 4) and located in two scattered geographic points. Moreover, establishing a strategy for Disaster Recovery Planning [DRP], and Operational Continuity, the solution allows generating value to project management and risk management in all three areas.

4.2 Economic Census of 2014 Performed by the National Institute of Statistic and Geography, México

- *Overview:* As part of the activities performed by INEGI (National Institute of Statistic and Geography 2014b). It was necessary to identify the economic indicators for the Mexican government decision-making, for which automated processes should be carried out for capturing, validating and visualizing statistical data using tools based on Software Engineering.
- *Business need:* In order to manage all elements involved in the work teams such as people, processes and technology, it was necessary to implement a collaborative way of working at national level through the 32 Mexican states.
- *Solution:* implementing a DevOps strategy enables INEGI to generate a collaborative environment based on software engineering standards; best practices and the information technology and infrastructure, that is implemented in fault tolerant controlled environments and in environments of risk management. Figure 8 shows the DevOps solution.

Table 3 Benefits of DevOps

Development (Software engineering)	Quality assurance (QA)	Infrastructure technology
15 people Rol's: Team developer WebMaster SysAdmin (SO) DBA Architected	2 people Rol Beta tester They deliver reports of QA and best practices [security, scalability, perception and user] by technology web 2.0	2 server applications 1 cluster Server's database (8 nodes) parallel process. 1 Server's storage and backup [10 TB SAN: 60% NAS: 30%]

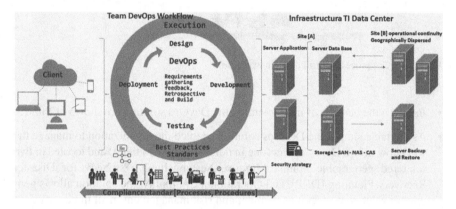

Fig. 8 DevOps processes (drill down in expertise)

- *Benefits:* the benefits of implement a DevOps strategy enables INEGI to manage a workflow of 32 Data Centers (Tier 2–4) located in different geographical points in Mexico. The DevOps solution allows establishing a strategy for Disaster Recovery Planning [DRP], and Operational Continuity and generating value to project management and risk management in the three areas as Table 4 shows.

One of the key aspects of a data center is to guarantee the processing, storing and deploying the information of an organization oriented to products or services in an automated way. The examples showed in this section highlight the benefits of DevOps as a solution to implement a strategy that allows establishing a level of services working together oriented to meet the needs among different IT areas of an organization. Then, A DevOps approach allows establishing a strategy through the iteration of workflows responsive and tolerant to failures. Besides, according to the experience we have had in the implementation of the DevOps approach, a set of recommendations have been identified and are showed in the next section.

Table 4 Benefits of DevOps

Development (Software engineering)	Quality assurance (QA)	Infrastructure technology
300 people Rol team developer 4 people Rol WebMaster 4 people Rol SysAdmin (SO) 4 people Rol SysAdmin (LAN, MAN,WAN) 4 people Rol DBA 32 people Rol architected	124 reports QA and best practices [security, scalability, perception and user] by technology web 2.0 and client-server 5 people Rol Beta tester	10 server applications 124 web containers 4 Server's database 2 Server's geographic information systems 2 server file transfer protocol 4 Server's E-mail services 4 Server's storage and backup [8.6 TB SAN: 52% NAS: 48%]

5   Main Recommendations and Cautions in the Implementation of a DevOps Approach

This section shows a set of lesson learned that we recommend taking into account in the implementation of a DevOps approach to maximize its powerfulness and performance.

- Use a common set of practices based on an agile methodology to maximize collaborative development between development and operation teams.
- Define a set of roles with responsibilities across the software development life cycle that promotes the enterprise-wide stakeholder collaboration.
- Define a set of processes that support all development life cycle from the governance politics to the deployment. Besides, they should include quality assurance practices and security.
- Deploy a set of organizational technologies and practices to be used through the development lifecycle.
- Automate of manual and overhead activities that push the continuous software delivery such as change spread and scoring, traceability, measurement, and the progress report while using the organization's technologies such as development, test, staging and production environments.
- Establish standards-based platforms that support the continuous software development life cycle feedback and improvement.
- Establish different communication channels to be used according to the communication needs that support the continuous software development life cycle.
- Define service levels for the organization's infrastructure technology using best practices of models and/or standards such as ITIL or ISO 20000.

6 Conclusions

Nowadays, Organizations are under pressure to achieve an advantage in the software development and delivery cycle to satisfy customer needs, and in Data Centers, which host the most critical systems of an organization, this pressure become critical element.

As a solution, DevOps offers an innovative and powerful solution to help an organization to reduce time for the software development life cycle, increasing quality, reducing risk and cost, and unifying process, culture and tools. Moreover, it enables an organization to reinforce and maximize the collaborative development between development and operation teams, integrating them with the use of organizational process and tools.

DevOps allows the interaction between organizational internal and external work areas generating added value getting a map of services oriented to risk management.

Finally, working under the DevOps strategy has allowed INEGI to establish communication between software engineers and information technology architects throughout the software development projects lifecycle, as well as, achieving stability in infrastructure, generating optimal service levels and reducing contingencies.

References

Bass L., Weber, I., Zhu L.: What is DevOps? In: Addison-wesley (eds.) DevOps a software Architect's perspective. SEI Series in Software Engineering. First version, pp.19–37 (2015)

Callou, G., Ferreira, J., Maciel, P., Tutsch, D., Souza, R.: An integrated modeling approach to evaluate and optimize data center sustainability, dependability and cost. Energies. 7, 238–277 (2014)

Cook, N., Milojicic, D., Talwar, V.: Cloud management. J. Internet Serv. Appl. 3, 67–75 (2012)

Curphey, M., Groves, D.: OWASP-SAMM (Open web application security project – software assurance maturity model) a guide to building security into software development Version 1.0 (2015)

Davis, J., Daniels, K.: Effective DevOps Building a Culture of Collaboration, Affinity, and Tooling at Scale. O'Reilly Media Inc, Beijing (2015)

De Meer, H., Klingert, S., Somov, A.: Energy efficient data centers, Springer link, ISBN: 978–3–642-33644-7 (Print) 978–3–642-33645-4 (Online) (2012)

Forsgren, N., Humble, J.: The role of continuous delivery in IT and organizational performance. In: Proceedings of the Western Decision Sciences Institute (WDSI) 2016, Las Vegas, NV, pp. 1–15 (2016). Available at SSRN: https://ssrn.com/abstract=2681909

Fylaktopoulos, G., Goumas, G., Skolarikis, M., Sotiropoulos, A., Maglogiannis, I.: An overview of platforms for cloud based development. SpringerPlus. 5(38), 2–13 (2016)

Gloger, B.: Scrum checklist. The hard facts: roles, artifacts. All meetings (2014)

IBM Software: DevOps: The IBM approach, Technical White paper RAW14323-USEN-01, pp 1–12 (2014)

ITIL/OGC: Scope and development plan Copyright TSO 2010. Retrived from: www.ogc.gov.uk (2010)

Kant, K., Mohapatra, P.: Internet data centers. Computer. IEEE Computer Society, pp 35–37 (2004)

Lwakatare, A.E., Kuvaja, P., Oivo, M.: Dimensions of DevOps. In: Lassenius, C., et al. (eds.) XP 2015, LNBIP 212, pp. 212–217, Cham, Springer International Publishing (2015)

National Institute of Statistic and Geography México: url http://www.inegi.org.mx/est/contenidos/proyectos/ce/ce2014/default.aspx (2014a)

National Institute of Statistic and Geography México: url http://www.inegi.org.mx/inegi/contenidos/investigacion/Experimentales/animotuitero/default.aspx (2014b)

Robertazzi, T.: Data Centers. In: Basics of Computer Networking, pp. 69–72. Springer, New York. Briefs in Electrical and Computer Engineering (2012)

Virmani, M.: Understanding DevOps & bridging the gap form continuous integration to continuous delivery. In Fifth international conference on Innovative Computing Technology (INTECH 2015), pp. 78–82 (2015)

Mirna Muñoz She is a PhD in Computer Science (Computer Languages, Informatics Systems and Software Engineering) from the Polytechnic University of Madrid. She has a Master in Computer Science from the Institute Technological of Orizaba University of México. She is working as a software engineering researcher at the Zacatecas Unit of the Mathematic Research Center in México. Her research field is Software Engineering. Her current research interest is on software process improvements focusing on the human factor, software process improvements using multimodel environments, the implementation of quality model and standards and the integration of high effective teams. She has collaborated in the translation of CMMI v1.2 and v1.3 to Spanish language. During her PhD she collaborated with everis consultants in research projects. She has published several technical papers on process improvement, project management, TSPi, CMMI and multi-model environments. She is the author of the book Multimodel methodology for implementing software process improvements.

Oswaldo Díaz He has been an Architect TI and Researcher for 18 years at the National Institute of Statistics and Geography (INEGI) México. He has expertise in processes oriented to DevOps for 32 Data Center nationwide and in Software Engineering performing 950 Web Technology Projects through 2005-2017 years, based on Risk Management and Security (Ethical (Hacking and Forensics) - Web 2.0, Mobile, Semantics, Cloud Computing).

Sustainable and Resilient Network Infrastructure Design for Cloud Data Centers

Ritchie Qi, William Liu, Jairo Gutierrez, and Mamta Narang

Abstract In this chapter we firstly review the state of the art of the data center networks (DCNs) topological structures and explain the challenges in this field, which motivates our work. Then we propose a method for evaluating the topological metrics related to network robustness and node centrality so as to identify the most critical nodes and links in DCNs, as well as measuring the overall DCN performance such as throughput, latency, packet drop ratio according to the various faults occurred in the network. Moreover, we have identified the energy consumption behaviours according to the change of DCN's internal structure. Our simulation studies showed that the DCN topology and traffic load have significant impact on its overall energy consumption and also on other network-related performance aspects.

1 Introduction

The trend of growing reliance on online services and the increasing demand for mobile devices have already converted many client-based applications into cloud services (Choo 2014).Therefore, data centers as the place where the service originates is increasingly the focus of service provisioning. Also, an efficient server arrangement and the appropriate placement of jobs can largely reduce the power consumption and the heat dissipation (Beitelmal and Patel 2007). According to a survey conducted by the Gartner Group, approximately 40% of data center's OPEX comes from the energy consumed by Information and Communications Technology (ICT) equipment, which is composed of computing servers (2/3) and communication links (1/3). The remainder 60% energy consumption comes from the cooling and

R. Qi • W. Liu (✉) • J. Gutierrez • M. Narang
Department of Information Technology and Software Engineering, School of Engineering,
Computer and Mathematical Sciences, Auckland University of Technology,
AUT Tower Level 1, 2-14 Wakefield St, Auckland 1010, New Zealand
e-mail: qjx167@hotmail.com; william.liu@aut.ac.nz;
jairo.gutierrez@aut.ac.nz; mnarang@aut.ac.nz

© Springer International Publishing AG 2017   227
J. Marx Gómez et al. (eds.), *Engineering and Management of Data Centers*,
Service Science: Research and Innovations in the Service Economy,
DOI 10.1007/978-3-319-65082-1_11

power distribution facilities, which constitute 45% and 15% respectively. On the other hand, the cooling costs generated by data center infrastructure ranges between two and five million dollar per year (Banerjee et al. 2011).Therefore an optimized data center architecture plays an important role in OPEX reduction (Kliazovich et al. 2012). Cloud computing is a natural evolution of the widespread adoption of virtualization, service-oriented architecture (SOA), and computing resources which are based on the networking paradigm. Cloud computing is a model for enabling convenient, ubiquitous, on-demand network access service to a shared pool of configurable computing resources (e.g., networks, storage, servers, applications, and services) that can be rapidly provisioned and released with minimal management effort or service provider interaction. The National Institute of Standard and Technology (NIST) (Mell and Grance 2010) states that the cloud computing resources are located in the data center and end users can reach the data centers through services and infrastructure providers. The IaaS (Infrastructure as a Service) is a provider that allows physical resources to be assigned and split dynamically by provisioning capacity in virtualization (Wang et al. 2012).There is an increasing number of companies that have already transferred their business to a cloud platform so as to mitigate the burden of management and maintenance of different resources (Wang et al. 2012). Furthermore, cloud computing follows a business model of "pay-as-you-go" strategy and the cloud users only pay for the services as they use them and based on the service type. On the other hand, the cloud computing infrastructure has critical key issues such as ensuring security and privacy of the hosted ICT resources and application data, meeting performance demands despite uncertainties, dynamic reliability, standardization, fault-tolerance, debugging, scalability, reducing operational costs, and carbon emissions (Sadashiv and Kumar 2011).

Reducing power consumption and energy dissipation have become significant concerns for making cloud services environmentally developable and sustainable (Berl et al. 2010). To elaborate, some recent research has investigated the optimization of energy utilization by monitoring the performance of virtualized ICT resources (e.g., servers) and hosted workload under variable CPU frequency (Elnozahy et al. 2002).Other approaches have focused on techniques of voltage adjustments by switching off unnecessary resources e.g., a display monitor, processors speed control, and using hibernate or sleep modes (Horvath et al. 2007). The data center core layer (Steere et al. 1999) is responsible of maintaining the connections to the remaining elements in a data center and the public Internet. While in the data center service layer, devices such as the router, Firewall, Ethernet switch, fiber channel switch, server load balancing (SLB), and volume based billing/control (VBB/VBC) are involved (Ge et al. 2013).

The rest of the book chapter is organized as follows. Section 2 surveys the state of the art of DCNs architectures. Section 3 presents the models of network performance and energy consumption. In Sect. 4 we conduct extensive simulation studies to reveal how the underlying network structure changes can impact on the overlay DCNs performance. The conclusion and layout of future work are drawn in Sect. 5.

2 Overview of Data Center Networks

A data center is the pool of servers linked together at one geographical location. It also has layers of networking that contain routers and switches connected to servers. According to (Google's Whitepaper 2011), the five key characteristics of cloud computing are: task centric, user centric, intelligence, powerfulness, and programmability. Cloud computing data centers employ virtualization technologies that allow scheduling of workloads on a smaller number of servers that may be better utilized, as different workloads may have different resource utilization footprints and may further differ in their temporal variations. According to (Gorti 2014), the demand for computing performance is increasing at an unprecedented speed which is prompted by realistic reasons. IBM reported that more than 90% of the data in this world has been generated within the past 2 years. To satisfy the growing demand for outstanding performance, an increasing amount of transistors has become the trend when manufacturing the cores. On the one hand, chips have become more and more complicated in order to make the cores much more powerful for computing tasks. On the other hand, the number of cores is increasing for each computing node, while the number of computing nodes in a computing platform is also increasing. Figures 1 and 2 below show the consequences of scale-in and scale-out respectively

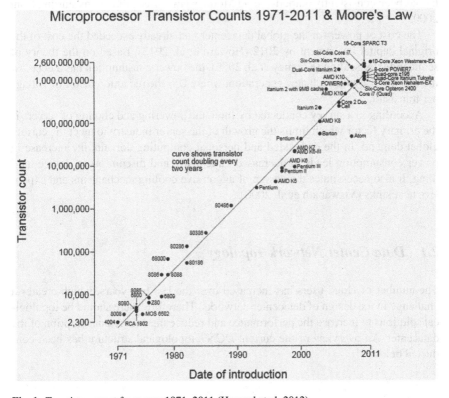

Fig. 1 Transistor count from year 1971–2011 (Howard et al. 2012)

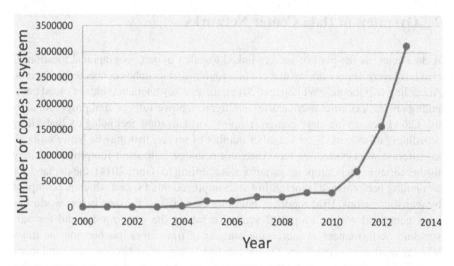

Fig. 2 Number of cores in system from year 2000–2014 (Viswanath et al. 2000)

in the IT industry over the last 14 years. In particular, we can observe that the industry has been consistently outperforming Moore's law-based predictions starting from 2000.

The cost of power for the global datacenter had already exceeded the cost of the original capital investment by 2012 (Howard et al. 2012). Based on the theory of semiconductor scaling (Koomey et al. 2009), the power consumption has a decreasing rate of U^2 with each new generation, where U is the reduction factor of voltage per transistor.

According to a survey conducted by Intel, the powering and cooling of servers is the primary factor which limits the growth of the server industry to meet the current global demand. In the embedded and personal computing domain, the increase in power consumption leads to decreased battery life and discomfort in device handling. It also necessitates the design of aggressive cooling mechanisms and expensive heat sinks (Viswanath et al. 2000).

2.1 Data Center Network Topology

The number of cloud users has increased over the last few years, which creates a challenge in the design of datacenter networks. Therefore, there should be topological solutions to increase the performance and reduce the energy consumption of the datacenter. An overview of the current DCN's topological structure has been conducted below.

2.1.1 Three-Tier

Three-tier DCN is the most commonly known architecture for cloud datacenters; it contains three layers of switches, including core, aggregate and access switches from the top to the bottom (Shang et al. 2002). The core layer allows for multiple aggregation switches to connect together, while aggregation layer switches are responsible for connecting access layer switches between each other. The access layer contains the connections between the pool of servers and access switches (Fig. 3).

2.1.2 Fat-Tree

Fat-tree DCN is the most widely adopted network configuration according to (Al-Fares et al. 2008); it follows the hierarchy architecture and contains a core, aggregate and access layers. This structure is composed of k pods, where in each pod there are (k/2) *2 servers, k/2 access layer switches, and k/2 aggregate layer switches. The core layers contain (k/2) *2 core switches, where each of the core switches is connected to one aggregate layer switch in each of the pods (Fig. 4).

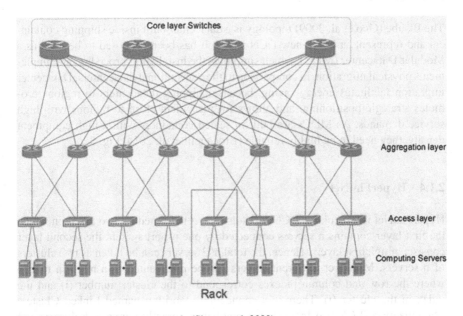

Fig. 3 Three tier architecture example (Shang et al. 2002)

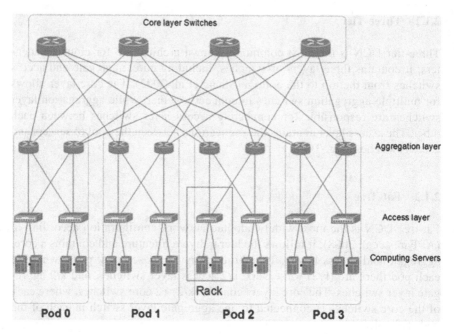

Fig. 4 Fat-tree DC architecture example (Al-Fares et al. 2008)

2.1.3 BCube

The BCube (Guo et al. 2009) topology is a datacenter built inside shipping containers and represents a brand-new DCN shape. It has been proposed to be used as a Modular Datacenter (MDC), which simplifies the installation procedure and implements physical migration, in comparison to the conventional datacenters. Datacenter migration facilitates energy saving, because shipping datacenters to regions promotes strategic positioning, and allows for placement close to regions with high service demands. As MDCs are built in sealed containers with a high equipment density, they need to be highly reliable (Brocanelli et al. 2014, Fig. 5).

2.1.4 HyperFlatNet

HyperFlatNet is a recursive DCN topology and it is formed by two layers in which the first layer contains n servers connected by one n-port switch; the second layer consists of n^2 first layers. Hence, the total n^3 servers can be taken as n^2 clusters of n servers. Moreover, different servers can be represented as a $n^2 * n$ matrix where the row and column indexes correspond to the cluster number (i) and the index in the cluster (j). There is a connection algorithm named Linked Clusters Maximization (LCM) to increase the number of directly connected clusters and reduce the number of intermediate hops used to transmit the packet to the destination. A 64-server HyperFlatNet DC architecture example is demonstrated in Fig. 6.

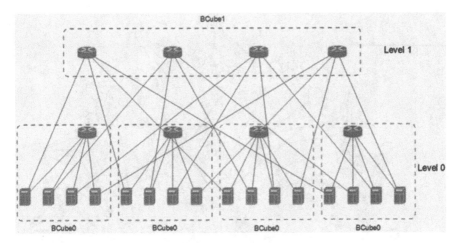

Fig. 5 BCube-2 layer DC architecture example (Guo et al. 2009)

Table 1 below summarizes the four DCN architectures. Both Three-tier and Fat-tree are Clos networks and have high transmission capacity, and BCube and HyperFlatNet are recursive networks which are highly reliable.

2.2 Traffic Load

When a cloud user accesses services such as instant messaging, content delivery, and social networking by using cloud applications from datacenters, a set of servers then generates different levels of workloads that are usually modelled as a sequence of jobs which can be divided into a set of tasks. The tasks are either dependent on the execution of other tasks, or independent. Furthermore, by the nature of grid computing applications such as biological, climate, or financial modelling, the jobs are usually computationally intensive, which needs high workloads to minimize the time required for the computation. The servers are Map-Reduced to accomplish this goal. Usually, the time taken to compute may vary by weeks or months when dealing with a large sequence of jobs. In cloud computing, the incoming requests generated are always less computationally intensive, but with a strict completion deadline based on the corresponding Service Level Agreement (SLA). The majority of cloud computing applications usually generate three types of jobs, which are as follows:

2.2.1 Computationally Intensive Workloads (CIWs)

This kind of job always requires High-Performance Computing (HPC) that aims to solve computation-intensive problems which load computing servers considerably (Choo 2014) e.g., huge data analysis which needs high computational ability from

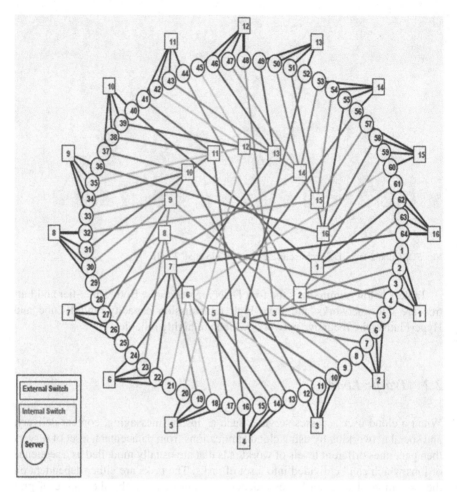

Fig. 6 HyperFlat bed

Table 1 Comparison of various DCN architectures

DCN type	No. of layer	No. of switch type	Architectural type	Characteristics	Cost level
Three-tier	3	3	Clos network, k-ary tree	High transmission capacity	Low cost
Fat-tree	3	3	Clos network, k-ary tree	High transmission capacity	Low cost
BCube	2	2	Recursive network	High equipment density, high reliable	Cost effective
HyperFlatNet	3	2	Recursive network	High performance	Cost effective

servers. Furthermore, CIWs also can be clustered into low data transferring (LDT) and high data transferring (HDT); the LDT requires less data transfers on the network so there is a very low probability of causing network congestion.

2.2.2 Data-Intensive Workloads (DIWs)

This type of job puts a heavy load on data transfers but produces almost no load at the computing servers (Choo 2014) For instance, the loads generated by the applications of video transferring or large file sharing from one simple user requires no computing capacity, but high demand for the interconnection of the DCN, so congestion always occurs through communication links for managing such jobs.

2.2.3 Balanced Workloads (BWs)

BWs are the jobs targeting applications that have both computing and data transfer requirements (Choo 2014). The computing servers are loaded proportionally to the communication links. The average load on servers therefore equals the average DCN load with this type of job.

2.3 Data Center Traffic Characteristics

Traffic in the datacenter is commonly flowing in three directions. The "North-South" traffic is usually flowing between end-users and servers, which is primarily comprised of traffic that enters and exits the datacenter, and generally contains commands, queries, and specific data either being retrieved or stored. Meanwhile, the "East-West" traffic, flows between DC nodes and applications that never leave the DC. It is primarily composed of communication between applications hosted on physical servers and virtual machines, coupled with virtual machine (VM) to VM, and physical to physical interactions within the DC. As the name implies, "Inter-DC" traffic is largely comprised of resource optimization and disaster recovery requirements between multiple DCs, and between DCs and the private/public cloud.

The Cisco's Global Cloud Index (Networking 2013) indicates that, the dominant volume of traffic in the DC traverses in an "East-West" direction (76%), followed by "North-South" traffic (17%), and finally, inter-DC traffic, which is currently only at 7%, but is gradually growing. Moreover, in campus networks, traffic is primarily (>90%) "North-South" traffic.

2.4   Energy Efficiency of Data Center Network

Reducing energy consumption is an important research topic and always a challenge for cloud computing organizations. Dynamic voltage and frequency scaling (DVFS) is the most common method in power management to deal with the challenge, where the supply voltage and frequency can be scaled dynamically within a computer component in order to achieve reduced energy consumption.

Dynamic Power Management (DPM) refers to a technique of selective shutdowns of systems for which components are in idle status or underutilized. Power management is a prediction problem; it seeks to forecast whether an idle period will be long enough to compensate for the overhead of power state changes. Although a server stays in an idle state, it generally consumes around 66% of energy compared to its full load energy consumption, which comes from the fixed component that is not related to the frequency but also consumes power.

2.5   Data Center Network Failures

Datacenter networks are subject to power failure, misconfiguration, firmware bugs, topology changes, cable damage, and malicious traffic. To implement failures concretely, each type of fault can be presented as component failures in a DC, where component failure is classified by link failure, server failure, rack failure, and switch failure. A server failure will immediately isolate the server from the rest of the network. A switch failure can cause significant influence on the network, as shown in Fig. 7 below. To implement failures concretely, each type of fault can be presented as component failures in a DC, where component failure is classified by link failure, server failure, rack failure, and switch failure. Figure 7 depicts the example of the fault types in a BCube DCN, where with under-redundant connections, a link failure cannot effectively stop the traffic between source node and destination node, and traffic can be still switched from an alternative route. A server failure will immediately isolate the server from the rest of the network.

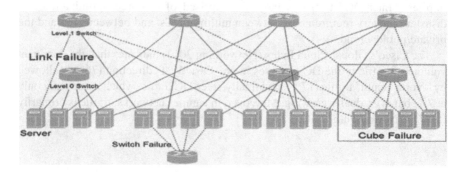

Fig. 7 DC component failure example

3 Topological Modelling and Metrics

A number of modelling and simulation techniques (Heymann 2014) are used to help us with our study. Both techniques are commonly used in networking due to the difficulties of experimenting with real configurations. The DCN architectures are modelled and studied by using the CloudNetSim++ (an extension of OMNeT++) cloud simulator, as well as the Gephi network analysis toolkit.

3.1 Network Modelling and Analysis Tools

OMNeT++ is an extensible, modular, component-based C++ simulation library and framework, with strong GUI support primarily for building communicational network simulation. It implements C++ language and offers powerful simulation class libraries. In OMNeT++, a network model consists of nested entities in hierarchical order which called modules. CloudNetSim++ (Malik et al. 2014) is a modeling and simulation toolkit to facilitate simulation of distributed datacenter architectures, energy models, and high speed data centers' communication network. It is the first cloud computing simulator that uses real network physical characteristics to model distributed datacenters.

Gephi is an open-source network analysis and visualization software package written in Java on the NetBeans platform initially developed by students of the University of Technology of Compiegne (UTC) in France. It adopts a 3D render engine to display large networks in real-time and to speed up the exploration of such networks. The flexible and multi-task architecture brings new possibilities to work with complex data sets and produces valuable visual results. It provides easy and broad access to network data and allows for spatializing, filtering, navigating, manipulating and clustering. Gephi (Heymann 2014) is an interactive visualization and exploration platform for all kinds of networks and complex systems, with dynamic and hierarchical graphs.

3.2 DCN Architectural Models

In this work, each DCN implemented a 64-server architecture for the sake of being able to compare their topologies. The link error rate was set as 0.8%, and various link bandwidths were adopted in the range from 1 Gigabit/second to 100 Gigabit/second to conduct a sensitivity analysis.

3.2.1 Three-Tier

The conventional Three-tier topology follows a tree-based architecture which has three layers, i.e., core layer, aggregation layer, and access layer. The core switches are responsible for connecting the network outside the DC, and also the aggregation layer. The aggregation layer switches the link between the upper core layer switches and the access routers, where access routers are normally placed inside the rack to connect a set of servers.

3.2.2 Fat-Tree

According to the architecture of Fat-tree DC, the tree-based architecture highly relies on the server Rack assembled that is modelled as sectionalized modules, and the rack can be regarded as an entirety which involves servers placed inside with the edge router connected. The rest of the architecture can be referred to as the interconnections among core switches, aggregation switches, and the Racks.

3.2.3 BCube Architecture Modelling

The BCube DC architecture complies with the shipping container principle that applies a "servers placed in a Cube" method to achieve the goal of portability. Similarly, a Cube module is much like a Rack module, where a Level 0 switch is connected with a set of servers. In fact, Cubes are always considered as Level 0 (L0) of a BCube DC, whereas in an upper layer, Level 1 (L1) switches are placed above the first level. Normally, a typical BCube consists of the same number of L0 switches and L1 switches. The number of Cubes is considered to be the same as the number of switch ports. Hence, in a 64-server BCube with two layers, eight servers are connected with each L0 switch, where there are eight for both L0 switches and L1 switches.

3.2.4 HyperFlatNet Architecture

According to the property of HyperFlatNet, this architecture has two layers where the first layer has n servers and only one n-port switch, and the second layer consists of n^2 first layers. Thus, there are n^3 servers in total which are connected by n^2 groups of switches; a group here can be considered as a cluster. The hyperFlatNet modelling can be deployed by a matrix function. n^3 servers can be treated as a n^2*n matrix.

3.3   Energy Consumption Modelling

Here we deployed an energy model by using the Dynamic voltage and frequency scaling (DVFS) technique and Dynamic Power Management (DPM) fixed timeout policy together as shown in the following algorithm, and the fixed timeout scheme was used as the DPM policy. When the servers are under loaded after a period of execution time at full load, the DVFS technique is adopted to save energy, while if the servers are transferred into idle state, a DPM policy can be implemented. The energy consumption algorithm is deployed by both the DVFS and DPM techniques. In DVFS (Shang et al. 2002) chip switching power decreases proportionally to $V^2* f$, where V is voltage and f is switching frequency. The core principle is that the average power consumed has a cubic relationship with the CPU frequency, moreover, the power consumption for the components which are not related to f that remains fixed, such as bus, memory, and disk. Therefore, the server power consumption can be stated as follows,

$$P = P_{fix} + P_f \times f^3 \qquad (1)$$

Where P_{fix} is the fixed power consumption by components not linked with frequency such as the bus, memory, and disk, P_f is CPU power consumption linked with frequency.

On the other hand, according to (Choo 2014) the total energy consumption for the DCN can be divided into three main portions: computing energy by servers, communication energy consumed by links and network equipment operations, and the power consumed by infrastructure for supporting datacenters (e.g., cooling/air conditioning system). Only a fraction of energy consumption has been delivered to the computing server directly, another considerable portion of the energy being consumed for maintaining interconnection links and network equipment operations. The power consumption for switches makes up a great proportion to the overall DCN power consumption. The researcher set up three scenarios with the Green Cloud simulator to compare the detailed network component energy consumed among Two-tier DCN, Three-tier DCN and Three-tier high-speed DCN. The results showed that the energy consumption for the switches accounted for 26.54%, 30.27% and 30.98% respectively, which take up around 1/3 of the total energy. The energy consumed by a switch can be expressed as:

$$P_{switch} = P_{chassis} + n_{linecard} {}^*P_{linecard} + \sum_{configs}^{i=0} nports_{configs_i} {}^*P_{configs_i} \qquad (2)$$

Where $P_{chassis}$ is the power consumed by the switch hardware, $P_{linecard}$ represents the line card power consumption with no ports turned on, $n_{linecard}$ represents the number of cards plugged into a switch, $P_{configs_i}$ is related to the power consumed for a port running at rate i, $P_{chassis}$ and $P_{linecard}$ are fixed due to the operation of a switch, so in this equation, only $P_{configs_i}$ is dependent on transmission rate which is proportional to the overall power consumption of the switch. In other words, the transmission workload directly influences the total energy consumption of a switch; more tasks go through a switch, more energy a switch consumed.

3.4 Network Performance Measurement

Based on the existing DCNs infrastructure, there are possibilities to conduct topological change to improve the DCNs performance. The communication components for networking such as the switches and links directly influence the network performance of the Cloud infrastructure. Normally, due to its geographical distribution character, the links which connect each data center are always equipped with relatively long distance cables, which means link delay cannot be neglected as a performance metric. The latency or packet delivery time indicates the time spent from the first bit sent from the transmitter to the last bit received by the receiver, which is composed of packet transmission time and link propagation delay. The average packet delay can be calculated as follows, where D_{avg} refers to the average packet delay and represents the number of packets received, d_i refers to the delay of the packet i.

$$D_{avg} = \frac{1}{n}\sum_{n}^{i=1} d_i \qquad (3)$$

On the other hand, when a data stream is transmitted over a communication channel, the possibility exists for the number of received bits to be altered due to link noise, interference, etc. leading to a probability of packets dropping. In addition, the packets also have the probability of being dropped when a large data stream traffic pass the switch especially when the switch load goes beyond its frame capacity, and the packets are dropped automatically by the switch queue mechanism. Furthermore, the simulation will adopt this model in the situation when traffic is forced to be transferred to alternative routes due to the link failures so that alternative switches will bear the extra load.

3.5 Topological Metrics

3.5.1 Network Graph Model

It is useful to define the term "graph" to assist in the understanding of our network analysis. In modern graph theory, a graph (Deo 2016) can be classified by different types of edges into two main kinds, a directed graph, or digraph, and an undirected graph. These two types of graphs are mainly distinguished by the edge property: the directed graph has oriented edges while the undirected graph has no oriented edges.

An undirected graph is a graph in which the edges have no orientation. If there is a graph G = (V, E), where V = {a, b, c, d} and E = {(a, b), (c, d), (d, a)} then the edge (a, b) is identical to the edge (b, a), i.e., they are not ordered pairs. In networking, the links are bidirectional with both "upward" transmitting and "downward" transmitting functionality. The maximum number of edges in an undirected graph without a loop is n(n − 1)/2. However, in a directed graph, the distinction appears from Edge set where E is a set of ordered pairs of vertices. Presenting as an expression, (a, b) is a different edge from (b, a), i.e., (a, b) is considered to be directed from node "a" to node "b". Often "a" is called the head and "b" is the tail of an arrow, and (b, a) is treated as the inverted arrow of (a, b).

3.5.2 Topological Metrics

Average Nodal Degree ($\bar{k}$)

This is the coarsest connectivity feature of any topology. The degree of a node is the number of edges neighbored to that node while the average nodal degree represents average of the degrees over all nodes in the network. For example, in Figs. 8 and 9, the degree of node X is 6 while the average nodal degree is 2.5.

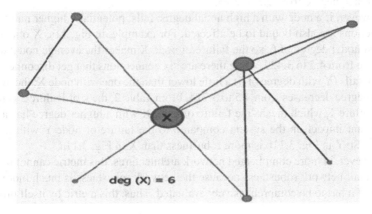

Fig. 8 Example of degree of a node X

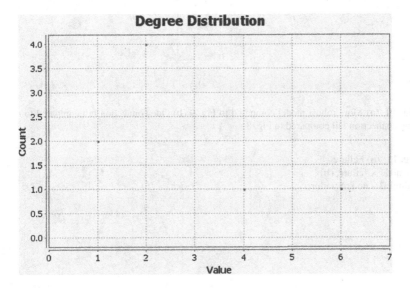

Fig. 9 Node degree distribution from Fig. 8 example

$$\deg_{avg} = \frac{node\ count \times value}{total\ number\ of\ node} = \frac{2 \times 1 + 4 \times 2 + 1 \times 4 + 1 \times 6}{8} = 2.5 \qquad (4)$$

Networks with higher k values are regarded as better-connected on average, and, consequently, are likely to be more robust. On one hand, "more robust" means that there are more chances to establish new connections such as the ones shown in Fig. 10, the average nodal degree increases to 4.5 when more connections are established based on Fig. 10c. When one connection (X <−>Y) fails, the average nodal degree decreases to 4.25 while the same scenario from Fig. 10c to Fig. 8 decreases the average degree from 2.5 to 2.25.

However, if a node with a high nodal degree fails, potentially higher numbers of connections are also bound to be affected. For example, in Fig. 11a, X obtains the highest nodal degree of 6, so the failure of node X makes the average nodal degree decrease from 4.5 to 3.429, while there are six connections that get disconnected. If node Y fails (Y with degree of 5) a little lower than the one with node X, the average nodal degree decreases from 4.5 to 3.714. From Table 2, the k of Failure 2 is higher than Failure 1, which means the failure of node X with a higher degree has a more significant impact on the system compared to the failure of node Y with a lower degree. So Y in Fig. 3.11b is more robustness than X in Fig. 3.11a.

However, in more complicated network architectures, this metric cannot indicate the overall network robustness because the network robustness is much more complex and it has to be comprehensively evaluated. Thus, this metric by itself provides

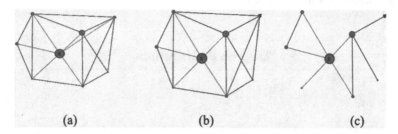

Fig. 10 (a) More robust model compared to Fig. 9 (b) One connection fail compared to (a), (c) One connection fail compared to Fig. 8

Fig. 11 (a) Failure 1 – node X failure, (b) Failure 2 – node Y failure

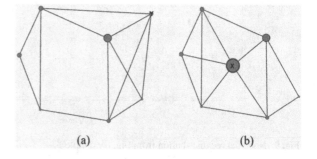

Table 2 Robustness
comparison: node failure with
different degree

Node failure	Failure 1	Failure 2
Node selected	Node X	Node Y
K – Initial	4.5	4.5
K – After failure	3.429	3.714
Robustness	Low	High

only a limited measure of the robustness of a network which is likely to vary depending on how the nodal degree is actually distributed over the graph.

Network Diameter

The diameter is, like the average nodal degree, another broad robustness metric of a network. It is the longest of all the shortest paths between pairs of nodes. In general, one would wish the diameter of networks to be low. Scale-free networks generally have small diameters, but are not particularly robust in response to deliberate attacks, due to their relatively low value of node connectivity. Nonetheless, small-scale networks represent a combination of the advantages of the properties of random networks (where no node is privileged by design) and scale-free networks (where there is a low diameter). We also note that expansion, the diameter of a network normalized by its size, could be also used in order to carry out a comparison analysis. The length $max_{u,v}d(u, v)$ of the "longest shortest path" (i.e., the longest graph geodesic) between any two graph vertices (u,v) of a graph, where $d(u, v)$ is the graph distance.

$$D = max_{u,v}\, d\left(u,v\right) \tag{5}$$

Average Shortest Path Length

The average shortest path length (ASPL) is calculated as an average of all the shortest paths between all the possible origin-destination node pairs of the network. Generally, networks with smaller ASPL are more robust in terms of network latency, but they are prone to lose connections due to having fewer linking cardinal numbers. Therefore, in order to comprehensively compare network performance, ASPL cannot tell to all the nodes about network latency. d_{ij} Denotes the distance between the vertices v_i and v_j, N is the vertices number, and the average path length L of an unweighted network can be calculated by the formula (Fig. 12):

$$L = \frac{2}{N(N-1)}\sum_{i \geq j} d_{ij} \tag{6}$$

Fig. 12 ASPL: 6 nodes example

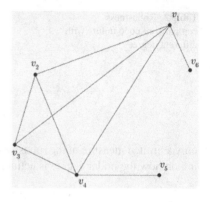

For example, $\displaystyle\sum_{i \geq j} d_{ij} = d_{12} + d_{13} + d_{14} + d_{15} + d_{16} + d_{23} + d_{24} + d_{25} + d_{26} + d_{34} + d_{35} + d_{36} + d_{45} + d_{46} + d_{56} = 1 + 1 + 1 + 2 + 1 + 1 + 1 + 2 + 2 + 1 + 2 + 2 + 1 + 2 + 3 = 23$,

then $L = \dfrac{2}{6 \times 5} \times 23 = \dfrac{23}{15}$.

Betweenness Centrality

The betweenness centrality for a node in a network indicates the proportion of the node that lies on paths between other nodes in the network. A high proportion implies an important node in a network which has a large influence on the transfer of messages through the network. The betweenness centrality of a node reflects the amount of control that this node exerts over the interactions of other nodes in the network.

The betweenness centrality of a node N is calculated as follows:

$$C_b(N) = \sum_{s \neq N \neq t} \left(\varphi_{st}(N) / \varphi_{st} \right) \tag{7}$$

Where s and t are nodes that different from N, φ_{st} refers to the number of shortest paths from node s to t, and $\varphi_{st}(N)$ **denotes the number of shortest paths from s to t that N lies on. For example, the betweenness centrality of** node b is computed as follows:

$$C_b(b) = \frac{\varphi_{ac}(b)}{\varphi_{ac}} + \frac{\varphi_{ad}(b)}{\varphi_{ad}} + \frac{\varphi_{ae}(b)}{\varphi_{ae}} + \frac{\varphi_{cd}(b)}{\varphi_{cd}} + \frac{\varphi_{ce}(b)}{\varphi_{ce}} + \frac{\varphi_{de}(b)}{\varphi_{de}}$$
$$= 1/1 + 1/1 + 2/2 + 1/2 + 0 + 0 = 3.5 \tag{8}$$

Closeness Centrality

Closeness centrality is a measure of how fast information spreads from a given node to other reachable nodes in the network. Nodes with high closeness centrality are important because they can reach the whole network more quickly than the other nodes. The node's closeness centrality is measured by the reciprocal of its average distance. The average distance of node v_i to other nodes is calculated as follows:

$$D_{avg}(v_i) = \frac{1}{n-1} \sum_{n}^{j \neq i} g(v_i, v_j)$$

(9)

where n is the number of nodes, $g(v_i, v_j)$ is the length from node v_i to node v_j.

The closeness centrality of node v_i is measured as follows:

$$C_C(v_i) = \left[\frac{1}{n-1} \sum_{n}^{j \neq i} g(v_i, v_j) \right]^{-1}$$

(10)

For example, the closeness centrality of node b in Fig. 13 is computed as follows:

$$C_C(b) = 1 / \left(\left(L(b,a) + L(b,c) + L(b,d) + L(b,e) \right) / 4 \right) = 4 / (1+1+1+2) = 4/5 = 0.8$$

Eccentricity

In graph theory, the eccentricity $E(v)$ of a vertex v is the greatest geodesic distance from v to another vertex. In a network, the eccentricity is regarded as the distance from a given starting node to the farthest node from it.

Eigenvector Centrality

Eigenvector centrality measures the influence of a node in a network. Each node is assigned a score on the basis of the concept that connections to high-scored nodes make more contributions to the score of the node than identical connections to low-scored nodes. PageRank by Google is a variant of eigenvector centrality measurement. The

Fig. 13 Betweenness centrality: 5 nodes example

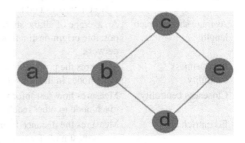

Eigenvector centrality can be measured by using adjacency matrix. For a given graph G = (V, E) with a set of vertex V and a set of edges E, and let A = $(a_{v, t})$ be the adjacency matrix, if the vertex v is connected to vertex t, then the score of vertex v is defined as:

$$s_v = \frac{1}{\mu} \sum_{t \in M(v)} s_t = \frac{1}{\mu} \sum_{t \in G} a_{v,t} s_t \tag{11}$$

where $M(v)$ is a set of neighbors of v and μ is a constant value (referred as eigenvalue). Generally, only the greatest eigenvalue μ can result in the desired centrality measure.

Metrics such as average nodal degree, average weighted degree, and network diameter and radius, are necessary parameters for evaluating the robustness of a network. A larger average nodal and weighted degree, and a shorter diameter and radius tend to represent a robust network. However, the centrality metrics are important metrics that have great influence on a network (Table 3).

4 Simulation Studies

For the case study, we firstly built an energy-aware DCN by conducting simulation studies in order to observe the impact of the underlying network connectivity on the DCNs' performance according to the fault tolerant perspective. A distributed DCNwas then setup so as to evaluate different DCNs' performance under the failure conditions based on the solution of the first study. Both studies were conducted using a Network Analysis Tool (Gephi 0.8.2) and a Network Simulation Tool (CloudNetSim++ version 1.0 based on OMNeT++ Version 4.1 and Inet network framework) (Table 4).

Table 3 Topological metric summary

Metric	Summary	Metric feature
Average nodal degree	Measures the number of edges neighbored to that node	Coarse metric
Network diameter	Measures the longest of all the shortest paths between pairs of nodes	Coarse metric
Average shortest path length	An average of all the shortest paths between all the possible origin-destination node pairs of the network	Shorter, less latency
Betweenness centrality	Measures the proportion that lies on paths between other nodes in the network	Large influence
Closeness centrality	Measures how fast information spreads from a given node to other reachable nodes in the network	Large influence
Eccentricity	Measures the distance from a given starting node to the farthest node from it	Medium influence
Eigenvector centrality	Measures the influence of a node in a network	Large influence

Table 4 Notice on notation representation of the use in simulation studies structure

Notation	Representation
NRM	Network robustness metric
NP	DC network performance
NPE	DC network performance evaluation
ECE	Energy consumption evaluation
LFR	Link failure ratio

4.1 Case Studies

In the first process, robustness metrics were evaluated based on the network established, according to the analysis for each metric, and important nodes and edges were determined in this process according to NRM values. Various types of component failure based on important nodes and edges were simulated in CloudNetSim++ simulator. The NP was analyzed and verified on the basis of node and link selection. Initially, a representative conventional balanced-DCN with unbalanced edge weight was constructed in Gephi; the reason for this was to find important nodes and weights in the network by using network robustness metrics measuring techniques so that the network performance simulation part could be treated as the verification of the results gained from Gephi. Moreover, the network QoS evaluation part in the first study was represented as the network performance and energy consumption versus the node failure scenarios so as to be able to compare between the different nodes. Initially, five DCN architectures were setup, and the architectures were comprehensively compared in topological view. Then the network performance of various DCNs was recorded and compared using CloudNetSim++.

4.2 Network Performance Evaluation

4.2.1 Topology Setup

We have set the topologies, as shown in Figs. 14 and 15 below for the simulation studies.

*The edge thickness is depicted according to the edge weight size, while the weight in this case represents the traffic flow.

4.2.2 Topological Measurement

In Fig. 16, we can see that Core switches and aggregation switches own the highest eigenvector centrality which indicates that they are the most important nodes in such network, with important neighbors connected as well.

As seen in Fig. 17 below, according to the rank, aggregation switches which lie on a high proportion of paths between other nodes in the network are the most important nodes, which is to say that aggregation switches held the greatest responsibility in this

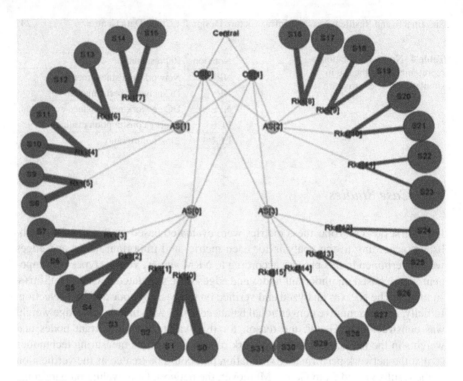

Fig. 14 Network setup

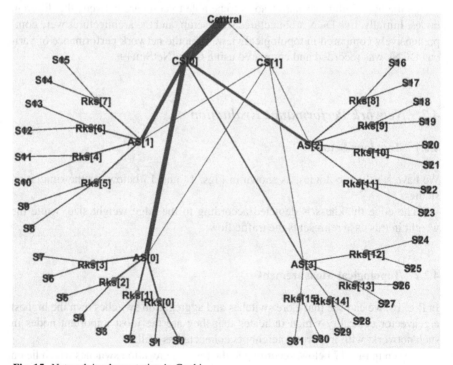

Fig. 15 Network implementation in Gephi

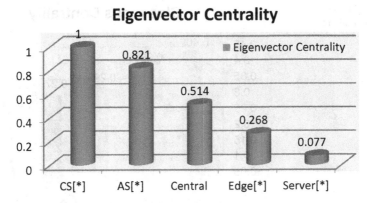

Fig. 16 Eigenvector Centrality

Fig. 17 Betweenness
centrality ranking

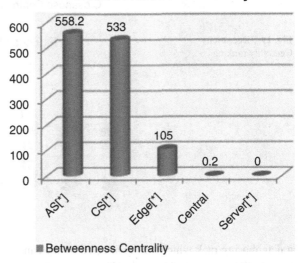

study. Similarly, core switches also hold an important position for relaying packets to farther destinations. On the other hand, each edge router had one in five chances of being walked through that packet than each aggregation switch.

As shown in Fig. 18, the core switches and aggregation switches obtained the largest value of closeness centrality which means that these two types of switches could quickly communicate with other nodes in the network. The less the average distance to other nodes, the more efficiently it can relay the message, especially in the role of a switch. The results showed that the core layer switches and aggregation layer switches gain the ability of fast communication with other nodes in the network (Fig. 19).

As expected, servers had the largest value of eccentricity. They had distance of six hops from one server to the farthest server. For example, the server connected by AS[0] had to go through six hops to the server connected by AS[1], but four hops to

Fig. 18 Closeness
centrality ranking

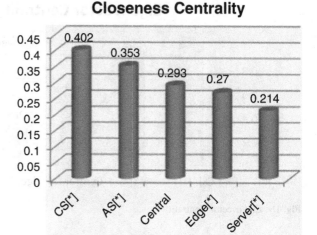

Fig. 19 Eccentricity
Centrality ranking

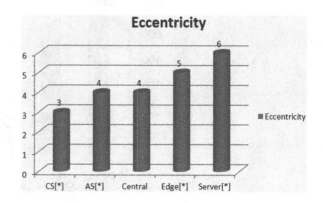

a neighboring rack which was connected by the same aggregation switch, and two hops to the server inside a rack. On the other side, core switches and aggregation switches had the lowest eccentricity value which means they were lying on the "center" of the network. Moreover, aggregation switches achieved highest nodal degree of 6 because each aggregation switch has six ways out to its neighbors as shown in Fig. 20 below.

According to above centrality metrics, CS and AS are the most important nodes in the network, and by the result shown, AS[0] was determined as the most important switch in this network. The Server[0] was regarded as the most important server, and Rack[0] was the most important rack. To verify this assumption, the simulation was conducted from latitudinal and longitudinal dimensions. Comparisons were carried out among servers; among aggregation switches; and between AS, Rack and server.

Fig. 20 Node degree
ranking

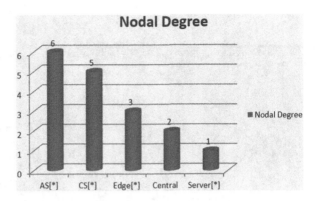

4.2.3 Simulation Studies

We have set up the network topology and parameters for the simulations as shown in Fig. 21 and Table 5 below.

As realized in CloudNetSim++, the traffic generated in this case used an unbalanced and skewed distribution, from the left to the right, and each server sent an equal number of packets (400) to other servers, while the servers located to the left, i.e., Rack[0].server[0], received the larger number of packets compared to the right, i.e., Rack[15].server[1], as shown in the figure below (Fig. 22):

The sampling servers were selected based on the principle of equipartition in the range of server size, so from the left to the right were, in order, the server with the lowest throughput received to the highest throughput received (Table 6 and Fig. 23).

From Fig. 24, it can be seen that the failure of the server with low throughput_rx remained with high average network throughput, and vice versa. The failure on different servers generated various average network throughputs for packet receiving (throughput_rx), while the network with no failures achieved 41,500 bits/s throughput_rx, but the failure on higher-workload server caused a larger impact on the overall network performance. Originally, Rks[0].server[0] was the node that made up the highest throughput to the network which contributes 9.82% to the entire network, while Rks[15].server[1] contributed the smallest portion of the network throughput of only 0.248%. However, the node failure would further degrade the entire network performance due to the completed cloud tasks being reduced because of the decreasing total number of packets received. The failure on Rks[15].server[1] made average network throughput decrease by 3.1% while Rks[0].server[0] decreased 12.9% on the overall network average throughput (Table 7 and Fig. 25).

The avg. packet delay did not vary too much on the basis of failures, which is still in the accepted range of 0.0039–0.0041 s (Fig. 26).

The packet drop ratio result presented a reverse graph to the one for an average network throughput. Failures on high-loaded servers produced a higher packet drop ratio. The packets which were originally going to the failed server had to be dropped by the switches taking charge of that data flow. The failure on the most important

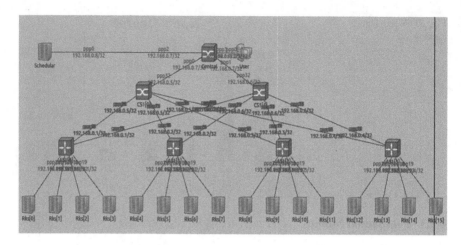

Fig. 21 Network topology

Table 5 Network parameters

Parameter	Value	Description
DCN	Three-tier architecture	Conventional DCN
No. of Core switch (CS)	2	Shown as CS[0] & CS[1]
No. of aggregation switch (AS)	4	Shown as AS[0]-AS[3]
No. of rack (Rks)	16	Shown as rack[0]-rack[15]
No. of server per rack	2	Shown as rack[*].Server[0], rack[*].Server [1]
Protocol	UDP	–
Traffic type	All-to-all	Server-to-server
Server workload distribution	Diverse	From high-load to low-load (Rks[0].Server[0] to Rks[15].Server[1])
Packet size	1000 bytes	–
Send interval	5 s	–
Queue type	Drop tail queue	Queuing mechanism
Queue capacity	1000	–
Power management	DVFS & DPM	Dynamic voltage/Frequency Scaling & Dynamic Power Management (Fixed timeout τ)
Simulation time	2500 sim-seconds	Simulation time

node generated the highest packet drop ratio which was 15.57%, five times higher than the original network's ratio.

The energy consumption for the network was considered to be the sum of computing servers and the communicational components (such as the switches). According to the GreenCloud results, the power for supporting the operation of the switches accounted for a large portion (approximately 1/3 under normal operating

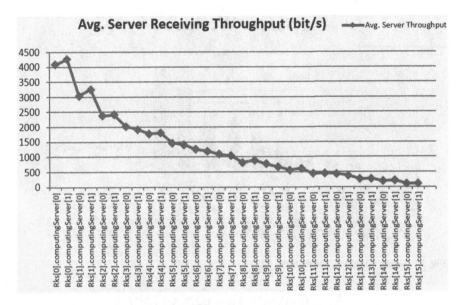

Fig. 22 Average server receiving throughput

Table 6 Sample servers' description and servers' receiving throughput

Rack[n] selection	Server[n] selection	Avg. throughput_rx (bit/s)
Rks[15]	Server[1]	103.0
Rks[13]	Server[0]	260.75
Rks[11]	Server[1]	453.9
Rks[7]	Server[1]	1036.57
Rks[5]	Server[1]	1413.21
Rks[3]	Server[1]	1912.18
Rks[2]	Server[0]	2378.96
Rks[1]	Server[1]	3257.79
Rks[0]	Server[0]	4078.67

conditions) of the total power consumption. The DVFS technique automatically decreased the energy consumption on the basis of CPU frequency adjustment, and servers with peak load corresponded to the ones with high CPU frequencies. According to the DVFS model, the power consumption of a server was proportional to the CPU frequency, and the high-loaded server consumed more power rather than the low-loaded server. When failure occurred on a server, packets may be dropped by a switch in varying degrees, and transmission to a failed server was blocked at the connected edge switch, which caused a high workload to the switch so that the energy consumption for the switch increased.

$$E_T = P_{switch} + P_{server} \tag{12}$$

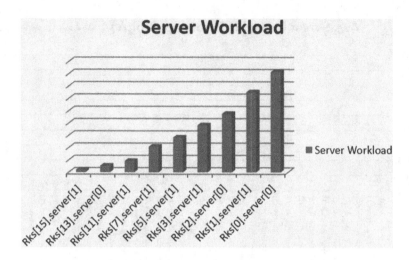

Fig. 23 Server workload distribution

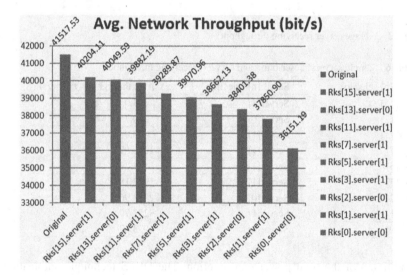

Fig. 24 Average network throughput (bits/s)

where E_T is the total network energy consumption, P_{switch} is the power supplied for switches and P_{server} represents the server power consumption. The failed server caused increment "a" on the switch power because of the increasing switch work load, and reduction "b" on the server power, so that the Total power consumption after failure can be calculated as:

$$E_T{}' = \left(P_{switch} + a\right) + \left(P_{server} - b\right) \tag{13}$$

So that

Table 7 Critical node throughput ratio and degradation after failure

	Rks[15].server[1]	Rks[0].server[0]
Contribution to overall avg. network throughput (%)	0.248%	9.82%
Avg. network throughput degradation after failure (%)	3.1%	12.9%

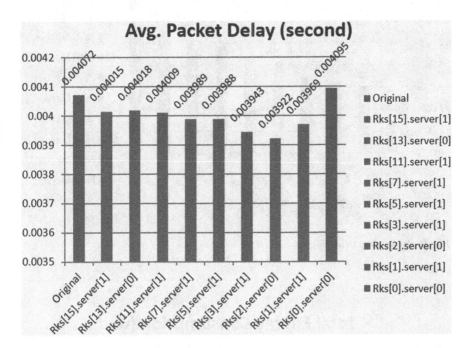

Fig. 25 Average packet delay (second)

$$E_T^{'} = P_{switch} + P_{server} + (a - b) \qquad (14)$$

where $E_T^{'}$ indicates the total energy consumption after server failure. While $|a| < |b|$ due to the reality of hardware components where the power needed for supplying components of a server is always higher than the one for a switch, and conditions change in a server so it needs more power supplementing compared to the switch. Therefore, the absolute increment for switch power cannot be beyond the absolute reduction for server power. This is to say, a − b is always <0, but various "a" and "b" makes the reduction of E_T in varying degrees. As Fig. 27 shows, as the servers failed in order from low loaded to high loaded, the reduction of E_T became larger, however, the value of (a − b) became smaller, so that the reduction of E_T was not so obvious. However, despite the theoretical assumption, in an extreme condition, the $E_T^{'}$ could be larger than E_T, which indicates that $|a| > |b|$, could, in this case, mean more power will be consumed for supplying the intensive workload for switches which could overwhelm the power reduction of the server, under various conditions of failure.

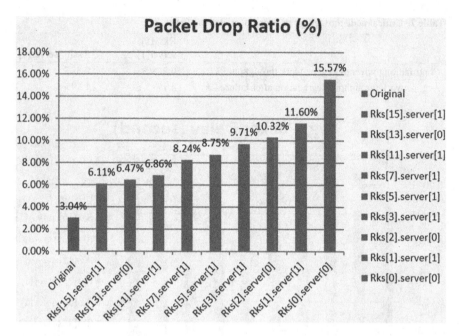

Fig. 26 Packet drop ratio (%)

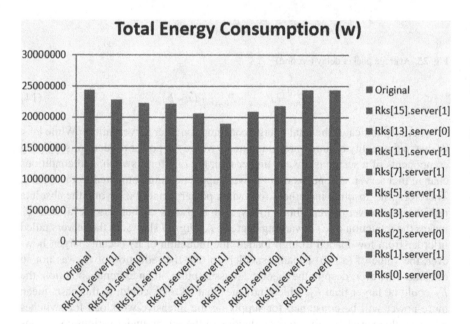

Fig. 27 Total energy consumption

5   Conclusions

In this chapter, the state of the art on the data center networks (DCNs) topological structures has been presented and then the challenges in this field have been identified to motivate our work. DCNs' performance is not merely a function of resource provisioning and allocation, but also it is a network-wide activity. We have revealed how the DCN QoS performance and robustness can be impacted by the underlying network structure in a cloud environment. Some topological metrics have been studied to reveal their impact on DCN performance and robustness. Then the robustness, in the presence of node/link failure for DCN architectures, are evaluated which also shows their correlations to DCN performance. Moreover, we have identified the energy consumption behaviours according to the change of DCN's internal structure. The simulation studies showed that the DCN topology and traffic load have significant impact on its overall energy consumption and also other network-related performance aspects.

References

Al-Fares, M., Loukissas, A., Vahdat, A.: A scalable, commodity data center network architecture. ACM Symposium conducted at the meeting of the ACM SIGCOMM Computer Communication Review (2008)

Banerjee, A., Mukherjee, T., Varsamopoulos, G., Gupta, S.K.: Integrating cooling awareness with thermal aware workload placement for HPC data centers. Sustain. Comput. Inform. Sys. 1(2), 134–150 (2011)

Beitelmal, A.H., Patel, C.D.: Thermo-fluids provisioning of a high performance high density data center. Distrib. Parallel Databases. 21(2–3), 227–238 (2007)

Berl, A., Gelenbe, E., Di Girolamo, M., Giuliani, G., De Meer, H., Dang, M.Q., Pentikousis, K.: Energy-efficient cloud computing. Comput. J. 53(7), 1045–1051 (2010)

Brocanelli, M., Zheng, W., Wang, X.: Reducing the expenses of geo-distributed data centers with portable containerized modules. Perform. Eval. 79, 104–119 (2014)

Choo, K.-K.R.: Mobile cloud storage users. IEEE Cloud Comput. 1(3), 20–23 (2014)

Deo, N.: Graph Theory with Applications to Engineering and Computer Science. Courier Dover Publications, New York (2016)

Elnozahy, E.M., Kistler, M., Rajamony, R.: Energy-efficient server clusters. Springer. Symposium conducted at the meeting of the International Workshop on Power-Aware Computer Systems (2002)

Ge, C., Sun, Z., Wang, N.: A survey of power-saving techniques on data centers and content delivery networks. IEEE Commun. Surv. Tutorials. 15(3), 1334–1354 (2013)

Gorti, N.P.K.: Application aware performance, power consumption, and reliability tradeoff. Diss. Iowa State University, (2014)

Google White Paper: Google's green data centers: network POP case study. Google. https://static.googleusercontent.com/media/www.google.com/en//corporate/datacenter/dc-best-practices-google. pdf, (2011)

Guo, C., Lu, G., Li, D., Wu, H., Zhang, X., Shi, Y., Tian, C., Zhang, Y., Songwu, L.: BCube: a high performance, server-centric network architecture for modular data centers. ACM SIGCOMM Comput. Commun. Rev. 39(4), 63–74 (2009)

Heymann, S.: Gephi. In: Encyclopedia of Social Network Analysis and Mining, pp. 612–625. Springer, New York (2014)

Horvath, T., Abdelzaher, T., Skadron, K., Liu, X.: Dynamic voltage scaling in multitier web servers with end-to-end delay control. IEEE Trans. Comput. **56**(4), 444–458 (2007)

Howard, A.J., Holmes, J.: Addressing data center efficiency: lessons learned from process evaluations of utility energy efficiency programs. Energy Efficiency. **5**(1), 137–148 (2012)

Kliazovich, D., Bouvry, P., Khan, S.U.: GreenCloud: a packet-level simulator of energy-aware cloud computing data centers. J. Supercomput. **62**(3), 1263–1283 (2012)

Koomey, J.G., Belady, C., Patterson, M., Santos, A., Lange, K.-D.: Assessing trends over time in performance, costs, and energy use for servers. Lawrence Berkeley National Laboratory, Stanford University, Microsoft Corporation, and Intel Corporation, Tech. Rep (2009)

Malik, A.W., Bilal, K., Aziz, K., Kliazovich, D., Ghani, N., Khan, S. U., Buyya, R.: Cloudnetsim++: A toolkit for data center simulations in omnet++IEEE. Symposium conducted at the meeting of the 2014 11th Annual High Capacity Optical Networks and Emerging/Enabling Technologies (Photonics for energy) (2014)

Mell, P., Grance, T.: The NIST definition of cloud computing. Commun. ACM. **53**(6), 50 (2010)

Networking, C.V.: Cisco global cloud index: Forecast and methodology, 2012–2017 (White paper): Cisco (2013)

Sadashiv, N., Kumar, S.D.: Cluster, grid and cloud computing: A detailed comparison. Symposium conducted at the meeting of the Computer Science & Education (ICCSE), 2011 6th International Conference on IEEE (2011)

Shang, L., Peh, L.-S., Jha, N.K.: Power-efficient interconnection networks: dynamic voltage scaling with links. IEEE Comput. Archit. Lett. **1**(1), 6–6 (2002)

Steere, D.C., Goel, A., Gruenberg, J., McNamee, D., Pu, C., Walpole, J.: A feedback-driven proportion allocator for real-rate scheduling Symposium conducted at the meeting of the OSDI (1999)

Viswanath, R., Wakharkar, V., Watwe, A., Lebonheur, V.: Thermal performance challenges from silicon to systems. Intel. Technol. J. (2000)

Wang, L., Chen, D., Zhao, J., Tao, J.: Resource management of distributed virtual machines. Int. J. Ad Hoc Ubiquitous Comput. **10**(2), 96–111 (2012)

Ritchie Qi received his master's degree in the School of Engineering, Computer and Mathematical Sciences, Auckland University of Technology in 2015. He received the Bachelor degree at Computing and Information Sciences at the same University. His research interest is in the sustainable and resilient network infrastructure design for cloud networking.

Dr. William Liu received his PhD and Master (with distinction) in Electrical and Computer Engineering at the University of Canterbury, Christchurch, New Zealand. He is currently a Senior Lecturer at the Department of Information Technology and Software Engineering, in the School of Engineering, Computer and Mathematical Sciences, Auckland University of Technology. In general, his research interests are in the design and performance evaluation of infrastructures and protocols for packet-oriented networks. He is working especially in the areas of network dependability, survivability, sustainability, and trustworthy computing.

Dr. Jairo Gutierrez is Deputy Head of the School of Engineering, Computer and Mathematical Sciences at Auckland University of Technology in New Zealand. He was the Editor-in-Chief of the International Journal of Business Data Communications and Networking (2004–2008) and received a Systems and Computing Engineering degree from Universidad de Los Andes in Colombia, a Master's degree in Computer Science from Texas A&M University, and a Ph.D. in Information Systems from the University of Auckland. His current research is on network management systems, networking security, viable business models for IT-enabled enterprises, next-generation networks and cloud computing systems.

Mamta Narang is a PhD student at the School of Engineering, Computer and Mathematical Sciences, Auckland University of Technology. She obtained a University degree in IT from Lovely Professional University in Punjab, India (2009) and a Master's degree from the Regional Institute of Management and Technology in Punjab, India (2012). From 2010 to 2014 she worked as an Assistant professor at the Lovely Professional University, after which she joined the City Institute of Management and Technology in Punjab as an Assistant Professor. Her research interests include Cloud computing and 5G technologies for Unmanned Aerial Vehicles or Drones.

Application Software in Cloud-Ready Data Centers: A Survey

Johannes Hintsch, Ateeq Khan, André Siegling, and Klaus Turowski

Abstract The digital transformation of the economy, as well as society in general, is in large part based on data centers' capabilities to process, store, and transport data. As the range of application requirements, the volume of data and system complexities, as well as security requirements increase, appropriate application system landscapes to support the tasks performed in a data center become crucial to success. Within this chapter we provide an overview on application software used to manage IT service production in data centers. With the advent of cloud computing, data centers increasingly face outside competition on all layers of the IT stack. Cloud service providers, such as Software as a Service companies, may even operate their own data centers. Furthermore, the people who use the investigated application software often themselves undergo an evolution from pure administrative to engineering responsibilities. Lastly, progress in the domain of application software, in general, has influenced application software discussed here. These phenomena are examined in order to compare common practice against competitive advantage of using the software from the presented taxonomy. The presented research has implications for practitioners because it provides an overview on the essential application fields of cloud-ready data centers. Additionally, the chapter contributes to the knowledge base by providing a taxonomy that is derived from a previously conducted case study. The taxonomy may be used in further research, for instance, in application system landscape maturity models.

1 Introduction

Digital transformation or digitization, the phenomenon of transferring tasks to machines, which were previously performed by humans (Hess 2016), is not new, but has been and is transforming company's business models (Cortada 2008; Hess 2016).

J. Hintsch (✉) • A. Khan • A. Siegling • K. Turowski
Magdeburg Research and Competence Cluster for Very Large Business Applications,
Faculty of Computer Science, Otto-von-Guericke University Magdeburg,
Universitätsplatz 2, 39106 Magdeburg, Germany
e-mail: johannes.hintsch@ovgu.de; ateeq.khan@ovgu.de; andre.siegling@ovgu.de;
klaus.turowski@ovgu.de

© Springer International Publishing AG 2017
J. Marx Gómez et al. (eds.), *Engineering and Management of Data Centers*,
Service Science: Research and Innovations in the Service Economy,
DOI 10.1007/978-3-319-65082-1_12

Consequently, consulting companies, such as Boston Consulting Group, argue that digital transformation should be on every business executive's agenda (Boston Consulting Group 2017). Governments, such as that of the Federal Republic of Germany (Die Bundesregierung 2017), also have digital transformation agendas. Furthermore, the phenomenon is addressed in prime research outlets as well. Digitization offers great opportunities for service innovation and thus the traditional socio-economic conception of what a service is can be questioned (Barrett et al. 2015). Use cases for digitization, such as smart or connected cities (Tucker et al. 2017), have strong implications for society as well as the ubiquity of social media and mobile computing (Andriotis et al. 2016). Finally, potential that is possibly ignored by European and North American practitioners and academics lies in Africa, Latin America and Asia (Best 2014).

Apart from stationary personal computers, mobile computing and communication devices, or sensors in the industry 4.0 enabling internet of things paradigm (Oesterreich and Teuteberg 2016) substantial computing power lies in data centers that offer services, which are often essential to products in the era of digitization. These data centers in their most general form can be found in any organization. For modern cloud service providers they are in some sense the factories of these companies (Abolhassan 2013). Cloud service providers with the highest depth of value creation must control the full IT stack. They often manage their own data centers and are thus not only concerned about problems regarding computer science or systems engineering, but also need to answer questions regarding, for instance, facility management.

IT service management (ITSM), as defined by the IT Infrastructure Library (ITIL), describes some of the common practices (Hochstein et al. 2005) that are employed by data center executives, managers, as well as operators to conduct their tasks. IT service management practices are tool-implemented by vendors such as BMC Software or ServiceNow (Matchett et al. 2015). However, especially in cases where companies are centered around the services that are offered by data centers, additional fields of application need to be considered by executives and managers, as well as by operators. In those cases, companies will use individual or standard application software from different fields.

In this chapter we provide an overview on the application software in data centers. Hence, we have chosen a title that explicitly addresses data centers that should be ready to offer cloud services if they have a consistent architecture that includes software from the application fields mentioned here. Therefore, for practitioners, this could be a worthy read because an overview of an integral part of their organization's information system, namely application software, is provided. For academics, we provide a taxonomy of the application software used by today's cloud-ready data centers or, more broadly, used by IT service providers.

The remainder of the chapter is structured as follows. In the next section the conceptual evolution from data center to cloud service provider, the convergence of systems administrators and systems engineers as well as the relevant aspects of the evolution of software will be discussed. In Sect. 3, results from a previously conducted case study on application system landscapes of IT service providers will be presented. Section 4 contains the taxonomy of application software. This taxonomy as well as the chapter in general are discussed in Sect. 5. And, finally, this chapter is concluded in the last section.

2 The Data Center

There are different perspectives on application software. Behavioral scientists focus, for example, on the value that application software can bring to the business. An example is the research on technology acceptance under which the "[...] troubling problem of underutilized systems [...]" is addressed (Venkatesh and Davis 2000). On the other hand, information systems researchers seek to "[...] extend the boundaries of human and organizational capabilities by creating new and innovative artifacts." (Hevner et al. 2004). Whereas for the former the management seems to dominate computer science, the latter require strong capabilities in computer science disciplines, such as systems engineering. As such, accurate understanding of the nature of the systems that a systems engineer is talking about is necessary. Within this chapter, we use the information system definitions as illustratively arranged in Fig. 1.

Information systems comprise the people, processes, and the IT system landscape of an organization. Other than Krcmar (2015, p.22) we do not position processes inside the IT system landscape as they may also be performed manually without system support. Of course, they are encoded in the application systems if supported. According to Porter (1985, p.37) "[e]very firm is a collection of activities that are performed to design, produce, deliver, and support its product.[...]". Within this chapter we will use the more contemporary concept of process. The illustration's processes are adopted from Porter's generic value chain (Porter 1985, p.37).

Some aspects are highlighted in the graphic while others are left out. Important aspects left out, for instance, include service level agreements (Hunnebeck 2011, p.100). Also, not only application services are offered by data centers. IT does not serve as an end in itself, but solutions are built to provide utility (Hevner et al. 2004). For instance, application services address functional requirements within one application field of the service's users. This ignores possible service offerings on a platform (e.g. test environment for developers) or infrastructure (e.g. virtual machines on demand). Software for providing infrastructure as a service (IaaS) itself can also be offered as a service. Traditionally, application software and system software are differentiated (Laudon and Laudon 2005, p.203), but this distinction is not always expedient. For example, consider the case of a hypervisor, "[...] computer systems that present a very basic user program interface-one which is so nearly identical to a particular computer machine interface that an operating system intended to support such machines may serve as a hypervisor user program without software modification." (Hendricks and Hartmann 1979) They may be considered as system software, "[which manages] the computer's resources, such as the central processor, communications links, and peripheral devices" (Laudon and Laudon

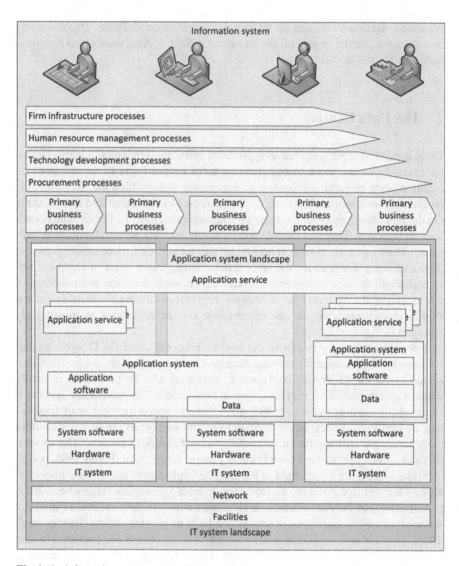

Fig. 1 An information system and its IT system landscape that contains application systems such as Enterprise Resource Planning (ERP) systems based on ERP application software and the corresponding data

2005, p.203), but it also is essential to the application of providing virtualized infrastructure services. Nonetheless, the term system software is still relevant, for example, to categorize operating systems (Laudon and Laudon 2005, p.204). System software, middleware as well as database systems in their own right will not be part of this chapter's taxonomy. It will focus on core data center application fields that need system support.

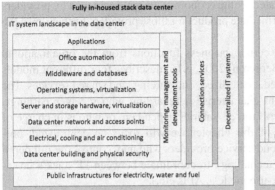
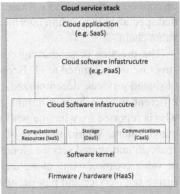

Fig. 2 Full inhoused stack data center adapted from Boersen et al. (2012) possibly evolving into cloud service stack where all or selected parts of the IT stack may be sourced as a service (Youseff et al. 2008)

In the following subsection some context on the subject of this chapter will be provided. We will describe the evolution from data centers to cloud service providers that shows how requirements of such organizations have changed. Those changes are also reflected in application software products of this chapter's taxonomy.

2.1 Evolution from Data Center to Cloud Service Provider

Data centers, which in their entirety may be understood as the *cloud* (Armbrust et al. 2010), underwent an evolution from various perspectives, for example, from an architecture perspective. Miller (1982) points to the increasing geographical spread of the IT systems of enterprises. He illustrates this with technological progress in mass storage systems that enable consistent data access, interface standardization, the advancement from monolithic operating systems to such with smaller kernels, or the ISO/OSI reference model for the network stack.

Figure 2 presents two architectural layer views of how data centers or cloud service providers may produce their services. Traditionally, the data center stack is likely fully insourced. With cloud computing (cloud service stack) the concept of application programming interface (API) based, elastic, and pay-per-use services questions if, for instance, mission critical infrastructure should be operated in a small organization's own data center. Another viable option now would be to leverage the infrastructure competence of larger providers, and to source this layer, potentially at a lower price with better quality.

Zarnekow and Brenner (2003) illustrate the increasing business-orientation and productization of IT service provisioning, e.g. from providing one MIPS computing power, over a billing application, over IT-support of a billing process, to pure business products like, for instance, software as a service offerings. This concentration on core competencies is facilitated by the economies of scale achieved by providers that specialize in a certain intermediate product for those providers further down the value chain.

The practice of separating certain business functions from the organizational structure is not limited to IT. Bergeron (2002, p.16) describes four different models of shared services: decentralized, centralized, outsourcing, and shared services. The different models have different characteristics regarding who receives earnings, who is reported to, what the workforce's salaries depend on, or who is in charge of management. Within the rest of this chapter we will focus on centralized, outsourced, and shared service cloud service providers who may control the full depth of value creation using cloud technology to coordinate between IT stack's layers (using self-service and pay-per-use models, APIs etc.).

Along with the architecture and business models, process maturity has increased. ITIL is often described as a de-facto standard (Wu et al. 2011) for ITSM. Yet, it underwent an evolution of its own. Finding its roots in management methodologies such as the Deming cycle (Deming 1986, p.88), ITIL has evolved from a British government agency created framework (Disterer 2009) to a globally used framework (Marrone et al. 2014). It contains detailed explanations, examples and some prescriptions on how to manage IT service provisioning. As such, it serves as a reference to researchers and practitioners in the field of ITSM or data centers that provide those services. However, companies may also practice ITSM without the ITIL as the discrepancy between ITIL implementation and practiced ITSM shows (Yazici et al. 2015).

An important part of any information system, if not the most important part, are the people that use the application services offered within the information system. The next subsection will discuss two other roles, not the users, that are responsible for operating and engineering the IT system landscape of an information system. For those two groups of professionals we argue that a convergence of their responsibilities can be observed.

2.2 Convergence of the Responsibilities of IT Systems Administrators and IT Systems Engineers

Those who operationalize ITSM, IT systems administrators, supervise the execution and use of IT systems. They play a crucial role in today's daily life due to the bespoken importance of IT systems. However, they are sometimes seen as "jack of all trades" who use trial and error rather than systematic approaches (Rowe et al. 2015). Rowe et al. (2015) took this as a reason to establish a graduate level university course for IT systems administrators. To overcome the trial and error approach and replace it with a systematic approach, they adopt systems engineering into their course, which already is a fundamental part of many computer science curricula (Rowe et al. 2015). IT systems administrators are often seen as those who are responsible for IT systems in their operation lifecycle stage. Regarding systems engineering on the other hand, Mobus and Kalton (2015) reuse an earlier definition characterizing engineering as "[...] the practice of organizing the [... design, construction, and operation ...] of any artifice which transforms the physical world around us to meet some recognized need." Subsequently, they define systems engineering as "[...] meta-engineering that involves the integration of complex subsystems that are often designed by different sub disciplines [...]". Systems engineering may include several sub disciplines, such as software, computer, or electrical engineering. We argue, however, that IT systems administration and engineering, in practice, often are practiced by the same individuals. Consequently, we argue that it is practical to appreciate the convergence of these two responsibility areas. In the following text we will abbreviatory use the terms systems administrator and engineer instead of IT systems administrator and engineer.

Today, most people, with varying levels of expertise, carry out administration tasks regarding their personal computers or smartphones. Here, personal use and correspondingly configuring the system are central. But, considering the systems administrator of a prospering small company, the borders between administration and engineering quickly become blurred. For example, administrators often administer the company's e-mail service. Technically, this service may be based on an arrangement of message transfer agents[1] that were tediously installed and configured to meet the company's demands. But, as the company grows, standardized calendar management, reliable smartphone synchronization as well as directory integration might be added to the feature list of the evolving e-mail service. Also, failover scenarios may be required. Several decisions, which ideally do not resemble a trial and error approach need to be taken in this situation.

Companies, for instance, need to take make or buy decisions. In the make case, for the prospering small company, tasks include clarifying whether a new e-mail software may be more effective, or sizing the new infrastructure to establish failover capability and more performance to satisfy an increasing user load. If the service is to be bought, questions regarding integration in the company's information system need to be answered, as well as assessing different software as a service offerings. As systems grow even more complex, increasingly engineering skills are required to evolve old and introduce new systems. This increasing professionalization of systems administrators and their convergence to systems engineers using scientific methodologies is reflected by the 31st Large Installation System Administration Conference (LISA) held in 2017 (USENIX 2017).

Table 1 presents a non-formal comparison of the two converging areas. Both responsibilities require to satisfy business needs. However, they can be distinguished. While administrators usually acquire their knowledge from practical experience and therefore, initially, use inductive reasoning, engineers acquire their knowledge through study and initially use deductive reasoning. Engineers may also use inductive reasoning, such as case study research (Eisenhardt 1989) or requirements engineering, to create new application software (see Fig. 3). Whereas the

---

[1] https://en.wikipedia.org/wiki/Message_transfer_agent

Table 1 Characteristics of IT systems administrators and engineers

IT systems administrator	IT systems engineer
The requirements of the business need to be the leading guideline for action	
– Practically acquired knowledge – Initially inductive reasoning – Needs to work in brownfield environments – Specific technology know-how – Organizational understanding (including personal politics) – Solution-oriented (pragmatic) – Mostly active in the service operation stage	– Knowledge acquired through study – Initially deductive reasoning – Sometimes in danger of admiring greenfield approaches (this preference will decrease when exposed to practical problems) – Methodological and theory know-how – Problem-oriented – Mostly active in the design stage, but also during continual improvement

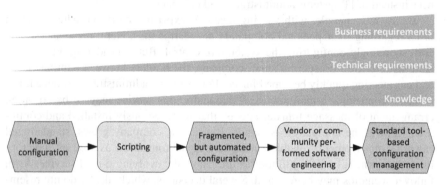

Fig. 3 Evolution from manual configuration to standard application software for configuration management

administrator usually needs to work in grown environments (brownfield), university educated engineers sometimes need a practice shock to understand the often unrealistic requirements of greenfield approaches. Whereas the administrator is often trained in specific technologies, the engineer can apply his methodological approach and theory knowledge more broadly including a potentially rigorous evaluation. By differentiating between solution- and problem-oriented, we hint at the pragmatism of being satisfied with one solution to a problem. However, carefully analyzing and understanding the root-cause of problems (Lloyd 2011, p.68) can be crucial. Using ITIL's service lifecycle terminology, administrators tend to be mostly active in the operation stage, while engineers are predominately working in the design and continual improvement stages.

The term DevOps (development and operations) points at another convergence: that of IT system administrators (used synonymously with IT system operators) with software engineers (Spinellis 2012). The term usually refers to the requirement of rapidly deploying functionality into production, which is achieved by strong collaboration between development and operation professionals. DevOps is also strongly associated with a set of tools emphasizing this style of cooperation (Ebert et al. 2016).

Figure 3 exemplifies how tools, such as those for configuration management, have evolved from manual administration work to standard application software used in data centers. With increasing business and technical requirements as well as with increasing domain knowledge of the systems administrators (business and technical), manual configuration is replaced (Talwar et al. 2005). Scripting requires generalizing concrete configuration actions of often recurring routines. Even if this automates configuration, the landscape of different scripts may be fragmented. Also, such a grown script-based automation environment may be hard to understand for new team members. With further increasing requirements and knowledge, vendor or community performed software engineering projects lead to standard tool-based configuration management. An example for such an evolution is the configuration management tool Puppet (Kanies 2006).

The proliferation of automation and management tools is facilitated by progress made in software engineering, which is described in the next subsection.

2.3   Progress in the Domain of Application Software

A key differentiator of a tool like Puppet in comparison with its proprietary counterparts is its declarative domain specific language (Delaet et al. 2010). In other configuration management software, general purpose languages might require a steep learning curve. Conversely, domain specific languages and their abandonment of the imperative in favor of the less error-prone declarative programming paradigm make such tools available to a wider audience of systems administrators without previous programming skills. The evolution from second to third generation programming languages had similar effects on the whole software engineering domain. Within this section, several aspects on the progress in the domain of application software will be discussed.

General issues that have been discussed in software engineering include managing development costs, time to market, dealing with incomplete requirements, software quality, as well as software maintenance (Naur and Randell 1969). These issues remain major challenges.

One strategy to achieve better maintainability was software decomposition into manageable pieces (Naur and Randell 1969). Different terms and approaches have been used for decomposable parts and decomposition itself. Naur (1969) refers to decomposable parts as action clusters, whereas McIlroy calls them software components (McIlroy 1969). Parnas (1972) proposed the modular design by decomposing software design into software units. Finally, Dijkstra proposed dividing software into sequential phases and hierarchical levels (Dijkstra 1968; Laplante et al. 2008).

These principles created the foundations for today's efficient and effective module-based software development. Loosely coupled modules or components can be easily adopted according to requirements without having to implement the functionality. Several paradigms, including component based software engineering (CBSE) and service oriented computing (SOC), have emerged based on the bespoken foundations.

In CBSE, new systems are engineered by building and combining components. Each component or module represents functionality and is considered as a building block for system development. Components can be combined or reused with reduced effort. This enables organizations to build components themselves or buy them from the market as commercial off the shelf software.

SOC, on the other hand, is a paradigm to create IT system landscapes. It aims at a high degree of flexibility, interoperability, and cost effectiveness (Josuttis 2007; Papazoglou and Heuvel 2007). SOC is based on CBSE as well as software evolution. But, whereas in CBSE a module architecture is necessary, in SOC, wrappers and adapters can be used to tie together a multitude of legacy applications of all architectural styles.

Another important factor is standardization. It can be observed in implicit or explicit standards, such as APIs, that enable a commonly known access to application functionality. Similarly, open standards and open source have played an integrating role in the global software ecosystem (Andersen-Gott et al. 2012).

But, software engineering is not the only computer science discipline that influences application software in cloud-ready data centers. Attempting to achieve an even higher degree of automation, the company Arago uses artificial intelligence in operations automation. Their concept is designed in such a way that a systems administrator may perform required administrative tasks and having the system perform these tasks from that point onwards (Boos 2014).

The progress described in this section has lead to the application software that is used in today's cloud-ready data centers. There, such application software forms the basis of application systems that are connected to landscapes (see Fig. 1). In the next section, results from a study on application system landscapes of IT service providers are presented.

3   The Application System Landscapes of IT Service Providers

The case study results (Hintsch et al. 2016) were published in the proceedings of the 2016 IEEE 4th International Conference on Enterprise Systems (ES2016) held in Melbourne, Australia. Its research questions were posed in the context of the research on the industrialization of IT. Key industrialization concepts include standardization and automation (Hochstein et al. 2007). In manufacturing, enterprise resource planning (ERP) systems implement these principles (Jacobs and Watson 2007; Romero and Vernadat 2016), but they are not the only application systems used by firms (Romero and Vernadat 2016). This research was conducted because literature lacks an account of the constituting systems of IT service providers' application system landscapes. The results contribute to the knowledge base by informing those needing to make pre-appraisals about a provider's current application system landscape (e.g. within merger and acquisitions projects) as well as allowing practitioners to proactively construct their landscapes during market entry.

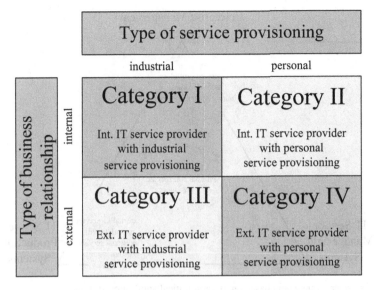

Fig. 4 IT service provider categorization framework (Becker et al. 2011)

Table 2 Case sample overview

Case	Categories				Case	Categories			
	I	II	III	IV		I	II	III	IV
Small hosting provider		x			Large consultancy		x		
Small integrator		x	x		Large integrator	x	x	x	x
Medium customizer			x		Large ASP	x			
Large telco			x		Large ASP	x		x	
Large integrator			x	x					

Abbreviation: *ASP* Application service provider

The case study, methodologically aligned with Eisenhardt (1989), did not specifically target data centers or cloud service providers, but more generally IT service providers. The nine analyzed cases were sampled using a categorization framework by Becker et al. (2011) depicted in Fig. 4.

Industrial is also referred to as equipment-based (Thomas 1978) IT service provisioning. Data centers usually are industrial IT service providers, whereas IT service providers who offer consulting services strongly depend on human expertise in each instance of service provisioning, and are thus referred to as personal IT service providers. The sampled cases usually were companies of more than one category. A more detailed description of the research methodology as well as the cases is contained in the original paper (Hintsch et al. 2016). Table 2 provides a brief overview of the sampled cases.

Figure 5 presents two main results. First and most importantly for this chapter, IT service provider's landscapes consist of systems to manage their enterprises.

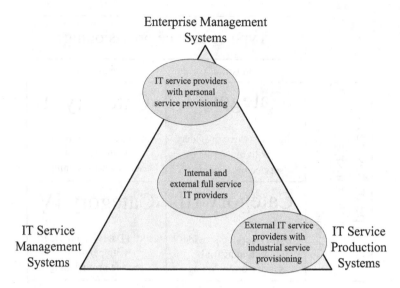

Fig. 5 Provider arrangement based on mission-critical application systems

Also, landscapes include systems for IT service management and for the actual production of IT services.

For IT service providers with industrial service provisioning who serve external clients, IT service production systems are mission-critical and these systems are highly customized. For those that provide internal industrial or a mix of industrial and personal services, standard application systems from all domains are purchased and tailored to the needs of the company. For IT service providers who practice personal service provisioning, enterprise management systems and ITSM systems are used.

The distinction into three application system categories acts as a basis for further differentiating application software in the taxonomy presented in the next section.

4   Application Software Taxonomy

In this section, the taxonomy for application software is presented. The complete set or a subset may be used by internal data centers as well, but it is likely most comprehensively used by full stack cloud service providers. Table 4 aligns the eight categories with the more general categories from the previous section.

The subsections for each application field include a definition, a broader description of the respective application software, specific proprietary and open source examples, as well as a mapping of the five lifecycle stages of ITIL.

Table 3 Mapping of the application software taxonomy with the categories from the case study on application system landscapes of IT service providers (Hintsch et al. 2016)

Classes of application software for cloud service providers	EM	ITSM	ITSP
Enterprise management	x		
IT service management		x	
Infrastructure management			x
Operations automation			x
Monitoring and analysis	x	x	
Security and compliance	x	x	
Systems engineering	x	x	
Miscellaneous	x	x	x

Abbreviations: *EM* Enterprise management, *ITSP* IT service production

Table 4 Maturity levels for tool landscapes of IT service providers

Level	Maturity
1	No requirements
2	Basic process support is implemented ("[...] stable service operation can be achieved.")
3	Integrated ("[...] most important processes are supported by tools and the central tools are interconnected in a way that they can share data in an efficient way.")
4	Comprehensive basic tool-support ("central processes can work very efficiently because of an optimized tool landscape.")
5	"all tool areas are fully implemented and processes can benefit from optimal tool support" ("continual improvement of the tool landscape is also addressed.")

All direct quotes are taken from the paper of Richter and Schaaf (2011)

Software that is provisioned as a service is not in the taxonomy's scope because this depends on each provider's' customers. Nonetheless, for example, enterprise management software may be provisioned as a service to customers also in cases where the same software is included in the enterprise management system of the provider (Table 3).

4.1 Enterprise Management

Definition Enterprise management software integrates all primary and secondary processes and functions of an enterprise as well as its resources into a common database to support transactional and analytical purposes.

Such systems provide managers with the comprehensive view of the company they need for decision making (Davenport 2000, p.2). By its design, ERP systems might be treated synonymously to terms such as enterprise applications. Gartner (2017a) defines enterprise applications ideally to be able to "[...] control all major business processes in real time via a single software architecture on a client/server platform [...]". That this is not the case in practice is reflected by the different products for ERP, customer relationship management (CRM) or business intelligence (BI) by vendors such as SAP or Microsoft. This differentiation is also reflected in literature (Botta-Genoulaz et al. 2005; Chen and Popovich 2003; Møller 2005).

The concrete enterprise management software products in the previously presented case study supported the following application fields: business intelligence, business support, communication, customer relationship management, enterprise resource planning, firm control as well as project management (Hintsch et al. 2016). Some of those application fields were quite specific, but we consider ERP, CRM, project management, communication as well as BI as most central for IT service providers in the area of enterprise management. IT service providers use ERP systems mostly for sales, finance and accounting, controlling, and human resource management (Botta-Genoulaz and Millet 2006; Hintsch et al. 2015b). Financially relevant information is also joined in ERP systems from different sources such as other application systems, for example, capacity and usage information from monitoring systems (Hintsch et al. 2015b).

Gartner sees SAP as the leader in the market for "Single-Instance ERP for Product-Centric Midmarket Companies" (Guay et al. 2015). A popular example from the open source community for enterprise management is odoo (Kapitsaki et al. 2017; Kountouridou et al. 2016).

Enterprise management systems are used in service strategy, in service design, and continual service improvement. The material master of an ERP system, for example, often acts as a service catalogue, which is part of the corresponding management process in service design stage. Furthermore, continual service improvement, for example, regarding process cycle times, may also partially be performed in enterprise management systems.

4.2 IT Service Management

Definition IT service management software supports "[t]he implementation and management of quality IT services that meet the needs of the business. IT service management is performed by IT service providers through an appropriate mix of people, processes and information technology." (Cannon 2011, p.16).

ITIL, the reference for ITSM software (Pink Elephant 2017), developed from version two to three in 2007 (Marrone et al. 2014). While the second version processes were grouped into service delivery and support, the current version additionally and explicitly focuses on strategy, design, and continuous improvement (Marrone et al. 2014). Numerous organizations have not yet transitioned from the second to the third version (Marrone et al. 2014), and, thus, it is not surprising that ITIL implementation still mostly comprises processes from the service transition and operation stages, as data from a broad international study shows (Marrone et al. 2014). For some of these organizations alignment with recommendations for these processes is. Implementing the newer parts of ITIL would appear as unnecessary complexity for them. Consequently, Gartner uses the term IT service support management tools for ITSM software and points to their origins as IT help desk tools (Gartner 2017b).

Nonetheless, ITSM software has evolved and now includes process support for all stages (Pink Elephant 2017). In the case study, we observed a trend by ITSM software vendors, such as ServiceNow, to include more of the functionality traditionally being in scope of enterprise management software (Hintsch et al. 2016). In any case, ITSM also needs to interface with enterprise management software. For instance, the tickets answered by a help desk can be used as a basis for allocation of costs to products or customers. ITSM software vendors provide interfaces to enterprise management software (BMC 2017; ServiceNow 2015).

According to Gartner (Matchett et al. 2015), software by the vendors ServiceNow and BMC is leading the market. ServiceNow, a software as a service vendor, dominates in the "ability to execute", whereas BMC is ahead in its "completeness of vision". An open source example of this application category is OTRS (Erek et al. 2014; Herrick et al. 2012).

ITSM software with comprehensive process support is used in all stages of the IT service lifecycle.

4.3   Infrastructure Management

Definition Infrastructure management software manages the lifecycle of bare metal and virtual hypervisor-based computing, storage, and networking resources, including boot image management.

Software for infrastructure management has dramatically changed through the pervasiveness of the x86 processor architecture as well as the related pervasiveness of virtualization (Bernstein et al. 2009). Whereas company data centers that grew with their company could have a multitude of processor architectures, data centers like those of Amazon Web Services focus on x86, only including the variability options of 32 and 64 bit (Barr 2012).

Nonetheless, even if virtualized, infrastructure management includes additional functionality, such as remote hardware configuration, backup, storage software, or network configuration, including software firewalls.

Infrastructure virtualization software, often including the aforementioned functionality, is lead by VMware, followed by Microsoft, with still considerably lower market share (Bittman et al. 2016). Placed third by Gartner is Red Hat, which is the largest contributor to OpenStack (Mirantis Inc. 2017). The open source cross-industry developed software OpenStack was predicted to "become a new de facto standard by the end of 2014" (Nelson et al. 2014) and has since seen increasing adoption rates (Talligent 2016).

Infrastructure management software is used during the stages service transition and operation, for instance, for the setup of test and production environments.

4.4   Operations Automation

Definition   Operations automation software automates functions performed during deployment, operation and retirement of IT systems or their components.

The name of this application software category is adopted from Wettinger et al. (2016). Operations automation (OA) software automates functions related to installation and configuration during service deployment, reconfiguration during service operation, and retirement of IT systems or their components. As services often span several physical or virtual hosts, orchestration is another function performed in OA. This includes reacting to alerts by the monitoring systems when, for example, capacity is close to being exceeded.

Although not its prime purpose, OA software is also used in the engineering activities involved for creating new services or integrating new features in existing system landscapes. In such cases, OA technology is used in the development, testing and or quality assurance environment. This will be elaborated on in section "Systems Engineering".

Wettinger et al. (2016) differentiate configuration management, image-based configuration management and model-based management. They further mention infrastructure management in the form of application programming interfaces for IaaS software and providers as well as platform-centric management where PaaS is used as a basis for performing OA.

Generally, OA technology evolved from manual administrative work. Talwar et al. (2005) motivate this evolution by complexity. They give the example of updating large installations spanning thousand or more nodes. The configuration of each node would already be time consuming, and very prone to human error, particularly due to complex system interdependencies. Focusing on configuration management, they point out that configuration management tools can improve correctness, speed, and documentation as compared to administrative work. But, they also point out that OA technologies have to be learned and that specifying automation costs developer time.

Delaet et al. (2010) provide an overview on configuration management tools. Tools generally provide the administrator with an interface, which is used to specify the configuration of the managed devices. These specifications are stored in a repository. Device-specific profiles, which represent the configuration specifications, are generated, and the deployment agents of the managed devices configure the device as specified.

Image-based configuration management refers to the practice of deploying pre-configured special-purpose virtual machine images rather than general-purpose virtual machine images and configuring machines at run-time. In other words, the machine's configuration state is not controlled in this approach. Using such heavily-baked images has reliability advantages and tools exist to modify such images without the need for them to be running in a virtual machine (Zhu et al. 2015). Container-based virtualization is similar, but also comes with the challenge of binding services from different containers together, thus effectively requiring configuration, but before run-time. Compared to hypervisor-based, containers enable a more fine-grained resource elasticity with less overhead. In this regard, the borders between OA and infrastructure management blur. However in OA, infrastructure management software is used, for example, through APIs to automate actions on the infrastructure layer that could also be performed manually, for example, through the software's user interface.

Model-based OA tools "enable the definition of a holistic application-centric model of a particular Cloud service for the deployment, its structure and behavior" (Wettinger et al. 2016). They often integrate the capabilities of traditional configuration management and infrastructure management.

Being closely tight to the emerging DevOps (Ebert et al. 2016) paradigm, Gartner names some of these tools application release automation tools. Such tools named leaders by Gartner include software, for example, by ElectricCloud, IBM, or CA technologies (Fletcher et al. 2016). Popular open source tools in this domain include Puppet (configuration management) or OpenStack Heat[2] (Model-based management), as well as runtime environments for the open topology and orchestration specifications for cloud applications (Palma et al. 2015).

OA, like infrastructure management, is performed in the stages service transition and operation.

4.5   Monitoring and Analysis

Definition Monitoring and analysis software raises operations data about infrastructure, platforms, as well as applications and provides means for analyzing the data to evaluate functional as well as non-functional properties of monitored IT systems.

Spring states, in two articles on cloud computing, which specific layers in data centers need to be monitored (Spring 2011a, b). These correspond to traditional data center layers (left side of Fig. 2). Monitoring facilities includes data from security cameras and building security in general. Network monitoring can be done with low granularity to high granularity, performing full package capture. Hardware monitoring includes different hardware components, hence overseeing, for example, memory load or processor utilization. When monitoring the operating system exemplary tasks include making sure that the same tested operating system version is installed under all production hypervisors and that only allowed operating system features are activated. The middleware and application layer both require scenario specific log data monitoring to detect abnormal behavior. Similarly, the user's behavior may be monitored to detect attackers or to detect characteristics in user behavior that are of interest to the provider (e.g. process execution).

Generated log data can be of large volume, for example, when full package capture is activated. In such cases it is feasible to store data only for a certain time

---

[2] https://docs.openstack.org/developer/heat/

span (Spring 2011b) and aggregate older data. Based on such historic or real-time data a broad range of analyses can be performed. Analysis reports as well as raw monitoring data may be requested by customers to verify that service level targets have consistently been met (Spring 2011a).

Monitoring and analysis software may integrate with software for security and audit, operations automation, in particularly for orchestration, or with IT service management, for example, regarding the user help desk or in capacity management.

Gartner differentiates two categories in this area. For application performance monitoring, they name Dynatrace and AppDynamics as the two leading vendors (Haight and Silva 2016), and for network performance monitoring and diagnostics, three vendors (NetScout, Viavi, and Riverbed) are rated to lead the segment (Ganguli and Bhalla 2017). Popular open source tools include Nagios for monitoring (Hernantes et al. 2015) and a plethora of other tools, such as logstash for collecting, parsing, and transforming log data[3].

Monitoring and analysis are performed during the lifecycle stages of service operation and continual service improvement.

4.6 Security and Audit

Definition Security and audit software "[keeps] the impact and occurrence of information security incidents within the [acceptable] levels" (Lainhart et al. 2012, p.113) as well as offering capabilities for internal and external security audits.

Particularly in cases where data centers store, process, and transport data of external customers and generally highly sensitive data, security programmes and audit processes to ensure high security levels are important.

Proactive measures against cyber attacks can include taking the role of the attacker and performing penetration testing with individual or standard security software (Foster 2006).

Additionally, controlling who may access information, physically or remotely, is another function of this type of software. Aligning the role-based access models with companies' realities as well as regulatory requirements marks a challenge in today's mission-critical application system landscapes (Fuchs et al. 2011).

Audit tools may base their assessments regarding the landscape's security on configuration management databases filled by IT service management and operations automation software (Desai et al. 2006) as well as monitoring and analysis software. Also, business intelligence (e.g. data mining) techniques, similar to those found in enterprise management, are applicable here (Fuchs et al. 2011).

Gartner named Okta and Microsoft as leaders for identity and access management services (Kreizman and Wynne 2016), as well as rating IBM and Dell leaders for managed security services (Kreizman and Wynne 2015). A multitude of open

---

[3] https://www.elastic.co/products/logstash

source tools exist in this area, some on the edges of legality. A popular example for network traffic analysis is WireShark[4].

Security and audit software is relevant in all service lifecycle stages.

4.7 Systems Engineering

Definition Systems engineering software supports activities ranging from requirements engineering, modelling and design, to construction and testing (Mobus and Kalton 2015).

Requirements engineering is crucial for systems engineering as well as for software engineering (Dardenne et al. 1993; Mobus and Kalton 2015). As errors made in this engineering stage can propagate to other stages, rigor is crucial, particularly when agile methodologies are not applicable (Nerur et al. 2005). Requirements engineering is supported by modelling languages, such as SysML (OMG 2015) or ArchiMate with the related enterprise architecture framework TOGAF (The Open Group 2016).

Modelling, particularly mathematical modelling, can then be the basis for simulations. In the early design stages such techniques guide systems design, for instance, regarding non-functional properties (Bosse et al. 2016). Furthermore, modeling languages or domain specific languages can also help in modeling different aspects of the system (structure and behavior). If the design of a system is sufficiently described, prototypical implementation may commence, possibly aided by model-driven engineering tools (Bordeleau 2014).

In the construction phase, operations automation software may be used to create a testbed for engineers, which then can also be used during production. In this phase, software engineering techniques are applicable. For example, configuration management together with desktop virtualization tools may be used to specify an application system landscape comprehensively enough so that production-like landscapes can be launched using an almost identical configuration compared to the production environment. Such testing environments may differ from production environments only in different passwords, different node sizes and quantities, and data stored in the databases.

Proprietary software in this area includes enterprise architecture software, in which area Gartner rates Software AG as a leader (McGregor 2016). A plethora of tools again exists in the open source community. A popular tool for systems engineering, based on SySML, is Papyrus (Bordeleau 2014).

Systems engineering is performed in the service design, transition, and operation service lifecycle stages.

---

[4] https://www.wireshark.org/

4.8 Miscellaneous

Because this category does not specifically target any application field of cloud service providers or data center operators, no definition is provided. This category includes the usual office software, such as word and spreadsheet processing tools. Proprietary as well as open source software are commonly known to be available and software of this category is used in all service lifecycle stages.

5 Discussion

Only focusing on tools may equal chasing mediocre ITSM implementation projects. Of course, tools cannot be of benefit to a company if the people are not properly trained or processes not efficiently and effectively implemented (Cater-Steel and McBride 2007). Excellence does not come from purchasing licenses and installing tools, but rather from excellent people and processes who use proper tools. Similarly, as people use software tools to fulfill functions in their companies' processes, tools have an effect and so does their quality, for example regarding user acceptance (Venkatesh and Davis 2000).

Application software, often originating in areas where work was performed manually, is usually designed around use cases. These use cases to some degree standardize how certain actions are performed. Such standardization, across entire processes, is one of the benefits sought when implementing ERP software (Gronau 2010, p.12). Thus, if large process improvement projects (e.g. in the form of infrastructure automation or operations automation) are carried out, we argue that it is more than a wild guess to assume that the critical success factors (Finney and Corbett 2007) observed in ERP implementation projects also apply to other application fields of the taxonomy (Pollard et al. 2009).

Similarly to the diverse and complex IT system landscapes of companies, where IT is not the product (e.g. manufacturers, insurers or retailers), IT service providers' tool landscapes have often grown very complex (Richter and Schaaf 2011). Richter and Schaaf (2011) therefore present a maturity model for tool landscapes of IT service providers. Table 4 lists these maturity levels.

They use the term tool area synonymously to our use of application field. They make no differentiation between application software and application system. As their work was labeled to be ongoing, they describe the need to identify a comprehensive list of tool areas (Richter and Schaaf 2011) as future work. This is a contribution of this chapter.

In the following, common practice and competitive advantage of using application software from the taxonomy will be discussed. We employ the presented maturity levels to guide this discussion.

5.1 Common Practice

All IT service providers who use application software to support their business need to have employees who understand how to use the tools. Without capable employees, great tools may not be of benefit. Similarly, the process architecture can be ineffective or inefficient, rendering capable employees as well as a mature application system landscape useless.

In particular, the first two maturity levels make clear that complete tool-support is not required for all data centers, or more generally, for IT service providers. This may be a sign of immaturity, but not necessarily of ineffectiveness. For instance, operations automation software may not be required for very small data centers. Similarly, personal IT service provisioning (see Fig. 4) may have an application system landscape with only low maturity, based on the maturity model, compared to that of an industrial IT service provider with a very mature landscape. Nonetheless, also the former landscape may be of utility to the personal IT service provider.

Size and type of the IT service providers should be considered when assessing a tool landscape (Hintsch et al. 2015b). Further, an application system landscape that would be sorted into the lower levels of the maturity level, or be labeled common practice, could also be sufficient for the IT service provider because of a different reason. If the data center is not under high efficiency or quality pressure, a common practice application system landscape may be sufficient. With increasing financial pressure in literally every type of organization (e.g. for profit, government or non-profit), IT service providers will have to compete with external service providers and therefore the provider's excellence is and will increasingly be required. Therefore, we will discuss how competitive advantage, in our view, is achievable for full-stack cloud service providers who act as outsourcers or shared service centers (Bergeron 2002) and, thus, need to compete in the market place.

5.2 Competitive Advantage

People and processes are again crucial to competitive advantage. In particular, understanding the requirements of the business, or in the case of external IT service providers, the customer's business, is crucial for achieving competitive advantage. For instance, if the IT service provider offers standard business application software to its customers, this requires a great deal of knowledge specific to the software's stack. This is similar to the understanding that may be required by IT service providers who support their corporation's main business, such as insurance or pharmaceutical, with domain specific application software.

Additionally, if the company is dependent on a standard software vendor, it may also be restrained exceeding beyond the software capabilities envisaged by the vendor. For instance, a standard software application service provider may be restrained in becoming a cloud service provider due to limitations of the legacy architecture of the standard software. Such providers may be able to use parts of the cloud stack (e.g. IaaS, see Fig. 2). But, aiming at rapid elasticity (Mell and Grance 2011) by using operations automation technology they would need to completely redesign the architecture of the standard software (Leymann et al. 2016).

Application software automates tasks previously performed by humans. When such software is well understood it may be aggregated together in automation scripts requiring the application software products to expose corresponding APIs. This also requires increasingly strong software engineering skills. As such application landscapes are augmented by custom glue and integration code. Additionally, as APIs grow more standardized or as further progress in artificial intelligence is made, even more tasks may be performed by software. Consequently, artificial intelligence tools specialized in IT service management are available and are even already being applied. This includes application fields such as incident and problem management including ticket correspondence and problem resolution respectively (Boos 2014).

The maturity model's highest level characterizes application system landscapes of IT service providers, such as cloud service providers, as follows. It is integrated, supports all processes and application fields, enables very efficient work, and is continuously improved. For assessing efficiency, the results of monitoring and analysis tools confronted with industry benchmarks are adequate guidelines. Continuous improvement may include replacing application software where better alternatives are available as well as reducing the number of parallel used software products. In this regard, landscape consolidation already practiced in industries, such as banking (Penzel 2005), will be necessary in order to stay flexible enough to meet varying business requirements and to manage costs related to the provider's IT system landscape.

The vision of ERP for IT is particularly relevant for continuous improvement and the industrialization of IT in general. The vision of an all-encompassing enterprise application (Gartner 2017a) is not in sight for any industry. For instance, application system landscapes that support manufacturers consist of a range of different products as well (Cupek et al. 2016), similarly to the situation in telecommunications (Wittgreffe et al. 2006). Nonetheless, a fully integrated application system landscape that is controlled via an enterprise management application where all information, technical and managerial, needed for the management of a cloud service provider is concentrated (Glohr et al. 2014; Hofmann 2009), could, in our view amount to competitive advantage. Similarly, operations automation and computer aided engineering software, potentially combined with an ERP for IT, may enable further industrialization of IT (Hintsch et al. 2015a).

Lastly, the question of make or buy is also applicable to application system landscapes of cloud service providers. For instance, consider the economies of scale of large IaaS providers in securing their systems. Their capabilities in security and audit, for instance penetration testing, manifested in application software, but also in their employees' skills, may outperform that of a small IT service provider. Some already call infrastructure and platform as a service utility computing (Armbrust et al. 2010). This can be seen as a direct answer to Nicolas Carr's provocation that

IT doesn't matter (Carr 2003). The operation of large IT infrastructures was until recently limited to capital intensive companies. Utility computing drastically lowers the barriers for entering a market where application services are offered to, potentially millions of, customers. The future will show if this commoditization also applies to application fields that are closer to traditional primary business processes. An example for this is software as a service customer relationship management software with its prime example SalesForce[5].

6 Conclusion

With the increasing digitization of our societies, digitization's back-bone, data centers and industrial IT service providers, become an ever more crucial part of the economy. Much research has been spent on application software, particularly on ERP software for traditional industries (Esteves and Bohórquez 2007; Esteves and Pastor 2001; Romero and Vernadat 2016). Therefore, we argue that studying the information systems of IT service providers and, particularly, their application system landscapes is necessary when trying to further increase the efficiency of providers' production processes. Hence, in this chapter, we have extended previous work and presented an application software taxonomy. The taxonomy is related to research on maturity models for application software for IT service providers.

The research in this chapter is based on a case study (Hintsch et al. 2016). The case sample of that study was limited to nine German companies. This is a limitation because the sample is not representative for all data centers or cloud service providers. However, parts of the taxonomy are also reflected in industry, for instance, in analyses of Gartner's (2017b) industry experts.

In future work, this taxonomy should be integrated with the existing work on maturity models as well as enterprise architecture management. Results of such work could guide the decision making process necessary to manage IT service providers' application system landscapes. Furthermore, the taxonomy should be hardened by analyzing it against comprehensive process maps for IT service providers (Lainhart et al. 2012, p.24).

References

Abolhassan, F. (ed.): Der Weg zur modernen IT-Fabrik: Industrialisierung, Automatisierung. Springer, Optimierung (2013)

Andersen-Gott, M., Ghinea, G., Bygstad, B.: Why do commercial companies contribute to open source software? Int. J. Inf. Manag. **32**(2), 106–117 (2012)

Andriotis, P., et al.: Highlighting relationships of a smartphone's social ecosystem in potentially large investigations. IEEE Trans. Cybernetics. **46**(9), 1974–1985 (2016)

---

[5] www.salesforce.com

Armbrust, M., et al.: A view of cloud computing. Commun. ACM. **53**(4), 50–58 (2010)

Barr, J.. EC2 Updates: New Medium Instance, 64-bit Ubiquity, SSH Client. Available at: https://aws.amazon.com/de/blogs/aws/ec2updatesnewinstance64bitbitubiquitysshclient/ (2012)

Barrett, M., et al.: Service innovation in the digital age: Key contributions and future directions. MIS Q. **39**(1), 135–154 (2015)

Becker, J. et al.: Industrialization of IT Services: Application of Industrial Concepts and their Implications from the Perspective of IT Service Providers (orig. title: Industrialisierung von IT-Dienstleistungen: Anwendung industrieller Konzepte und deren Auswirkungen aus Sicht von IT-Dienstleistern). In: Bernstein, A., Schwalbe, G. (eds.) Tagungsband der 10. Internationale Tagung Wirtschaftsinformatik, pp. 345–354. AIS Electronic Library, WI. Zurich, Switzerland (2011)

Bergeron, B.: Essentials of Shared Services. Wiley, Hoboken (2002)

Bernstein, D., et al.: Blueprint for the intercloud-protocols and formats for cloud computing interoperability. In Internet and Web Applications and Services, 2009. ICIW'09. Fourth International Conference on. IEEE, 328–336 (2009)

Best, M.L.: Global computing: Thinking outside the continent. Commun. ACM. **57**(4), 27–29 (2014)

Bittman, T.J., Dawson, P., Warrilow, M.: Magic Quadrant for x86 Server Virtualization Infrastructure. Gartner Inc. (2016). Stamford

BMC. Remedy AR System API and Integration Interfaces Overview (C, Java, .NET, Web Services, email, Ruby, Jython, VB, direct SQL). Available at: https://communities.bmc.com/docs/DOC17512 (2017)

Boersen, H. et al., 2012. Strategic choices for data centers. Compact, 0, pp. 3–13

Boos, C.: Entering effectiveness: Approaching the big chance with smart automation. Gartner Newsl. **1**(23), (2014)

Bordeleau, F.: Model-Based Engineering: A New Era Based on Papyrus and Open Source Tooling. In Proceedings of the 1st Workshop on Open Source Software for Model Driven Engineering, pp. 2–8. Valencia, Spain (2014)

Bosse, S., Splieth, M., Turowski, K.: Multi-objective optimization of IT service availability and costs. Reliability Eng. Syst. Saf. **147**, 142–155 (2016)

Boston Consulting Group. {Digital Transformation}. Available at: https://www.bcg.com/expertise/capabilities/technology-digital/digital.aspx (2017)

Botta-Genoulaz, V., Millet, P.: An investigation into the use of ERP Systems in the Service Sector. Int. J. Prod. Econ. **99**(1), 202–221 (2006)

Botta-Genoulaz, V., Millet, P.-A., Grabot, B.: A survey on the recent research literature on ERP systems. Comput. Ind. **56**(6), 510–522 (2005)

Die Bundesregierung. Digitale Agenda 2014–2017. (2017) Available at: http://digitale-agenda.de/Webs/DA/DE/Home/home_node.html

Cannon, D.: ITIL – Service Strategy. The Stationery Office, Norwich (2011)

Carr, N.G.: IT doesn't matter. Educ. Rev. **38**, 24–38 (2003)

Cater-Steel, A., McBride, N.: IT service management improvement-actor network perspective. In: ECIS, pp. 1202–1213 (2007)

Chen, I.J., Popovich, K.: Understanding customer relationship management (CRM) people, process and technology. Bus. Process. Manag. J. **9**(5), 672–688 (2003)

Cortada, J.W.: Patterns and practices in how information technology spread around the world. IEEE Ann. Hist. Comput. **30**(4), 4–25 (2008)

Cupek, R., et al.: Agent-based manufacturing execution systems for short-series production scheduling. Comput. Ind. **82**, 245–258 (2016)

Dardenne, A., Van Lamsweerde, A., Fickas, S.: Goal-directed requirements acquisition. Sci. Comput. Program. **20**(1–2), 3–50 (1993)

Davenport, T.H.: Mission Critical: Realizing the Promise of Enterprise Systems. Harvard Business School Press, Boston (2000)

Delaet, T., Joosen, W., Van Brabant, B.: A Survey of System Configuration Tools. In: van Drunen, R. (ed.) 24th Large Installation System Administration conference, LISA, USENIX (2010)

Deming, W.E.: Out of the Crisis. MIT Center for Advanced Engineering Study, Cambridge (1986)

Desai, N., Bradshaw, R., Lueninghoener, C..: Directing Change Using Bcfg2. In LISA, pp. 215–220 (2006)

Dijkstra, E.W.: The structure of the"THE"-multiprogramming system. Commun. ACM. **11**(5), 341–346 (1968)

Disterer, G.: ISO 20000 for IT. Bus. Inf. Syst. Eng. **1**(6), 463–467 (2009)

Ebert, C., et al.: DevOps. IEEE Softw. **33**(3), 94–100 (2016)

Eisenhardt, K.M.: Building theories from case study research. Acad. Manag. Rev. **14**(4), 532–550 (1989)

Pink Elephant: PinkVERIFYTM 2011 Toolsets. Available at: https://www.pinkelephant.com/en-us/PinkVERIFY/PinkVERIFYToolsets (2017)

Erek, K., Proehl, T., Zarnekow, R.: Managing cloud services with IT service management practices. In: Engineering and Management of IT-Based Service Systems, pp. 67–81. Springer (2014). Berlin, Heidelberg

Esteves, J., Bohórquez, V.W.: An updated ERP systems annotated bibliography: 2001-2005. Commun. Assoc. Inf. Syst. **19**(1), 386–446 (2007)

Esteves, J., Pastor, J.: Enterprise resource planning systems research: An annotated bibliography. Commun. Assoc. Inf. Syst. **7**(1), 8 (2001)

Finney, S., Corbett, M.: ERP implementation: A compilation and analysis of critical success factors. Bus. Process. Manag. J. **13**(3), 329–347 (2007)

Fletcher, C., Williams, D.P., Wurster, L.F.: Magic Quadrant for Application Release Automation. Gartner Inc. (2016). Stamford

Foster, J.C.: Writing Security Tools and Exploits. Syngress (2006). Rockland

Fuchs, L., Pernul, G., Sandhu, R.: Roles in information security–a survey and classification of the research area. Comput. Secur. **30**(8), 748–769 (2011)

Ganguli, S., Bhalla, V.: Magic Quadrant for Network Performance Monitoring and Diagnostics. Gartner Inc. (2017). Stamford

Gartner. Enterprise Applications. In IT Glossary. (2017a) http://www.gartner.com/it-glossary

Gartner. ITSSM Tools (IT Service Support Management Tools). In IT Glossary. (2017b)http://www.gartner.com/it-glossary

Glohr, C., Kellermann, J., Dörnemann, H.: The Road to a Modern IT Factory. Springer (2014). Berlin, Heidelberg

Gronau, N.: Enterprise Resource Planning – Architecture, Functions and Management of ERP Systems (Original German Title: Enterprise Resource Planning – Architektur, Funktionen und Management von ERP-Systemen). Oldenburg, München (2010)

Guay, M., et al.: Magic Quadrant for Single-Instance ERP for Product-Centric Midmarket Companies. Gartner Inc. (2015). Stamford

Haight, C., Silva, F.D.: Magic Quadrant for Application Performance Monitoring Suites. Gartner Inc. (2016). Stamford

Hendricks, E.C., Hartmann, T.C.: Evolution of a virtual machine subsystem. IBM Syst. J. **18**(1), 111–142 (1979)

Hernantes, J., Gallardo, G., Serrano, N.: IT infrastructure-monitoring tools. IEEE Softw. **32**(4), 88–93 (2015)

Herrick, D.R., Metz, L., Crane, A.: Effective zero-cost help desk software. In Proceedings of the 40th annual ACM SIGUCCS conference on User services, ACM, pp. 157–160 (2012)

Hess, T.: Digitization (original German title: Digitalisierung). In: Gronau, N., et al. (eds.) Enzyklopädie der Wirtschaftsinformatik – Online-Lexikon. GITO (2016). Potsdam

Hevner, A.R., et al.: Design science in information systems research. MIS Q. **28**(1), 75–105 (2004)

Hintsch, J., Schrödl, H., et al.: Industrialization in Cloud Computing with Enterprise Systems: Order-to-Cash Automation for SaaS Products. In Thomas O., Teuteberg F. (eds.) Tagungsband der 12. Internationale Tagung Wirtschaftsinformatik. pp. 61–75 WI. Münster, Germany. http://wi2015.uni-osnabrueck.de (2015a)

Hintsch, J., Kramer, F., Turowski, K.: ERP Systems' Usage in the German IT Service Industry: An Exploratory Multi-case Study. In IEEE 19th International Enterprise Distributed Object Computing Conference (EDOC), pp. 169–178 (2015b)

Hintsch, J., et al.: The Application System Landscapes of IT Service Providers: A Multi Case Study. In Li G., Yu Y. (eds.) Proceedings of the 4th International Conference on Enterprise Systems (ES2016). Los Alamitos, California, Washington, Tokyo: IEEE, pp. 122–131 (2016)

Hochstein, A., Zarnekow, R., Brenner, W.: ITIL as common practice reference model for IT service management: formal assessment and implications for practice. In Cheung W. K. Hsu J. (eds.) International Conference on e-Technology, e-Commerce and e-Service. EEE. Hong Kong, China: IEEE, pp. 704–710 (2005)

Hochstein, A., et al.: IT industrialization: What is it? (original German title: IT-Industrialisierung: Was ist das?). Computerwoche. 15(3), 5 (2007)

Hofmann, G.R.: Interview with Bettina Uhlich on IT controlling. Bus. Inf. Syst. Eng. 1(3), 266–268 (2009)

Hunnebeck, L.: ITIL – Service Design. The Stationery Office, Norwich (2011)

Mirantis Inc: Stackalytics for OpenStack Pike based on Reviews Metric. Available at: http://stack-alytics.com/ (2017)

Jacobs, F.R., Watson, F.C.: Enterprise resource planning (ERP)—a brief history. J. Oper. Manag. 25(2), 357–363 (2007)

Josuttis, N.: SOA in Practice: the art of Distributed System Design. O'Reilly Media, Inc, Sebastopol (2007)

Kanies, L.: Puppet: Next-Generation Configuration Management. ;login:, 31(1), pp.19–25 (2006)

Kapitsaki, G.M., Kramer, F., Tselikas, N.D.: Automating the license compatibility process in open source software with SPDX. J. Syst. Softw. 131:386–401 (2017)

Kountouridou, N., Antoniou, P., Stamelos, I.: A comprehensive approach for implementing an open source ERP in a Greek industry. In Proceedings of the 20th Pan-Hellenic Conference on Informatics. PCI '16. Patras, Greece: ACM, pp. 23:1–23:5 (2016)

Krcmar, H.: Informationsmanagement. Springer, Berlin/Heidelberg (2015)

Kreizman, G., Wynne, N.: Magic Quadrant for Managed Security Services. Worldwide, Gartner Inc (2015)

Kreizman, G., Wynne, N.: Magic Quadrant for Identity and Access Management as a Service. Worldwide, Gartner Inc (2016)

Lainhart, J.W., et al. (eds.): COBIT 5 – Enabling Processes. ISACA, Rolling Meadows (2012)

Laplante, P.A., Zhang, J., Voas, J.: What's in a name? Distinguishing between SaaS and SOA. IT Professional. 10(3), 46–50 (2008)

Laudon, K.C., Laudon, J.P.: Management Information Systems: Managing the Digital Firm, 8th edn. Recording for the Blind & Dyslexic, Princeton (2005)

Leymann, F., et al.: Native Cloud Applications: Why Virtual Machines, Images and Containers Miss the Point! In Proceedings of the 6th International Conference on Cloud Computing and Service Science (CLOSER 2016). SciTePress, pp. 7–15 (2016)

Lloyd, V.: ITIL – Continual Service Improvement. The Stationery Office, Norwich (2011)

Marrone, M., et al.: IT service management: A cross-national study of ITIL adoption. Commun. Assoc. Inf. Syst. 34(49), 865–893 (2014)

Matchett, C., Lord, K., Bandopadhyay, T.: Magic Quadrant for IT Service Support Management Tools. Gartner Inc. (2015). Stamford

McGregor, M.: Magic Quadrant for Enterprise Architecture Tools. Gartner Inc. (2016). Stamford

McIlroy, M.D.: Mass produced software components. In Naur P., Randell B.,(eds.) Software Engineering. Scientific Affairs Division of NATO. (1969). Brussels

Mell, P., Grance, T.: The NIST Definition of Cloud Computing. National Institute of Standards and Technology (NIST), Gaithersburg, MD (2011)

Miller, S.W.: Mass storage systems and evolution of data center architectures: Guest Editor's intro-duction. Computer. 7(15), 16–19 (1982)

Mobus, G.E. & Kalton, M.C., 2015. Systems Engineering. In Principles of Systems Science. Springer, pp. 699–731. Berlin, Heidelberg

Møller, C.: ERP II: A conceptual framework for next-generation enterprise systems? J. Enterp. Inf. Manag. 18(4), 483–497 (2005)

Naur, P.: Programming by action clusters. BIT Numer. Math. 9(3), 250–258 (1969)

Naur, P., Randell, B. (eds.): Software Engineering. NATO Science Committee, Garmisch (1969)

Nelson, L.E., Staten, J., Williamson, K.: State Of Cloud Platform Standards: Q1 2014 – OpenStack Steps Forward To Become The New De Facto Model. Available at: https://www.forrester.com/State+Of+Cloud+Platform+Standards+Q1+2014/fulltext/–/E-res112621 (2014)

Nerur, S., Mahapatra, R., Mangalaraj, G.: Challenges of migrating to agile methodologies. Commun. ACM. **48**(5), 72–78 (2005)

Oesterreich, T.D., Teuteberg, F.: Understanding the implications of digitisation and automation in the context of industry 4.0: A triangulation approach and elements of a research agenda for the construction industry. Comput. Ind. **83**, 121–139 (2016)

OMG: OMG Systems Modeling Language. Version 1.4, (2015)

Palma, D., Rutkowski, M., Spatzier, T.: TOSCA Simple Profile in YAML Version 1.0, OASIS Committee. Available at: http://docs.oasis-open.org/tosca/TOSCA-Simple-Profile-YAML/v1.0/TOSCA-Simple-Profile-YAML-v1.0.html (2015)

Papazoglou, M.P., van den Heuvel, W.-J.: Service oriented architectures: Approaches, technologies and research issues. VLDB. **16**(3), 389–415 (2007)

Parnas, D.L.: On the criteria to be used in decomposing systems into modules. Commun. ACMs. **15**(12), 1053–1058 (1972)

Penzel, H.-G.: Vorgehensweise zur Industrialisierung des Bankbetriebs. In D. Bartmann, ed. Die Industrialisierung des Bankbetriebs, pp. 95–114. Wiley (2005). Hoboken

Pollard, C.E., Gupta, D., Satzinger, J.W.: Integrating SDLC and ITSM to'servitize'systems development. AMCIS 2009 Proceedings, p.415 (2009)

Porter, M.E.: Competitive Advantage – Creating and Sustaining Superior Performance. The Free Press, New York (1985)

Richter, C., Schaaf, T.: A maturity model for tool landscapes of IT service providers. In Integrated Network Management (IM), 2011 IFIP/IEEE International Symposium on. IEEE, pp. 1050–1057 (2011). Piscataway

Romero, D., Vernadat, F.: Enterprise information systems state of the art: Past, present and future trends. Comput. Ind. **79**, 3–13 (2016)

Rowe, D.C., Moses, S., Wilkinson, L.: Systems Administration at the Graduate Level: Defining the Undefined. In Proceedings of the 16th Annual Conference on Information Technology Education. ACM, pp. 77–82 (2015). New York

ServiceNow. Product Documentation: List of Available Integrations. Available at: http://wiki.servicenow.com/index.php?title=List_of_Available_Integrations#gsc.tab=0 (2015)

Spinellis, D.: Don't install software by hand. IEEE Softw. **29**(4), 86–87 (2012)

Spring, J.: Monitoring cloud computing by layer, part 1. IEEE Secur. Privacy. **9**(2), 66–68 (2011a)

Spring, J.: Monitoring cloud computing by layer, part 2. IEEE Secur. Privacy. **9**(3), 52–55 (2011b)

Talligent. 2016 State of OpenStack Report. (2016)

Talwar, V., et al.: Approaches for service deployment. IEEE Internet Comput. **9**(2), 70–80 (2005)

The Open Group. ArchiMate, Version 3.0, (2016)

Thomas, D.R.E.: Strategy is different in service businesses. Harv. Bus. Rev. **56**, 158–165 (1978)

Tucker, R., et al.: Connected OFCity: Technology innovations for a Smar City project [invited]. IEEE/OSA J. Optical Commun. Networking. **9**(2), A245–A255 (2017)

USENIX. LISA Conferences. Available at: https://www.usenix.org/conferences/byname/5 (2017)

Venkatesh, V., Davis, F.D.: A theoretical extension of the technology acceptance model: Four longitudinal field studies. Manag. Sci. **46**(2), 186–204 (2000)

Wettinger, J. et al.: Middleware-oriented deployment automation for cloud applications. IEEE Transactions on Cloud Computing, PP(99), pp. 1–1 (2016)

Wittgreffe, J., Trollope, C., Midwinter, T.: The next generation of systems to support corporate grade ICT products and solutions. BT Technol. J. **24**(4), 93–112 (2006)

Wu, M.-S., Huang, S.-J., Chen, L.-W.: The preparedness of critical success factors of IT service management and its effect on performance. Serv. Ind. J. **31**(8), 1219–1235 (2011)

Yazici, A., Mishra, A., Kontogiorgis, P.: IT service management (ITSM) education and research: Global view. Int. J. Eng. Educ. **31**(4), 1071–1080 (2015)

Youseff, L., Butrico, M., Da Silva, D.: Toward a unified ontology of cloud computing. In Grid Computing Environments Workshop, 2008. GCE'08. IEEE, pp. 1–10 (2008). Piscataway

Zarnekow, R., Brenner, W.: A Product-Based Information Management Approach. In R. Claudio U.and Mercurio Ciborra et al., eds. Proceedigns of the 11th European Conference on Information Systems. ECIS, pp. 2251–2263. AIS Electronic Library, Naples (2003)
Zhu, L., et al.: Achieving Reliable High Frequency Releases in Cloud Environments. Software, IEEE (2015). Piscataway

Johannes Hintsch studied computer science and business informatics at the universities of Regensburg and Magdeburg, respectively. He earned his Master's degree in business informatics from the University of Regensburg in 2012. In the same year, he started his research at the Magdeburg Research and Competence Cluster for Very Large Business Applications. His research focuses on integrated application systems for IT service providers, and is complemented by a practitioner-proven interest in most things related to DevOps.

Ateeq Khan studied Data Knowledge Engineering at the Faculty of Computer Science of the Otto von Guericke University Magdeburg and earned his Master's degree in 2009. Since then, he has been working as a researcher at the Faculty's Institute of Technical and Business Information Systems. His research interests include Digital Manufacturing, Industry 4.0, Service-oriented Computing, and Software as a Service. He is a member of program committees and reviewer of many conferences and journals.

André Siegling, born in 1980 and having studied business informatics, worked in different SAP projects and has been a member of the SAP University Competence Center (SAP UCC) team at the Otto-von-Guericke University since 2002. After working with different SAP solutions he is now responsible for the customer support at SAP UCC. He was one of the driving forces when the organization started to follow ITIL paradigms. Now, the SAP UCC service offering is being evaluated regarding IT service automation potentials. Here, André again has a great share among other colleagues.

Klaus Turowski (born 1966) studied Business and Engineering in Karlsruhe, achieved his doctorate at the University of Münster and habilitated in Business Informatics at the Otto von Guericke University Magdeburg. In the year 2000, he held the Chair of Business Informatics at the University of the Federal Armed Forces München and, from 2001, he headed the Chair of Business Informatics and Systems Engineering at the University of Augsburg. Since 2011, he has been heading the Magdeburg Research and Competence Cluster which encompasses the world's largest SAP University Competence Center (SAP UCC Magdeburg).

Printed in the United States
By Bookmasters